Militant
Mediator

Militant Mediator

WHITNEY M. YOUNG JR.

Dennis C. Dickerson

THE UNIVERSITY PRESS OF KENTUCKY

Publication of this volume was made possible in part
by a grant from the National Endowment for the Humanities.

Published by The University Press of Kentucky
Scholarly publisher for the Commonwealth,
serving Bellarmine University, Berea College, Centre
College of Kentucky, Eastern Kentucky University,
The Filson Historical Society, Georgetown College,
Kentucky Historical Society, Kentucky State University,
Morehead State University, Murray State University,
Northern Kentucky University, Transylvania University,
University of Kentucky, University of Louisville,
and Western Kentucky University.
All rights reserved.

Editorial and Sales Offices: The University Press of Kentucky
663 South Limestone Street, Lexington, Kentucky 40508-4008
www.kentuckypress.com

Library of Congress Cataloging-in-Publication Data

Dickerson, Dennis C., 1949 –
Militant mediator—Whitney M. Young, Jr. / Dennis C. Dickerson.
p.   cm.
Includes bibliographical references and index.
ISBN-10: 0-8131-2058-6 (acid-free paper)
ISBN-10: 0-8131-9081-9 (pbk)
1. Young, Whitney M. 2. Afro-American civil rights workers—Biography.
3. Civil rights workers—United States—Biography. 4. Afro-Americans—
Biography. 5. National Urban League—Biography. I. Title
E185.97.Y635D53   1998
323'.092—dc21
[B]   97-43456
ISBN-13: 978-0-8131-9081-5 (pbk)

This book is printed on acid-free recycled paper meeting the requirements of the American
National Standard for Permanence of Paper for Printed Library Materials.

Manufactured in the United States of America

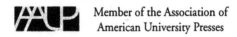

Member of the Association of
American University Presses

To my wife,
Mary,
with love

Contents

Illustrations follow page 198

Acknowledgments

M y awareness of Whitney M. Young Jr. began fortuitously at my brother Charles's 1965 graduation from Lincoln University in Pennsylvania. As Mr. Young, the commencement speaker, marched in the procession I inadvertently took his picture while taking several shots of my brother. When I undertook to research and write this book, Charles, who had been my history professor, strongly encouraged me but did not live to see this project completed. My debt to him is only one of many that I have accumulated.

Generous financial support has come from a Chairman's Special Fellowship from the National Endowment for the Humanities, a grant-in-aid from the American Council of Learned Societies, and an Albert J. Beveridge Grant for Research in American History from the American Historical Association. A Moody Grant from the Lyndon Baines Johnson Foundation enabled me to do research at the Lyndon Baines Johnson Presidential Library in Austin, Texas. The Rockefeller Foundation Research Fellowship Program for Minority Scholars supported a sabbatical from Williams College in 1983-84, and the Rockefeller Foundation Residency Fellowship Program in the Humanities allowed me to spend the 1987-88 academic year at the Carter G. Woodson Institute for Afro-American and African Studies at the University of Virginia. Other financial assistance at Williams College included grants from Division II research funds, from a Presidential Discretionary Fund, from the Named Chair Account, and a residency during the 1992 spring semester at the Center for the Humanities and Social Sciences. Dean of the Faculty David L. Smith expeditiously provided funds to reproduce photographs from the Rare Book and Manuscript Library at Columbia University. Rhodes College aided with Faculty Travel Funds.

Many librarians and archivists facilitated research at Williams College, Columbia University, Kentucky State University, the University of Louisville, the University of Massachusetts at Amherst, the University of Minnesota, the Atlanta University Center, Emory University, the John F. Kennedy Presidential Library, the Lyndon Baines Johnson Presidential Library, the Library of Congress Manuscript Division, the Federal Bureau of Investigation, the Minnesota Historical Society, the Martin Luther King Jr. Center for Nonviolent Social Change, the Rockefeller Archive Center, the Carnegie Corporation of New York, the Taconic Foundation, the Alfred P. Sloan Foundation, the Ford Foundation Archives, and the Great Plains Black Museum in Omaha, Nebraska. Arthur C. McCaw allowed me to examine his private papers. Leonard Garment gave me access to his personal papers at the Library of Congress Manuscript Division.

I extend my many thanks to colleagues who read all or part of the manuscript and shared perceptive and helpful comments. At Williams College they include Thomas Kohut, John M. Hyde, Frederick Rudolph, Russell H. Bostert, Charles B. Dew, David L. Smith, Alex Willingham, and Reginald Hildebrand, now at the University of North Carolina at Chapel Hill. I am also appreciative to James H. Cone of Union Theological Seminary in New York City, George C. Wright of the University of Texas at Arlington, Kenneth M. Hamilton of Southern Methodist University, and the late Armstead L. Robinson of the University of Virginia. A. Bernice Manns-Hutchinson also read early portions of the manuscript and gave me the benefit of her evaluation.

Georgia Swift, secretary of the Williams College Department of History, typed various versions of the manuscript. Donna Chenail, Shirley Bushika, Becky Brassard, and Peggy Weyers of the Williams Faculty Secretarial Office typed the final drafts. They performed these tasks punctually and efficiently. They have my thanks.

Mrs. Margaret B. Young, widow of Whitney M. Young Jr., granted me three formal interviews, shared her private papers, read the manuscript, and answered innumerable questions over the telephone and by mail. Dr. Marcia Young Cantarella and Mrs. Lauren Young Casteel, the daughters of Whitney and Margaret Young, also aided the research through my interviews with them. I am grateful for their assistance and respect for my scholarly independence.

My family has been unusually supportive through the several years of research and writing. My mother, Oswanna Dickerson, and my late father, Carl O. Dickerson, always cheered me on. My brothers Carl and James provided me with lodging during various research trips. My children, Nicole, Valerie, Christina, and Dennis Jr., always wanted to know about Whitney M. Young Jr. and why he was so important. My wife, Mary A.E. Dickerson, to whom this book is dedicated, extended to me her unwavering love, unstinting encouragement, and enormous patience. She tolerated my frequent absences when traveling to numerous repositories and my marathon work on this project. She made its completion possible. Only I, however, bear responsibility for any shortcomings my efforts may have produced.

Introduction

B lack Americans seldom have spoken with a single voice. While a consensus has always existed concerning the urgency of freedom and equality, blacks have disagreed about how these objectives were to be achieved. During the black struggles of the 1950s and 1960s, despite intergroup conflicts, leaders of the major civil rights organizations spoke with rare unanimity about their quest for an integrated American society. Although they pursued common goals, they chose different tactics to attain them. Moreover, each played a special leadership role and made unique contributions to the civil rights movement.

These national leaders, the "Big Six," defined the goals of the civil rights struggle and encouraged blacks and whites to respond to the call for "Freedom Now." James Farmer of the Congress of Racial Equality (CORE), Martin Luther King Jr. of the Southern Christian Leadership Conference (SCLC), and John Lewis and James Forman, spokesmen for the Student Nonviolent Coordinating Committee (SNCC), represented activist organizations that used marches, freedom rides, sit-ins, and aggressive voter registration as their principal tactics.[1] They believed that confrontations with racist institutions and protests against odious racial practices, particularly in the South, would result in progress for blacks. Although not on the frontline of civil rights protest, Dorothy Height headed an important federation of black women's groups, the National Council of Negro Women. She lent valuable support to efforts to achieve racial equality. Roy Wilkins served as the executive director of the oldest and largest civil rights group, the National Association for the Advancement of Colored People. Although the NAACP often sponsored marches, the organization stressed change through the legal and political system, particularly in the courts and through legislative lobbying.

Whitney M. Young Jr., the militant but diplomatic head of the National Urban League, also belonged to this leadership cadre. Like Farmer, King, and Forman, Young possessed impeccable activist credentials. In the early 1950s, while he served as executive director of the Omaha Urban League, he planned strategy with the combative De Porres Club, a forerunner of the Nebraska affiliate of CORE. Later in the decade, when he was dean of the School of Social Work at Atlanta University, he became an officer in the local NAACP and an adviser to student protesters who challenged racial segregation in downtown Atlanta stores. Young appreciated the importance of activism to achieve civil rights, and he supported these efforts throughout his career. At the same time, he asserted with equal fervor that the National Urban League with its programs for job training and social services was best equipped to translate de jure victories into de facto equality for black Americans.

Young's style of leadership differed significantly from that of King, Farmer, Wilkins, and Lewis and Forman. Other black leaders articulated the demands of black Americans with urgency and eloquence. Young voiced these same grievances, but he tried to reconcile them to the social and economic concerns of major white institutions. He interpreted the goals and grievances of black Americans to government, business, and foundations. He also sought ways to persuade powerful whites within these institutions that their support of the civil rights movement was consistent with their interests. He stressed that the achievement of political and economic equality would give blacks a stake in American society and would create a black middle class of entrepreneurs and consumers and a group of professional, technical, and blue-collar workers whose skills and productivity would enhance the American economy. While he helped government, business, and foundation leaders understand black demands, he developed specific programs to involve these officials in efforts to allay racial tensions and to ameliorate the black social and economic condition. Young was a black ambassador to elite white leaders and institutions. He interpreted the grievances and concerns of each group to the other.

Two perspectives have shaped assessments about Young. Tom Buckley, a *New York Times* reporter, in a 1970 article in his newspaper's Sunday magazine posed the provocative question, "Whitney Young: Black Leader or 'Oreo Cookie'?" Buckley validated the idea that Young's successful interactions with establishment whites signaled compromises that disfavored the black population and undermined his own racial militancy. So widespread was this misperception that, even before the Buckley article appeared, some militant blacks and antiestablishment whites called the League leader "Whitey" Young. A second perspective was promulgated by Nancy Weiss in *Whitney M. Young Jr. and the Struggle for Civil Rights*. Weiss stressed that the essence of Young's leadership lay in his cultivation of wealthy and influential whites in business, philanthropy, and government. His emphasis on these constituencies shaped the perspectives and programs he inaugurated through the National Urban League.

Missing from both perspectives are acknowledgments of how much the integrationism of middle- and working-class blacks influenced Young both as a local leader in the Twin Cities, Omaha, and Atlanta and as the executive director of the National Urban League. *Militant Mediator* carefully chronicles how Young in his public career drew unprecedented contributions to the civil rights movement from powerful and influential whites. At the same time this biography argues that Young vigorously sought and received endorsements of his leadership from blacks through their numerous churches, fraternities, voluntary organizations, and other institutions. While Young aggressively pursued the support of whites in Fortune 500 corporations, major foundations, and the federal government, he made similar efforts to mobilize integrationist blacks whose views became increasingly overshadowed by smaller groups of Black Power proponents. Moreover, Young did not concede that black nationalists exclusively spoke for black ghetto residents. Through various League initiatives he impacted their social and economic conditions and devised programs through which inner city blacks articulated their own perspectives and aspirations.

As a leader, Young balanced the interests of middle- and working-class blacks with those of powerful and influential whites. His credibility with whites relied on his broad support within the black population. Although he was never viewed as a grassroots black leader like Martin Luther King Jr., Young still had as much tangible black support as his colleague in SCLC. This dimension of Young's leadership does not appear in the Buckley/Weiss interpretations.[2]

Three influences shaped the leadership of Whitney M. Young Jr. First, his parents had a profound impact on him. Loved and encouraged by both, he became a confident adult unashamed of his race and unintimidated by whites. From his father he learned how to negotiate with influential whites and reconcile his objectives with their interests. The elder Young headed Lincoln Institute in Lincoln Ridge, Kentucky. This secondary school provided high school training to blacks from numerous Kentucky communities with limited educational facilities for their minority students. The elder Young consciously emulated the pragmatism of Booker T. Washington and his stress upon practical education. Also, like the Tuskegeean, Young successfully courted wealthy Kentucky whites and state officials and drew needed support to his financially vulnerable institution. By observing his father, Young learned how to negotiate skillfully and effectively with powerful whites. From his mother, he learned that in some instances militant confrontation with racial injustices was necessary. Whenever her children were slighted or when a white sales clerk treated her family discourteously, Laura Ray Young almost never held her tongue. She also defended Lincoln Institute students in their encounters with local police. She and her husband helped to mold Young into a black leader skilled in the art of persuasion but ready to protest when white leaders and institutions seemed deaf to black demands.

The Urban League was the second major influence that shaped Young's leadership. He spent nearly two decades as an official in this organization. Established in 1911, the National Urban League grew rapidly in the 1920s and succeeding decades because it provided a wide range of employment and social services to recent black arrivals to the cities. Since individual philanthropists, foundations, and corporations traditionally financed the group, most League officials knew that effective dealings with wealthy whites were required for success. Additionally, negotiations with employers, unions, and various government units, especially about jobs for blacks, required diplomacy. Although Whitney Young injected greater militancy into the National Urban League and involved it in more controversial issues, he expanded corporate, foundation, and government contributions to the organization. His skill in presenting urgent racial issues in a nonconfrontational manner won him numerous supporters within these important institutions.

Escalating black militancy during the 1950s and 1960s was the third major influence on Young. The Brown decision of 1954, in which the Supreme Court outlawed public school segregation, inspired blacks to undertake greater activism to bring about the total demise of Jim Crow. One historian has written that the Brown decision was a "second emancipation proclamation" and that it "heightened the aspirations and expectations of Afro-Americans as nothing ever had before."[3] A burgeoning civil rights movement resulted. The Baton Rouge, Montgomery, and Tallahassee bus boycotts of the 1950s, the Little Rock crisis of 1957, and the Greensboro sit-ins of 1960 mobilized blacks and sympathetic whites to demonstrate and protest until the federal government moved to end second-class citizenship for the nation's largest racial minority. When Young became executive director of the National Urban League in 1961, he wanted to revive a conservative organization that viewed its role as narrowly oriented toward social service. His desire to make this change came mainly from two sources. First, Young had experience as an activist. Second, the growing militancy of that civil rights struggle compelled him to make forthright statements in support of black demands for political and economic equality. With freedom rides, sit-ins, and marches occurring throughout the South and some parts of the North, Young wanted the National Urban League to get involved directly in the black struggle. He wanted blacks unmistakably to identify him and the National Urban League with such activist groups as CORE, SCLC, SNCC, and the NAACP. At the same time, Young was able to persuade powerful whites that in the midst of these unsettled racial conditions, the National Urban League was the best equipped organization to implement programs to achieve actual black equality. As a result, funds flowing into the civil rights movement went not only to such activist leaders as King, Farmer, and Forman and the groups they represented, but also to Whitney M. Young Jr. and the National Urban League.

Young made a major contribution to the civil rights movement through his audacious advocacy of creative programs for racial advancement and as a gifted and effective organizer and mediator. He suggested in 1963, for example, that the federal government undertake a bold initiative, a "domestic Marshall Plan," and spend $145 million over the following decade to rehabilitate black Americas. In 1968 he secured from the Ford Foundation a grant of $1,050,000 for the National Urban League to initiate a grassroots program relevant to the immediate needs of particular black communities. This "New Thrust" effort allowed the National Urban League "to change . . . from . . . a bridge between black and white communities to that of an advocate for . . . large, low-income ghetto areas." The League was to become less concerned with interpreting black demands to powerful whites than with developing the capacity of blacks to define their own objectives and solutions. The League would deemphasize its ambassadorial role, assume the position of facilitator, and empower ghetto blacks. Young never understated the seriousness and depth of racial realities when trying to enlist corporate, government, and foundation assistance in attacking these problems.

Moreover, Young played a key role in organizing black leaders and the groups they represented. With substantial backing from Stephen Currier of the Taconic Foundation and other contributors, Young helped to form the Council for United Civil Rights Leadership (CUCRL). The group consisted of the heads of major civil rights organizations, and they divided funds given to the coalition by several philanthropists. Young also realized that the National Urban League could assist blacks if organizations with similar goals became involved in tackling urban problems. Accordingly, he became a founder of the National Urban Coalition, a group which attempted in 1966 to forge formal alliances between business and government to solve urban ills. Young also reached out to Black Power advocates who espoused racial separatism and physical resistance to white racism. In the late 1960s he helped Imamu Amiri Baraka in efforts to revive Newark, New Jersey, by deepening black participation in the city's political and economic decision making. He endorsed the application of CORE, now a black separatist group, when officials sought foundation funding for a special project in Cleveland. Young never allowed his rapport with powerful whites to undermine his credibility with grassroots black organizations. He wanted blacks who populated the pews of black churches and filled the membership rolls of social, fraternal, professional, and service organizations to ratify his leadership and endorse the interracialism he articulated.

Each of the "Big Six" brought unique contributions and perspectives to the civil rights struggles of the 1950s and 1960s. With his stirring oratory, King drew upon the rich religious and cultural heritage of blacks to articulate in moral and democratic terms their hopes and aspirations. Wilkins used the NAACP's numerous contacts in the White House and in Congress to get important civil rights legislation enacted. Farmer, Lewis, and Forman represented organizations that worked at the grassroots mobilizing blacks to register to vote and urging them to challenge unjust racial practices through sit-ins, freedom rides, and marches. Height injected an organized female presence in a movement largely dependent on women's support, but one in which men held the most visible and influential positions.

Whitney M. Young Jr., alone among these civil rights leaders, drew unprecedented financial support, mainly from foundations and corporations, to the civil rights movement. Although foundations had been involved in racial affairs for several decades, Young persuaded them to give larger amounts to the National Urban League and to other civil rights groups. Also, most businessmen, except for a notable few, had remained aloof from racial betterment organizations. Whitney Young changed that. He persuaded corporate leaders to give substantial contributions to his group, and he involved them more conspicuously in civil rights and urban affairs. He capitalized on his relationships with Presidents Kennedy, Johnson, and Nixon to influence the appointment of blacks to key subcabinet and agency positions within the executive branch and to attract federal money to important League projects.

Young was a pragmatist, an organizer, and a facilitator who built coalitions between factions of black integrationist leaders and later reached out to include younger and more militant Black Power advocates. At the same time, he solidified relationships with corporate leaders and foundation executives and involved them in the civil rights movement. He moved the once conservative National Urban League into the thicket of the black struggles of the

1960s. Moreover, he changed its focus and direction when rioting in major cities and the rise of Black Power convinced him that the League clientele required greater input in the creation and implementation of programs aimed at assisting them. No longer would the organization confine its role to speaking to powerful whites for poor urban blacks. It would now help inner-city residents to design programs and spearhead groups to express their needs and aspirations to white-controlled public and private institutions.

Whitney M. Young Jr. was a mediator between deprived blacks and powerful whites, who tried to reconcile their different perspectives and interests. He also communicated to white Americans the integrationist vision of millions of middle- and working-class blacks who wanted an end to social and economic barriers based on race. What follows is a critical assessment of his leadership and his ambitious attempt to mobilize the resources of government, corporations, and foundations to end the poverty, deprivation, and discrimination that lay at the core of racial inequality in the United States.

_1_

As the Twig Is Bent

Whenever Whitney M. Young Jr. mentioned his background in Kentucky, he identified himself and his native state as southern. He remembered that Jim Crow was as deeply entrenched in this border state as it was anywhere in the Old Confederacy. Segregated housing, schools, restaurants, libraries, and other public facilities were as much a part of Kentucky's racial landscape as they were Alabama's or Mississippi's. Yet, in some ways, Kentucky was different. Sixty years before Young was born, the state's nonslaveholding majority and its indigenous abolitionist movement limited the influence of slaveholders. When the Civil War occurred, Kentucky, while retaining its commitment to the "peculiar institution," sided with the North and stayed in the Union.[1] Nonetheless, in ways that mattered most to blacks, Kentucky was no different from other southern states.

During Reconstruction most white Kentuckians denounced the Thirteenth, Fourteenth, and Fifteenth Amendments. As Jim Crow evolved into legal form in the South in the late nineteenth and early twentieth centuries, white Kentuckians imposed rigid racial segregation and discrimination on blacks. They were segregated as customers on public transportation, as patrons of white businesses, and as clients of health and welfare agencies. Employment discrimination locked them out of better paying jobs and relegated them to menial occupations. Racial violence, like that which plagued Alabama and Mississippi, was also present in Kentucky. Although blacks eventually secured the franchise, hostility from Democrats and indifference from Republicans limited their political influence. Louisville enacted a residential segregation ordinance in 1914 to lock in the physical separation of the races. Although the U.S. Supreme Court struck down the law in 1917 in _Buchanan v. Warley_, the desire to maintain second-class citizenship for black Kentuckians in no way disappeared. Any effort to promote racial equality and full integration met stiff resistance from white Kentuckians who wished their state to observe the doctrine of separate but unequal as tenaciously as any Deep South state. Hence, Berea College, an interracial institution, yielded to the majority white sentiment, which espoused Jim Crow. The founding and fate of this interracial experiment was a part of Kentucky's ambiguous legacy to Whitney M. Young Jr.[2]

Established in eastern Kentucky in 1855 by two white abolitionists, Berea College admitted both black and white students. In 1904, however, during the spread of legalized Jim Crow throughout the South, the Kentucky legislature passed the Day Law, which banned integrated education. Berea supporters sympathetic to black Kentuckians wanted to build another school for them. As a result, Berea trustees raised funds and founded the Lincoln Institute near Simpsonville, Kentucky, in 1910. The Eckstein Norton School for Girls in Cane Spring, Kentucky, also merged into this new institution. Strongly influenced by Booker T. Washington's Tuskegee Institute, Lincoln stressed vocational training in agriculture, business, industrial and building trades, and steam and maintenance engineering. Women could enroll in home economics and pre-nursing courses. In 1912, eighty-five students, including Young's father, enrolled in Lincoln Institute. Within the next few years, his mother, Laura Ray, also enrolled.[3]

Lincoln Institute, a high school, emerged out of Berea College separate and unequal. Since Young's parents spent most of their lives at this struggling institution as teachers and administrators, he learned firsthand about the realities of race relations and the methods that black leaders used to improve the condition of their followers. Created in the image of Tuskegee Institute, Lincoln required its black faculty and staff to adopt an accommodationist philosophy and to emphasize practical education. To woo white benefactors and reassure white Kentuckians, Whitney M. Young Sr. did not present himself or Lincoln Institute as threats to the racial status quo. As a teacher at Lincoln from 1920 to 1935 and afterwards as president, the elder Young, who depended heavily on white contributors, seldom antagonized powerful Kentucky whites with strident demands for black equality. In numerous speeches and articles he extolled vocational education and promoted hard work and religious piety. He emulated the leadership style and educational aims espoused by Booker T. Washington. At the same time, Young searched for any cracks or openings in Kentucky's Jim Crow system to advance his students and other blacks beyond the restraints of racial segregation and second-class citizenship. The techniques and strategies he employed to draw white support to Lincoln Institute later proved instructive to his son.

Whitney Moore Young Jr. was born on July 31, 1921, in Lincoln Ridge,

Kentucky, a village that embraced the Lincoln Institute campus and the residences of the school's faculty and staff. He grew up with his two sisters, Arnita and Eleanor, born in 1920 and 1922. Their mother, Laura, was born in Lebanon, Kentucky, in August 1896. Her parents, Richard and Ella Ray, were native Kentuckians, both born in 1860, probably as slaves. Married in 1881, Richard Ray operated a sulphur well and sold its special water to an interracial clientele to support his wife and ten children. For a time, Laura's older siblings worked to supplement the family income. Mary taught school, and Abe and George became farm laborers. In spite of these financial struggles, the Rays lived in their own mortgage-free home in 1900. Laura met Young at Lincoln Institute, and they married in 1914. She continued her education at Kentucky State College and taught school. After graduation, the Youngs lived in Detroit before returning to Lincoln Institute in 1920. Until her death in 1962, Laura Ray Young assumed numerous roles in the small Lincoln Ridge community.[4]

She was a firm disciplinarian who required her children to dress impeccably and to conduct themselves in a courteous and respectful manner. Although she was strict with her daughters, her jovial son, Whitney, whom everyone called Junior, frequently could get her to smile even when she attempted to teach him a serious lesson in proper behavior. Affectionately known as "Mother Dear" by her children and later her grandchildren, Laura Ray Young was a gracious and formal woman who wanted her offspring to be credits to their family and set positive examples for Lincoln Institute students who were sometimes deprived of such parental guidance.[5]

Mrs. Young's conscientious rearing of her three children, however, did not preclude deep involvement in the lives of Lincoln Institute students. To numerous Lincoln youth, her home-cooked meals were far superior to food prepared by the campus dietitians. Those audacious enough to knock on her door were seldom turned away. Occasionally, she went to nearby Simpsonville and Shelbyville to buy clothing for needy students. She also intervened with the police whenever Lincoln youth were wrongly accused of misconduct. During her husband's teaching and administrative career at Lincoln Institute, she became a campus matriarch, always ready to correct a pupil's poor English or offer advice to a troubled student. Unlike her spouse, Laura Ray Young openly defied Jim Crow practices and flouted them whenever she could. It was the custom in Simpsonville and Shelbyville stores that blacks were prohibited from trying on garments before purchase. Mrs. Young firmly and successfully resisted this policy when it involved her children and Lincoln Institute students. In 1945, she became the postmistress at Lincoln Ridge,

Kentucky. This position provided her with an independent, professional identity unusual among black women in Kentucky.[6]

Young probably inherited his assertive and outspoken attributes from his mother. He learned different lessons, however, from his father. For nearly fifty years, the elder Young served Lincoln Institute as a teacher, athletic coach, and administrator. Working in a border state riddled with Jim Crow, Young was tied to a school that stressed vocational education. Whites believed such training would prepare blacks for practical occupations that would not challenge the racial status quo. Like Booker T. Washington, the elder Young did not articulate black aspirations or define black goals in ways inimical to white interests. He also worked surreptitiously to limit the influence of white prejudices upon black education and to circumvent Jim Crow whenever integration was an attainable objective. When he wished to introduce electrical engineering into his school's curriculum, for example, he presented the proposal to white supporters as a janitorial course. Although his professional standing in Kentucky education depended on the existence of segregated institutions, Young initially endorsed efforts to integrate schools in his state. A pragmatic, resourceful educator skilled in racial diplomacy, he set a compelling example for his son, who achieved similar success in his dealings with influential whites in government, business, and philanthropy.

Born in Midway, Kentucky, in November 1895, Whitney M. Young Sr. grew up in poorer circumstances than his wife. Taylor Young, his father, was born in March 1855, and his mother, Anne Henderson, was born in May 1864. Taylor worked as a farm laborer, and his wife earned money as a cook. In 1900, they did not own the home in which they reared their daughter and two sons. Although Whitney knew little about his father's ancestors, he learned plenty about his maternal relatives.[7]

His mother's parents were Harve and Winnie Henderson. Grandfather Harve, born a slave near Georgetown, Kentucky, took the surname Henderson from the wealthy white family who held him in bondage. He did not remember his parents because he had been sold away from them while still a small boy, "a fact he mentioned with considerable pain." "A full-blooded Negro," Harve Henderson died at the age of eighty-four early in the 1900s while married to his fourth wife. Whitney Sr. knew less about his grandmother, Winnie Henderson, "a half-blooded Indian." While still in slavery, Winnie's physical beauty and "her long wavy black curls . . . brought her favour with her old master." Whether this meant that she received better treatment than other slaves or that she had a personal relationship with her owner is unclear. In any case, Harve Henderson fathered all five of their children, one son and four daughters: Harve, Polly, Birtie, Bettie, and Anne. In 1880 Anne married Taylor Young, and they became the parents of five children, not all of whom survived infancy. Whitney M. Young Sr. was the second oldest.

Unlike the Rays, the relatives of his future wife, Young's immediate family lacked even an elementary education. His father, Taylor Young, was literate, but neither his mother nor his brother could read or write. Perhaps his brother who worked as a house servant stayed out of school to supplement the family income. Apparently, the Young family encouraged Whitney to get an education. He attended elementary school in Frankfort, Kentucky, and enrolled at the Chandler Normal School of Lexington, Kentucky, where he finished the ninth grade. When he was graduated in 1912, a white teacher persuaded him to enter the new Lincoln Institute. Because Taylor Young was too poor to offer his son any financial assistance, Whitney found a job at the Lincoln Institute dairy farm.[8]

The founders of Lincoln Institute greatly admired Booker T. Washington and aimed to make Lincoln a "Tuskegee in Kentucky." Two trustees visited Tuskegee Institute to find ways to mold Lincoln in the image of Washington's school. Consequently, when Lincoln Institute opened in 1912, it offered industrial and agricultural courses. As a student at Lincoln, Young pursued engineering. His training included the repair and maintenance of electrical fixtures and boilers, plumbing, and other practical skills. He was graduated from Lincoln in 1916, but school officials were so impressed with him that they invited him to return the following year to teach mathematics and social studies.[9]

World War I inaugurated a massive black migration from the agricultural South to the industrial North that lasted from 1916 to 1930. Thousands of blacks went to Chicago, Pittsburgh, Cleveland, and Detroit to take advantage of better employment opportunities and a freer social environment. Whitney and Laura Young joined this migration to the Motor City. His training at Lincoln Institute proved attractive to the Detroit United Railway Company, which hired him as an engineer.

On March 21, 1918, however, the U.S. army drafted him. Mustered in at Georgetown, Kentucky, Young received his basic training at Camp Sherman, near Chillicothe, Ohio. He served in Company F of the 317th Engineers, 92d Division. Shipped overseas on June 10, 1918, he saw action in France from late August until November 11 when the armistice was signed. He returned to the United States on April 14, 1919, and was honorably discharged at Camp Sherman, Ohio, two weeks later.[10]

Cosmopolitan experiences in France and other parts of Europe transformed black soldiers, many of whom came from the racially restrictive South. Their enlarged perspectives made it difficult for some to return to provincial southern towns where their sophistication posed grave threats to the racial status quo. Young resumed his job in Detroit. Although he made more money there than in Kentucky, Young felt possessed by a mission. Lincoln Institute was in his blood. Apparently, he envied the numerous black and white administrators and teachers who educated the hundreds of underprivileged students who matriculated at the school. In any case, after another year in the Motor City, Young joined the staff of his alma mater at a sharply reduced salary.[11]

Between 1920 and 1935, Young served Lincoln Institute as an engineering teacher, football coach, and dean of men. Like Booker T. Washington, he believed that vocational training met the educational and employment needs of the black population. For Young, education provided a means to reduce "friction between the races." He contended that training in the trades helped blacks to develop economically and morally: "When the Negro shall have become a greater producer rather than a consumer, a lender rather than a borrower, an economic asset rather than a liability, he will have a proper foundation for building the higher things." He further asserted, "All labor is dignified when done in a dignified manner." Young praised two Lincoln Institute alumni who worked as Pullman porters. They advanced to porters in charge "due to lessons in reliability and promptness taught them at Lincoln."[12]

Young also declared that his field of engineering imparted a wide range of employable skills to Lincoln students. He noted that janitors needed a knowledge of electricity, plumbing, steam fitting, and steam boiler operation. Blacks who worked as factory employees, managers and supervisors of large office buildings, and power plant operators would find engineering useful in their occupations. Optimistically, he pointed out that blacks had opportunities to open plumbing, electrical, and repair shops in cities and that "many sympathetic white architects and contractors are not prejudiced and will give work to trained, dependable Negro men." Again Young cited a successful Lincoln alumnus who wisely chose to study engineering: "After leaving the Institute he secured work as a chauffeur at the Kentucky Children's Home. Seeing a new power plant being erected, he went to the superintendent and asked if he might have the position of running the plant. . . . He told him he had finished a course in it at Lincoln Institute. . . . Not only did this boy make good and is still operating the plant . . . but he came back to the school and got six more boys when the superintendent told him he could use six more like him." Also like the Tuskegeean, Young contended that "trade

and business men make the middle class of the race. . . . The middle class is
the feeder for the professional class and the masses." Hence, "the plight of the
Negro . . . is traceable to this malicious and suicidal neglect."[13]

Young worked under four white presidents. These administrators, however, failed to strengthen the school financially and increase enrollments. Between 1925 and 1935 the student body decreased from 131 to 81. In 1935
the trustees decided to close Lincoln Institute, pay off its debts, and use the
remaining funds to send students to other institutions. Before final action
was taken, Young and J. Mansir Tydings, the white business manager, presented a "Faith Plan" to the trustees. Young and Tydings believed that deep
religious faith would resurrect this moribund institution. Specifically, the plan
freed the trustees from their fiscal responsibilities to the school. Bills would
be paid before funds were disbursed for salaries. Since black support was
crucial, a black, preferably Whitney Young, would assume the presidency.
Since the trustees had no other options, they endorsed this last-ditch effort to
keep the school open.

The confidence of Young and Tydings apparently impressed Lincoln
teachers and potential benefactors, both black and white. At Young's urging,
the faculty traveled throughout Kentucky to recruit students. Within two
weeks 125 applied for admission. Fortuitously, a wealthy black in Lexington,
Kentucky, died and left $10,000 to Lincoln Institute. Embarrassed white
trustees and supporters, shamed by such generous black philanthropy, followed with their own contributions. Young coaxed free health services from
black doctors and reorganized the farming operation with greater student
participation. Within two years, Young had turned Lincoln Institute around.
Enrollments climbed, salaries rose, financial contributions increased, and even
the institute farm showed a profit.[14]

Young, the pragmatist, accepted the reality of racial segregation in Kentucky education and used it for Lincoln's maximum benefit. Charles W. Anderson Jr., a Louisville lawyer and the state's only black legislator, sponsored a
bill in 1938 that directly aided Lincoln Institute. Since most Kentucky communities failed to provide high schools for blacks, the new law offered state
funds to underwrite transportation costs and tuition for students who wished
to attend Lincoln Institute or some other high school within the state. Young
corresponded with Anderson, supported his efforts, and later advocated more
state involvement with Lincoln Institute. By 1944, for example, Lincoln was
designated a teacher training laboratory high school for Kentucky State College for Negroes. Much to Young's pleasure, the state commenced a biennial
appropriation of $42,000 to support the program.[15]

As Lincoln deepened its relationship with Kentucky's education department, the credentials of Young and his faculty came under closer scrutiny. In 1938 Young earned his B.A. from Louisville Municipal College after several years of night school, summer school, and extension courses. Soon the state educational commissioner urged him to pursue a master's degree. Segregation forced him to go out of state to the all-black Fisk University in Nashville, Tennessee, where in 1944 he received the M.A. Compelled to emulate their president, Lincoln faculty in 1952 included ten teachers with credits beyond the master's, five with work above the bachelor's, and three with specialized technical training.[16]

Young's visibility as an educator drew him into Kentucky's black leadership class. Although he publicly eschewed partisan politics, he learned to deal successfully with Kentucky politicians and gain support for his school. His friend Charles H. Parrish Jr., a professor at Louisville Municipal College, admired Young's "detailed knowledge of Kentucky" and his "appraisal of the political crosscurrents" of their native state. A succession of governors and other state officials appointed him to numerous positions and committees. From 1935 to 1943 Young served as the state's assistant supervisor for Negro education. In 1944 he served on the Governor's Commission on Negro Affairs. The state superintendent of public instruction commended Young in 1945 as an effective coordinator of the Negro High School Principals Conference. In 1952 the state director of vocational education appointed him to evaluate the West Kentucky Vocational Training School for Negroes in Paducah. In each of these positions Young approached the separate-but-equal doctrine in a serious and, at times, self-serving way. In 1947, for example, as a state supervisor for Negro education, he investigated schools in Carroll County. He angered whites and blacks in the town of Ghent when he suggested that black students seek their education elsewhere, perhaps at better black facilities in Paducah, Louisville, or Lincoln Ridge. He had harshly criticized Ghent for its "antiquated" and "dilapidated" Negro school. Although residents wanted to build a new Negro school, Young probably wanted blacks to get a Class A education, with state aid, beyond Carroll Country, probably at Lincoln Institute.[17]

A succession of state appointments and his presidency of Lincoln Institute made Young an important spokesman for Kentucky blacks. He became president in 1948 of the Negro Section of the Kentucky Education Association, after an unsuccessful bid in the 1930s. In 1950 Young joined with Frank L. Stanley, publisher of the *Louisville Defender*, a black weekly, to launch a Commission on Negro Affairs. Young wanted to include civil rights groups, churches, and political organizations to "make democracy a reality" and improve "all Negro institutions and living conditions of the masses of our people." As a columnist for the *Defender,* he challenged Stanley and other black Louisville leaders to "extend your influence beyond the city." He noted that there was "tremendous . . . suffering in every section of the state due to the lack of intelligent organized leadership," and he asked, "Why not use some of your fine leadership qualities in helping the people in the rural areas?" He soon joined the Kentucky Division of the Southern Regional Council, an interracial organization devoted to the study and improvement of race relations.[18]

As an educator, Young articulated a conservative philosophy in part to attract white support to Lincoln Institute and other black Kentucky schools. He advocated the expansion of agricultural and shop courses in secondary schools, and he urged a greater emphasis on business, engineering, and science. The manager of the Foust O'Bannon School in Louisville, an institution that trained domestics, seamstresses, stenographers, and shoe repairmen, praised Young for his cooperation. Apparently the O'Bannon School had accepted students whom Young had recommended. His educational philosophy seemed confirmed when Fred Njilima, a Lincoln Institute classmate, built a school in Africa's Nyasaland modeled after their alma mater.[19]

Although Young remained cautious, he desired an immediate end to legalized racial segregation. In 1954, he greeted news of the landmark Brown decision, which outlawed public school segregation, like a second emancipation proclamation. The attainment of integration, however, placed some black institutions and organizations in jeopardy. Young pragmatically proposed that such groups devise plans to demonstrate their importance in a desegregated Kentucky. At the time of the Brown decision, Young presided over the Kentucky Negro Education Association (KNEA) and promoted the interests of black teachers and students. Nonetheless, he backed a merger between the KNEA and its white counterpart, the Kentucky Education Association. Despite the failure of this early effort, Young suggested that his organization change its name to the Kentucky Teachers Association (KTA) because the inclusion of the word *Negro* in KNEA "delimits" and "prevents others from joining our ranks."[20]

Young also envisaged a special role for Lincoln Institute in the desegregation of public facilities in Kentucky. He asserted that his school was well positioned among state-supported institutions to offer vocational education in engineering, agriculture, construction, pre-nursing, and home economics. "Kentucky has a great opportunity to expand its vocational services by developing Lincoln Institute," Young contended. The promise of Brown, however, remained unfulfilled for Young despite Kentucky's acquiescence to the court decision. In 1955 it seemed clear that black Kentucky students who attended Lincoln Institute, a Class A high school, would have to integrate white institutions of lesser quality. Young candidly told a federal official that some people thought that "because a thing is white it is all right. They disregard the . . . enriched curriculum of Negro schools because they are Negro schools. There are thousands of white children in Kentucky that need the services of Lincoln Institute and we do not object to opening our doors to all races."[21]

Clearly, Young saw integration as a mutual effort to desegregate both black and white schools so that outstanding institutions like Lincoln would survive. He sadly predicted that Negro schools with poor equipment and dilapidated buildings would close and cause black teachers "to lose out completely." He hoped that well-trained black educators would be hired in previously all-white schools. To reciprocate he advised black colleges to hire white faculty. Mournfully, he wrote in 1954, "It is . . . a sad commentary on American democracy that a people should be held down for over two hundred years and denied the necessary funds to build decent schools and then should be called upon in the name of justice to give up the little they have so that justice might be done to all."[22] The onus of integration, he believed, unfairly burdened and jeopardized black institutions worthy of financial support and further academic development.

Subsequent events seemed to justify whatever fears Young may have had about the future of Lincoln Institute. Since the 1950s he believed that desegregation harmed black institutions and the black professionals affiliated with them. Within a decade after the Brown decision, black school closings in Kentucky reduced the number of black principals whom Young knew from twenty-five to four. This unpleasant reality compelled Young to insist that his successor at Lincoln should be black. To safeguard Lincoln Institute, Young lessened his enthusiasm for integration and defended the integrity of predominantly black schools. As his enrollments declined, Young proposed two strategies to keep his school open. They included unsuccessful attempts to preserve Lincoln as a black facility and several plans to develop the school as an integrated institution.

Throughout Young's tenure as head of Lincoln Institute, the school owed its survival to legalized racial segregation. Numerous local and country school boards in Kentucky found it cheaper to send black students to Lincoln Institute rather than to build separate educational facilities. After the Brown decision, however, more black students entered previously all-white schools. As a result, enrollments at Lincoln dropped. For a time, Young depended on the school boards in nearby Simpsonville and Shelbyville to maintain their traditional arrangement. In the early 1960s one-third of Lincoln's student body was black. The addition of evening classes, an expanded vocational curriculum, and high school equivalency courses helped to bolster sagging enrollments. Despite the general decline in Lincoln's student population, white and black supporters of the institution agreed to keep it open until Young's retirement in 1966.

Young did not want Lincoln to close. Between 1966 and 1970 he and other Lincoln supporters pursued and discussed numerous strategies to keep it open. Efforts to establish it as a private boarding school for children of black professionals failed. In 1967, Lincoln Institute became part of the University of Kentucky and functioned as an interracial preparatory school for gifted but disadvantaged youth. For the three years that this program existed, Samuel Robinson, whom Young hired in 1960 as a biology teacher and later as his administrative assistant, served as principal. In 1970 the effort ended. Young believed that the state discontinued funding because "interracial boy-girl relationships" were "too much" for whites in surrounding Shelby County.

Soon thereafter, the trustees of the Lincoln Foundation, an independent philanthropy which had aided Lincoln Institute since its inception, discussed ways to revive the school. One proposed that Lincoln Institute become a branch of Berea College and educate urban blacks either in vocational subjects or in remedial courses needed for college admission. Under the terms of another proposal, Lincoln would serve as a state-supported vocational high school for "Appalachian white and ghetto black students from the Louisville area." In other recommendations Lincoln would become a community college in the University of Kentucky system or an academy for Seventh-Day Adventists. Trustees discovered, however, that each possibility had limitations. One board member thought, for example, that "reestablishing Lincoln as a *vocational* high school is turning the clock backward. The old Booker T. Washington concept of what was good for black people in his time does not speak to the present aspirations of the people to learn how to *think* for themselves, and for their community, rather than to learn how to serve the white man for better wages." Ironically, the death of Whitney M. Young Jr. in 1971 created another alternative. In 1972 the campus of Lincoln Institute became the site of the federally financed Whitney M. Young Jr. Job Corps Center. True to the Lincoln heritage, the center imparted skills and vocational training to disadvantaged black youth.[23]

As an important black Kentucky educator and leader, the career of

Whitney M. Young Sr. held profound significance for his son. Legalized racial segregation shaped southern black leadership in the generation before the civil rights movement. Black spokesmen developed close ties with sympathetic but conservative whites who, while believing in the racial inferiority of blacks, supported efforts to improve their social and economic conditions in ways consistent with Jim Crow.[24] To attain such support black leaders articulated goals for blacks that did not threaten white interests. This style of black leadership exemplified by Booker T. Washington influenced Whitney M. Young Sr., who stressed diplomacy and caution in his dealings with whites. He was not an "Uncle Tom." He believed strongly in black institutions under proud black leadership. He promoted racial integration whenever he could exploit a crack in the Jim Crow system. Ultimately, however, Young was a pragmatic leader who recognized that black objectives had to be reconciled to racial realities. His son learned these leadership techniques, but he used them to change racial realities and redefine and harmonize black and white interests in ways that enhanced racial equality. The elder Young was effective in his interaction with powerful whites. Despite his success, he negotiated with whites not as an equal but as a shrewd supplicant. His equally wise and diplomatic son approached whites with a directness and an urgency which would have been anathema to his father's generation.

The relationship between father and son was especially close. The elder Young gave advice and kept careful watch over his son's evolving career. On several occasions, he wrote to his son's employers, all of whom were black, hoping that they, like surrogate fathers, would promote and oversee Whitney's professional development. He asked S. Vincent Owens, executive director of the St. Paul Urban League, who hired Young as industrial relations secretary, to give his son the training and experience he needed to advance within the National Urban League. He expressed similar sentiments to his friend Rufus E. Clement, president of Atlanta University, where Whitney would spend six years as dean of the School of Social Work. "I want to take this opportunity," wrote Young, "to express our appreciation for your interest in our son. We realize that it was largely through your influence that he was employed at Atlanta University."[25]

At critical junctures in Young's evolving career he received advice and instruction from Owens, Clement, and Lester B. Granger, executive director of the National Urban League. All were contemporaries of his father, born between 1895 and 1909. They exposed him to effective black leadership strategies in dealing successfully with powerful white businessmen, philanthropists, and politicians. Young learned the uses of caution and diplomacy. Since

these men, especially his father, were also proud black leaders who were assertive when whites perpetrated egregious injustices against blacks, Young learned
that circumspect advocacy for blacks at times had to yield to urgent and
militant articulation of black demands for equality and fair play.

Whitney Jr. matured into a polished, versatile, diplomatic, but assertive
black leader. His father acknowledged this fact in comments about Omaha
residents who praised his son's successful efforts in race relations. The elder
Young noted, "It is a rare thing . . . for anyone to receive such complimentary
letters from so many important people." In amazement he added, "We all
have a few enemies . . . but, it seems that . . . you have manipulated things so
skillfully that you made friends of potential enemies."[26] Native ability partially explained Young's career successes. Parental example and nurture were
also responsible. Perhaps the relationship between another important black
leader and his parents will illustrate this point.

In writing about Martin Luther King Jr. and his unusual capacity to
love, sacrifice, inspire, and lead, the noted black psychologist Allison Davis,
in *Leadership, Love, and Aggression,* asserted that the civil rights leader "had
the incredible good fortune to be loved by both his mother and father. . . .
His personality seems to have combined his mother's intelligence and tender-
ness with his father's stubbornness, endurance, and fortitude." Davis further
noted that King's "ego was strengthened in his very first years by learning to
deal with a father who was tenacious, stubborn, enduring, and responsible."
Moreover, his "identification with his father made Martin . . . increasingly
stubborn but patient, determined, but enduring and responsible—the image
of his father." Consequently, King became "the first great Negro-American
leader born of securely married parents of good economic position. He was
also the only leader whose father did not early desert or deny him. Martin
was his father's pride and joy."[27]

Davis could have added that Martin Luther King Jr., like his father, became a Baptist preacher committed to social activism. In 1935, for example,
the elder King led a black voter registration demonstration to Atlanta's city hall,
an unprecedented display of black assertiveness. King gained from his father a
concept of the black church ministry that required militant leadership from the
pulpit.[28]

Davis was wrong, however, when he asserted that Martin Luther King Jr.
was "the first great Negro-American leader born of securely married parents of
good economic position" who deeply loved their son. Young shared this distinction. Both had fathers who achieved unusual success despite the constraints
of legalized racial inequality. Both imbibed characteristics that shaped their

leadership style and how they dealt with whites. As sons deeply cherished by their parents, King and Young developed into confident, courageous, and creative black leaders.

Their fathers, both integrationists, made them heirs to two different traditions in black leadership style. Martin Luther King Sr., an assertive black Baptist preacher, passed on to his son the mantle of militant ministerial leadership. The son brought this tradition into full flower in the Southern Christian Leadership Conference. The Kings as pastors in the black church possessed greater independence than the Youngs, who labored in black institutions dependent on white financial support. Whitney M. Young Sr. headed a black secondary school that relied on the favor of whites. Caution and diplomacy offered the best means to achieve his objectives. Once he told Whitney, "I hope you will continue to be constructive and liberal in all your thinking. . . . Many problems connected with human beings cannot be solved in a day or even a thousand years, therefore it is highly important that one should exercise sound judgment and patience in trying to find a solution to many human problems."[29] His son observed the success of these methods and used them in the Urban League, an organization whose existence depended on such leadership strategies. Nonetheless, King and Young became noted black spokesmen in the 1960s at a time when the civil rights movement had become increasingly militant. Black leaders, including Young, no matter how moderate, adapted their rhetoric and programs to fit these new realities in the black struggle for equality. Whatever inclination Young had toward militancy came largely from interaction with his mother. She resisted Jim Crow and refused to submit to its required practices. Diplomacy and circumspection characterized Young's leadership, but he blended these approaches with demands for immediate attention to racial problems and for urgent action to eliminate the "tangle of pathology" which afflicted the black population. This impatience with racial injustice clearly came from his mother.

Young also deeply respected and admired his father. In 1955, Monrovia College, a missionary school in Liberia run by the African Methodist Episcopal Church, conferred upon the elder Young an honorary doctor of education degree. His son wrote to him with "extreme pleasure and pride" upon learning of this achievement. "It is reassuring and encouraging to see" honors "come to those who . . . merit and deserve them."[30] Seldom did Young miss an opportunity to bring his father's hard-won accomplishments to the attention of others. Ralph Edwards of the popular *This Is Your Life* television program considered a tribute to Whitney M. Young Sr. When his son learned of this possibility, he wrote to Edwards to urge a commitment. Young reviewed his father's long years of service and sacrifice at Lincoln Institute. He told of his father's struggle to earn his B.A. and M.A. degrees. He added, "In the midst of all this he remained the ideal father and husband and companion to all of his children. . . . In spite of continuous limited financial resources, we, as children, were never made to feel any insecurity. His burden in this respect was shared only by his wife and consequently each of the children was sent off to school and received the necessities and even some of the luxuries, unaware of the very great sacrifice that was being made." Unfortunately, Edwards never did the show.[31]

Young did not learn from his father in Pavlovian fashion. He had a mind of his own and used it in mature interaction with the elder Young. As his career evolved, he advised and consulted with his father as a peer, especially on Lincoln Institute affairs. Young Sr., respectful of his son's expertise, drew him to the Lincoln Foundation board of trustees in 1964. Young's unanimous election came at a time when integration challenged the existence of Lincoln Institute as a segregated school with a special mission to Kentucky blacks. The elder Young told his son, "I am particularly interested in your selection because . . . the Foundation money belongs to Lincoln Institute as long as it is a school" and because the endowment should be increased to $125,000, "the point where it was originally." He added, "Lincoln Institute will continue to serve some special needs of the Negro people." With his impending retirement in mind, Young told his son that he wanted him to be actively involved in Lincoln Foundation affairs, "so that you can know exactly what is going on at the institution which gave you life and your first big boost into the arena of the great." He advised his son to draw his own conclusions from the reports.[32]

His son did just that. As more black students took advantage of educational options created by public school integration, enrollments at Lincoln Institute declined. Young advised his father to consider alternative programs for the school. Lincoln, he believed, had served its purpose and had to change.[33] Young used his influence with the Rockefeller Foundation, to whose board he belonged, to support the joint application of the Lincoln Foundation and the Academic Affairs Committee of the National Association of Intergroup Relations Officials for $166,000 to establish university-based Intergroup Relations Study Centers. The program would train students for careers "in intelligent social action." Leading scholars would develop a curriculum. The Lincoln Foundation would administer the grant and operate centers at three universities in Oklahoma, Massachusetts, and Georgia that would test the effectiveness of the program.[34] Although Rockefeller did not fund this proposal, Young's influence probably persuaded the agency to support a special project at Thomas More College in Covington, Kentucky. The Lincoln School, short-lived successor to the Lincoln Institute, educated gifted but disadvantaged black students. Since this state-funded effort ended in 1970, the Rockefeller Foundation agreed to grant $68,000 to assist Lincoln juniors and seniors. An accelerated summer program allowed juniors to finish their senior subjects and graduate. Ten Lincoln seniors would receive two years of full financial support to attend Thomas More College.[35] Such examples of Young's influence pleased his father and probably reinforced his respect for his son as a peer whose advice and counsel even the elder Young felt compelled to seek.

Whitney M. Young Jr., a major black spokesman who mingled with powerful whites in business, government, and philanthropy, bore the imprint of his parents and other black leaders in the years preceding the civil rights movement. Diplomatic advocacy for black concerns became part of his leadership style. Deeply loved by both parents, Young became a confident and secure adult. He was sure of his talents and goals and was unafraid to challenge major white institutions with both caution and militancy to open opportunities to aspiring black Americans.

2

Growing Up
with Jim Crow

Whitney M. Young Jr. grew up in the segregated South. Separate and
unequal conditions existed in every facet of black life including education, employment, housing, and public accommodations. For Young, however, racial segregation did not affect him seriously. He was sheltered by his
mother and father and exposed to unusually talented black professionals at
Lincoln Institute, at Kentucky State College, and in Louisville among his
parents' social peers. Reared in a comfortable middle-class environment, Young
was occasionally cushioned from the harsh realities of Jim Crow. From child-
hood to early manhood, separate black institutions shaped his experiences
and perspectives. Educated by black teachers, including his father, Young's
exposure to whites was limited. After he was graduated from college, where
he was a pre-med major, he worked as a teacher and coach at a black high
school. He wished eventually to join the black elite as a physician. Within the
black community as Whitney M. Young, M.D., he would command a high
income and attain social prestige. Although some black doctors became noted
leaders who challenged the racial status quo, most were content to practice
medicine inconspicuously and enjoy their status as valued participants in
black bourgeois society. As a physician, Young probably would have had a
black clientele, belonged to black fraternities and social clubs, and joined
black medical groups. There would be little need to venture beyond the black
community for professional or social associations.[1]

Young's World War II experiences, however, turned him in another direction. As a noncommissioned officer in a black army company overseas, he
discovered that his talents lay in interracial mediation. He settled numerous
disputes between black soldiers and their white superiors. As a result, Young
now knew that he could move blacks beyond Jim Crow institutions and practices toward broader social and economic opportunities. He no longer viewed

segregated institutions as shelters from a hostile white world but as impediments to fuller black advancement.

In Kentucky Jim Crow affected every aspect of Whitney Young's immediate environment. In nearby Shelbyville he had to sit in segregated theater balconies. He also saw white and colored signs above water fountains and rest rooms. On trips to Louisville with his father he could eat meals only in the black section of town. The same racial restrictions existed for him in education. Because Young was a precocious youngster, the local white postmistress volunteered to teach him to read and write, skills which he attained by age four and a half. His tutorials continued until he was nine years old. At that time he entered a segregated elementary school in Simpsonville. Called the Lincoln Model School, this facility was maintained for the town's black students. Children of Lincoln Institute faculty and staff and those from the all-black village of Montclair also attended. Fortunately, the school benefited from teachers and various instructional aids made available by Lincoln Institute.[2]

Racial segregation mandated disrespect for blacks and subjected both adolescents and adults to incredible indignities. Not only did Young hear "nigger, nigger" on the way to Simpsonville's segregated elementary school, but he watched white townspeople, many of whom needed the patronage of Lincoln Institute, struggle to call his father Professor or Reverend, but never Mister. Segregation was a fact of life. No matter how many times his mother disregarded white signs over water fountains and rest rooms, her defiance failed to protect her children from other more egregious examples of American apartheid.[3]

Young experienced some integration at Lincoln Institute. His father hired a few white teachers who, like their black colleagues, worked closely with students. Despite their presence, Young and others knew that Lincoln Institute was another manifestation of Jim Crow in Kentucky. The practice of separate but unequal allowed Simpsonville to provide a high school for whites, but none for blacks. So Young and his two sisters transferred to Lincoln Institute for their high school training.[4]

Lincoln was not inferior to white schools, because Whitney M. Young Sr. attracted an able faculty. In 1937, for example, he brought in several new black teachers, most of whom were graduates of black colleges. They included Joseph A. Carroll, a graduate of Kentucky State who taught agriculture and later chemistry and biology, and Kathleen A. McClain, an alumna of Louisville Municipal College and an M.A. from Indiana University who became assistant principal and later a teacher of mathematics. Also in the group were

Anna Howard Russell, another Kentucky State graduate and an M.A. from Atlanta University who became dean of women, and Medora F. Hayes, who held a B.S. degree from Tennessee Agricultural and Industrial State College and who served as librarian and taught commercial courses.[5]

Young enjoyed Lincoln as though it were a college campus. Physically small early in his adolescence, he participated in athletics as an unofficial manager to the Institute teams. By the time he reached his senior year, he was tall enough to make the basketball team. Young, who in earlier years skipped a grade, learned quickly from the Lincoln faculty. His academic achievements sometimes embarrassed his father. He took several classes from his dad and would make the highest marks on examinations or finish problems much faster than other students. As graduation day, June 2, 1937, approached, grades were tallied and Young was chosen valedictorian and his sister, Arnita, became salutatorian. Fearing the appearance of faculty favoritism, their father tried in vain "to modify the situation." Lincoln teachers, however, refused to deny these honors to the Young siblings.[6]

Whitney and Laura Young tried to shield their children from the worst aspects of Jim Crow. One way was to join with other members of Kentucky's small black elite and promote social interaction between their children. Frequently, Young and his sisters went to social events in Louisville and reciprocated with invitations to parties at Lincoln Institute. They mingled with the Wilson sisters, whose father was principal of Louisville's Central High School. They also saw Alice Clement, daughter of Rufus E. Clement, a Northwestern University Ph.D. and dean of Louisville Municipal College. Charlotte Smith, whose father was an executive in a black-owned insurance company, was another member of this small circle of friends.

His father's colleagues in the Kentucky Negro Education Association opened still other friendships for Whitney. William Shobe, a teacher in Middlesburg and Lynch in western Kentucky brought his son, Benjamin, for visits to Lincoln Institute. Similarly, Harvey C. Russell, a teacher and school official at various times in Louisville, Frankfort, and Paducah, brought his son, Harvey Jr., to Lincoln Ridge where he came to know Young and his sisters. Some of these relationships were solidified at Kentucky State College where Shobe became Young's roommate and Russell became a lifelong friend and confidant.[7]

Young's decision to attend Kentucky State seemed as natural as going to Lincoln Institute. First, he won an athletic scholarship, then his sister Arnita and numerous friends entered with him, and finally, his father knew the president and several faculty members. Moreover, like the segregated schools in

Simpsonville and Lincoln Institute, Kentucky State was another experience in Jim Crow education. Established in 1886 by the state legislature as Kentucky State Normal School for Colored Persons, the institution achieved land grant status in 1902 and added "Industrial Institute" to its title. When Young entered in 1937, it was called Kentucky Industrial College for Colored Persons, but before his graduation the school became Kentucky State College for Negroes. Fortunately, Kentucky State, like Lincoln Institute, possessed able, dedicated administrators and faculty. It probably had a greater proportion of Ph.D.s than most state institutions.[8]

Numerous administrators and faculty strongly influenced Young. Perhaps Rufus B. Atwood, president of Kentucky State since 1929, knew him best. Born in Hickman, Kentucky, Atwood earned an A.B. degree from Fisk University in 1920, a B.S. from Iowa State, and the M.A. from the University of Chicago. A World War I veteran, he served six years as dean at Prairie View Agricultural and Mechanical College in Texas before coming to Kentucky State. A close friend of Young Sr., Atwood was active with him in the Kentucky Negro Education Association and in the Psi Boule of the prestigious Sigma Pi Phi Fraternity, an elite organization founded in 1904 for black male college graduates. Like the elder Young, Atwood's experience as head of a black school dependent on white financial support proved instructive to the future black leader. As with his father, Young observed Atwood use his skills of negotiation and persuasion to maintain funding from the state legislature for black higher education.

Perhaps second to Atwood in their influence on Young were Henry C. Cheaney and Henry A. Kean. Cheaney, Young's history professor, was a native of Henderson, Kentucky. He earned his A.B. degree from Kentucky State and the M.A. and Ph.D. degrees, respectively, from the University of Michigan and the University of Chicago. He joined the Kentucky State faculty in 1936. Kean was Kentucky State's athletic director. Young served him as trainer to both the football and basketball teams.[9]

A popular personality of Kentucky State, Young participated in a broad range of campus activities. Initiated with six others into the Beta Mu chapter of Alpha Phi Alpha, he became the fraternity's vice president. He was also elected class president during his junior year. Now six feet two inches, Young played intramural basketball on a three-man team called "the Louisville." As football manager he accompanied the Kentucky State team to games with other black colleges in the Midwest Athletic Conference including Tennessee State, West Virginia State, Virginia Union, Wilberforce in Ohio, and Lincoln in Missouri. Occasionally the team played Florida A&M and Lane and

Knoxville Colleges in Tennessee. Whether the games were played at home or away, Young and other black students remained in a separate Negro world. When he traveled with the team to meet rivals in Tennessee or Virginia, only segregated facilities were available to them. Even if they played a home game, they were largely restricted to Kentucky State's hilltop campus, which overlooked a segregated Frankfort.[10]

When Young met Margaret Buckner, a shy and reserved student from the Midwest, this event proved to be more important than any other occurrence during his stay at Kentucky State. Born in Campbellsville, Kentucky, Young's future wife moved to Aurora, Illinois, at the age of three or four. Her mother, Eva Carter Buckner, already had siblings in this Midwest factory town and had allowed an older daughter to board with an aunt and attend the local schools. Margaret's father, Frank W. Buckner, arrived in Aurora before his wife and daughters. They followed after he found a job at the Commonwealth Edison Company as a fireman. Frank and Eva Buckner settled in Aurora at great professional sacrifice. Both had normal certificates and taught school in Kentucky. Frank Buckner also supplemented the family income with a grocery store. Schooling for their five daughters became crucial. Kentucky provided inferior schools for black children. In most communities no high school existed at all for black students. Since the Buckners did not want their children to attend Lincoln Institute or West Kentucky Vocational School in Paducah, they opted for a move north. The remote possibility of finding teaching jobs in Aurora did not dissuade them from leaving Kentucky. What seemed most important was a better public school education for the Buckner children.

Growing up in Aurora exposed Margaret to minimal racial segregation. Although her maternal relatives lived in a predominantly black enclave known as Cartersville, the Buckners lived where whites were a majority. In 1920 Aurora had 627 blacks within a population of 35,765. Since blacks made up a tiny percentage of all Aurora residents, housing segregation was not an urgent concern to whites. Margaret attended integrated schools where all of her teachers were white. Several took a special interest in her, and she excelled in her studies. She supplemented her formal schooling with an avid interest in reading. Not surprisingly, the public library had her as a regular patron. Her parents encouraged her academic development by allowing her to skip a grade.[11]

Like most of her white peers, Margaret wanted to attend either Northwestern University or the University of Illinois, the leading institutions in her state. She wanted to study journalism, earn her degree, become a "bachelor girl," and live in her own apartment. Margaret's superb academic record clearly qualified her for admission, but her parents lacked the money to send her to the institution of her choice. Her older sister, Eugenia, a graduate of Louisville Municipal College and a teacher in Kentucky, suggested that Kentucky State College for Negroes was affordable and would provide an antidote to Margaret's predominantly white environment and acculturation in Aurora. Another sister, Virginia, who subsequently enrolled in the Chicago Musical College, was graduated from high school along with Margaret. For the Buckners to finance a college education for two daughters simultaneously was difficult enough without Margaret attending an expensive institution. Kentucky State seemed the best alternative.[12]

When Margaret arrived at Kentucky State, her roommate remembered that she seemed far ahead of most students in both poise and cultural awareness. Studious and serious, Margaret commenced her stay at Kentucky State mostly in the library or in her dormitory. Unaccustomed to racial segregation, it took time for her to feel comfortable within the predominantly black environment of Kentucky State. At her job selling tickets at football games, she displayed minimal interest in the outcome of the competition between her alma mater and its black college rivals. As soon as the ticket window closed, Margaret returned to her room to listen to Illinois and Northwestern games on the radio. She had black hometown friends on both teams, and their athletic exploits mattered more to her than those of the Kentucky State players.[13]

Eventually, Margaret felt more comfortable at Kentucky State. Since she had never been exposed to black teachers, the quality of the Kentucky State faculty impressed her. Her friendship with Ann Heartwell, a psychology instructor and dean of women, helped her adjust to her new environment. Moreover, she became involved in several extracurricular activities. She served as president of Alpha Kappa Alpha Sorority, Tau Sigma Honor Society, and the Kentucky Players. She was secretary of both the Student Council and the Pan Hellenic Council. She belonged to a few other groups including the Committee on College and National Defense.[14]

The school newspaper, the *Kentucky Thorobred*, on which Margaret served as associate editor, provided her with the perfect outlet for her journalistic interests. She wrote on a broad range of topics including propaganda, FDR's election to a third term, and campus gossip. In all her articles Margaret experimented with satire, sarcasm, and other literary devices to develop her writing skills. Like Langston Hughes, who created the comic figure "Simple," Margaret brought her own character, "Needless Ned," into being.

Ned, a campus resident always on the sidelines, always a spectator, was the first to complain about meals and to sneer at campus organizations and programs, but he never participated in any of the groups and activities, "To him," wrote Margaret, "the athletic program was o.k. but Needless was the type who cheered the team when it was going strong and deserted it when it went down."[15]

During her final year at Kentucky State, Margaret wrote an essay in the *Thorobred* on "Passing the Buck" in which she discussed school spirit and made a parting shot at the Needless Neds who populated the student body. She thought that Kentucky State needed more "oneness of purpose, ideal, and creed" and should "strive together for a definite culture and intelligence that we can and should represent." She added, "To me it represents a thought which arises from four years of living in a different environment with a different group of people." Ironically, through Margaret's critique of her alma mater came an acceptance of Kentucky State as her school. She had overcome her earlier suspicion and alienation from this thoroughly black institution.[16]

Beyond these extracurricular activities, Margaret, an attractive sophomore, drew closer to Kentucky State and its campus life when she started to accept dates from male admirers. For a brief time, a member of Kappa Alpha Psi, Oscar Long of Louisville, succeeded in getting her attention. Generally, the male students from Chicago, Louisville, and other large cities seemed more urbane and sophisticated than their rivals from Kentucky's rural communities. Nonetheless, Long had a formidable competitor in the boyish and unpolished Whitney Young. He had noticed Margaret during a chapel service. Although Young received no reply to the note he wrote to Margaret, he did not give up. Since Ersa Hines of Paducah, Kentucky, a friend of his sister Arnita, was Margaret's roommate, he tried in vain to win her as an ally in his romantic pursuit. Finally, during a campus homecoming, Young, in a brazen move, jumped into the taxi cab in which Ersa and Margaret were riding to a movie. Margaret was at first taciturn, but eventually she found Young to be both "charming and disarming." Over time, as she warmed up to him, they dated steadily and each became off-limits to other potential suitors.[17]

Young was graduated from Kentucky State in 1941, and Margaret finished a year later. Although he did well in his major, natural sciences, Young depended on Margaret for help in other courses. His mastery of syntax was deficient, so she edited some of his term papers. Clearly, a deepening commitment was developing between the two; nonetheless, graduation compelled each to choose a vocation and find a place in the separate black world for which Kentucky State had prepared them.[18]

Young still wished to become a physician. Although some northern white medical schools admitted blacks, none in Kentucky did. Howard in Washington, D.C., and Meharry in Nashville, Tennessee, the nation's only black medical schools, remained the most realistic options for potential black doctors. Young applied to each institution, but both turned him down. Since he could try again the following year, Young took a job as mathematics instructor, basketball coach, and assistant principal at the all-black Rosenwald High School in Madisonville, Kentucky.[19]

Young enlisted in the army reserve on July 22, 1942, and worked as a mechanic learner with the War Department Signal Service at Large at the Lexington Signal Depot. He was reassigned on October 1, 1942, and became a junior repairman trainee and an assistant radio mechanic. On May 6, 1943, he was ordered to active army duty and was accepted into specialized training. Although he had hoped that the army would send him to medical school, he was assigned instead to an engineering training program. He studied electrical engineering at the Massachusetts Institute of Technology along with two other blacks. From January 10 to April 1, 1944, he studied at Rhode Island State College in Kingston. He continued the program for a brief time at the Army Air Force Technical Training Command in Kerns, Utah. Abruptly, the army ordered Young and others to report overseas. He was put into an all-black combat engineers battalion that built bridges and roads for the infantry.[20]

Occasional furloughs allowed Young to visit Margaret. While still in the United States, he wrote her to propose marriage. Margaret accepted, and the ceremony took place at the Buckner home in Aurora, Illinois, on January 2, 1944. They had a short honeymoon in Chicago. In September 1944 he was shipped to Europe. Margaret was now a war bride.

During the war, both Margaret and Whitney made important vocational decisions. Margaret was graduated in 1942 from Kentucky State with a B.A. in English and French. Financial necessity required her to work during her entire stay at Kentucky State. A fifteen-dollar-per-month job funded by the National Youth Administration (NYA) helped with a large portion of her board. After graduation, she remained on campus as an instructor in freshman English. She also worked for the superintendent of buildings and grounds at Kentucky State and later as cashier in the business office under J.D. Stewart. While in the business office Margaret interacted extensively with students and frequently talked with them about their vocational plans. Most of them chose such traditional fields as teaching and preaching without realizing that broader career options were available to them. This experience persuaded

Margaret to seek a graduate degree in counseling so that she could help such students to develop their potential more fully. Dean J.T. Williams urged Margaret to choose either Indiana, Michigan, or Minnesota. Margaret opted to do further study at the University of Minnesota.[21]

Young's ultimate career plans were less certain. He still wanted to study medicine. Engineering had also become an option. Nonetheless, a final decision had to await the end of the war. In the meantime, in confronting America's unpleasant racial realities in the army, Young discovered that his talents lay in ameliorating these conditions.

The U.S. army and the other branches of the armed services mirrored the segregation and discrimination prevalent in American society. All army units were segregated and under the command of white officers. Separate facilities existed for black and white soldiers. When blacks who were stationed in southern towns left their bases, they were subjected to disrespect and ridicule. At times racial violence occurred between black soldiers and white civilians. As in previous wars, the army was reluctant to dispatch blacks into combat. They were usually assigned to engineering and labor battalions.[22]

Whitney Young became a part of this segregated army. Because he held a college degree and had done some graduate work at MIT, he advanced quickly from private first class to first sergeant. When he arrived in France, Young remained in an all-black company commanded by white officers. Their duties required them to travel ahead of the infantry to build roads and bridges. Recalcitrant black soldiers, however, frequently disobeyed white officers and continued their disobedience even when reprimanded. The white officers became so intimidated by such insubordination that they refused to leave their tents at night. To protect themselves against German air raids, American military camps put the lights out at night. Under these circumstances, white officers did not wish to tempt black soldiers, with darkness as the perfect cover, to provoke a fight.[23]

Young decided to intervene. He probably felt empowered by his position as a noncommissioned officer to address these racial issues. In any case, Young offered to relay orders to black soldiers in return for concessions from their military superiors. He stressed that blacks wanted to be treated with respect, get passes regularly, suffer less severe punishments for petty offenses, and receive promotions. Moreover, white officers agreed to share the liquor that they hoarded for themselves, and they became more tolerant toward black soldiers dating European women. Because continued insubordination was the alternative, Young's proposals were given a try. Improved treatment made these black soldiers more willing to obey orders, and Young discovered his own hidden talents, which loosened his commitment to a medical career.[24]

It had not occurred to Young to choose a vocation related to race relations. If he continued his pursuit to become a physician, he would avoid substantial interaction with whites, especially if he remained in the South. He would probably attend a black medical school, intern at a black hospital in the South or a large northern city, and treat black patients. Minimal contacts with whites would be required. While a student at Kentucky State, Young had once been a delegate to an interracial national YMCA conference. This was one of a few brief encounters with whites. Young had never thought that he could articulate black demands and mobilize white support for the achievement of these objectives. Experiences in a segregated American army that fought Nazism and racism brought the subject of race relations to a new level of consciousness in Young's mind. Success in finding common ground for white officers and black soldiers to deal with each other with civility and compromise caused Young to think of other career possibilities in which to employ these newly found talents.[25]

World War II was a watershed in Whitney Young's life. Aside from the usual rigors of military life, he came to realize the urgency of allaying mounting racial tensions in both the armed services and American society in general. At home, blacks dissatisfied with residential segregation and police brutality rioted in urban areas, including Detroit and New York City. In major defense industries black workers went on strike to complain about employment discrimination. Overseas, as Young himself observed, black soldiers disobeyed white officers who enforced Jim Crow practices. "As an American Negro," he wrote aboard ship in December 1945, "I don't expect to find any great liberal changes" upon return to the United States. He would be involved, however, in finding solutions to his country's nagging racial problems.[26]

Moreover, Young pondered the meaning of World War II, especially for black soldiers who encountered segregation for the first time in the army. Again he expressed uncertainty as to whether he and other black soldiers would be received and accepted "gratefully" in postwar America. Yet for what did they fight? "To appease mad politicians in their thirst for power. Maybe to prove or disprove racial or national superiority. Maybe, but I still would rather think of it as the most vivid portrayal of a man's conviction as to what is right and what is wrong." Whatever the reasons for war, Young wished freedom for all the "little peoples of the earth, a miner in Bolivia, a coolie in

China, a beggar in India, yes, even a little colored boy in Miss[issippi]."[27]

After Young's ship arrived in New York City, he went to his separation center at Fort Knox, Kentucky, where he was honorably discharged from the army on January 12, 1946. He reenlisted in the army reserve and served honorably until January 12, 1949.[28]

After his discharge from active duty, Young joined his bride in Minneapolis. Margaret was certain of her vocational goals, but the young first sergeant was not sure of his. As his interest in medicine waned, his attraction to social work grew. Social work appeared to offer the best opportunities to do on a grander scale what he had accomplished during the war in getting better treatment for black soldiers in a Jim Crow army. The choice seemed clear. As a social worker, he could address the societal ills that afflicted blacks in post–World War II America.

3

Maturing in Minnesota

Whitney Young's later effectiveness as a national black leader owed much to his early professional experiences in Minnesota and Nebraska. From his work with National Urban League affiliates in Minneapolis and St. Paul he learned important lessons in mobilizing interracial support for black advancement. He persuaded influential whites in these communities, especially in business, to cooperate with League efforts to broaden employment opportunities for blacks and to become permanent backers of these local affiliates. At the same time, Young recognized that black activism represented another effective means to break down racial barriers. Both as a participant and as a behind-the-scenes supporter, Young reasoned that on appropriate occasions, black protest could achieve some League objectives faster than the patient, less confrontational efforts of sympathetic whites and cautious blacks.

Nonetheless, when Young arrived in Minneapolis in 1946, he was still uncertain about his vocational objectives. Margaret had lived at the Phyllis Wheatley House, a social settlement in a predominantly black section of the city. When her husband arrived, they rented space in a family home.[1] As Young debated whether a medical career or race relations work suited him better, Margaret continued study toward the master's degree in psychology and prepared for the arrival of their first child, Marcia, in the late autumn. In the meantime, Mr. and Mrs. Ashby Gaskins, one of whom studied at Kentucky State with Margaret, helped Young to overcome his indecision. They observed that his interpersonal skills, so ably demonstrated overseas in the army, made social work the better career choice. Besides, they had jobs in the social services and could certainly identify a potential colleague.[2]

Young probably possessed greater certainty about pursuing a career in social work and race relations than those around him suspected. His pivotal role in the amelioration of racial tensions in his Jim Crow army unit resulted in tangible gains for black soldiers and greater understanding of the inequities of racial discrimination among once insensitive white officers. These experiences influenced Young's decision to enroll at the University of Minnesota School of Social Work on March 29, 1946.

Since the late nineteenth century, blacks had been graduating from the University of Minnesota. Between 1880 and 1909 only eight blacks received degrees, but the university remained open to other blacks, and an increasing number earned undergraduate and graduate diplomas. Moreover, numerous black alumni and alumnae achieved unusual success in the professions and in agencies for racial advancement. During the 1940s the School of Social Work accepted black students and reached out to black communities in the Twin Cities through graduate student field assignments in the Phyllis Wheatley Social Settlement in Minneapolis and the Hallie Q. Brown Community House in St. Paul. When Young entered the University of Minnesota, he enrolled in an institution with a tradition of racial liberalism where he could refine and discipline his considerable interpersonal skills.[3]

The Youngs sometimes speculated on what would have happened if she had chosen Michigan or Indiana rather than Minnesota to pursue her graduate work. Surely, Young's life would have taken a different turn. He would not have met John C. Kidneigh and Gisela Konopka, two social work professors who strongly shaped his graduate education and his approach to race relations. Kidneigh came to the University of Minnesota from a varied career in government social service on the municipal, state, and federal levels, especially while living in Utah and Colorado. Born in 1907 in Oregon, Kidneigh earned the B.A. from the University of Utah and the M.A. from the University of Denver. He worked as a high-level official in Social Security from 1943 to 1946 when he became an associate professor and associate director of the School of Social Work at the University of Minnesota. In 1947, at Kidneigh's strong urging, the institution hired Gisela Peiper Konopka. Born in Berlin in 1910, she studied at the University of Pittsburgh and earned her doctorate from Columbia University. From 1943 to 1947 she served as a psychiatric group worker for the Child Guidance Clinic in Pittsburgh before she went to the University of Minnesota to develop its group work curriculum. Kidneigh also brought in Ruby Pernell, a black social work alumna from the University of Pittsburgh, to assist Konopka in group work courses.[4]

Kidneigh's presence at the social work school helped to make it unusually receptive and relevant to blacks. For example, Gisela Konopka's experience as an inmate in a German concentration camp made her a unyielding foe of racism in any form. The addition of Ruby Pernell to the staff integrated the teaching faculty for the first time. Moreover, Kidneigh maintained a close relationship to the black communities of St. Paul and Minneapolis. He employed the executive directors of the St. Paul and Minneapolis Urban Leagues as paid field instructors who helped train social work students, both black and white. Also, other black institutions in the Twin Cities received UM students for field assignments. Furthermore, Kidneigh, Konopka, Pernell, and others accommodated Urban League staff from the two affiliates who wished to take courses.[5]

Dean Monica Doyle admitted Young to the social work program because of a recommendation from his army superior. Still dressed in his sergeant's uniform, Young came to graduate school on the GI bill. Although he was not unusually studious, he approached his graduate education with greater certainty about his vocational objectives than if he had entered earlier in the 1940s. Young enrolled in standard social work courses, but he concentrated on the group work curriculum. His performance was outstanding in such courses as the history of social work, the dynamics of human behavior, and community organization, which he took from John Kidneigh. He received B's in other courses in psychology, statistics, public welfare, and the principles of group work. Apparently his disinterest in social pathology earned him an embarrassing C.[6]

Young exerted little energy in those courses which he deemed unrelated to his carefully focused concerns with race relations. Kidneigh recalled that an annoyed psychiatrist, who taught Young in a course related to psychopathology, complained that he was bored and unenthusiastic. Young's attitude about the psychiatric course related to some other academic deficiencies that Kidneigh identified. He remembered that Young should have studied more history, political theory, and other subjects that stressed the ability to conceptualize issues, put them in theoretical frameworks, and understand them in historical contexts. What Kidneigh and others eventually understood was that Young preferred the pragmatic and applied aspects of education. For him solutions depended on the discovery of a successful strategy and appropriate methods to ameliorate racial tensions and broaden social and economic opportunities for blacks. Perhaps for these reasons Young excelled in his fieldwork assignments where interpersonal skills rather than academic abilities seemingly proved more useful.

Despite these shortcomings, Kidneigh wrote in January 1947 that Young's record was very good and that he had impressed the faculty with his "sincerity, integrity, sound reasoning and grasp of social work principles." Additionally, Young satisfactorily completed one phase of his field experience in basic casework at the UM training center at the Hennepin County Welfare

Board.[7] He was not interested in casework, however, but in race relations as pursued by the National Urban League.

Founded in 1911 in New York City by middle-class blacks and wealthy and philanthropic whites, the National League of Urban Conditions among Negroes aimed to assist southern blacks new to northern cities to find gainful employment and decent housing. The League resulted from a merger of three interracial New York City organizations: the Committee for Improving the Industrial Condition of Negroes in New York, the National League for the Protection of Colored Women, and the Committee on Urban Conditions. After the merger, a national office stabilized with the appointment of Eugene Kinckle Jones as a full-time field secretary in 1911 and executive director from 1917 to 1941. The League also authorized the founding of affiliates in several cities. In 1918 there were twenty-seven affiliates, although some of them had failed by 1935. By this date permanently established Leagues existed in Pittsburgh, Philadelphia, Chicago, Newark, Cleveland, Detroit, and St. Louis. Under Jones's successor, Lester B. Granger, who served as executive director from 1941 to 1961, the League grew from thirty-seven to sixty-six affiliates. Funded nationally by the Rockefeller and Rosenwald philanthropies and locally by community chests, the League generally eschewed militant agitation for black political and constitutional rights, but it tended to stress to potential white employers the need for broadened economic opportunities for urban blacks.[8]

The League movement spread to St. Paul in 1923 and to Minneapolis in 1925. To ensure greater financial efficiency, the two affiliates merged in 1926 to form the Twin Cities Urban League. Not until 1938 did they separate and become autonomous again. The University of Minnesota School of Social Work listed the two Leagues among two dozen social agencies whose supervisors provided fieldwork instruction to students. Young could have chosen among various welfare agencies including religious and secular hospitals, the state psychiatric institute, veterans' facilities, and family and children's services. His interest in race relations and social change drew him to the Minneapolis Urban League to enhance his social work training.[9]

Before Young arrived at the offices of the Minneapolis affiliate, he already had made work in the League his vocational objective. While he was living in Kentucky, his father's extensive professional contacts allowed him to meet Julius A. Thomas, the executive director of the Louisville Urban League. Thomas's distinguished appearance and impeccable attire impressed Young, who aimed to emulate him. Whether Young wanted to imitate Thomas's stately mien or his leadership of Louisville blacks is unclear. Nonetheless, two other factors that more decisively drew him into the League can be identified. First, Young probably knew since his Kentucky years that the League offered the best opportunity to improve the socioeconomic condition of blacks and to involve whites in a direct way in black advancement. Moreover, the organization needed precisely the kind of interpersonal skills he had demonstrated in the army. Second, the social work school at the University of Minnesota, especially under Kidneigh's direction, made the St. Paul and Minneapolis Urban Leagues a part of its field education program. As a result, Whitney Young was thrown into constant contact with the two affiliates.[10]

James Tapley Wardlaw, who had studied sociology at Atlanta University under W.E.B. DuBois, served as the executive director of the Minneapolis Urban League. As Young's field instructor, Wardlaw supervised his earliest work in the League and broadened his contacts within the national organization. Under Wardlaw's direction, Young completed a wide range of assignments that immersed him in routine League activities. He accompanied the industrial secretary to personnel offices, union halls, and employment bureaus to explore job opportunities for prospective black applicants. He counseled with some applicants who experienced placement problems. He also made field visitations to other agencies from which the Minneapolis Urban League needed technical assistance. Moreover, Wardlaw sent him to the state capitol in St. Paul to compile summaries of all bills pending in the legislature that pertained to social welfare issues. Young also contacted knowledgeable persons in the Twin Cities to solicit their views on these legislative matters. He performed his duties so thoroughly that Wardlaw permitted him to present his findings to a meeting of the Minneapolis Urban League board of directors.

To Young's field consultant at the university, Wardlaw wrote that he showed "positive evidence of growth." Young has the "capacity for objectivity in his relationships with both clients and office staff, and very favorable responses were made as [a] result of his contact with our board members and representatives of other agencies." Because Young wanted a job with the League, an elated Wardlaw told Ann Tanneyhill, the director of vocational guidance at the national office, "I have been greatly impressed with Mr. Young's capacity for initiative, thoroughness, and sincerity." Although Young had another quarter to spend at the Minneapolis Urban League, Wardlaw did not believe that his favorable assessment had been premature. Young was his apprentice, and clearly Wardlaw was proud of him.

To complete Young's introduction to the League, Wardlaw took him to St. Louis to attend a meeting. There Young met some of his future colleagues.

Although he expressed a lingering desire to attend medical school, Young now seemed convinced that the League was where he wanted to be. Wardlaw had shown him the wider world of this national organization, and Young wanted to be a part of it.[11]

Proximity to two League affiliates gave Young unusual opportunities to observe and compare the operations of both the Minneapolis and St. Paul organizations. Although the Minneapolis affiliate provided him with valuable fieldwork experiences, the St. Paul affiliate offered what seemed a useful subject for his M.A. thesis. John Kidneigh and Monica Doyle, who served as his field consultants while he worked with the Minneapolis affiliate, approved his proposal to write a history of the St. Paul Urban League.

The thesis discussed the League's philosophy of social work as applied to race relations. The League, an interracial social work agency, recognized that blacks needed allies to overcome oppressive societal conditions. It employed a group work strategy to ameliorate these seemingly intractable obstacles which blocked the progress of disadvantaged blacks. Like the parent organization, the St. Paul Urban League emerged in response to massive black migration to the cities and the racial discrimination that blacks encountered in employment and housing. In the thesis Young recounted the development of the St. Paul affiliate. Mainly a narrative account, Young uncritically presented the League's functions in housing, job placement, vocational guidance, and other efforts to increase economic opportunities for blacks.[12]

Although Young believed in interracial cooperation, he was not naive. Moreover, he clearly understood why blacks in St. Paul initially greeted the League's interracialism with suspicion. When efforts to start the St. Paul Urban League commenced, blacks gained the assurance of the local community chest that regular financial assistance would be forthcoming. To allay fears that the community chest and another white agency would dominate the infant organization, St. Paul blacks agreed to raise their share of the League's operating funds. Not until both blacks and whites were elected to the board did agreement occur about the necessity for the board to be interracial. Young understood that without black representation on the board and black financial support to match white contributions, the League's famed interracialism would be a dead letter. Otherwise, whites would control, and equal participation in setting League policy would not exist.[13]

Despite a promising beginning, the St. Paul Urban League had some problems in implementing its interracial power sharing. The NUL mandated that the executive boards should be equally represented by both white and black citizens. Attempts were also made to achieve an occupational balance among white board members. Young thought the policy foolhardy, since it meant "having some officers who have never employed Negroes." Still, as Young observed, "It was many years before all of these men retired or were replaced." He also noted that their presence on the St. Paul board not only tended to destroy the confidence of the already suspicious Negro, but their activities inhibited some efforts to improve significantly the condition of League clients. Insightfully, Young identified a crucial issue that he would encounter as a League executive, that is, how to balance black input and white participation in League affairs on a basis of true equality and articulate objectives behind which both groups could rally.

Young's thesis revealed a thorough knowledge of the Urban League movement. Moreover, his complete mastery of the development of the St. Paul affiliate gave him valuable historical information and a pragmatic understanding of its operations that would prove especially useful in his future dealings with the agency. His intimate study of the St. Paul Urban League also emboldened him to make suggest ways to stabilize fiscal support from the community chest, to continue cooperation with the University of Minnesota School of Social Work in encouraging students to enter the League movement, and to revive the Urban League Guild to allow black and white women to work together for black advancement.

Although he was certain that the League, as a service agency, had a large role to play among blacks in the Twin Cities and elsewhere, Young remained uneasy about the differing ways that blacks and whites understood the term *interracial.* To blacks it usually meant white financial support and consultation. To whites it frequently implied significant input into the major decisions of the affiliate, since their monies mainly sustained the organization. Most local executives wanted white contributions and assistance, especially when a white board member could intervene with a recalcitrant employer who refused to deal seriously with a League representative. Clearly, blacks wanted whites to be silent partners!

In many League cities there were efforts to make affiliates black community organizations whose objectives blacks defined, albeit with white financial support. What Young identified in his thesis as suspicion by St. Paul blacks of white attempts to control the League through the community chest were ambivalent feelings about the League's emphasis on interracialism. Unsure himself, Whitney Young entered the League movement with similar perspectives about the group's interracialism. Although he stressed the importance of black community support of League objectives, he grew to recognize the importance of increased white involvement and support of the organization.[14]

In August 1947 Young's thesis earned him the M.A. degree in social work from the University of Minnesota. Although he did his major field assignment with the Minneapolis Urban League, S. Vincent Owens, executive director of the St. Paul Urban League, had been interested in Young from the time he entered the School of Social Work. Apparently Young's thesis topic solidified their relationship. Young filled an unexpected vacancy at the St. Paul affiliate when its industrial relations secretary left to resume his teaching career.[15]

Born in 1909 in Kansas, Owens was graduated from the University of Kansas and studied at the New York School of Social Work as an Urban League fellow. Later he earned the M.A. degree in social work from the University of Minnesota. He acquired broad experience in social service administration in Atlanta as an official in the Federal Emergency Relief Administration, at the Maryland State Transient Bureau, in Louisville as head of the Negro Division of the United States Employment Service, and in New York City in the Service Bureau for Negro Children. He became the executive director of the St. Paul Urban League in 1941.[16]

Owens earned a reputation for militancy among St. Paul blacks. In 1947, for example, James S. Griffin, a six-year veteran on the St. Paul police force, was denied a promotion because of his race. Owens called the civil service board to request a copy of its employment manual. Promptly, he showed police officials how they had violated the rules in dealing with Officer Griffin. As a result Griffin received his promotion. In another instance, Owens intervened when a theater owner refused entry to a group of black youths. Although tall, husky, and broad shouldered, Owens talked gently to the proprietor and pointed out that televisions would soon be common in most households and might damage his business. It was foolhardy for him to turn away customers under these circumstances. Apparently, Owens persuaded him to open the cinema to blacks.[17]

While Owens established his legitimacy as a black community leader, he also gained credibility among whites in business and government. His tenure as head of the St. Paul Urban League during the entire span of World War II put Owens in a pivotal position to influence white politicians and white employers who were fearful of the epidemic of black unrest that affected other parts of the country. At military installations both in the United States and overseas, recalcitrant black servicemen, tired of segregation and mistreatment, became restive, disobedient, and at times violent. Black workers, equally impatient with the persistence of employment discrimination, ignored federal, union, and company officials and staged wildcat strikes during the war to protest unfairness in the workplace. Additionally, black urban residents, especially in New York City and Detroit, rebelled against crowded and substandard housing, police harassment, and other racial injustices. These conditions caused serious riots in several major cities.[18] Governor Edward Thye wanted to avert such catastrophes in his state, particularly in the Twin Cities.

While seated next to Michigan governor Harry F. Kelly at a governors' conference in Columbus, Ohio, in 1943, Thye noticed his colleague leave to take an important telephone call. Kelly returned and informed Thye that a major race riot had erupted in Detroit. Resolved that this would not happen in Minnesota, Thye appointed an interracial commission to study any significant conditions that might cause serious social disorders. The commission included fourteen members of whom five were black, including S. Vincent Owens.

Although the commission met in the governor's office, it had neither budget nor staff. Despite this lack of resources, the members believed that a study of job discrimination against black workers in Minnesota would provide needed information to political and business leaders who wanted to improve race relations. Owens offered the commission office space at the League and allowed the affiliate's industrial relations secretary, Charles F. Rogers, to direct the study. Predictably the report observed that the St. Paul and Minneapolis Urban Leagues possessed both the skills and the personnel to ameliorate difficulties in employment placement for blacks. Moreover, it was noted that Duluth needed an Urban League. The report suggested that municipal and civic leaders in that community should use the services of the Twin Cities affiliates to help improve employment prospects for Duluth blacks. Completed in 1945, the interracial commission report drew upon data which the two affiliates provided and depended on personnel from the St. Paul agency. In the process, Owens brought his affiliate into statewide prominence and enhanced his position as a leader. Thye credited Owens and Rogers with producing the essential elements of the report. Even Thye's successor, Governor Luther Youngdahl, in response to Owens's continued involvement in state affairs, told NUL director Lester B. Granger that Owens was "a high class gentleman, of fine personality and unusual ability." Such commendations proved important to Whitney Young, since Owens became his mentor in the League.[19]

Owens had few if any qualms about hiring Young to replace Charles F. Rogers as industrial relations secretary and director of vocational guidance. Others in the Twin Cities already marked him as a "comer" in the area's community affairs. While he was still at the university, the Minneapolis Junior Chamber of Commerce elected him a member. When he assumed his duties at the St. Paul Urban League, the president of that city's junior chamber of commerce accepted his membership transfer. As an associate to the increasingly influential S. Vincent Owens and newly affiliated with an important, predominantly white civic organization, Young started work in the St. Paul Urban League with promising connections.[20]

Whitney Young became aware of the twofold challenge that lay ahead of him in St. Paul. First, he grew to recognize the importance of white financial contributions to the League and the indispensable assistance of civic and business leaders in softening employer opposition to job advancements for blacks. At the same time, like S. Vincent Owens, Young realized that black community support of League leadership and programs was crucial to the group's credibility as the representative voice of the city's largest racial minority. In another context, one black scholar has noted that black leaders need external sources of white political and economic support "while they simultaneously require legitimation internally among blacks."[21] Young started to learn that effective leaders had to articulate the integrationist aspirations of middle- and working-class blacks.

This dialectical tension between two different constituencies put the League in difficult circumstances. Simultaneous satisfaction of both groups was hard to achieve and maintain. Yet, for the three years that Young worked with Owens, that seemingly impossible feat was accomplished. Young was fortunate to work in Minnesota during the terms of two governors and other political leaders who responded effectively to the national wartime militancy of black Americans. Wishing to avoid the racial violence and protest prevalent in other cities, the military, and the workplace, Minnesota's political and business leaders moved to establish commissions, enact legislation, and pressure racially recalcitrant employers to take the offensive, anticipate black demands, and respond to them before significant unrest occurred. Ironically, S. Vincent Owens, Whitney Young, and others, inspired by that same militancy, mobilized blacks to press for broader opportunities, particularly in employment. Their organizational skills and credibility among blacks brought success in breaking down racial barriers. Additionally, the presence of a sympathetic white elite that disdained Jim Crow and actively cooperated with League leadership proved equally crucial to the advancement of blacks in the Twin Cities.

At the time that Young assumed his duties at the St. Paul Urban League, Governor Luther Youngdahl, a devout Lutheran, continued the racial liberalism of his predecessor. Youngdahl pushed, though unsuccessfully, for a Fair Employment Practices Committee bill in 1947, 1949, and 1951. By executive order he desegregated the Minnesota National Guard in 1949, and he mandated nondiscriminatory hiring in state government. In an important symbolic gesture, Youngdahl joined the St. Paul NAACP, and he personally investigated racial discrimination at a Lutheran-run invalid hospital.[22] Hubert Humphrey's efforts as mayor of Minneapolis complemented the governor's racial egalitarianism. He sponsored legislation to create a municipal FEPC. With lobbying from his human relations committee, headed by Reverend Rueben H. Youngdahl, the governor's brother, the measure passed in 1947. Humphrey, who held membership in the Minneapolis Urban League, also solicited its advice concerning some nominees to the agency.[23] Youngdahl and Humphrey, a Republican and a Democrat, helped to develop a bipartisan consensus among some officials in both government and business to effect advancement for blacks. Work in such an atmosphere greatly aided Whitney Young and others concerned with the improvement of race relations.

Young aimed his efforts at major breakthroughs in employment, and he challenged numerous Jim Crow practices in St. Paul. Vincent Owens, his boss, and Charles Rogers, his predecessor, had already written most of "The Negro Worker in Minnesota," the first report of the governor's interracial commission. In it they surveyed Minnesota's principal employers and labor unions and their record in race relations. As a result, when Young assumed the job of industrial relations secretary, he had relevant information available. Additionally, Charles Washington and Owens, the successive directors of the League, within the previous decade persuaded some employers to hire blacks in formerly lily white positions. To maintain this momentum, Young was relieved of routine job placement responsibilities. He transferred, for example, household employment to the Minnesota State Employment Service. "The Urban League is not an employment agency," Young declared in his annual report. Consequently, he focused his energies on opening jobs in fields where blacks had not worked before.[24]

With an experienced superior on hand and with modest improvements in the racial environment, Young commenced his work. To enhance his effectiveness, he secured assistance from League board members and other influential whites. For example, when he tried to persuade a St. Paul laundry owner to offer jobs to blacks, white board members Walter Rock, a school administrator, and Carl Schuneman, a major retailer, accompanied him on a visit. The presence of Rock and Schuneman helped Young to persuade the

proprietor to end his discriminatory practices. On another occasion he succeeded in getting blacks hired at Minnesota Mining and Manufacturing (3M).
Again, intervention from influential whites, friendly to League objectives,
probably helped.[25]

Although Young's predecessors had made some employment advances
for blacks, much remained to be achieved. In 1948, for example, Young reported that only 100 area manufacturing companies out of 800 employed
blacks. In 1949, he added sixteen firms to that list. In 1950, however, he
persuaded ten companies to hire blacks, especially in nontraditional jobs. In
each instance, blacks secured employment in occupations that had been exclusively white, including jobs as a chemist, laboratory technician, watch repairman, and bookkeeper.[26]

Young pursued numerous other methods to advance the occupational
interests of St. Paul blacks. Probably with assistance from S. Vincent Owens,
Young developed working relationships with several persons and agencies in
the state government. When the Governor's Interracial Commission authorized a follow-up study of Minnesota black workers, committee members
chose Whitney Young and William Seabron, the industrial relations secretary
of the Minneapolis Urban League, to research and write the report. In 1949
they produced "The Negro Worker's Progress in Minnesota." Young and
Seabron reported significant black employment gains in the public utilities,
where a dozen black males, for example, became motormen and conductors
at Twin City Transit and four black females took jobs as switchboard operators; both were unprecedented developments. They also noted gains in local
department stores, in state, county, and municipal employment, and in several factories.

Employers in beverage production, trucking, milling, railroads, and food
processing resisted hiring and upgrading black workers. Predictably, Young
and Seabron placed collective responsibility for the lack of progress in some
occupational areas on timid or racist employers, unfriendly labor unions,
restricted access to apprenticeship programs, and poorly administered vocational guidance efforts in public schools. They also noted racial discrimination by various employment recruitment agencies, both government and private.[27]

This special assignment with the governor's interracial commission represented only one of several ways that Young sought to influence public officials to promote broader employment opportunities for blacks. In St. Paul,
the seat of Minnesota's state government, he grew to understand politics better, specifically the role of reciprocity in achieving important League objec-

tives. In 1949, for example, he helped Governor Youngdahl by testifying before legislators in support of various mental health proposals. The bill's passage pleased Youngdahl, who thanked Young for his support and asked him "to stand by for continued help." He wanted Young's further assistance to get patient-centered hospitals as well as detection and preventive services for the mentally ill. Mental health was an important issue within social work, Young's chosen profession, but League objectives to improve black employment were uppermost in his mind. In return for his support for Youngdahl's mental health legislation, Young probably pressed the governor to hire black professionals once public agencies in the field were established. So Youngdahl informed Young that representatives from the Citizens Mental Health Committee and the Minnesota Civil Services would contact him with notices about "job openings and methods of calling these to the attention of your community." Apparently, the governor and Young tacitly agreed that two deprived minorities could benefit equally from this new legislation.[28]

Similarly, Young intervened with Bernhard LeVander, Minnesota's Republican state chairman, to help Louis Moore, a St. Paul black with training in agricultural economics, to become a meat inspector. Through LeVander's efforts and Young's persistence, an aide to the governor contacted the state commissioner of agriculture to urge employment for Moore. Although it is unclear whether Young successfully assisted Moore, this episode further illustrated his attempts to enlist the support of state government to broaden employment opportunities for blacks.[29]

Young also supported efforts to enact laws against job bias. Despite legislative opposition to a Minnesota Fair Employment Practices Committee (FEPC), Governor Youngdahl repeatedly introduced bills in the late 1940s to outlaw discriminatory hiring practices. Wishing vainly for the eventual success of these bills, Whitney Young, in several speaking engagements, tried to mobilize backers for the governor's proposed legislation. In 1949 during legislative hearings for the bill, Young argued the Negro's case for FEPC. At a meeting of college YMCA-YWCA chapters hosted by Macalester College in St. Paul, Young spoke on "Practices Which the Fair Employment Practice Bill Would Eliminate." Although the legislature rejected various FEPC proposals, Young succeeded in informing Minnesotans about those barriers which restricted job advancement for blacks.[30]

For over a decade, the National Urban League strongly promoted a vocational guidance program to alert and prepare black youth for jobs in new and developing occupations. The effort also aimed to inform whites that opposition to black employment advances was detrimental to society. At the

St. Paul Urban League, vocational guidance was included in Young's job port-folio. Like his other efforts in improving employment opportunities, Young used the vocational guidance program to broaden job prospects for the League's future clients. In 1948, for example, Young invited his predecessor, Charles F. Rogers, to show films to area youth about becoming skilled workers. In 1949, Young held numerous meetings with school personnel, private and public counselors, parents, employers, labor organizations, authorities on the state level, and black youth. During Vocational Opportunity Campaign Week, Young employed the print media, radio, and several community groups to discuss new occupational fields for which black adolescents needed to pre-pare. Young noted that the week was "climaxed with a program at Hallie Q. Brown House . . . [where] several young people who have been successful in a variety of occupations told of their work and the preparation needed." Shortly thereafter, Young shared his experiences with other Urban League officials at a national vocational guidance meeting in Chicago. How many black youth in St. Paul benefited from these efforts is unclear. Nonetheless, this educa-tional program provided information about new occupations still unaffected by racial discrimination.[31]

Young recognized that appeals to whites in government and business were not enough to effect racial advancement. He learned that black commu-nity mobilization supplemented traditional League approaches and would help to end many unfair racial practices. Like Young, numerous college-edu-cated blacks in Minneapolis and St. Paul also wanted to eliminate racial dis-crimination. Consequently, Young, who counted a number of these indi-viduals as friends, led some and assisted others in selectively challenging Jim Crow practices in the Twin Cities.

Young's social life drew him into numerous group affiliations. He re-mained an active member of Alpha Phi Alpha. The Alphas, the nation's old-est black fraternity, established Mu chapter at the University of Minnesota in 1912. When university officials banned graduate members from all campus fraternities, adult Alphas in 1946 started Gamma Xi Lambda Chapter. Young played an important role in developing the new affiliate. The Duke and Duch-ess Club and the No Name group, though less formal than Alpha Phi Alpha, claimed an equal amount of Young's time. The former was a couples club whose members were recent graduates of black colleges. Deliberately bour-geois in outlook and behavior, the Dukes and Duchesses wished to demon-strate in social events and other activities that blacks could be classy and sophisticated. The No Name group included Ashby Gaskins, the social worker, Carl T. Rowan, the *Minneapolis Tribune* reporter, Charles Rogers, the teacher, and Young. They met monthly to dine, play cards, and discuss current events. Each of these groups provided Young, an avid partygoer, with opportunities to blend good times with social action.[32]

Although socializing remained the raison d'être for the Alphas, the Dukes and Duchesses, and the No Names, serious issues were always present in discussions, and frequently direct action resulted. Often Young, usually with a drink in hand, turned frivolities toward topics on the state of American race relations. Although his friends knew him as the life of the party, they also acknowledged Young as the one most serious about black advancement. In 1949, Frank Stanley, editor of the *Louisville Defender* and a family friend, wrote to tell Young that he was considering running for president of Alpha Phi Alpha. In his reply Young noted that opposition to the incumbent stemmed in part from his uncertainty as to whether Alpha involvement with civil rights was desirable. His favorable response to Stanley seemed to indicate that the Louisville editor believed in Alpha participation in civil rights. That won Young's support and his promise to get delegates in his section to endorse Stanley.[33]

Although fraternities existed primarily for social interaction, Young believed that they should not hide from pressing societal issues. During the winter of 1949-50, Arthur McWatt represented Mu chapter of Alpha Phi Alpha on the University of Minnesota Interfraternity Council. He also served on a special subcommittee that made appeals to the national officials of campus fraternities to urge their chapters to eliminate discriminatory clauses from their constitutions. McWatt invited Whitney Young to join him and a white student from Sigma Nu to meet the several fraternities and sororities about this matter. They succeeded in two or three instances in persuading the groups to end racial exclusion.[34]

Young's influence moved the Duke and Duchess Club to activism. On one occasion he persuaded fellow members to attend the performances of a well-known musician who was appearing at a local ballroom. Since the establishment barred blacks, one of the club members, a person of very fair complexion, went to purchase tickets. To the utter astonishment of the proprietor, the Youngs and other black couples arrived at the ballroom. Of course, they were refused service and asked to leave. Within a short time, the League and NAACP of St. Paul jointly filed a suit. As a result, the court fined the proprietor one hundred dollars. The No Name Club did not have any such dramatic protest to its credit. Nonetheless, two of its members, Whitney Young and Charles Rogers, cooperatively and aggressively pressured the St. Paul school board to hire more black teachers.[35]

Young enhanced his activist credentials with a membership in the St. Paul NAACP. In 1948 he was nominated to the executive board of this 265-member chapter.[36] He and several black professionals in 1949 founded a Twin Cities chapter of the Frontiers service organization. Established by Nimrod Allen, executive director of the Columbus Urban League in Ohio, the Frontiers promoted various projects to improve their communities and to encourage leadership and excellence in the business and professional lives of the members. Carl T. Rowan was elected president, and Young was named to the board of directors. The Frontiers deliberately held their meeting in desegregated hotels in St. Paul and Minneapolis to make sure that the facilities remained open to blacks.[37]

In these groups Young either spearheaded or participated in efforts to effect racial change in the Twin Cities. He was successful partly because he had become well connected in the local black leadership network. Affiliation with important organizations and his leadership role within them legitimized Young as a community spokesman and emboldened him to move against racial injustices. His network expanded and his legitimacy enhanced as he became involved in St. Paul's black religious community. Young joined St. James African Methodist Episcopal Church, a leading congregation, and within a short time the pastor, Reverend Benjamin N. Moore, appointed him to the board of stewards. Moore and St. James members James W. Crump and Lillian Parks Balenger served on the board of the St. Paul Urban League. Young also developed ties with St. Paul's oldest black congregation, Pilgrim Baptist Church. The pastor, Floyd Massey Jr., also belonged to the League board. Young spoke at Pilgrim in 1949 to the church's Baptist Youth Fellowship on "The College Will Open the Door." Moreover, his wife, Margaret, taught in the church school at Pilgrim.[38]

Young became a successful spokesman in the Twin Cities for another reason. The thrust of the NUL movement in the postwar period aimed at placing qualified blacks in middle-class occupations. Those in St. Paul with whom Young associated were blacks who could benefit from this new thrust. They wanted broader social and economic opportunities, heretofore denied to the black middle class. Sue Williams exemplified these aspirations. A graduate of Fisk University, Mrs. Williams came to St. Paul as a bride in 1943. At that time the St. Paul Urban League supplied personnel to work in a local National Youth Administration project. S. Vincent Owens gave her an NYA position that lasted until 1944. Subsequently, she organized an Urban League Guild, an interracial women's support group for the St. Paul affiliate. When Young became industrial relations secretary, Mrs. Williams and her husband,

Alfred, joined the Youngs and other black college-educated couples to form the Duke and Duchess Club. Through the organization she put on an annual Cotton Ball to raise money for the St. Paul Urban League. She was much impressed with Young's successes in opening new employment opportunities for St. Paul blacks. Both she and Young tried in vain to persuade Alfred Williams, who held a baccalaureate degree, to forego more lucrative pay as a railroad worker in exchange for one of the more prestigious positions that Young had wrested from once recalcitrant employers.[39]

It must be stated, however, that what seemed to be community mobilization against racial discrimination in employment and public accommodations was actually black bourgeois activism designed to achieve special class benefits. Although the rhetoric signified racial advancement for all blacks, in reality much of what the League accomplished through Young's efforts primarily helped upwardly mobile blacks. It was therefore ironic that in 1949, Young complained that less than 12 percent of the adult black population supported the Urban League of St. Paul. Perhaps the city's lower-class blacks, especially those who were marginally employed, had a clearer view of League objectives than Young himself.[40]

Despite this lack of unanimity within the St. Paul black community, Young learned a valuable lesson. He discovered that an atmosphere of racial liberalism created and maintained by such influential political leaders as Governors Thye and Youngdahl and Mayor Hubert H. Humphrey facilitated League efforts in breaking down various discriminatory barriers. This setting also made the protests of numerous black middle-class groups more certain of success. In a different environment such strides would have been in vain. After all, St. Paul blacks in 1950 numbered only 5,666, a miniscule percentage of a total population of 311,291.[41] Even if middle-class blacks had the solid support of other segments of their community, their numerical strength would remain inconsequential. Therefore, influential white support for desegregation accounted more for significant racial advancement in St. Paul than the vigor and effectiveness of black middle-class protests. Nonetheless, such demonstrations of black resolve contributed greatly to Young's leadership training. Despite the goodwill of white business and government leaders, whites were reminded that blacks were dissatisfied with their status and were unwilling to wait indefinitely for basic social and economic improvements. These were lessons that Young did not forget.

Most important of all, in Minnesota, Young became increasingly committed to racial integration. No doubt he gained much satisfaction from his ability to lead and mobilize middle-class blacks. That was not difficult. A product of the black middle class himself, Young understood and embraced its values and aspirations. At the same time, much of what middle-class blacks wanted in terms of broader social and economic opportunities required the vigorous support of whites. Young came to enjoy his visits to white groups to advocate black advancement, to educate his listeners about black aspirations, and to enlist their help in achieving these goals. As his invitations to such gatherings increased, he undoubtedly gained greater confidence in his ability to communicate with whites, challenge their misperceptions about blacks, and attract their support to black betterment groups.

Apparently, Young made significant headway toward enlisting white support for black advancement. The Jewish War Veterans' Auxiliary benefited from his "thorough" discussion of the special report on civil rights written by a Truman presidential panel and indicated a desire for more programs of this nature. He also made a successful appearance in 1948 at Iowa State Teachers College at a social issues conference. Later, he spoke at Peace Evangelical and Reformed Church in St. Paul, where the pastor congratulated him on "a splendid job of presenting the issues in a manner that deepened friendship between the races."[42]

When Young talked about integration, he referred to broadened social and economic opportunities that drew blacks into mainstream institutions as equal participants. Integration meant more than better jobs and access to public facilities once closed to blacks. It also allowed blacks to reach for social and cultural possibilities beyond their separate black communities. He thought that blacks should be emancipated from the narrow confines of an isolated Negro world. For Whitney and Margaret, an early flirtation with Unitarianism helped to serve this purpose.

American Unitarianism had its roots among dissident New England Congregationalists who in the nineteenth century opposed the trinitarian view of the deity, denied the divinity of Jesus, and believed in the perfectibility of human character and the ultimate salvation of all souls.[43] Unitarians stressed the importance of independent thought and encouraged unusual liberalism in theological matters. The organization had never attracted many blacks. Around 1949, when the Youngs expressed interest in the denomination, no more than a few hundred blacks nationwide affiliated with Unitarian churches.[44] Yet, for the Youngs, Unitarianism seemed to satisfy a desire to ponder transcendent issues without the baggage of race.

Neither Whitney nor Margaret could seriously criticize the pastors of the churches they attended. In the pulpit of St. James AME Church stood the Reverend Benjamin Nelson Moore. He had earned degrees from both the college and seminary at Northwestern University, and he held a master's degree from the University of South Dakota. A fervent advocate of social activism, Moore promoted the passage of a federal FEPC, belonged to the governor's interracial commission, and served on numerous social welfare boards. Similarly at Pilgrim Baptist, where Margaret attended, Reverend Floyd Massey Jr., who was graduated from Johnson C. Smith University and Colgate Rochester Divinity School, believed strongly in a social gospel. With Moore, he served on the board of the St. Paul Urban League, and he belonged to the Minnesota Council for the FEPC and to the board of the community chest. With ministers of this caliber, why would the couple consider leaving congregations that projected such influence and relevance to the St. Paul black community?[45]

No matter how impressive were the credentials and social activism of Moore and Massey, they met with stiff competition from fellow League board member Arthur Foote. As pastor of the Unity Church of St. Paul, Foote's social involvements hardly matched the more extensive affiliations of his black ministerial colleagues. It is likely that Foote drew the Youngs to Unity Church, although Margaret recalled in later years that some black friends probably had invited them. Foote's congregation represented opportunities for broader interracial fellowship and intellectual interaction beyond the black community that St. James and Pilgrim could not offer. So the couple occasionally attended Unity Church. Certainly to Whitney and Margaret, that's what integration ultimately meant: to move beyond race in the totality of one's social, economic, and cultural interactions.

Nonetheless, the Youngs remained ambivalent. For Margaret, Unitarianism was too intellectual and too removed from the day-to-day realities of black life. She and Young did not join Foote's congregation. In a few years, however, their doubts would be resolved, and they would move closer to the Unitarian Church.[46]

Besides positive experiences with white Unitarians, there was much in the general climate of race relations to instill optimism in Whitney Young and to deepen his commitment to racial integration. The Roosevelt and Truman administrations made unprecedented efforts to include blacks in federal programs and to promote their advancement. Moreover, in the 1948 national election, President Truman and other influential Democrats, including Hubert Humphrey, made civil rights an important item on the liberal agenda.[47] Additionally, in Minnesota, both Democratic and Republican leaders gave increased attention to civil rights matters and proposed major governmental initiatives against employment discrimination. Mindful of these developments,

Young became optimistic about further improvements in race relations, and he was certain that integration had become an achievable goal. In 1948 he told his father, "I see a new day dawning in this whole field of race relations. Never before in history has public opinion been stronger for a more democratic society. All about the country we see evidence, small as they may be of changing patterns." In affirmation of his belief in integration, Young added, "More and more, Negro youth are going to be called upon to identify themselves, not as Negroes, but as people whose success or failure in life depends on their own initiative and perseverance."[48]

A short time later, in an interview with Carl Rowan in the *St. Paul Recorder*, Young, fresh from a trip to Atlanta, said that social forces were "hammering out interracial progress in Dixie." At a Henry Wallace presidential campaign rally, he noted, whites and blacks had expressed a common interest in civil rights. Moreover, Young claimed not to have encountered any discrimination in transportation while in the city. He also indicated the presence of whites at a social work conference at Atlanta University. He said, "It was interesting to see those students from white southern schools come out to . . . talk over the nation's problems. They came without the patronizing of 'working for you people' attitude. They didn't just discuss race relations with Negroes, but all the problems now facing America."[49] Clearly, Whitney Young was convinced that racial equality was both a desirable and an attainable objective to which he could devote his energies.

A committed integrationist and community activist, Young had learned and accomplished a great deal between 1946, when he entered the University of Minnesota, and 1950, when he left the Twin Cities. He was becoming a polished and sophisticated leader. Integration was the objective, and he knew that blacks could not rely entirely on whites but had to use a range of activist tactics to achieve the goal. When such techniques proved inappropriate, he enlisted the help and intervention of sympathetic whites to accomplish what protest could not. S. Vincent Owens, from whom he learned many of these lessons, believed Whitney to be an exceptional young man with a lot to offer. In 1949 he told NUL officials that Young deserved "a promotion in terms of leading a department or serving as an Executive Secretary of one of our affiliates." He added, "We should make use of him at the earliest possible date. I don't feel that he should be permitted to become discouraged because his talents are not utilized to the fullest extent." Owens believed that he had done all that he could for his colleague in both training and compensation. "We have recognized Mr. Young's ability and interest by increasing his salary within a two-year period from $2,700 to $3,500."[50]

Moreover, Owens encouraged Young to write to Lester Granger, NUL executive director, about job possibilities. Owens believed that Baltimore and Omaha were good prospects. At his boss's urging, Young successfully applied to become executive director of the Omaha Urban League. Now he would have to demonstrate independent leadership in a new setting without the helpful instruction and protection of his numerous Minnesota friends and supporters.

4

Becoming a Leader:
The Omaha Years

A tough job lay ahead of Whitney Young in racially conservative Omaha, Nebraska. Segregationist practices barred blacks from most downtown hotels. Restaurants did not welcome black patrons, and even the airport cafeteria refused them service. Housing for blacks was sharply restricted to designated areas bordering 24th Avenue. Even some churches steadfastly resisted efforts to integrate their congregations. Most appalling to Young was the refusal of Omaha's biggest firms to hire blacks. Even when exceptions were made to these racial customs, they yielded only to minor modifications. For example, in the 1940s, the exclusive Fontenelle Hotel agreed to provide lodging to the nationally acclaimed contralto Marian Anderson--but only if she compromised her dignity by riding to her room on a freight elevator! In public accommodations, housing, employment, and even religion, Omaha drew a color line that disfavored blacks in ways resembling the Jim Crow South.[1]

Clearly, greater liberality in racial matters existed in the Twin Cities than in Omaha. Although Young would now fight on a different battlefield, he found that methods he developed in Minneapolis and St. Paul held similar promise in a more recalcitrant Omaha. Young promoted militant but nonviolent action against Jim Crow practices and acknowledged its importance as an effective instrument for social change. At the same time, he encouraged influential whites serving on his Urban League board to strongly encourage employers, proprietors of public facilities, and realtors to drop the color barrier. Young believed that only when these simultaneous efforts occurred would his skills of persuasion, negotiation, and diplomacy be used most productively. He built on other lessons he learned in the Twin Cities. He increasingly recognized that his effectiveness as a leader depended on how well he advanced the integrationist objectives of middle- and working-class blacks.

When Young assumed leadership of the Omaha affiliate in 1950, he found a thriving organization. During the previous decade as Omaha's black population grew from 12,015 to 17,011, the League shifted from a community center with programs in public health, recreation, scouting, and social services for black soldiers and defense workers to an organization increasingly focused on civil rights activism. The affiliate deepened its commitment during World War II to job training for unskilled black workers and initiated referrals of such laborers to various placement agencies. Between 1939 and 1950 the League made some employment breakthroughs in jobs once off-limits to blacks. It also helped to agitate successfully for a local branch of the federal Fair Employment Practices Committee. As the affiliate displayed increased militancy in advancing job and housing opportunities for blacks, it completed the transition from a social service agency to one of civil rights advocacy.[2]

Within this context, the board of directors of the Omaha Urban League sought to replace M. Leo Bohanon, one of two executive directors who guided the affiliate through these recent changes. The associate executive director of the National Urban League, R. Maurice Moss, submitted Young's name along with some others. Six candidates were considered. The committee eliminated half of them and interviewed the remaining three including Young. One had been on the industrial staff of both the New York and National Urban Leagues. Another candidate had experience as a League executive in Warren, Ohio, and in the Baltimore Housing Authority. Another contender had been a successful industrial relations secretary in the Washington Urban League. Concerning Whitney Young, Moss wrote that he "is younger than the others . . . but his work in the Minneapolis area has stamped him as one of the most promising men in the industrial ranks. . . . He has an outgoing personality and impresses one with his quick grasp of total situations and his ability to plan and to carry through programs."

Whether Moss pushed Young's candidacy beyond this written recommendation is unclear. Surely he and other national officials knew that Young had become restless in the Twin Cities and was eager for greater independence and responsibility. Apparently, they helped him to get an interview for the Omaha position. Predictably, his interaction with local board members was so successful that his competitors quickly paled in comparison. They offered Young the job, and he wisely accepted.[3]

Young was fully prepared for this new challenge by the lessons he had learned in Minnesota. He knew that League objectives needed steadfast endorsements from the local white elite and from the black community. If either group withdrew its support, Young believed that his effectiveness would be seriously compromised. Trying to reconcile different white and black perceptions of progress, pace, and objective truly put Young in the middle. How well he managed this paradoxical position would determine his success in Omaha.

Young quickly discovered that local board members were his biggest assets. The presence of Otto W. Swanson and Alfred C. Kennedy proved to be a real boon. Both were veteran white businessmen who knew many members of Omaha's economic establishment. Swanson, the president of the Nebraska Clothing Company and an active Lutheran layman, was already involved in a host of civic and charitable endeavors. Kennedy was president of McFarland and Kennedy Realty, and he held a number of influential positions in local and national real estate organizations. Both men, while believing strongly in racial equality, preferred conservative and noncoercive methods to achieve this objective. Kennedy, for example, opposed laws that penalized employers who refused to hire blacks. He and Swanson favored voluntary compliance. Nonetheless, the two businessmen frequently accompanied Young to meetings with recalcitrant employers to urge the hiring of blacks in skilled and white-collar occupations. They also put their reputations on the line in pursuit of broader social and economic opportunities for blacks. Swanson not only hired two black salesmen in his company but backed Young in a vain effort to get other clothiers to do the same. Kennedy firmly supported blacks who settled beyond the 24th Avenue ghetto in all-white neighborhoods and helped them find mortgage money to finance these efforts. Such a stand was unprecedented among Omaha realtors.[4]

Equally eager to support Young in encounters with racially insensitive employers and proprietors of various public establishments were two young white entrepreneurs, William Ramsey and N. Phillips Dodge. More militant than Swanson and Kennedy, they were Young's contemporaries and shared his impatience with white Omaha businessmen who preferred that black progress proceed at a snail's pace. A lawyer by training, Ramsey was vice president and manager of the American Road and Equipment Company. Dodge worked in his family's realty company, one of the oldest and largest in Nebraska. Margaret R. Fischer, a veteran board member and lawyer, and June H. Vance, a prominent civic leader, joined Ramsey, Dodge, and Young in developing the Omaha Urban League into a forceful advocate for racial advancement.[5] Blacks on the board backed Young's efforts to establish an even more activist League affiliate. Board members Charles Davis, a lawyer and bank official, and Eugene Skinner, Omaha's first black principal, had wanted to hire Young because of his forthright leadership in the Twin Cities.[6]

Young knew that a strong board of diverse influence within the city would be key to any success he might enjoy. He carefully added new members as terms expired. With Alfred Kennedy's help, Young persuaded leading white businessmen to join the board, including Lloyd Skinner, the food manufacturer, and Roman Hruska, the politician and future U.S. senator.[7]

A strong board was not enough, however. The infrastructure of the Omaha affiliate, although improved under Young's predecessor, M. Leo Bohanon, required additional growth and change. Increased contributions from the community chest, which pulled the annual budget from $12,000 to $28,000 between 1950 and 1953, laid the groundwork. Also, Young aggressively urged new supporters to aid the League through the purchase of memberships. In 1953 the Omaha affiliate claimed one thousand members, up from seventy-five in 1950.[8]

These financial developments allowed Young to increase the staff from three to five. Marion M. Taylor, the industrial relations secretary, held this post and functioned as acting executive director until Young's arrival from St. Paul. Although he claimed an excellent relationship with his new boss, difficulties occurred and he resigned in 1953. To replace Taylor, Young brought Milton Lewis from Erie, Pennsylvania. The board also allowed him to hire a community services secretary to coordinate activities with local black organizations. The new appointee, Wesley T. Cobb of Toledo, Ohio, like Lewis, held a master's degree. With an expanded staff, including two office secretaries, the affiliate became an increasingly efficient operation prepared to precipitate and implement important social changes.[9]

Beyond these personnel matters, Young was most concerned about employment opportunities for Omaha blacks. He believed that improved job prospects were key to all other advancements for his constituents. He spoke out constantly about the issue. Soon after his arrival in Omaha, he declared to local businessmen that "eliminating discrimination against racial groups is good business." Greater economic opportunities for blacks meant "an increasing market for business." He challenged businessmen to "take the initiative in ending job discrimination against Negroes." Young further noted, "We are going to give employers a chance to set a precedent--to show that the Sermon on the Mount is more than just pretty words."[10]

Of course, Young was not about to pay mere lip service to this objective. He used private persuasion and negotiation, the assistance of influential white board members, agitation for governmental intervention, and nonviolent direct action to improve job possibilities for Omaha's restless black population.

Young knew firsthand from his Minnesota experiences that fair employment practices legislation helped to expand job opportunities for blacks. The federal FEPC during World War II had been very effective in curtailing employment discrimination. Federal investigators had statutory authority to recommend the withdrawal of government contracts from recalcitrant employers. Although the federal FEPC expired in 1946, ten states established their own agencies by 1950. Efforts to enact a Nebraska FEPC started shortly before Young's arrival. Omaha's black state legislator, Senator John Adams Sr., introduced a bill in 1949. It was defeated, and he resubmitted it in 1951.

Young did much to urge passage of the bill. In an Omaha Personnel Association panel discussion, he explained why legislation was needed given the discriminatory behavior of white employers. He traveled to Lincoln, the state capital, to plan strategy with Theodore Sorensen, a University of Nebraska law student, who had advised Senator Adams in drafting the original proposal. Young also testified as a witness before the legislative committee considering the bill. He brought other people to the hearings to display grassroots support for the proposed law.[11]

Again the bill was unsuccessful. Organized Nebraska businessmen thought that the proposal was too radical, and some even referred to Sorensen, the son of a former Nebraska attorney general, as a communist. Apparently the same view prevailed within Nebraska's unicameral legislature. In an earlier effort to gut the bill, one legislator proposed that cities and towns pass their own ordinances. Although Senator Adams opposed the substitute motion, the idea bore some fruit for Whitney Young. When the Adams bill met defeat, Young, always the pragmatist, spearheaded a new effort to induce the city council of Omaha to establish a local FEPC. He gave a hard-hitting speech to the white Omaha Ministerial Union in which he was critical of its silence on a city FEPC, and he strongly urged its members to support it. He also asked attorney Elizabeth Pittman to write a draft ordinance for consideration by the city council. They enlisted further assistance from Mary Frederick, a prominent white civic leader, but even with her influence, Young failed to get a hearing from the council.[12]

It was apparent that influential white Nebraskans, especially those in business and in state and local government, strongly opposed coercive measures to end employment discrimination. Those concerned about limited job mobility among blacks advocated voluntary efforts to achieve equal opportunity. Such individuals encouraged Whitney Young and his industrial relations secretary, Marion Taylor, to work through Omaha's Mayor's Committee on Human Relations. As the two officials moved to increase opportunities for blacks in public sector jobs, the agency's support proved crucial to their success. They urged the Metropolitan Utilities District to hire blacks as electrical engineers and mechanics. After a series of meetings with the MUD board and the Mayor's Committee, a resolution was passed promising that blacks would work in all departments and would be upgraded and promoted on the basis of their ability to perform. At the recommendation of the League, at least two black women were hired in clerical positions in Omaha municipal offices, and two other secretaries were placed in the county public assistance agency and in the city-county health department. Moreover, discussions with city officials yielded commitments to give blacks a fair chance to take both police and firefighter exams. For the latter positions Young even urged black candidates to come to the League office for advice in passing the test. Although these negotiations with municipal officials yielded major commitments, only a few jobs were immediately offered to blacks. That's why Young preferred a state or local FEPC to compel the city, the utilities board, and private employers to make good on their promises and apply concrete actions to their "pretty words."[13]

In neither instance did Young get everything that he wanted. No FEPC was forthcoming. From municipal and county agencies came merely promises to give black applicants fair consideration, and only a few clerical jobs became available to black women. Young turned to other strategies. To gain greater access to local businessmen, Young asked influential white board members to accompany him to meet employers and urge them to be more receptive to blacks seeking jobs. In some cases, he motivated white board members themselves to set the right tone by opening jobs to blacks in their own establishments. Lloyd Skinner, for example, already employed three black women at his Skinner Manufacturing Company. In 1951 he hired four black men to work in semiskilled positions.[14]

During encounters with fellow white businessmen, board members discovered the entrenched position of racism in the Omaha job market. They were amazed when so few large employers expressed interest in the important but conservative work of the League and its goal of enhancing black employment. In such circumstances N. Phillips Dodge was astounded by Young's patience in dealing with raw racial prejudice. Dodge accompanied him to a meeting with the president of a large Omaha firm. The employer, attempting casual affability, told Young about the several Negroes whom he knew. Of course, those individuals were his personal stewards! After Young cordially but firmly pressed him about hiring blacks in such responsible positions as lawyers, engineers, draftsmen, and surveyors, the employer seemingly yielded to his argument. Although he promised to hire some black trainees, however, he insisted that they work among the white employees with glass partitions around them. Young held his temper and agreed to the employer's terms, at least for the moment. He and Dodge returned for one or two follow-up meetings. Helped by Dodge's presence and his own persistence, Young ultimately convinced the businessman that the glass partitions were a needless and bothersome expense.[15]

On another occasion, Young, Dodge, William Ramsey, and Lloyd Skinner plotted a preemptive strike on employment discrimination in Omaha. Western Electric planned to build a new plant in the city on land that Dodge's realty company sold to the firm. Young and his three board members visited company officials to urge a fair employment policy. Western Electric agreed but then reneged. With Dodge, Ramsey, and Skinner behind him, Young persuaded the company to honor their original agreement on open employment.[16]

Black board members, although less influential in the larger business community, assisted Young's efforts to improve job opportunities. Arthur McCaw, perhaps Young's closest friend and confidant, came in contact with all the city's businesses as chief tax examiner. As a result, McCaw knew where employment breakthroughs would likely occur. Whenever possible during his tax interrogations, McCaw would mention Young, the League, and their employment goals. Another board member, pharmacist Lillian Dorsey, wrote to Mutual of Omaha to protest its discriminatory employment policies. Unfortunately, a conversation with the insurance firm's president failed to produce any openings.[17]

Young valued board members' assistance in breaking employment barriers, but he remained convinced that protest and other nonviolent direct action tactics proved equally effective in routing job discrimination. Although the Urban League was not a protest organization, Young cooperated with groups that were. When such groups aimed to increase employment opportunities, Young enthusiastically, though at times surreptitiously, aided their efforts. His close ties with Father John Markoe, a Jesuit priest, and the De Porres Club clearly illustrate the point.

Father Markoe, whom Young esteemed and greatly admired, had been a 1914 graduate of West Point. Service in the southwest leading units of black soldiers exposed him to racial issues. His departure from the army and his triumph over alcoholism preceded his entry into the Society of Jesus in

1917. After ordination, he served two black parishes in St. Louis. In 1944 Markoe integrated the Jesuit-sponsored St. Louis University. So great was the hostility that he transferred to Omaha's Creighton University, another Jesuit institution. A group of Creighton students in 1946 had become dismayed over the disappointing state of race relations in Omaha. One of them, Denny Holland, asked Father Markoe to help them organize a group to promote interracial justice and charity. Formally chartered in 1947, the De Porres Club, named after a black Catholic saint, drew an interracial group of students, social workers, and other Omahans to its membership.[18]

Young was most attracted to the militancy of Markoe and the new organization. De Porres members staged boycotts, formed picket lines, and precipitated sit-ins whenever employers discriminated against blacks. Some of their tactics were quite creative. To prod the Omaha and Council Bluffs Street Railway Company to hire black drivers, Markoe and others boarded buses during the rush hour. Each of them deposited the fare of seventeen cents into the receptacle, one cent at a time, an action which stalled the bus and its driver during the worst part of the day. Whenever Young had difficulty persuading recalcitrant businessmen to hire blacks, the De Porres Club and its militant tactics helped to cast the League director as much more moderate and reasonable than the unmanageable Markoe and his compatriots. Frequently, businessmen preferred to negotiate with Young rather than with De Porres spokesmen. Young and Markoe encouraged each other in the discharge of their different duties.[19] Sometimes when De Porres demonstrators put up picket lines to protest an offensive employment policy, Young would make a symbolic appearance at the scene. One contemporary remembered that Young had actually walked a picket line with club members.[20]

Young's deepest involvement in a De Porres demonstration focused on the Omaha Coca Cola Bottling Company. Based on information requested from the Omaha Urban League, De Porres criticized the firm for discriminatory hiring practices in the fall of 1950. When the manager agreed to interview blacks within the next several months, the club withheld its protest. It was evident by April 1951 that no blacks had been hired. Consequently, the club organized a boycott. Businessmen in Omaha's black neighborhoods heeded the club's request and refused to sell Coca Cola. After six weeks, the firm wanted to negotiate. Whitney Young and Denny Holland handled the talks and subsequently announced that two blacks had been hired and that no further discrimination would take place.[21]

The alliance between Young and Markoe's De Porres Club had been so close that when breakthroughs occurred, credit in some instances belonged to both. De Porres members and the Omaha Urban League probably shared the honor of persuading cab companies to hire black drivers. Similarly, Markoe rejoiced over the Reed Ice Cream Company's decision to hire a black saleslady at the main store. Apparently, Young knew about the De Porres effort and consulted with Markoe and Holland during the long hard pull to bring that small victory to fruition.[22]

Young also built upon efforts that Leo Bohanon and Marion Taylor had initiated prior to his arrival. In the brewery industry, for example, Young's predecessors had been working with personnel officials at Pabst, Blatz, Schlitz, and their counterparts in the Brewery and Distillery Workers Union in softening white employee opposition to blacks. That effort paid off after Young came to Omaha, and by August 1950, those companies started to hire blacks. Young worked closely with the Nebraska Employment Service and inaugurated a new policy with the agency. He reported in 1950 that the service placed more blacks than in previous years because of "our increased contacts with industry selling them on the idea of including Negro workers in their requests." Consequently, the state employment office made more frequent requests to the League to refer qualified blacks for job openings.[23]

Because Young skillfully mobilized support from influential members of the League board, state and local government officials, the militant De Porres Club, and other allies, major employment breakthroughs for Omaha blacks occurred. In December 1952, Young reported ninety-three new openings. These positions included architects, milktruck driver-salesmen, a claims official at the Nebraska State Employment Service, an assistant librarian in a municipal public library, stenographers in various firms, and numerous other jobs never before held by blacks. In some instances, it was simply a matter of calling employers' attention to qualified blacks already on their payroll. At Northwestern Bell, for example, two black women advanced from elevator operators to long-distance operators. One was an alumna of a technical school, and the other had taken business courses in high school and college. Young and Marion Taylor persuaded Northwestern Bell that their training could be utilized better in these new positions.[24]

To achieve these gains, Young occasionally yielded to embarrassing compromises. J.L. Brandeis, a major Omaha department store, refused to hire black women as salespersons. Young had much help from white board members in trying to break this employment barrier. Otto Swanson intervened with a high Brandeis official to argue for a change in policy. The wives of William Ramsey and N. Phillips Dodge anonymously went to Brandeis and other department stores to tell managers that they would welcome a black salesperson. Ultimately, with constant prodding by Young, Brandeis agreed. Store officials insisted, however, that the employee start in the infant wear department, where her race would be least offensive. The person assigned to the job was already on the payroll as an elevator operator. Some blacks then complained that Young accomplished these changes at Northwestern Bell and J.L. Brandeis because he consented to employer preferences for light-skinned blacks, since they would presumably mingle better with whites. Some Omaha blacks believed that Young acquiesced to these experiments because their likely successes would later open jobs to darker-skinned applicants.[25]

While the broadening of employment opportunities proved a difficult barrier to penetrate, Young found efforts to promote integrated housing equally hard. According to Alfred Kennedy, blacks were restricted to older neighborhoods where the houses had been built in the late nineteenth century on lots only thirty feet wide. He further noted that in a number of cases more than one house had been built on a single lot. Although Omaha's black population increased by 38.3 percent between 1940 and 1950, Kennedy observed that only thirty new homes had been built for black occupancy. Young discovered that segregated housing patterns compelled the city's 1940 black populace to occupy an area thirty blocks long and eight blocks wide. Although their numbers grew by at least 5,000 persons a decade later, only one additional block in Omaha's black section became available for housing. Shortly before Young's arrival, his predecessor completed a survey which indicated that 50 percent of all appraised homes in Omaha's black community met minimum standards for occupancy. Approximately 9.2 percent required major repairs, and 15.2 percent of black housing needed to be condemned![26]

Blacks bold enough to move beyond the 24th Avenue corridor met reluctant lenders, frightened sellers, and hostile white neighbors. Dr. A.B. Pittman, a black veterinarian, started his practice in a building in nearby Benson. Resentful whites, however, pressured his landlord to cancel the lease. When Pittman decided to build a home on the outskirts of Omaha, he tried to get a loan from a local insurance company. After he cared for the pet of the wife of the company's founder, she dispatched him to the firm's treasurer to get a loan. The official refused, and surprisingly the woman then concurred with the treasurer. They believed that the neighborhood needed to be saved from Pittman and other blacks. Numerous white homeowners, despite the Supreme Court's ruling in *Shelley v. Kraemer* (1948), held deeds that barred sales to blacks.[27]

Young had trouble finding decent housing, and so did his new black secretary, Lavonne Curtis of Pierre, South Dakota. Phil Dodge intervened

and helped Young find a home in a transition area on the periphery of the
24th Avenue area. Because a number of Catholics lived nearby, Father Markoe
helped Whitney and Margaret to move in. Devout parishioners were reluctant to start trouble around the well-known Jesuit priest. Markoe and the De
Porres Club did the same when a black air force veteran, Woodrow Morgan,
bought a house in a white neighborhood. Although anger was directed at the
white owner, the realtor, and the finance company, neighbors threw stones
into the house of the new black residents. Young called up Father Markoe
and De Porres members, who came the next morning to assist the Morgans.
No altercations occurred. Again, Markoe's priestly garb helped to preserve
the peace.[28]

Overcrowded black neighborhoods and resistance from white residents,
realtors, and mortgage bankers convinced Young that housing, like employment, was an urgent issue that he could not ignore. Two tasks lay ahead of
him. First, he had to educate white realtors about the harmful effects of residential segregation and mobilize their support to end it. In this effort, Young
persuaded Alfred C. Kennedy and N. Phillips Dodge, successive presidents
of the Omaha Urban League, to intervene with fellow realtors and convince
them of the importance of desegregated housing. Second, to further expand
the pool of available homes, Young believed that public housing agencies
needed to relieve the overcrowded conditions in Omaha's black neighborhoods.

As with employment issues, Young asked Kennedy and Dodge to play
major roles in the fight against segregated housing. Neither man opposed the
principle of open housing, and both tried to persuade their colleagues to
adopt the same attitude. Clearly, it was their influence which drew to the
League's housing committee five members of the Omaha real estate board,
three of whom had been past presidents.

Kennedy discredited the notion that poor housing conditions among
blacks were attributable to their alleged racial inferiority. They lived in slum
areas because they could not afford better residential areas. "If the Negro were
employed on the basis of his ability, without discrimination," Kennedy declared, "he could afford reasonably good housing." Racial discrimination also
caused slum conditions. "White citizens," he believed, had "an arbitrary, un-
reasonable and wholly unjustified attitude" toward blacks. He added, "In
complete disregard of the law, custom has pushed the minority group into a
small area of older houses, drawn an imaginary line, . . . and said, 'Stay there.'"
Kennedy was impressed with the newly integrated air force with its black and
white officers living side by side, without friction, at Offutt Field near Omaha.

The same could be accomplished among civilians, he contended. If local and county government condemned substandard homes, if mortgage companies lent to qualified borrowers regardless of color, and if inexpensive existing housing in good neighborhoods became available to blacks, then slum areas would eventually disappear. Ultimately, Kennedy contended, "The barrier around the Negro neighborhood must be removed. Negroes must be free to move into neighborhoods where their economic status permits them to live."

To translate these sentiments into action, Kennedy intervened for Dr. A.B. Pittman when he could not find favorable mortgage terms to build a new home in a white area. Kennedy helped Pittman get a loan from the New York-based Aetna Life Insurance Company.[29]

Apparently, the efforts of Kennedy and Dodge had some salutary effect upon Omaha realtors. In 1950, for example, the League's housing committee sponsored a forum in a black church on housing. The real estate board deemed the meeting important enough to send a representative to appear on the panel. When NUL head Lester Granger visited Omaha in early 1953, he addressed 125 members of the real estate board. Theodore Maynor, former president of the National Association of Real Estate Boards, responded favorably both to Granger's speech and to Dodge's general attempts to sensitize him to the work of the Omaha affiliate. Maynor noted that businessmen "promised to sit down and work out a program to improve local housing conditions." Moreover, some realtors became more willing to sell to blacks in transition areas.[30]

Dodge attempted to liberalize other Omaha realtors, but those efforts met with less success. He managed to get antidiscrimination resolutions enacted by the local and state real estate boards during his presidency of the latter group. He also persuaded the local organization to go on record against blockbusting. None of these efforts, however, resulted in any substantive improvements. In fact, when he accompanied Father Markoe to stand with a black family moving into a white neighborhood, the real estate board concluded that Dodge was "nuts."[31]

While Young encouraged Kennedy and Dodge in their attempts to sensitize realtors to racial issues, he neither waited nor depended on these efforts to end segregated housing. Instead, he and independent white realtors, builders, and lenders brought relief to those in substandard and overcrowded housing. In 1950 Young initiated a joint effort to build homes for Omaha blacks. He selected sites, chose contractors, and gained the cooperation of various white businessmen in the housing field. To underwrite the venture, Young secured support from the League housing committee chairman, Charles Davis. Davis headed the black-controlled Carver Savings and Loan Association, which promised to lend money to prospective home buyers. Young also received advice from De Hart Hubbard of the Federal Housing Authority, and he attracted FHA guaranteed loans.[32]

One firm finished two houses in 1952 and 1953. Another group started construction on four houses in 1953. The success of these undertakings motivated an Omaha life insurance company to make available $150,000 in FHA-insured mortgages to the black community. Young correctly boasted that more new homes had become available to Omaha blacks within three years than in the preceding decade.[33]

Young had reason to be heartened by these developments. He noted, "With the tacit approval and cooperation by these various groups, Negro citizens have been permitted to buy homes in at least ten adjacent blocks of the heretofore almost completely segregated neighborhoods." He went on to tell a National Urban League official, "I believe that all too often many of our staff in the Urban League movement adopt a hopeless attitude with regard to real estate men, bankers [and others]. My experience has shown that there are individual realtors like individual employers who may be educated in spite of the policies of the National Real Estate Board and the National Manufacturers Association, which in many cases we are opposed to." While undocumented, Kennedy and Dodge must have helped Young make contact with various realtors, builders, and lenders. Their moral exhortations persuaded few, but once Young injected pecuniary benefits in his League objectives, the assistance of Kennedy and Dodge became more effective.

Young knew that businessmen held the key to improved housing for blacks. He contended, "In presenting our need we should minimize public housing and emphasize the need for private enterprise." The truth of that contention had been demonstrated to Young's satisfaction. Nonetheless, public housing was a fact of life in Omaha, and although private sales were preferred by Young and the leading realtor on his board, he could not overlook the rampant racial discrimination in housing projects that eroded black living standards. Two major issues confronted the League executive director. First, he wanted to end racial separation in existing public dwellings, and second, he tried to prevent residential segregation in newly built projects.[34]

With federal funds in 1936, Omaha built 1,078 public housing units for blacks and veterans. City officials located the dwellings on two sites in North Omaha and South Omaha. Arbitrarily, the Omaha Housing Authority permitted blacks to rent apartments on both sites, but compelled them to live in segregated buildings. To accommodate other low-income blacks and whites in need of decent but affordable housing, the Omaha City Council in 1949 authorized the construction of seven hundred additional units. Building began in 1951 at three sites, all of which were located within Omaha's black community. At this point, Young and the League's housing committee announced their intention to prevent residential segregation in the new units and to initiate desegregation in the older projects as vacancies in the buildings occurred. Black members of the committee vigorously pushed the issue over the objection of some whites. Young sided with the black members, and they gradually persuaded their fellow members to present a united front.

Arthur McCaw initially stirred Young on this issue. While driving past the public housing units, McCaw noticed the construction of an earthen embankment designed to further segregate black and white tenants who were already living in separate buildings. McCaw told Young, who then called together his housing committee to press for the desegregation of Omaha public housing.

Armed with information from the Federal Housing Act and the experience of other cities with integrated public housing, Young and the housing committee asked Omaha's mayor to eliminate race as a criterion for any public housing assignments, to appoint a black to an upcoming vacancy on the housing authority, and to employ blacks in the agency. Within three weeks the mayor appointed a black to the housing authority. The new official then proposed that the agency consider the League's other requests. A housing authority member who wished to delay any further changes persuaded the other officials to postpone action until William Hill, the race relations adviser of the Federal Public Housing Administration, came to Omaha from the Chicago regional office to discuss matters with them.

Hill arrived and met with the housing authority and with the League's housing committee. League members assured Hill that their protest was not a smokescreen for efforts to sabotage future public housing. Young bluntly told Hill that he and his committee strongly advocated public housing, but if future projects were "dependent upon continued segregation, then the Negro community would not support it." Hill ultimately recommended that the mayor and the housing authority approve the League request to end segregation in public housing along the lines that Young and the housing committee suggested.

The housing authority stalled again. After a few months, at a closed meeting, a divided agency voted for the principle of integration and gradual implementation. At this point Young and the League mobilized biracial community support from labor, industry, churches, and numerous organizations.

He urged them to appear at the housing authority meetings, write letters, and otherwise pressure for complete acceptance and action on public housing integration. Young and the committee also visited the mayor and warned that if the housing authority failed to act, they would ask the city council to pass an ordinance to authorize and implement integration. The mayor retreated from this potential source of political embarrassment and urged housing officials to respond to League demands. Representatives from a host of organizations attended the next housing authority meeting. Alfred Kennedy reiterated the League's request and then called on other speakers from the community to state their support. Finally, the housing authority, after some disunity, enacted a policy of no segregation in new and future public housing and desegregation of existing units as vacancies occurred.

Again Young demonstrated his consummate leadership skills in mobilizing blacks and whites behind League objectives. He responded speedily to militant black members on his League housing committee who wanted to take an uncompromising stand against residential segregation. At the same time, he persuaded reluctant white members to join him and their black colleagues in taking the moral high ground against public housing segregation. Perhaps the involvement of federal monies with their strictures, however vague, against segregation also strengthened the resolve of whites on the housing committee. In any case, once Young drew whites into the fray, they and the blacks attracted support from numerous other community groups. Ultimately, the mayor and the housing authority could ignore neither the biracial support that desegregation attracted nor the endorsement of William Hill of the FHA. Young's leadership produced the appointment of a black to the housing authority and a forthright policy against segregation, as well as screening of black applicants for assistant manager, tenant counselor, and clerical positions in the agency. "All in all," wrote Young, "we feel this is another example of how the Urban League, through its interracial social work approach and utilizing the processes of community organization, brings about improved conditions for Negro citizens." What Young failed to stress, either because of strategy or oversight, were the pivotal roles of black militant demands and federal support, both of which moved whites in the local League and in city government to end segregation in public housing.[35]

Although encounters with Omaha city authorities had been successful over public housing matters, Young fell short of his goals on slum clearance issues. The Federal Housing Act of 1949 included a Slum Clearance and Redevelopment Program. Responsibility for administering the initiative belonged to the Omaha Housing Authority. Before action commenced, the agency chose six areas within the city to study as potential targets for the program. Without the knowledge and advice of Whitney Young and the League's housing committee, the housing authority selected an inappropriate area within the black community to investigate. Once again city housing officials aroused Young's ire. He and the housing committee emphatically asserted that this particular Negro section had not been chosen "with the thought of improving what was obviously our worst slum." Instead, the housing authority preferred to beautify the area surrounding the new public housing project, a decision that would do little to further expand housing for blacks.

Young charged the agency with an egregious oversight. He and other League officials met with housing authority members to suggest that they study a ghetto area in need of much greater attention than the newly furnished housing project. The neighborhoods that the League's interracial housing committee recommended for investigation contained some of the city's worst housing. Young noted that the 1950 census figured that one-third of the dwellings had no indoor toilets and one-tenth had no hot and cold running water. Additionally, Young observed that in the neighborhood was "our greatest incident of illness, crime, delinquency, and definite fire hazard." Furthermore, banks consistently refused to grant loans for home improvement, and insurance companies refused to insure most of this property. To make matters worse, the rate of absentee ownership of these slum dwellings exceeded 50 percent. The housing authority's six recommended areas nearly became a fait accompli before Young and others conferred with the agency and persuaded it to abandon its earlier beautification proposal. Instead, the housing authority agreed to investigate the blighted area suggested by the League's housing committee.

So that black leaders in Omaha would understand his impromptu meeting with the housing authority, Young met with the black clergy, the Federation of Colored Women's Clubs, the Omaha NAACP, and other organizations. He informed them that an opportunity existed to improve living conditions in the city's most depressed black neighborhoods. He probably explained that the League's singular action was not an attempt to upstage other groups but an attempt to get substantive improvements in Omaha's black ghetto. He drew additional support from black physicians and black lawyers as well as from the chamber of commerce and the real estate board to petition the city council to pass an ordinance that included the blighted black neighborhoods as areas needing investigation by the housing authority.

Young's new effort failed miserably. He accused the white Small Property Owners Association, whose members held title to much of Omaha's slum property, of misrepresenting League actions and recommendations to the housing authority. Young noted, "They were successful in getting a couple of 'jackleg' Negro ministers and a political 'Hanger-on'" to convince black slum residents that the League would get them evicted from their homes.

Young fought back. In a long letter to Omaha's black ministers, he reminded them of the disgraceful condition of the targeted black neighborhoods. He stressed that all the proposal required was an investigation of the area. He emphatically declared, "If the study comes up with the specific recommendations that certain areas be cleared, but does not reveal a satisfactory plan of relocation of families into private homes, does not promise more than fair return for the homes bought, or does not assure us that new individual dwellings will be built in the area available for Negro citizens and at prices they can afford, then we will of course withdraw our support." What Young wished to accomplish was not a blanket condemnation of the entire blighted area, but identification of salvageable houses susceptible to rehabilitation. It was necessary, however, to refer to the whole area in the ordinance "so that the truly run-down and deteriorated homes will be weeded out." Finally, Young put on the line his own credibility and that of his organization. He said, "The Urban League--which has demonstrated its concern for Negro citizens by opening up jobs in department stores, the utility district, the telephone company, and the public library; and has demonstrated its interest in housing by securing a policy of no segregation in public housing and has educated real estate men so that Negro citizens are now able to move peacefully" beyond the ghetto "does not need to sell you on its sincerity and value to our community." The ministers responded favorably to Young's appeal and repeated his analysis to their congregations. Unfortunately, their efforts were not enough.

Young claimed that those who opposed the program either had too little information or were "deliberately misinformed by persons who exploit this area for their own purposes." Clearly, the Small Property Owners Association through its black henchmen successfully stirred the fears of blacks in the targeted neighborhoods and convinced them that evictions were imminent. Protests from these persons persuaded the city council, which had been favorable to Young's proposal, to table the issue. As a result, black Omaha lost an opportunity to rehabilitate several incredibly debilitated neighborhoods with federal funds.[36]

Reginald A. Johnson, the League's national coordinator of housing activities, and Frank S. Horne, assistant to the administrator of the Federal

Housing and Home Finance Agency, assessed Young's leadership in the redevelopment effort and still hoped to salvage success from the endeavor. Horne, a former member of FDR's famed "black cabinet," suggested that Johnson forward to Young an appraisal on why he failed. The lengthy evaluation, which consisted of poignant questions prepared by Horne's staff, stressed Young's negligence in communicating the local League's perspectives on the study areas in a full and timely manner to the relevant parties in the controversy, especially those in the affected slum neighborhoods. Horne acknowledged that the Omaha Housing Authority did not contact Young about the existence of a housing investigation. Nonetheless, he chose to brief black middle-class leaders and organizations but not the grassroots residents who would be potentially affected. This oversight cleared the way for white slumlords and their black sycophants "to succeed in developing and corralling a degree of Negro opposition" to Young's wiser and more beneficial efforts in their behalf. Horne also believed that Young should have had banks and fire insurance companies ready to communicate their assurances to potentially displaced slum residents.[37]

Horne's hindsight proved partially perceptive. The League and Young clearly neglected to talk directly to the tenants and homeowners in the blighted area. That would have happened, however, even if the Omaha Housing Authority had informed him of its plans earlier rather than later. Young viewed his role and that of the Omaha Urban League as coordinator, facilitator, and troubleshooter. Young and the League equipped other organizations and spokespersons with the information, objectives, and programmatic assistance to improve the condition of the black community. Hence his failure to communicate with ghetto residents, while wrong, was not the result of negligence but the consequence of a particular leadership tactic.

Although employment and housing issues claimed most of Young's energies, he eagerly attacked other examples of racial discrimination and segregation. Some of these concerns took him beyond what League executives normally addressed. Young acted on any urgent issue or practice that degraded blacks or limited their opportunities. At times these matters drew him deep into politics, into protest, and other spheres that League officials usually eschewed. Young seldom demurred but became a versatile local leader cognizant of the smallest injustice perpetrated against blacks.

When Young arrived in Omaha in 1950, the public schools employed twelve black teachers, including Wanasebe Fletcher and Eugene Skinner. Both men along with two white principals belonged to the board of the Omaha Urban League. Like board members Kennedy and Dodge, who advised Young on housing issues, the four educators told him about pressing concerns in the public schools. Skinner helped to acquaint Young with the school system shortly after his arrival. He invited the new executive director to give the commencement address at Long Elementary School, where he was principal.[38]

Unexpectedly, the issue of black teachers and their segregated status in the Omaha public schools was thrust upon Young. Before Young officially assumed his duties, League board members selected Harry A. Burke, the school superintendent, as one of their four achievement award recipients. Although saluted by the League for educational innovations in black schools, Burke was blamed for the system's poor representation of black professionals. G. Aneita Hayes spoke for those blacks who opposed the honor for Burke. In a telegram to Lester Granger, the League's national head, she accused Burke of paying black teachers less than their colleagues and assigning them exclusively to all-Negro schools. She held that if the League board insisted on the award for Burke, this would be detrimental to the League's national program and would weaken community support for the affiliate. Hayes promised a public protest against the presentation.

Lester Granger had warned Young about Mrs. Hayes before his arrival in Omaha. "In fact, she came in the first day I was in the office," replied Young, "and [she] went into a tirade: about Burke and the 'reactionary, anti-Negro, anti-labor' local League board that chose him." Young personally believed that "there might possibly be some question" about Burke's attitudes toward blacks, but her "charges are greatly exaggerated and some only hearsay." Although he told Mrs. Hayes that he would take her concerns under advisement, he was most interested in thwarting her planned demonstration. He informed her that "any public protest would be in poor taste" and would harm the League. With difficulty, Young persuaded her to say which groups would back her. Actually no community protest existed. Young was further assured when he met with the black ministers' alliance and others mentioned by Mrs. Hayes. All noted that she lacked their support. Ultimately, she called off the protest and promised Young her utmost cooperation. Although he doubted her sincerity, he preferred not to have her as an enemy.

Mrs. Hayes had competed with Young for the League position, so he questioned her support of his leadership. Nonetheless, he concluded that "there was some justification for the protest and sufficient community interest surrounding it to warrant our taking some positive action." Young further believed that Omaha blacks had numerous problems that took precedence over the school situation. Nevertheless, the presence of twelve black teachers in two all-Negro schools and the negative sentiments expressed toward Burke by blacks other than Mrs. Hayes gave Young ample justification to look further into this matter.

Young probably believed that the board used the award to Burke as a wedge to improve his performance on issues that mattered to blacks. That strategy met with only partial success. Within three years the number of black teachers more than doubled to twenty-six in six schools, five of which were integrated. Moreover, offensive minstrel shows at some high schools were discontinued. Despite these important gains, Young did not succeed in getting black teachers hired in the high schools nor did school officials authorize the faculty to participate in training programs on teaching human and race relations courses. The probable intervention of the three principals who served on the League board helped Young with some hiring gains. How much of his successes and setbacks were attributable to Burke or the school board is uncertain. With over two dozen teachers now in the school system, Young was correct to support his board's decision to give an award to such a dubious recipient as Harry Burke.[39]

Whatever the case, Young believed that blacks should no longer depend on Burke and other white school officials to advance their interests. He directed his new industrial relations secretary to collect data on the school system. He also persuaded attorney Elizabeth Pittman to campaign for a seat on the school board. Eleven candidates were running, but Young told blacks to vote only for Pittman. The strategy apparently worked because in 1953 she became the first black school board member in Omaha, beating the school board's endorsed slate. Again, Young used unorthodox methods behind the scenes to achieve ends that the League's traditional tactics could not accomplish.[40]

Young also attacked racial discrimination in Omaha's public facilities. Although the NAACP usually tackled such issues, the Omaha Urban League had developed an early concern with these unfair practices. During the 1940s, the League board tried to promote integration by holding its annual banquet downtown. Since no hotel would accommodate them, the chamber of commerce offered its facilities. When Young arrived in the 1950s, only one hotel and two downtown restaurants served blacks. This venture, like those in employment and housing, became a direct effort between Young and members of his board. Black and white board members would go separately to selected restaurants to query the management on integration. Later, each reported at a board meeting on what happened. Young and Phil Dodge also began dining together in segregated restaurants. The two would enter the

establishment and Dodge would introduce Young either to the proprietor or
to the maitre d'hotel. The Dodge family name not only ensured service for
the two but accomplished integration. To make certain that service for blacks
continued, Young would return to the restaurant with another white or with
a member of his staff. If a problem arose, Young called Dodge, and he would
come back to make sure that these integration efforts would be maintained.
"Whit was a good quarterback," remembered Phil Dodge. "He knew how to
use his blocking backs!" With these precedents set, Young commenced working with the Hotel and Restaurant Association and eventually achieved complete integration of downtown hotels and eating places. His persistence and
strategizing played an important role in this victory, but Dodge's backing
made the difference.[41]

     In Omaha, Young developed a mature understanding of leadership.
Whether ideas to initiate action against discrimination in employment, housing, education, or public accommodations came from him or emanated from
others, Young wisely sought support from both blacks and whites to achieve
these objectives. Although he supported League methods of persuasion and
closed-door negotiations, he seldom hesitated to abandon these tactics when
direct action and protest promised better results. He appreciated his associations with important Omaha whites, especially those on his board, but never
was he awed by them. Instead, he tried to steer their influence toward effecting swift social change in Omaha's racial environment and practices. Whenever these efforts were unsuccessful, Young, who never seemed to run out of
alternatives or potential allies, turned to government, on the federal, state,
and local level, to strengthen his thrust against racial discrimination and segregation. Jockeying among white businessmen, board members, the militant
De Porres Club, politicians, fellow blacks, and liberal whites, Young sought
support and action, depending on the issue, from some or all of these groups
and individuals to achieve his goals.

     During his three years in Omaha, Young gained increased visibility
among Omaha whites and eventually among some with statewide influence.
Because of his activism in employment and housing, he had already become
familiar to local employers, the real estate board, the chamber of commerce,
contractors, and mortgage bankers. Not surprisingly, his name also became
better known within other influential circles. Never one to pull any punches
about the urgency of ending racism, Young was outspoken about discrimination and segregation to whatever white organizations he addressed or with
which he associated. The president of the local B'nai B'rith thanked him for
his "very revealing and interesting discussion of your people." She agreed that

resolution of racial issues was vital to ensure domestic peace. The general secretary of the Omaha YMCA admitted, "You had a rather stormy start with our Y's Men's Club, but I think it all added up to definite growth on the part of the members."[42]

Increasingly, this wider exposure made Young more active in various organizations with few if any black members. In 1953, for example, the Nebraska Welfare Association elected Young its first black president. The group consisted of 250 professional and lay social workers concerned with health and welfare issues. Young's statewide fame also brought him to the attention of Nebraska governor Robert B. Crosby. Crosby asked him to serve on his human relations committee, an agency to study whether discrimination on the basis of race, creed, or nationality existed in Nebraska. After the survey was completed, the governor solicited recommendations on how to solve the problem. Since no funds had been budgeted for the committee, Young and other potential members had to bear their own personal expenses. In any case, the request came too late, because Young's departure from Omaha was imminent.[43]

That whites were not all alike was a significant lesson that Young learned in Omaha. His increased ability to discern differences enhanced his effectiveness in enlisting their help in specific causes they would likely support. Moreover, he discovered the boundaries beyond which some whites could not be pushed in pursuit of racial equality. His intimate associations with Alfred Kennedy, Phillips Dodge, and John Markoe illustrate these points.

Kennedy typified the conservative Republican businessman. Appeals to his conscience and to his sympathies for wronged African Americans were not enough to draw him into the fight for black equality. Rather, racial justice was a practical matter, an issue of common sense and fair play. How could you ask black soldiers to risk their lives in the Korean War, yet deny them decent jobs and housing in the States? With a war going on in Asia and "an impending shortage of manpower" at home, Kennedy told businessmen, "This is no time to discriminate." Because "foxholes have no color line," neither should employers. At the same time Kennedy held firm views on a range of subjects with which Young disagreed. He opposed empowering government to end job discrimination among private employers and he was unfriendly to federally subsidized public housing. Kennedy also believed that blacks bore a major responsibility for integration and becoming a part of the mainstream. He criticized them because so few attended the opera, symphony performances, and community playhouse productions. He contended that their presence at such events would increase white acceptance of blacks.[44]

Young worked amiably with Kennedy despite some of his dubious perspectives. Because Kennedy believed strongly in the private sector, he vigorously endorsed Young's efforts to increase the supply of housing for blacks through voluntary cooperative efforts among mortgage bankers, realtors, and contractors. Kennedy also contended that greater involvement by white businessmen in League affairs would yield voluntary moves to end employer discrimination, a better alternative than government coercion. Although Young was a staunch FEPC advocate, he encouraged Kennedy's efforts to enlist greater voluntary support among white employers.

Young understood that the Omaha realtor, despite his conservatism, was far more progressive than most of his peers on matters of race. That explains why Young encouraged Kennedy's League involvement by urging him to lead a discussion at the 1951 national convention in St. Paul, Minnesota. And that's why Young defended him even when Kennedy expressed his conservative views to a clearly irritated black audience. Legislation is not the way to solve racial problems, declared Kennedy. Although Young disagreed with him, he rescued Kennedy from this monumental faux pas.[45]

Perhaps Kennedy perceived that Young had sacrificed his own credibility to salvage the dignity of a middle-aged white man trying to grapple with the complexities of race relations. Maybe such sentiments shaped the letter Kennedy wrote to Young's parents before his departure from Omaha. He admired Young and noted, "I knew we could not expect to keep him here, too long. I was confident he would outgrow his job." Kennedy predicted that Young would eventually make a national contribution "to the cause of good relations which is the cause of these United States of ours."[46]

Whether Young's presence had a mediating influence upon Kennedy cannot be determined. After Young left Omaha, Kennedy's growth in race relations seems to have ended. When a black member of the community chest board suggested that Young return to replace the fired executive director at the latter's lavish $15,000 salary, Kennedy opposed the idea. He was also against the governor's proposal to name Arthur McCaw, the veteran tax examiner, as director of the tax assessor's office. In later years, as urban decay overtook downtown Omaha, Kennedy blamed blacks. Perhaps it is too far-fetched to argue that the absence of Whitney Young in Omaha left no black of sufficient influence to prevent Kennedy's ideas from degenerating from conservative to reactionary.[47]

Greater familiarity and ease, however, characterized Young's relationship with N. Phillips Dodge. They were about the same age and well educated. Dodge held a degree from Harvard, and Young possessed a master's degree from Minnesota. As veterans of World War II, they viewed race relations from a broadened, cosmopolitan perspective. Because they held liberal theological views, Young and Dodge shared an interest in the Unitarian Church.

Dodge served on an Omaha Urban League committee in 1949 and became aware of "the shocking condition of housing for Negro citizens." He accepted an invitation to join the League board in 1950 and later succeeded Kennedy as president of the Omaha affiliate. Young was cognizant of his friend's important family name and his enviable connections as a board member of the local utilities company, as a bank trustee, and as a director of the real estate board. Young's relationship with Dodge rested on a mutual regard for their friendship and on Young's desire to use Dodge's considerable civic and business influence to open doors for Omaha blacks. There was nothing manipulative about Young's objective. Phil Dodge fully understood the nature of their relationship, and he acquiesced.

Far from functioning as a black spokesman anxious to win the favor of influential whites, Young independently articulated his own objectives as a leader and creatively chose different strategies to achieve them. While Young never eschewed direct action protest, he knew that the presence and intervention of important whites sometimes accomplished the desired end with less trouble and fuss. Young called Dodge one day and asked that they meet immediately at a certain local hotel. Young had learned that blacks on a visiting baseball team had arrived in Omaha and were refused service at the hotel despite their reservations. The white teammates vowed not to room there if black players could not stay. A minor scene resulted. As Young and Dodge talked with hotel officials, some visiting white salesmen, who regularly lodged at the hotel, learned of the dispute and staged their own protest against this discriminatory conduct by taking rooms in another establishment. Young and Phil Dodge could not reason with the management. Consequently, Dodge went to his friend, Gene Eppley, proprietor of the exclusive Fontenelle Hotel, told him of the situation, and persuaded Eppley to invite the team to lodge at the best hotel in Omaha. Although the Fontenelle had a reputation for treating blacks rudely, Dodge's intervention changed that. Young wisely chose an influential white businessman to achieve what protest could not resolve in the short run. Phil Dodge was acutely aware of his role.

Dodge allowed Young to push him further into the fight for racial equality than Young could ever shove Kennedy. Nonetheless, neither Young nor Dodge could predict the heavy emotional toll that Phil's racial liberalism extracted from him in conservative Omaha. Dodge tried repeatedly to get other influential whites to join him on the local Urban League board. His neighbor, a prominent surgeon, was a prime candidate. Dodge thought that the surgeon would contribute much to the League. When he refused, Dodge accepted his answer without rancor. Later, when Dodge attempted a run for the Nebraska legislature, the surgeon led a surreptitious effort in their neighborhood to thwart his candidacy. He told fearful neighbors that, if elected, Phil Dodge would move blacks into their area to live. When Dodge learned of his friend's duplicity years later, he was astonished and deeply offended. Perhaps he, unlike Kennedy, came to a better understanding of what Young wanted to accomplish in Omaha and the odds that were stacked against him.[48]

Young's dealings with John P. Markoe were more formal than his relationship with Phil Dodge, perhaps because Markoe was a priest and a generation older than Young. Markoe often exhibited fatherly pride in Young's work. Young, in turn, esteemed Markoe's longtime concern for blacks and his unstinting support for their full equality. Never before had Young met a white man who so willingly and consistently sacrificed his reputation and vocational advancement to identify with the struggles of blacks. In Roman Catholic circles, especially in St. Louis and Omaha, Markoe was often criticized because of his conspicuous and unyielding opposition to Jim Crow, whether practiced by the Church or by secular society. Markoe affirmed for Young the existence of some whites whose advocacy for black advancement grew beyond occasional liberalism to total commitment and complete disregard for damaged reputations and other personal consequences. Young and Markoe were not simply acquaintances. They were fellow warriors who battled discrimination and segregation with seriousness and urgency.[49]

Young participated in several De Porres Club projects to desegregate various facilities in Omaha. By the same token, Markoe and his organization also helped Young and his affiliate. In 1952, for example, the club assisted Young in a drive to increase League membership. Additionally, neither Markoe nor Young believed that the Church was exempt from desegregation. Originally, the Omaha Roman Catholic diocese established St. Benedict's parish as a segregated congregation to serve blacks. As they moved slowly but steadily beyond the confines of the ghetto, St. Benedict members wanted to attend churches and parochial schools that were closer to them. To maintain the existence of St. Benedict's, but as an integrated congregation, Markoe and Young drew new boundaries within which St. Benedict's would draw new parishioners. These new areas included those originally assigned to white parishes.[50]

Young must have been proud of his association with Father Markoe. In

1951 the Omaha Urban League awarded the Jesuit its outstanding service award. Later that year, Markoe appeared as a discussion leader at the NUL convention in St. Paul.[51]

Kennedy, a conservative, believed in private voluntary efforts to end the mistreatment of blacks; Dodge, an upper-class liberal, contended that white elite intervention and influence would break down racial barriers; and Markoe, a grassroots activist, advocated protest and other direct action techniques. All three enlightened Young on the different roles and approaches whites could employ to further League goals. He learned that any one of these strategies, depending on the issues and circumstances, was useful in broadening opportunities for blacks. The attitudes and actions of Kennedy, Dodge, and Markoe taught Young valuable lessons on the multiple ways that whites could function in battles against racial inequality.

While Young mobilized different segments of white support for racial advancement, he found it equally important to mirror and represent the perspectives of Omaha blacks. To maintain his credibility as a black leader, Young worked to convince blacks that he promoted their objectives rather than the agendas set by influential whites on his League board. Obviously, he occupied an uncertain middle position! Sandwiched between a conservative white community and an expectant, perhaps impatient, black constituency, Young had a delicate balancing act to perform. Although he showed deftness in dealing with powerful Omaha whites, Young tried to demonstrate similar skill in cultivating black supporters.

Young made a sustained effort to cooperate and coordinate activities with other black leaders and organizations in Omaha. Every Saturday morning, the local "black cabinet" met at the YMCA to discuss the week's events, vent grievances against one another, and use the session to prevent divisions among them. Whitney Young and Marion Taylor regularly attended. The cabinet also included Ralph Adams, an attorney and president of the Omaha NAACP, Charles Davis, a lawyer, banker, and exalted ruler of the local black Elks, Alyce Wilson, director of the Woodson Settlement, and the executive secretaries of the "colored" YMCA and YWCA. Eugene Skinner also came to describe conditions in the public schools.

Besides serving as a clearinghouse for information, grievances, and strategy, the local black cabinet attained some concrete goals. Their unity persuaded the municipal government to hire more black policemen, and they lobbied for the appointment of Ralph Adams as chairman of the police community relations board. That agency oversaw police activities and conduct within the black community. Whatever success Young achieved as a spokesman derived in part from his intimate involvement with Omaha's council of black leaders.[52]

Young further developed these associations through active participation in other black organizations. Because the cabinet functioned as an interlocking directorate, Young's efforts to broaden his contact with blacks was enhanced. For example, Charles Davis, Eugene Skinner, and Ralph Adams of the NAACP were board members of the Omaha Urban League. At the same time, Young served on the Omaha NAACP board and supported NAACP marches against racial injustice. When Adams invited him to address his organization's mass meeting in March 1950, Young told the audience that blacks needed to use two principal tactics to improve their condition. He emphasized support from local and national civil rights groups, and he urged "sound political action." Young believed that blacks should discuss and decide which issues "vitally affect the masses of Negroes and let political representatives know what we expect of them." Young and the League cooperated with the NAACP, labor unions, Americans for Democratic Action, and other groups to lobby for the passage of an Omaha fair employment practices ordinance. While committed to traditional League methods of negotiation to effect change for blacks, Young never hesitated to supplement this approach with political mobilization and direct action strategies.[53]

Young further enhanced his credibility as a black leader when he joined Hiram Lodge #10 of the Prince Hall Masons. He also spoke frequently in Omaha's black churches. In 1950, he addressed a career institute at Zion Baptist Church. Soon thereafter he was the Men's Day speaker for St. John African Methodist Episcopal Church and Hillside Presbyterian Church. Although Young became a regular participant in fraternal and religious events, he regularly loitered, if only for a few minutes, on 24th Avenue, the center of Omaha's black community. There one heard the familiar refrain, "Hey, Whitney," from scores of black men who would ask, sometimes seriously, other times jovially, "Can you get me a job?" Young's standard response was, "Come down to the League office and we'll see what we can do." He was clearly in touch with the grassroots institutions of black Omaha and with its people.[54]

Most Omaha blacks held Young in high regard, but he could not always garner consensus among black leaders. Arthur McCaw, Young's best friend, was probably his closest ally and consistent supporter. As chief tax appraiser in Omaha and then as state budget supervisor, McCaw had become an important political figure. Moreover, he had been an Omaha Urban League official serving in the 1940s as boys' work secretary and also as president of the Omaha NAACP. These experiences further solidified Art's friendship with Whitney. McCaw's stature as a Nebraska state official had advanced to the point in 1953 that President Eisenhower considered his candidacy for governor of the Virgin Islands. Young praised him for the respect he earned as tax appraiser from Omaha's top businessmen and his ability to relate to the black community. These attributes, Young contended, qualified McCaw for the post. McCaw did not get the job, however.[55]

Whatever envy McCaw's prominence engendered among rival blacks, some of the fallout rained on Young. When Young and the League persuaded the housing authority to name a black to the board, municipal officials wanted McCaw, whose credentials also included a license in real estate. Young thought it was a good idea, but the local black cabinet opposed it. Instead of McCaw, they urged the appointment of Charles Davis. Because McCaw did not want the position and had not sought it and because Davis was acceptable to both him and Young, a conflict was averted. Young felt sufficiently uneasy about some of the local black leaders that he told McCaw they seemed "to be losing steam but will bear watching!"[56]

Young's continued flirtation with Unitarianism imposed a subtle but serious threat to his credibility as a black community spokesman. Although many blacks eschewed regular church attendance, nearly all agreed that the black church lay at the heart of their community life. Accordingly, Young cultivated Omaha's black clergy and involved them in League programs and initiatives. Perhaps his best ministerial friend and admirer was the Reverend Sanders H. Lewis, the pastor of Omaha's oldest and largest black congregation, the 700-member St. John AME Church. Young liked Reverend Lewis because of his broad interest and involvement in the civil rights struggle. The cleric had been president of the Omaha NAACP. Always hungry for the latest information about progress against Jim Crow, he often asked Young about the state of the black struggle. Young would then outline progress on state and local FEPC laws, Eisenhower's civil rights stands, southern black voter registration, integration of the armed forces, and other crucial issues.

Young visited all of Omaha's black churches, and despite a rumor that he would join the exclusive St. Philip Protestant Episcopal Church, the League director, at least publicly, did not favor one congregation over another. Nonetheless, Young had a fondness for St. John. Some of his board members and coworkers worshiped there. Moreover, his attachment to Reverend Lewis and his superb preaching made it difficult for Young to remain neutral. At the same time, Reverend Lewis grew increasingly concerned that Young had not been saved. During a series of sermons on faith, Lewis preached "And Enoch Walked with God" and drew Young to the altar to confess Jesus Christ.[57]

Although Young claimed to be an officer of St. John on his résumé, few others knew of his affiliation. Better known to black Omahans was his association with the Unitarian Church.[58] Phil Dodge belonged to the First Unitarian Church and served on the trustee board. The Reverend John Cyrus was a member of the Omaha Urban League board and attempted to educate white clergy about the black struggle. Young's previous exposure to the Unitarian Church in the Twin Cities gave Dodge and Cyrus an edge in attracting him to their church. Margaret Young taught the Sunday school class that daughter Marcia attended. Ultimately, Young discovered that affiliation with the Unitarians harmed his credibility among blacks. He knew that his seeming abandonment of the black church for a white congregation was perceived as an act of racial disloyalty. In fact, one black board member recalled negative reactions to the news that Young was becoming a Unitarian. Young returned to the black church, although Margaret and Marcia remained with the First Unitarian congregation. Perhaps Young was moved by Reverend Lewis's fervent preaching, but clearly his deepening ties to St. John AME Church helped to save his leadership as much as his soul.[59]

Although Young may have stumbled because he embraced Unitarianism, his increasingly visible accomplishments in the League rescued his reputation. Achievements in employment and housing won the applause of blacks and some influential whites. Other initiatives in health, recreation, and education broadened the involvement of the Omaha Urban League. For example, Young cooperated with efforts of the city health department to provide free X rays for tuberculosis in the black community. In joint sponsorship with the board of education and the city recreation department, Young drew black youth to the New Kellom School and Recreation Center to use the swimming pool and other athletic facilities. Also, the League administered a special fund, the Osmond scholarship, to encourage blacks to enter technical fields. As a result, two black physicians were able to finish their postgraduate training.[60]

These achievements drew praise from Young's boss, Lester B. Granger, head of the National Urban League. Granger made at least two visits to Omaha during Young's tenure. After the second trip in 1953, he was heartened by the increased support of the League by the large "colored" attendance at the annual dinner. Young also arranged for him to speak to 125 members of the Omaha Real Estate Board, and he set up interviews for Granger on television and with a major newspaper. Granger told others in the national office, "I got the impression of an extremely successful League program being operated in Omaha. The type and size of the attendance at the Annual Meeting was itself impressive, but even more impressive were the comments made . . . by practically everyone with whom I came in contact."[61]

Young's stature in the League also grew because he helped to shepherd the faltering affiliate in Lincoln, Nebraska. When veteran executive secretary Clyde W. Malone died in 1951, Young went to Lincoln as the League's national representative to give the eulogy at Quinn Chapel AME Church. Despite dissatisfaction with Malone's successor, Young worked with George Randol, the deceased's brother-in-law, to expand housing for Lincoln blacks. The reactivation of the air force base promised to draw hundreds of new black residents to a sharply restricted housing market. Randol had studied for a real estate license to help relieve the housing shortage. Young consulted with Randol about strategies to get mortgage monies available and put him in contact with a Federal Housing Administration official. Young's intervention also drew Alfred Kennedy and Phil Dodge to assist Malone's successor, Sydney Alexander, with real estate matters. Kennedy came in 1953 to speak on housing at a Lincoln Urban League dinner.[62]

Young was one of a group of up-and-coming League executives who became increasingly disenchanted with Granger's leadership. Willingness to employ direct action techniques and politics characterized Young's leadership tactics in Omaha. Local executives used similar methods to press more vigorously for black advancement. In employment, for example, Young and his colleagues at other affiliates thought that FEPC legislation would be indispensable to their efforts to prod resistant businessmen to hire blacks. Granger opposed these efforts. He believed that during World War II, the federal FEPC had been ineffective. Moreover, he felt that since Congress would not resurrect the agency after its 1946 expiration, it was a lost cause.

Granger's lack of militancy irritated other affiliate executives, including Edwin "Bill" Berry in Portland, Oregon, Alexander Allen in Pittsburgh, Sidney Williams in Chicago, Leo Bohanon in St. Louis, and Whitney Young in Omaha. Both Young and his predecessor, Bohanon, for example, had worked for the passage of a Nebraska FEPC. These five men called themselves the "Disturbed Committee." They also deplored the strained relations between Granger and the successive heads of the NAACP, Walter White and Roy Wilkins, and the lack of cooperation between the national offices of each organization. Young and Ralph Adams of the Omaha NAACP served on each other's board, and so did their counterparts in other cities. The Disturbed Committee wanted the same unity on the national level.[63]

Young had his own personal problems with Lester Granger. In 1950, while Granger was visiting Omaha, Walter White arrived, apparently to promote his latest book. To avoid conflict and to convey the idea of cooperation with the Omaha NAACP, Young scheduled Granger to speak a day before White. Mindful of the friction between the two leaders, Young assured his boss that White's appearance "came out a poor second" to his own.[64]

Young's desire to defuse Granger's potential irritation over White's speaking engagement was understandable. Less tolerable was Granger's cavalier manner toward League officials. The NUL board of directors already complained that he implemented programs and initiatives without its full backing.[65] Young had been trying to get an increase in Omaha's dues allocation to the national organization. Soon after his arrival in 1950, he sent in a $295 check in response to an appeal from Granger. Young said, "I recognize it is a very small amount, but hope it will help in meeting the immediate needs mentioned in your request." He was nonetheless surprised and much irritated to learn that Granger had already requested an increase in a separate letter to Omaha's community chest, the affiliate's principal funding source. That appeal was rejected. With his anger seemingly under control, Young told Granger that if he had known about the correspondence, "I could possibly have prepared our local Chest so that it might have received a more receptive reply." In the end, Young's intervention with Alfred Kennedy, who belonged to the boards of both the League and the community chest, got approval for the increase.[66] Granger's highhandedness and insensitivity reinforced Young's doubts about his leadership.

Young now began considering other vocations. Fortunately, the School of Social Work at the University of Nebraska needed a part-time instructor in the group work course. Astonishingly, Young and a part-time lecturer in community organizations were the only social workers in the whole state who were academically qualified to teach these subjects. In 1951 Young's board permitted him to teach one afternoon each week from January to June at the Lincoln campus. Soon after he broke the color line on Nebraska's faculty, Creighton University in Omaha invited him to teach in its adult education program. With these academic experiences now on his résumé, Young could look beyond his three years in Omaha to a broader range of alternatives, perhaps outside the League movement. Interest in Young from the School of Social Work at Atlanta University raised the issue for him. He thought he had done all he could in Omaha and now was the time for a change.[67]

In a conversation with Granger, Young learned that his boss had no plans for him. When Granger mentioned the top post in the dispirited and disorganized Washington Urban League, Young politely demurred. With few opportunities in the League available, Young decided to go to Atlanta University to head its School of Social Work. He resigned his job in Omaha in November 1953[68] and took Margaret and their daughters, Marcia and infant Lauren, to Georgia.

Young left the conservative midwestern city as a polished, pragmatic leader. Although devoted to the League and its emphasis on negotiation, persuasion, and pleading for sharp improvements in the social and economic condition of blacks, Young refused to be satisfied with these tactics alone. He was results oriented. If direct action, political involvement, or surreptitious plotting of boycotts wisely supplemented traditional League methods, then Young unhesitatingly embraced these approaches. Although he gained a sophisticated understanding of whites and their different perspectives and preferences on effecting racial advancement, Young occasionally failed to consult a sometimes fractured black community. Perhaps he was so relieved when he exploited an opening in the otherwise closed mind of an Omaha employer that he forgot that cultivation of his black constituency required the same expenditure of time and energy as he devoted to winning over recalcitrant whites.

5

An Activist Educator

Young did not choose to become a full-time social work educator because the ivory tower suddenly held greater attractions than the untidy world of social work practice. Rather, he reached a vocational dead end in a constrained League structure with limited opportunities for ambitious and restless local executives eager for promotions. While Atlanta University represented an alternative, it was not necessarily the most desirable. As Young grew accustomed to his new environment, however, he became increasingly aware of a burgeoning civil rights movement throughout the South. As dean of the region's only accredited school of social work primarily for blacks, Young envisaged a pivotal role for graduates in effecting social change, and he developed an academic program to achieve that result. Moreover, as a social worker with activist credentials, Young developed into a strategist and consultant to those in the forefront of the emergent civil rights revolution.

Young entered social work during the Truman administration, a period that one scholar has called the coming of age of civil rights as a national issue. Harry Truman, the first president to go to Harlem to seek black votes, compiled such impressive initiatives in civil rights that it became a federal priority. They included the desegregation of the armed forces, executive orders banning government contracts to discriminatory employers, and a hard-hitting commission report, *To Secure These Rights*, which condemned Jim Crow.[1] With that momentum, even the reluctant Eisenhower administration acknowledged the increased importance of civil rights in national politics. A hesitant and at times hostile Dwight D. Eisenhower advanced the civil rights agenda extending from efforts to eliminate Jim Crow from public facilities in the District of Columbia, to pressure on employers voluntarily to end job discrimination, to the armed enforcement of school desegregation in Little Rock, Arkansas. The 1954 Brown decision, a unanimous Supreme Court opinion written by an Eisenhower appointee, outlawed public school segregation and put the civil rights struggle on a new plateau of legitimacy and importance.[2]

Young knew that black grassroots activism in politics and protest had moved these diffident presidents to act. He had participated in broad-based efforts to enact FEPC legislation in Minnesota and Nebraska. Hundreds of blacks, primarily in the North and West, crusaded to get FEPC laws on the regional and local levels. Southern blacks focused on unequal treatment on local transit systems. In 1953, 1955, and 1956 in Baton Rouge, Montgomery, and Tallahassee, respectively, successful bus boycotts taught blacks that their economic power gave them sufficient leverage to end some Jim Crow practices. These actions, especially those which drew upon the growing militancy of southern blacks, culminated in a sustained thrust for racial equality. Successful challenges against seemingly impregnable white institutions and practices helped to transform these disparate and random efforts into a civil rights movement.[3] In this general setting of heightening consciousness and action on civil rights issues, Whitney Young led the School of Social Work of Atlanta University.

Young was one of more than a dozen candidates who competed to succeed Forrester Washington, who headed the school from 1927 until his retirement in 1954. Although Washington preferred another applicant, Atlanta University president Rufus E. Clement chose Young.[4] Social work faculty and graduates expressed puzzlement over his selection. Some professors noted that Young would be the only one of the five deans without a doctorate. Others scorned his lack of published scholarship. Doubts about his suitability also surfaced within the school's alumni chapter in New York. Apparently his age, thirty-two, and his academic inexperience annoyed some chapter members. In a vigorous defense of his credentials, Young observed that most alumni and alumnae did not know of his teaching stints in social work at the University of Nebraska and that he had supervised social work students from the University of Minnesota and Atlanta University. He also possessed "top recommendations from the key persons in the Council on Social Work Education" including his former dean at the University of Minnesota, John Kidneigh. Ersa Hines Clinton, the president of the New York chapter and a fellow Kentucky State graduate, assured Young that no one felt any resentment toward him personally. Rather, chapter members wanted to participate in the selection process and perhaps offer themselves as candidates for the position.[5]

Fortunately for Young, most of Atlanta's social work faculty already knew him. He had been a field supervisor for their students and a participant in their school's annual institute for off-campus instructors. Moreover, some faculty remembered him from various professional meetings. They found their new dean more than a full generation younger than their previous boss and possessed of an entirely different management style. Whereas Forrester Washington operated the school autocratically, Young believed in shared governance. He relied heavily on the advice of senior faculty, and he yielded decisions on curricular reform to them.[6] Moreover, he vigorously prodded President Clement to raise faculty salaries and provide extra funds for professional travel. For example, Young told his boss that "the wide gap between what we pay our faculty and what is paid in other schools" made it difficult to hold top-notch teachers. Clement then directed Young to inquire about faculty salaries at comparable schools of social work in the South. Young wrote to fellow deans at Tulane and Washington Universities. Their prompt replies, noted Young, "confirm quite definitely my concern about our faculty being considered underpaid." These testimonies apparently swayed Rufus Clement, because Young thanked him several months later for increasing salaries.[7] He also asked Clement to increase the professional travel allowance from $4,000 to $5,000 in the 1954-55 budget. He wanted funds to pay partial expenses for four additional faculty members to attend the 1954 convention of the National Conference on Social Work. Despite this "abnormal representation," it was important because several professors had not attended the annual meeting in five or six years. Young was told that his request was impractical, and he was only allotted enough to pay the partial expenses for one professor to attend the conference.[8]

Outside funding enabled Young to hire new faculty and field supervisors and to enhance the curriculum. His predecessor, for example, left him $22,000 from a Rosenwald Fund grant. Young used it to support psychiatric social work courses and to send a faculty member to the Menninger Clinic for further study. An $8,300 federal grant from the Office of Vocational Rehabilitation compensated three part-time instructors and paid for an institute course for one of his professors.[9] A $9,600 grant from the National Institute of Health increased the staff associated with the School of Social Work.[10]

As Young increased the number of field supervisors to mentor his students and the range of agencies where they did their practicums, he wanted to deepen connections to the Atlanta campus. He asked Clement for money to sponsor an annual institute for field supervisors so that they could continue to place students in their agencies.[11]

Each institute focused on a timely theme in social work practice. The 1954 conference discussed curricular issues, and the 1955 gathering dealt with teaching methods in supervision. Young also hired consultants for the institutes: John Kidneigh in 1954 and Florence Poole of the University of Illinois in 1955. Field supervisors, both black and white, attended these conferences, representing such diverse organizations as the Veterans' Administration, settlement houses, family courts, hospitals, YMCA/YWCAs, and League affiliates. Even with the diversity Young constantly tried to increase the number of participating agencies in his school's field supervision. He had the opportunity in 1954, for example, to involve potential supervisors at Atlanta's Family Service Society. Although officials were willing to train students without a fee, $500 was needed to rent downtown office space. In his successful bid for assistance from President Clement, Young noted that "the Family Service Society is . . . considered the top agency for training case workers." He added, "In most schools the full-time faculty person is employed to handle a student training unit in this type of agency. However, we have sold the local agency on using its very fine staff and giving the School supervision free of charge."[12]

While mindful that the School of Social Work played a special role in educating blacks, Young wanted it to conform to all the norms and regulations of the profession. Meeting the expectations of the National Conference of Social Work and especially the Council on Social Work Education meant enhancing the school's reputation and retaining its accreditation. Young often told Clement that he tried to maintain a top-notch accredited school and faculty whose program was always under review by the Council of Social Work Education. He added, "This Council, and I believe rightly so, gives no consideration to the fact that we are a Negro school." Rather, the agency compared Atlanta's program with the programs of other schools and refused to consider race as a mitigating factor. With this kind of scrutiny, Young knew positively that whatever his school gained in curricular innovation or faculty achievement met a universal standard.[13]

Just as Young arrived at Atlanta University, the Council on Social Work Education issued a new manual on curriculum that would become the basis for future accreditation. It required new or reorganized courses and special team-taught subjects in such areas as human growth and development. Professors in medicine, social work, and psychology were required. Young and his faculty also revised substantially the objectives of the curriculum and put greater stress on students acquiring a variety of conceptual and research skills and a specific competence either in casework, group work, or community organization. They also wanted "to stimulate in the student a desire to continue his professional growth through continuous study and participation in professional activity." The council had once regarded the school's unclear curricular objectives as its number one problem, but after a year's study, Young and the faculty hammered out these substantially revised academic aims.[14]

Young made certain that as many social work educators and consultants had input in Atlanta's curricular changes as possible. Sure acceptance from the council would more easily result from such contacts, and greater respect for the school would also occur. Even before he left Omaha, Young visited several institutions and talked with "people responsible for accreditation and some who have made the greater contributions toward curriculum formation." After he assumed his position, Young drew consultants from the National Institute of Mental Health, the American Association of Social Workers, the Office of Vocational Rehabilitation, and the American Foundation for the Blind to advise the faculty about curricular reform.[15]

Perhaps Katherine A. Kendall, consultant on educational services at the Council on Social Work Education, was Young's most important visitor. She met with the faculty and observed that its work on curriculum development was "truly remarkable." She advised Young to evaluate the new programs and their impact on the fieldwork of students during their matriculation and in their jobs after graduation. She also commended Atlanta for special curricular innovations that she wanted other schools of social work to emulate. Young was particularly pleased when Kendall praised the faculty's up-to-date information from recent council meetings. Kendall observed that they knew of new developments in curriculum and utilized information from the various program and workshop sessions. Discussions with colleagues from other institutions also seemed to inform the faculty's comments. Clearly, Young's vigorous encouragement of greater faculty attendance at professional meetings paid off.[16]

Winning recognition and congratulations from social work educators for his work at Atlanta University had become an important goal for Young. After Kendall reported her findings to the executive director of the council, he told Young, "I do not know what it is you are doing in Atlanta, but Mrs. Kendall has come back starry-eyed about the work which you and your faculty are doing in your curriculum studies. We find this exceedingly hopeful and want you to know what a real contribution this is to the field."[17]

Accreditation from the Council on Social Work Education and the American Association of Medical Social Workers for courses in that field was the tangible result of curricular reform. The association financed two visits for its representative to determine whether the dean and the faculty were competent to carry out a program in medical social work. Ultimately, both the association and the council granted their approval in May 1955. Since

Young credited Professor Hortense E. Lilly with developing the field, he prodded Clement to send her a commendation. He also cultivated support from
the university administration and from a wide range of social work educators
to bring this curricular change to fruition.[18] These efforts helped Young to
push his institution into the mainstream of social work education and to
alert others to the academic ascent of the school. Young started to think boldly
of a Ph.D. program. He conceded that the endeavor was five to ten years into
the future, but such projections indicated Young's growing confidence in his
school and its prospects.[19]

Perhaps the best barometer of Young's achievements as a university dean
was the stabilization of enrollment in the School of Social Work. Toward the
end of Washington's stewardship, enrollment fluctuated. During the 1951-
52 academic year, for example, Washington reported ninety-seven students.
Within two years, however, Clement called attention to decreased enrollment. Washington replied, "Our decrease was less than the decrease in general for all schools of social work in the country." In 1954-55 enrollments
during the Washington-Young interregnum stood at eighty-nine students
during the first semester and sixty-nine students during the second semester.
Those numbers improved substantially during the 1955-56 academic year to
ninety-two and eighty-six in the first and second semesters, respectively.[20]
While the previous figures reflect combined full-time and part-time enrollments, Young's achievement in increasing the student body is best seen in the
growth from sixty-four full-time students in 1954 to ninety-two in 1958,
when Young noted that applications had grown so much that "we are able to
be increasingly selective in our admissions process."[21]

Young's lead in expanding financial aid to students was probably the
biggest factor in the growth and stabilization of enrollments. Some of these
efforts built on programs that his predecessor started, and others stemmed
from Young's initiatives. Forrester Washington cooperated with the Southern
Regional Education Board in accepting funds from southern states that paid
tuition for black social work students to attend Atlanta University rather
than challenge segregated institutions closer to home. During the 1953-54
academic year a dozen students from Alabama, North Carolina, and Tennessee came to Atlanta under this program. That arrangement continued under
Dean Young. For example, Tennessee paid $3,550 for the 1954-55 academic
year for state students, and a few months later Alabama made a partial payment of $1,500 for its residents enrolled in the School of Social Work. Wash-
ington, however, seemed sure that Young agreed that "any right thinking
Negro" would be glad to see that practice end.[22]

At the same time Young asked Clement to increase university scholarships to social work students from $3,000 to $5,000 annually, since the former figure "constitutes very little financial help to students." Echoing Washington's warning that the Brown decision of 1954 would prompt white institutions to admit blacks to their schools of social work, funds from the Southern Regional Education Board would end. Additional scholarship assistance made it imperative to offset these potential losses.[23]

Funds from grants that Dean Young helped to secure earmarked financial aid for students. In 1956, for example, the National Foundation for Infantile Paralysis Fund provided two scholarships totaling $1,700. Funds to assist students also came from the National Institute of Mental Health and the Office of Vocational Rehabilitation.[24] Various alumni chapters made important contributions as well. The National Alumni Association set up the Forrester B. Washington Loan Fund, and the New York chapter initiated its own annual scholarship. Overall, Young increased scholarship aid from $6,000 in 1954 to about $32,000 in 1958.[25]

The admission of white students was another strategy that Young used to stabilize enrollments. Even before he came to Atlanta, he and Clement discussed the potential impact of desegregation on Atlanta University and the social work program. They concluded that the opening of other social work schools in the South to black students would not threaten enrollments at the Atlanta School. Young added that the school could become the most attractive center for social work education in the region. Since 1950, his predecessor had presented the applications of white students to the university as "test cases." The trustees, however, demurred because they feared Georgia would withdraw their tax-exempt status if whites were admitted. The Brown decision removed that threat, and in 1956, Young admitted the first white full-time students. No doubt, the curricular innovations, especially the recently accredited medical social work field, brought Young's ambition to make the school attractive to both whites and blacks closer to fruition.[26]

Young also inaugurated a program of continuing education for employed social workers who lacked the master's degree. To explain the curriculum and other requirements, Young arranged meetings between his faculty and local agency executives who would employ the potential pupils. They discussed various methods of scheduling, means of funding, and the subjects for study. When one agency executive asked whether the Georgia Merit Commission approved the program, Young quickly and proudly declared that the school was accredited by the Council on Social Work Education and had the highest rating that any school could have and that its curriculum was accepted by all agencies and boards. Young's answer demonstrated increased confidence to this interracial audience about the school as a mainstream institution that could serve social workers, both black and white.[27]

The placement of graduates was further evidence of the institution's growing interracial clientele. The involvement of whites as field supervisors helped Young to build on another of his predecessor's initiatives, that of placing graduates in predominantly white agencies. The school regularly awarded degrees to students who became officials in various League affiliates and in black community centers. Increasingly, Atlanta University graduated social workers for hospitals, public welfare agencies, charities, juvenile and criminal justice facilities, and other organizations that served an interracial constituency.[28]

Although administrative responsibilities claimed most of his time, Young taught courses on social services and served in the university senate, as chairman of the university faculty, and on a committee to oversee the sociology department. He was an ex officio member of all social work committees, both administrative and academic, including fieldwork and admissions, social work practice, human growth and development, and social services.[29] The onetime community leader and organizer had become a full-fledged academic. Some who were skeptical of Clement's choice had many of their doubts allayed, especially since Young's national and regional visibility and prominence as a social work educator became evident to administrators and faculty at Atlanta University.

Young's achievements at the School of Social Work resulted in numerous committee appointments. Clement urged Georgia governor Ernest Vandiver to appoint Young to a statewide committee to improve services to "colored inmates" at the Milledgeville mental hospital. His professional colleagues, most of whom were white, nominated him to executive boards of major national organizations in social work, including the Council on Social Work Education and the Planned Parenthood Federation. Similarly, Young's reputation drew him to executive boards of social work groups on the state and local levels. They included the Georgia State Welfare Conference, the Georgia Association for Mental Health, the Atlanta Tuberculosis Association, and the Atlanta chapter of the American Association for the Physically Handicapped.[30]

Perhaps more important, Young became a consultant to several public and private agencies, thus enhancing his influence and posture as a national expert on a wide range of social welfare issues. The Southern Regional Council, an influential interracial commission for gradual racial change, chose Young in 1955 as a paid consultant to its program on Mental Health Training and Research. He was reappointed in 1957. Young was also a consultant with the Georgia Committee on Interracial Cooperation, which was affiliated with the SRC. Also in 1955 Young accepted a three-year appointment as a consultant to the federal Bureau of Public Assistance and Children's Bureau Committee on Training. In a letter to Clement, Young revealed his hope that contacts with this small, select group of committee members would bring prestige to the school and alert him to federal funds that might be available for training social workers. That probably led to his later appointment to President Eisenhower's White House Conference on Youth and Children. He also belonged to a commission established by the National Council of Churches to help prepare its conference on the Church and Social Welfare.[31]

Moreover, Young maintained a phenomenally busy speaking schedule. He delivered addresses to a broad array of professional social welfare and social work organizations, university groups, civil rights agencies, fraternities, and alumni. For example, his topics ranged in 1958 from "Education for Citizenship" to the Albany, Georgia, chapter of Alpha Phi Alpha to "The South's Role in World Leadership" to Atlanta's Hungry Club to "Racial, Social, and Religious Tensions" to the International Conference on Liberal Religion and Religious Freedom at the University of Chicago.[32]

What must have pleased his once skeptical colleagues, especially in the arts and sciences, was Young's modest but growing list of publications. Before coming to Atlanta University, Young had written privately printed pamphlets on black employment in retailing, racial barriers in public housing, and health conditions among blacks. After becoming dean, he contributed articles on his transition from the League to higher education and one on blacks and the social work profession. These essays were published in minor journals, but his article on "The Role of the Community Organizer in Desegregation" was published in the prestigious *Journal of Orthopsychiatry*. A decade earlier, W.E.B. DuBois had founded *Phylon,* a serious interdisciplinary journal on racial issues. Young contributed an article and reviews and later joined the editorial board. His brief essay on urban renewal urged black participation. His reviews summarized the 1954 *Social Work Year Book* and critically assessed a study on southern attitudes toward desegregation.[33]

These achievements in social work education increasingly brought Young to the attention of influential leaders within his profession. In 1959, Joseph Golden, an able Ph.D. whom Young had hired a few years earlier, secretly nominated him for the coveted Florine Lasker Award for outstanding accomplishments in social work. He credited Young with enhancing the reputation of his institution and encouraging faculty "to proceed with curriculum revision on bold lines." He cited Young's involvements with numerous national and local social welfare, social work, and civil rights organizations. Golden also lauded Young's "action research," which resulted in important publications on "pressing problems." Golden's sentiments obviously reflected those of the larger social work profession, since Young was named the 1959 recipient of the Lasker Award. He received the $1,000 prize at the San Francisco meeting of the National Conference on Social Work. Young had now ascended to the top of his profession. Whites and blacks nationally recognized him as a preeminent social work administrator and educator. Nonetheless, he seemed to yearn for more.[34]

President Clement became increasingly aware that Young had been an effective dean and that other institutions might seek his services. Probably to preclude such possibilities, Clement granted Young yearly raises in salary. Between 1956 and 1959, his compensation rose from $6,800 to $8,300 annually.[35] Nonetheless, Clement's persistent reluctance to authorize leaves for Young to respond to numerous fellowship and consultant opportunities constrained his academic circumstances and perhaps increased his inclination to consider other offers.

Since coming to Atlanta University, Young was probably sensitive about his lack of a Ph.D. During his regular sabbatical year, he considered returning to the University of Minnesota for advanced work in administration and community organization. While Minnesota had few funds, ample money seemed available at the University of Kentucky. The Southern Education Foundation funded three fellowships for blacks to complete the Ph.D. Young, however, declined. He had not been at Atlanta University long enough to justify a leave. Moreover, Kentucky offered doctoral degrees in sociology, not in social work, his preferred field.[36]

Nevertheless, Young, with a terminal M.A., had become a respected social work educator. Increased demands for his expertise showed both national and global esteem for his Atlanta achievements. Notwithstanding these developments, Young refused two offers from the United Nations. Despite his interest in international social welfare problems, he rejected offers to serve as an overseas welfare adviser in 1956 and as a technical consultant in Syria.[37] He also turned his back on a full professorship at the University of Chicago and a visiting lectureship at UCLA.[38]

Young was willing to leave Atlanta University. Inquiries about permanent United Nations employment showed how unsettled he had become by 1957. Moreover, Margaret, his wife, thoroughly detested Jim Crowed Atlanta and refused to adjust her attitudes and behavior to it. Their daughters, Marcia and Lauren, attended a private school run by Atlanta University, but they could expose them to only a few cultural amenities in a racially segregated city. In 1958, Young himself acknowledged, "There are personal factors which make it difficult for me to live in the South with children."[39]

Why did he stay? Various factors combined to keep him in Georgia, at least for a few more years. Clement's reluctance to grant Young any extended leaves of absence to work for the United Nations was one reason. Young was not tenured and did not want to jeopardize his Atlanta job in favor of seemingly attractive offers elsewhere. Moreover, numerous administrative changes seemed to cause Clement to develop ulcers. Young felt obligated to stand by a Kentucky family friend during a time of administrative turnover.[40] The principal reason why he remained in Atlanta related to his deepening involvement in the burgeoning struggle for racial equality. His growing reputation as a race relations specialist stemmed from his civil rights activism.

Young arrived in Atlanta a few months before the landmark Brown decision of 1954, and he remained in the South during a surge of black activism within the region. Young became a recognized expert on the burgeoning movement from two vantage points. First, as a writer, speaker, and consultant he developed a national reputation as an advocate for relating the social work profession to social change. Hence, he became an acknowledged scholar on desegregation. Second, Young evolved into a skilled strategist and activist during escalating black militancy in Atlanta. These involvements, which would eventually define Young's vocational direction, cemented his commitment to remain at Atlanta University for a few more years.

When Young received the Florine Lasker Award in social work, the citation commended him for "vigorous, wise and unafraid leadership in the field of desegregation and civil rights." Drawing attention to this aspect of Young's efforts as a social work educator indicated how much he stressed the role of his profession in spearheading social change. At his school he told faculty and students to develop strategies to change conditions for blacks rather than push adjustments to inequitable circumstances. Young exhorted them to effect equality in services rendered to blacks, to analyze American society to understand how the unequal status of blacks evolved, and to integrate these perspectives into whatever phase of social work they either taught or practiced.[41] Young disseminated these views through numerous speeches, especially to fellow professionals.

Young declared to the National Social Welfare Assembly that "social action, social reform, conscious efforts to promote better intergroup relations

[are] not an incidental extramural activity for social work. . . . It is social work." He added, "If we fail to recognize this . . . then we shall have done a tragic disservice to our profession." He then criticized fellow professionals because they had not taken "forthright and courageous positions" in favor of racial equality. "In fact, we have often lagged behind other professional groups which have been denied the benefit of our daily experiences with the results of racial discrimination." Young cited instances at national conventions when social workers ignored issues of concern to blacks. He was especially dismayed that when the Democrats and Republicans received input from the National Association of Social Workers for their 1960 platforms, the organization excluded civil rights as a major concern. Young deplored this colossal oversight because he held that social workers should be the primary troubleshooters for fundamental changes in the condition of blacks. At another professional meeting, Young challenged his colleagues to "reflect the basic concepts in social work in our services as well as in administration." In categorical terms, Young declared, "The agency that discriminates on a racial basis in its admissions policies is no longer a legitimate social work agency, nor is its staff legitimate social workers." As a social work educator and as an activist in several national and regional professional groups, Young advanced the notion that social workers should effect social change, especially when the issues related to race.[42]

It was in the field of desegregation, however, that Young earned a reputation as one of the nation's foremost experts. He did some writing on the subject, including a detailed review in *Phylon* of *Desegregation: Resistance Readiness,* a book which surveyed opinions among whites in a typical North Carolina county. The study discussed which groups would probably accept desegregation and which would probably resist. Young was not surprised to learn that "the least educated, the least exposed to mass media, those in the lowest occupational class" would mount the most opposition. While Young generally agreed with these results, he questioned modestly the premises and methodology of the researchers. He noted that, in not including blacks in the sample, the author wrongly assumed that "all Negroes are for desegregation and . . . that they can play no significant role in the process." He also objected to the staff of white interviewers and "highly emotionally toned words . . . which encouraged negative responses." He simply believed that questions were phrased badly. "Researchers have learned that regarding the public attitude toward a Fair Employment Practices Law, for example, you get one response when you ask the question, 'Should employers be forced to hire Negroes?' and another, completely opposite response when you ask, 'Shouldn't there be a law preventing an employer from refusing to hire a person solely on the basis of his color?'" Young wondered if the authors would have gotten different results if they had asked, "Do you believe that Negro tax-paying citizens of this community should have the right to use those public facilities that are tax-supported?"[43]

Perhaps Young's clearest scholarly statement on dismantling Jim Crow appeared in the *Journal of Orthopsychiatry* to which he contributed an essay on "The Role of the Community Organizer in Desegregation." He stressed how those trained in social work could effectively function as catalysts for change in race relations. In five specific ways, contended Young, the community organizer affected the desegregation process. First, as an enabler, the organizer gathers facts, interprets them, and facilitates their implementation through meetings, reports, and coordination of various groups concerned with the issue. Second, the organizer appreciates the uniqueness of his setting and approaches problems without prejudice. For example, he does not assume that because a community is in the Deep South, its attitudes or traditions are necessarily like those of another southern community. Moreover, he would not assume that all southern white citizens oppose desegregation. Third, the status quo, since most are comfortable with it, should not be frontally attacked. Rather, "a suggestion or a review of another community's experience tactfully placed is helpful; but more important, praise where the slightest positive movement is shown and a careful avoidance of a condemning or self-righteous approach are mandatory." Fourth, while change is often painful, it is an attainable goal. "The community organizer," he wrote, "never forgets, then, the capacity and ability of all people for change." Finally, the community organizer must put together the genuine leaders and best groups to achieve desegregation. Young declared that the "organizer must be especially skillful in the process of interpretation and in the involvement of citizens who are for and against segregation. . . . Compromise on method may be desirable, but never on principles or goals. He should attempt to set up a time schedule that is realistic, but not one that is obviously an effort to delay or postpone what the highest court in the land has proclaimed to be the law."[44]

Young's practical understanding of how to implement desegregation strictly adhered to basic social work principles. These moderate tactics appealed to numerous activists eager to learn the best techniques to achieve their goals. Carlton B. Goodlett, a black physician and publisher of the *San Francisco Sun-Reporter,* sought Young's advice on methods for involving more blacks in the local schools. Bayard Rustin, a pacifist who emerged as a major civil rights strategist, hitchhiked from New York City to Atlanta to elicit reactions from Young on initiating interracial civil rights workshops. A Columbia University social work professor also urged Rustin to consult with Young on whether sit-ins, mass protests, and other militant tactics were feasible in the burgeoning civil rights struggle. Rustin had been told that Young was the nation's best sociologist with insight on this timely topic.[45]

The Montgomery bus boycott in 1955 and 1956 greatly impressed Young. He went there and spoke with Reverend Martin Luther King Jr. and attended dozens of meetings. Young felt that this was "not mere boycott" but represented a watershed in the struggle against segregation and discrimination. Montgomery movement leaders respected Young as a knowledgeable observer with valuable advice to offer. Reverend Ralph D. Abernathy, King's chief lieutenant, knew Young when he studied for the M.A. in sociology at Atlanta University. When Abernathy returned to the campus to speak about the Montgomery movement, he spent time with the dean. Young admonished Abernathy that communists might try to infiltrate the movement. He advised Abernathy to investigate all unknown volunteers to learn their identities and political motivations. Abernathy and Rustin were exposed to Young during the early stages of the civil rights movement, as was Kenneth B. Clark, the already famous black psychologist whose memoranda on the psychic impact of racial segregation on black school children influenced the Brown decision. On trips to Atlanta University where Clark visited faculty friends, he and Young discussed the impact and implementation of the seminal Supreme Court decree.[46]

Young was also no stranger to the NAACP. He knew Roy Wilkins, who became executive secretary in 1955. Young was a veteran board member of NAACP chapters in St. Paul and Omaha, and he continued on the board of the Atlanta branch and chaired its Labor and Industry Committee. When the NAACP branch at Atlanta University commemorated the first anniversary of the Brown decision with a forum on "The Meaning of Integration," Young agreed to participate on the panel. In 1958 he attended the NAACP national convention in Cleveland. While there he became increasingly concerned about the lack of democracy within the organization. On both the national and local boards there was a tendency "to perpetuate in office a small clique of people." That structure gave the impression that the NAACP was not a mass organization. That problem, contended Young, required Wilkins's attention. Young also believed that the group's traditional techniques needed to be supplemented. Young thought that the NAACP was "the foremost organization for the elimination of legal barriers that remain toward securing citizenship." At the same time, he argued, the group needed to develop initiatives "in community organization and skills other than legal, which are necessary to change community attitudes once the legal barriers are removed." Young was interested in helping the NAACP project itself as a relevant player in the broader area of civil rights activism. As a member of the planning committee for the 1960 White House Conference on Children and Youth, Young worked with a subcommittee on studies. This group solicited suggestions for books, articles, and other data related to the conference theme. Young asked Wilkins to submit a list of recommended readings. Young reasoned, "This will be an opportunity to show the NAACP's concern and activity in the broader areas of human relations."[47]

Although Young was a full-time educator, his connections with the League grew stronger. Several graduates of the School of Social Work became League officials. The affiliates also sought his recommendations on persons they wished to hire. Moreover, Young maintained a heavy schedule of speeches to various League gatherings. In 1959, for example, he delivered addresses to affiliates in Memphis, Tennessee, and Massillon, Ohio. Young's speeches at national meetings, however, made him a familiar and influential voice within League circles. He spoke at meetings in 1955 in Milwaukee, in 1958 in Omaha, and in 1960 in Denver and San Diego.[48] Additionally, Mahlon T. Puryear, vocational guidance secretary of the League's southern field division, persuaded Young to participate in career conferences in 1954 and 1955.[49]

Other League officials involved Young in the organization's affairs. When Young addressed a national meeting in Omaha on "What the Urban League Is Not," numerous local executives became excited. John C. Dancy, executive director of the Detroit Urban League, told him that "the young fellows coming into the organization should have some material such as you suggested which would give . . . guidance and a perspective of what the Urban League is or is not." Dancy thought that affiliates should use Young's ideas on that matter. William E. Hill, race relations adviser in the Chicago office of the Federal Housing Authority, worked closely with the League's national office and the local affiliates. He asked Lester Granger for several copies of Young's speech for use in Urban League board discussions throughout his region.[50]

Lester Granger deepened Young's involvement in the organization. He noted, "In a very real way we stand to gain by your Atlanta experience more than we lose by your Omaha resignation. For the Atlanta School provides you with an opportunity to see social work in-the-large, as such, as very few Urban League posts would provide. You are too young to be 'encased' in an educational frame permanently at this stage of your career, and so we expect to see you back in League harness in the future." To ensure that Young would not become isolated while at Atlanta University, Granger extended invitations to important League functions and pressed him for advice on organization programs.[51]

In 1958 Granger told Young about efforts of the Social Planning Council of Philadelphia to fund programs of the Armstrong Association, the League's affiliate in the Quaker City. He wanted Young to consider becoming the executive director of the Philadelphia agency. "My interest, convictions and dedication," wrote Young, "continue to remain very close to the Urban League program, and I would . . . consider any challenging opportunities." Substantial community conflict surrounding the Armstrong Association, however, compelled him to withdraw any interest in that affiliate.[52] In congratulating him in 1959 for getting the Lasker Award, Granger wished Young to know that he considered him "a good Urban Leaguer and a personal friend in whose development I have been deeply interested."[53]

Young's interaction with Granger aimed at pushing the League and its aging executive director to the cutting edge of the surging civil rights struggle. While serving on the planning committee for the 1960 White House Conference on Children and Youth, Young wrote to Warren Banner, the League's national research director, to solicit suggestions about studies on illegitimacy, divorce, values, and education. "I believe this is a good opportunity," declared Young, "for the Urban League's role and function to be highlighted before an important national body."[54] In 1960 Young asked Granger for advice on a Taconic Foundation project. Young was the only black on a committee working on recommendations to the foundation "for the most effective expenditure of its funds." Young was given "the almost impossible task of trying to cover the whole racial problem." He wanted Granger's input in order to "interpret the Urban League as a significant organization to be supported toward the amelioration of some of these [racial] problems."[55]

By 1960 Young had become a keen observer and critic on race relations. Samuel Z. Westerfield, dean of the School of Business Administration at Atlanta University and a respected economist, shared ideas with Young on the lack of economic growth in the Southeast due to underutilization of "Negro manpower." He hoped that the 1960 White House Conference on Youth and Children would address that issue. Westerfield had developed enormous respect for Young. Hylan Lewis, a former sociology professor at Atlanta University who went on to the Health and Welfare Council in Washington, D.C., wanted his advice on a project to help low-income families. Lewis also wanted Young to be a consultant. Young critiqued the proposal and suggested better training for teachers who would interact with poor families, better use of social agencies, and the need for blacks in policy and planning aspects of the project.[56]

Although invitations to serve as a consultant to the Taconic Foundation and to the 1960 White House Conference on Youth and Children were impressive, Young's address to the United Steelworkers of America was perhaps the most unexpected request of all. Young had dealt with League board members in St. Paul and Omaha who worked in labor unions, but he had never interacted with national union officials. That Young was asked to speak to the influential United Steelworkers of America was further evidence of his increased visibility as a race relations expert. It also meant that his ties with the National Urban League remained strong. Boyd Wilson, a black official in the steelworkers' union and a member of the National Urban League board, got the invitation for him.[57]

Young spoke on "Integration: The Role of Labor Education" to a national conference of steel union officials at Indiana University. He told his audience that because the union traced its origins to a time of social injustice and protest, it should "sympathize with those who now face the same fate." He added that the union should not "forfeit its historical mission of concern for the little guy." Since blacks, like militant workers in the previous generation, needed allies to assist in their uplift, Young called on the United Steelworkers to implement antidiscrimination efforts within organized labor. He said that where there is a closed shop or an apprenticeship program, unions could clearly act to ensure the hiring of blacks. Young also pointed out the dismal absence of blacks in high-level positions within union hierarchies. Although Boyd Wilson's presence was evidence that the steelworkers' union had made some strides in this area, unions had to move beyond tokenism. Finally, Young urged union support of civil rights groups and other organizations fighting for black advancement.[58]

To Young such sentiments were more than just rhetoric. He genuinely wanted to see organized labor involved in the civil rights movement. He followed up his speech with personal appeals to officials of the steelworkers' union. When Emery Bacon, head of the education department, received a copy of the speech from Young, he acknowledged the legitimacy of black demands and the need for labor's support. Young told President David McDonald that the steelworkers had "a magnificent opportunity to be the labor union to stand out among all others as the leader in helping to bring about equal opportunities for the Negro."[59]

Young was at his best when he discussed the emerging civil rights movement. Although he preferred the methodology of the League, he deeply understood and insightfully interpreted the new militancy of the black struggle. He knew that the southern civil rights movement was developing into an unprecedented grassroots phenomenon. Fundamentally, the movement represented attitude changes among black southerners. Young noted:

> Buses and lunch counter demonstrations are merely. . . dramatic symbols to protest the institution of segregation and give tangible proof to the lie that the Southern Negro is satisfied with his conditions. . . . The disturbances of the past few years are symptomatic not of regression, but of forward movement, bitterly contested. The South's troubles are not caused by a resurgence of an old order; they are results of the last desperate rally of the old order against new forces. The old answers will not silence the new spokesmen. The old order neither understands nor can control these forces. The older Negro of the South was brought up in a rural area and soon learned that the white men had absolute control. Today's youth never had a chance to learn that fear. Raised in cities, having more contact with world conditions through travel and modern means of communication, he now demands the same dignity and respect for his person [that whites demand].[60]

Young applauded civil rights militancy. To a San Diego audience he declared:

> Words like gradualism and moderation are phantom words, meaningless. . . . You either hire a man or you don't. You either let him join your organization or you don't. . . . Gradualism results from some people taking the point of view that Negro citizens should have equal opportunity . . . and be judged solely on their merit, while there are other citizens who insist that the Negro is by nature inferior. . . . In between these two points of view we get gradual change. The person who insists on standing in the middle is much like the individual standing in the center of a rope during a tug-of-war with a hand on each side. In the final analysis he is more interested in keeping everybody happy than he is in effecting change.[61]

Although Young fully backed the burgeoning civil rights movement, he felt that "too much leadership potential and ability among Negro citizens is spent fighting for first class citizenship, and too little spent preparing and helping a previously disadvantaged group from taking full advantage of it when it arrives." He became convinced that the League needed to maintain its social service orientation. In correspondence with a local League executive, he criticized "some Urban Leaguers who are more interested in the dramatic kind of protest action which gets into the newspapers, than in the day-to-day important work which is so greatly needed today as we make efforts to become integrated in the total community, and which is not duplicated by many other organizations."[62]

Young contended that no American agency had more experience than the League. He described it as a "social agency . . . not a mass protest group or a direct Civil Rights organization, as important and necessary as these are." Moreover, the League did not possess "the dramatic tools of legal action." Instead, its "tools are facts logically presented to an intelligent community that cares." For these reasons the existence of League affiliates in racially troubled areas proved crucial. The League, he argued, was "one of the few instrumentalities in a community where intelligent communication takes place across racial lines."[63]

Young would readily admit that militant mass action, legal and legislative remedies, and moderate social service solutions were indispensable to effective desegregation. Throughout his career, he promoted and participated in efforts that stressed all of these strategies. While he preferred the Urban League approach, he never eschewed protest and direct action pressure to achieve racial advancement. As in St. Paul and Omaha, Young combined protest activities and traditional League methods of fact-finding and behind-the-scenes negotiation during burgeoning civil rights struggles in Atlanta.

Despite Atlanta's recent history of active black political participation, the city still dragged its feet on obeying the Brown decision to desegregate schools and on ending separate but unequal practices in a host of other public facilities.[64] Moreover, Atlanta joined such southern cities as Baton Rouge, Montgomery, Tallahassee, and later Greensboro as an early scene of civil rights activity. Backed by an increasingly militant black middle and working class closely connected to autonomous black churches, less timid black colleges, and other institutions, black urban southerners financed and courageously participated in direct action efforts to challenge economically and legally the faltering foundations of Jim Crow. Young was in the thick of the battle in Atlanta.[65]

In ways similar to his role in Omaha, Young, while occasionally visible during direct action campaigns, participated behind the scenes as an important but inconspicuous strategist and adviser. As in Baton Rouge in 1953, Montgomery in 1955, and Tallahassee in 1956, Atlanta confronted bus boycotts by blacks disenchanted with transit segregation. In the summer of 1957, Atlanta's mayor, William Hartsfield, the head of the Atlanta Transit Company, and local black leaders met to discuss an "orderly transition" to integrated buses. Atlanta Transit was willing to lose because the company wanted the judiciary to settle the issue. Militant blacks, especially students, were impatient with court cases because they usually took too long. Instead, some tried the sit-in approach on the city buses. Even with this tactic, the issue still had to be adjudicated in court. Although the state court supported the bus company, federal judges sided with the demonstrators. The Reverend William Holmes Borders of Wheat Street Baptist Church and older black ministers initially challenged bus segregation, and Young urged Atlanta University students to get involved in the effort. He also helped with research that showed how much the transit system depended on black patronage. Young joined the black delegation that tried to negotiate with transit officials on hiring black drivers and integrating passengers.[66]

When Young worked with the St. Paul Urban League, he saw an occasional need for alternative organizations consisting mainly of young black professionals to spearhead racial advancement. In Atlanta Young saw a similar and perhaps more urgent necessity for such a group to augment the activities of an older and more cautious of local black leaders. With the presence of several black economic, religious, and educational institutions, Atlanta's large and prosperous black professional and business elite provided a seemingly inexhaustible supply of community spokesmen. Concomitant with the rise in the 1940s of the racially liberal William Hartsfield as mayor of Atlanta, the Atlanta Negro Voters League, led by a bipartisan group of leading businessmen and professionals, functioned as influential spokesmen for black aspirations and as liaisons between Hartsfield and the black community. The Voters League was proud of its seemingly productive relationship with Hartsfield and its ability to negotiate concessions from him on public education, law enforcement, and minor desegregation. In light of these dubious achievements, the Voters League firmly forbade Martin Luther King Jr., the head of the new Atlanta-based Southern Christian Leadership Conference, to become involved with racial issues in "the city too busy to hate."

Although respectful of his elders, Young was dissatisfied with the Voters League's cozy but sometimes slow and unproductive alliance with Mayor Hartsfield. In the mid-1950s, after Hartsfield won reelection, Young and

other black professionals wanted to press the mayor vigorously on desegregation. Young attended a meeting with some older black leaders in the Voters
League to discuss several issues that Hartsfield should address. These veteran
spokesmen had worked hard to elect the mayor, and some made excuses about
why he could not act swiftly on issues of great concern to blacks. For example, the city's weak mayor system, they claimed, restricted Hartsfield's authority. Perhaps older blacks, accustomed to race-baiting politicians, were
impressed with Hartsfield in 1955 when he refused to close municipal golf
courses to prevent integration. He ordered removal of all racist remarks painted
on benches and buildings and threatened to fire employees who insulted blacks
using the golf courses. Such actions created a large reservoir of patience for
the mayor among elders of the Voters League.[67]

However, Young and his peers knew that civil rights activity throughout the South had reached a point where such minor concessions as integrating a golf course would not suffice. "There is no such thing as painless change,"
he wrote to a fellow social worker. Integration could not occur only on the
periphery. It also had to occur in fundamental areas of southern life such as
public education. He argued, "Change will only take place when people are
forced to by some tragedy." For example, when white southerners closed public
schools to avoid desegregation, this created conflicts with federal courts that
were ultimately desirable. Young believed that "the tensions while unfortunate are . . . positive in that they manifest a long suffering minority determined to change the status quo."[68]

These attitudes clearly set Young and his peers apart from such stal-
warts as A. T. Walden, Martin Luther King Sr., C.A. Scott, and other elders of
the black community. Although Young successfully interacted with older black
leaders, he was not convinced that their patience with Hartsfield was war-
ranted. Their bipartisan Atlanta Voters League, while an important political
organization, could not respond effectively to the new mood of southern
black militancy. Young and his peers believed that another organization was
required to reflect the impatience of younger blacks toward token desegregation.

A new group was needed for another reason. Southern NAACP chapters
were under sustained attack from state and local government officials. The
attorneys general in Louisiana, Alabama, and Texas requested NAACP membership lists in 1956, hoping to harass and shut down the organization. Other
southern states instituted legal action against the organization, and in Alabama it was completely outlawed. The president of the Atlanta NAACP was
jailed briefly for refusing to furnish chapter financial records to the state leg-

islature. In fact, the attorney general of Georgia tried to outlaw the NAACP, but two Atlanta chapter officials filibustered on the witness stand until the case was dismissed. When Ruby Hurley, the NAACP southeastern director, moved from Alabama to Atlanta, Young and others believed that if Georgia followed Alabama's lead, they needed a strategy to preserve the NAACP. In that eventuality, Young suggested to Hurley that they get support from Martin Luther King Sr., William Holmes Borders, and other leading ministers to form a surrogate group for the NAACP.

The unsettled relationship between the Atlanta Voters League and Mayor Hartsfield and the attacks on the NAACP persuaded Young and other young black professionals to establish the Atlanta Committee for Cooperative Action. Young's colleagues included M. Carl Holman, an English professor at Clark College, Samuel Z. Westerfield, dean of business administration at Atlanta University, and Jesse Hill, an insurance executive. The committee was neither a political organization like the Voters League nor a direct action group like SCLC. Rather, it pressed municipal agencies, businesses, and sports organizations to hire blacks in responsible positions. Discriminatory practices in the media and the professions also attracted committee attention. Threats to mobilize black economic resources through boycotts and black electoral strength to urge concessions from city government were the principal weapons in the committee's arsenal.

As chairman of the business committee of ACCA, Young wrote to the Atlanta office of the National Biscuit Company (Nabisco) to inquire about the firm's practices and policies on hiring blacks. Young expressed concern "about the migration to the North of most of our talented young people because of the lack of economic opportunities here." The committee also tried to get the Los Angeles Dodgers, which was considering expansion to Atlanta, to employ black players and initiate integrated seating. Leroy Johnson, an attorney and future Georgia state senator, belonged to ACCA and pressed the Fulton County sheriff to hire more black deputies. The sheriff promised to appoint a black deputy within two months. Jesse Hill pledged ACCA to help black Atlanta nurses to persuade their national professional organization "to suspend or eject Georgia . . . unless Negro nurses were accepted" in the state affiliate.[70]

Perhaps ACCA's boldest move concerned the *Nat King Cole Show*. Cole, the popular singer, became the first black entertainer to get a prime time series on NBC. When the series could not find a sponsor, the network and potential sponsors required "proof of strong interest and support" for the show. Young suggested that ACCA members ask college classmates, fraternity brothers, and others to write NBC "expressing enjoyment of the *Nat King Cole Show* and the desire that the show be continued." The show was ultimately canceled, but the letter writing campaign may have prolonged its run.[71]

Atlantans took much pride in the racial liberalism that Mayor Hartsfield exemplified. Whites pointed to him as evidence that their city was a progressive, cosmopolitan oasis in a backward region. Blacks, happy that the mayor eschewed the race-baiting that characterized many southern politicians, joined whites in touting Atlanta's seemingly liberal reputation. Members of the Atlanta Committee for Cooperative Action, especially Young and Holman, knew better. They were already aware that the city's reputation for racial liberalism frequently belied reality.

Young and Holman also wanted to expose Atlanta's undeserved reputation for racial liberalism. As a consultant to the Great Atlanta Council on Human Relations, Young did a study on the public library system. Blacks had access to only three "Negro branches," although the main library was closer to predominantly black neighborhoods. Several southern cities, including Austin, Baton Rouge, Charlotte, and Norfolk, had quietly desegregated their library facilities. But "the city too busy to hate" would not follow suit. Young noted that efforts by the interracial American Veterans' Committee and the Committee on Interracial Cooperation to integrate the library system received no response from the library board of trustees. Young declared that blacks felt that some on the board and staff and racists who had deep prejudices were more influenced by the Klan and White Citizens Council than by sound democratic practices. Such conditions were but one example of how Atlanta's white and black boosters glossed over unpleasant racial realities in order to support an undeserved reputation for progressive race relations.[72]

He and Holman discovered that within some elements of the local black leadership no one could say anything critical about Atlanta because it had a reputation of being "so good." Young urged the Southern Regional Council to commission Holman to write a pamphlet, "Toward a Balanced View," to reveal the hypocrisy of Atlanta's superficial advances in race relations and to advocate total desegregation. Young and Holman also brought these ideas to the Atlanta Committee for Cooperative Action and proposed that the group publish its own report on Atlanta race relations. Although Holman prepared the text, nearly all the ACCA members participated, with each assigned to research one aspect of the black condition. Young conceptualized the project and chose subjects that required study. The result was a well-researched publication, *A Second Look: The Negro Citizen in Atlanta.*[73]

The report chronicled the unequal expenditures of funds in the state and city for public school and higher education for blacks. It noted the lack of health facilities, which produced higher death rates for blacks, while opportunities to enter or advance in the health professions were already restricted. Housing was also limited with blacks "paying a proportionally higher percentage of income for rental and purchase of generally lower quality property." Moreover, only two blacks worked at the regional FHA, and they had segregated offices. The same was true for the regional Public Housing Administration. Perhaps the section on black employment prospects yielded the most dismal findings. For example, over 3,300 firms were located in the city, but "the prevailing pattern is to adopt discriminatory employment patterns and to exclude Negroes partially or wholly from the training programs." Blacks also had trouble making major advances in municipal justice and law enforcement agencies.[74]

Although Young disagreed with established black Atlanta leaders about Hartsfield and his effectiveness, he managed to maintain a respectful and trusting relationship with them. In fact, Young frequently functioned as the liaison between older black leaders and their younger and more militant colleagues. It became Young's responsibility to approach Norris B. Herndon, president of the Atlanta Life Insurance Company, to pay the printing costs of the report. Young frankly told Herndon that the pamphlet "discussed the gross discrimination that still remains in . . . health, housing, recreation, employment," and other areas. He also showed "the great hypocrisy on the part of the Democratic Party, which unlike the Republicans has absolutely no Negro representatives in the state organization." Hartsfield was a Democrat. When Herndon acquiesced, Young should have viewed it as a good barometer on the reactions of Herndon's elite black peers.[75]

Young, Holman, and other ACCA members anticipated anger from the old guard. They believed that the ACCA should meet with older black leaders to explain A Second Look. Their reaction surprised the entire ACCA. The response of President James P. Brawley of Clark College, Holman's boss, was typical. In a letter to Young, he said, "No one should become angry or insensed [sic] by this careful and painstaking presentation of facts, but every responsible citizen should be shamed by the ugly picture of inequality, injustice, and unfairness . . . and should be moved to join those who would make every sincere effort to correct these evils." The old guard urged the ACCA to do a second printing of the report and offered to pay the costs. Nearly 4,000 copies were distributed between January and April 1960.[76]

Even before the 1960 Greensboro sit-ins, Young urged students to play important roles in direct action efforts. To President Albert Manley of Spelman College he wrote, "Schools like ours in the South have a particular responsibility to do more than adjust young people to a maladjusted environment." Instead, educators should "intelligently sensitize them to social problems and inequities to the extent . . . it becomes desirous of trying to effect change." As students at the six colleges in the Atlanta University Center became involved in a local bus boycott and in attempts to desegregate facilities at downtown department stores in 1957 and 1960, respectively, Young, Holman, and Howard Zinn, a white professor at Spelman College, advised them. During the sit-ins at Rich's Department Store, Young was quite pleased that students drew data from *A Second Look* to substantiate their claims against the firm. Young and the Reverend William Holmes Borders of Wheat Street Baptist Church formed a two member panel that discussed the 1960 Atlanta sit-ins. Young commended the students "for not involving unnecessary participants and for keeping protests directed and channeled." He said, "Their aim should be to dramatize injustice, prevent apathy and complacency, release hostility, and secure action." He advised students to select their leaders carefully and not lose sight of the motive for protest.[77] Concerning the Greensboro sit-ins, Young urged a colleague from Harvard University to go to North Carolina to meet two of the four people who had begun the sit-ins. Young's friend agreed with his assessment that "these students have shown an unusual degree of maturity and purposefulness in their actions."[78]

Young also maintained his belief that whites should play an important role in the black struggle against segregation and discrimination. In St. Paul and Omaha, Young learned that there was a wide range of white opinion on the tactics and objectives of the black movement. In the South, Young confronted another dimension of the problem. In Omaha, for example, persons as diverse as Alfred Kennedy, N. Phillips Dodge, and John Markoe espoused different methods for black advancement, but they all agreed that improvements in race relations were paramount concerns. Although the same range of consensus existed within some elements of the southern white population, the number of such persons was small and their willingness to speak in behalf of black rights happened too infrequently. Although Young was not employed as a full-time agency head, he still worked to win white allies to the black struggle.

Young contended that blacks would gain allies only if they expressed concern about the religious and ethnic oppression of other groups. That's why Young swiftly wrote to Rabbi Jacob M. Rothchild and enclosed a personal contribution to help rebuild his bombed Atlanta synagogue. Young noted that five black churches in Montgomery a year earlier had been bombed in one night. "If the bombing in your Temple does nothing more than make the citizens aware that unless lawlessness is curbed everywhere," Young declared, "it cannot be expected to be curbed anywhere." Rothchild thanked Young for his response and noted, "You and I think alike in these matters."[79]

Young, his wife, and two daughters attended the Unitarian Church, and he found allies within this important group. On occasion he addressed the morning worship at the United Liberal Church and cooperated with some of its members who worked with the Greater Atlanta Council on Human Relations. Young also lectured to the Thomas Jefferson Unitarian Southern Regional Conference.[80]

Although Young was impressed with Unitarian pastor Edward Cahill and his advocacy of equal rights for blacks,[81] he had no patience with the vast majority of southern white ministers who either refused to endorse racial integration or explicitly spoke for segregation of the races. One white Atlanta minister, Roy McLain, preached on integration from his pulpit in 1956. Young criticized him for citing "disproportionate disease, immorality, and common law marriage among Negro citizens" without noting the undesirable social conditions that created them. He added that pointing out racial problems in the North did not excuse legalized southern segregation. While Young agreed that morality could not be legislated, the Supreme Court was certainly correct in invalidating "enforced segregation" in public schools. McLain was misguided, but Young commended him for at least discussing a crucial issue, an act that put him "ahead of practically all of his fellow ministers who apparently are more concerned with the safety of the pocketbook than the safety of the soul." Since McLain's racial attitudes were like those of most white clergy, Young was justifiably pessimistic about finding allies within this segment of the white population. The Reverend Charles L. Allen, an Atlanta Methodist pastor, however, surprised him. Allen spoke to the Hungry Club at the black Butler Street YMCA about his changed perspectives about segregation. Allen could no longer find any moral justification for Jim Crow. Young complimented him on his "forthright and honest answers." He also told Allen, "I hope you will continue to be a witness to the things you know are right." While Allen's new views were important and welcome, southern white clergy remained either hostile or ambivalent to civil rights struggles and lent little help to that moral crusade.[82]

Young had never dealt with southern white liberals. His extensive participation in the Southern Regional Council, the Greater Atlanta Council on Human Relations, and the Unitarian Church exposed him to the vast major-

ity of such persons living in Atlanta. Practically anyone who eschewed the
uglier aspects of racial segregation and expressed some willingness to countenance gradual integration could gain admittance to this small circle of dis-
senters. Few were willing to go as far as federal judge J. Waites Waring of
South Carolina, whose ruling presaged the Brown decision, or novelist Lillian
Smith, who demanded full and immediate integration.[83] Most southern white
liberals probably resembled Mayor Hartsfield, whose rhetoric made him an
ally of the evolving civil rights movement but whose actions seldom matched
his lofty ideals. Southern white liberals like Hartsfield annoyed Whitney Young.
When a Jewish synagogue was bombed, Hartsfield blamed "the rabble-rous-
ing of politicians on the state level." Young disagreed. He told Hartsfield that
this was "the harvest from the many nice, respectable people who do not
rabble-rouse but who do and say nothing." Young reminded Hartsfield that
on several occasions he had asked for an official mayor's commission on human relations. Hartsfield claimed, however, that power figures in the community did not support the idea. Young advised that if he ever formed such a
high-level committee, he hoped in his appointment of blacks that Hartsfield
would not "as you have done in the past" name only blacks "who praise you
and always agree with you but will consider those who have the respect of the
Negro community" and "who will stand up for principle."[84]

Ralph McGill of the *Atlanta Constitution* was the best-known southern
white liberal with whom Young developed a relationship. McGill, a native of
east Tennessee, had been a consistent advocate of black advancement. Young
admired McGill's forthright defense of desegregation and other issues important to black progress. When "extreme racist pressure" aimed to oust the
Atlanta Urban League from the community chest, McGill denounced the
effort. Young commended McGill and credited him with helping keep the
community chest and the city out of the control of the Ku Klux Klan and the
state's rights councils. McGill's progressive views persuaded the Pulitzer committee to award him the coveted journalism prize in 1959. "In light of your
convictions," Young told McGill, "this award is quite significant and will
certainly encourage other journalists in the South who all too often feel they
must reflect rather than . . . mold public opinion." Their relationship progressed to the point that Young sought McGill's response to some speeches he
wrote.[85]

By 1960 Young had developed ambivalent feelings about living in the
South. He was an active participant in various struggles to achieve desegregation. Young noted that he along with other black professionals shouldered "a
daily burden of financing all of the litigation now going on . . . to acquire

elementary civil rights." Perhaps Young suffered burnout from his exacting positions as dean, social work educator, desegregation expert, and civil rights activist. While proud of these accomplishments, he seemed ready to leave the South.[86]

Rearing his two daughters amid southern segregation and social turmoil weighed increasingly on his mind. Moreover, Margaret Young, though she taught at Spelman College, refused to submit to Atlanta's Jim Crow. To a friend in Lincoln, Nebraska, Whitney Young in 1958 confided that Atlanta was not a place "sufficiently far along in human relations to warrant our making this a permanent place of residence." He wondered if his continued presence in the city was inhibiting his daughters' growth and development. At the same time, he "never regretted coming to Atlanta during a period of great change." He added, "I have . . . learned not to expect painless social change and to realize that tensions are often times more positive than negative, in that they suggest man's attempt to improve his status."[87]

His opportunity came in 1960 when the General Education Board awarded him a fellowship for postgraduate study at Harvard. President Clement granted him a leave of absence from September 1, 1960, to September 1, 1961. Clement probably knew that Young would never return.[88]

6

Crossroads

Those who saw an animated Whitney Young deliver speeches, advise movement activists, and counsel student protesters believed that he was ill-suited for academia. Scholarly reflection and writing, while not beyond his intellectual grasp, were less satisfying than frontline involvements in the burgeoning civil rights movement. Although unsure of his vocational direction, Young wanted to join with an organization that pursued social change.

While Young provided technical advice to scores of activists seeking to destroy southern segregation, he never forsook his first love, the Urban League. During the late 1950s his became a familiar voice at national and local League meetings as he exhorted the organization to stay abreast of the emerging civil rights movement. He wanted the League to reformulate a special role in the black fight for equality. If the League failed in this task, it would become a peripheral player among the other civil rights groups and lose an opportunity to influence the direction of the black struggle.

As the main speaker at the 1959 annual conference of the National Urban League in Washington, D.C., Young spoke on "The Role of the Urban League in the Current American Scene." He noted that the group had an important place in the black struggle because any program which asserted that "judicial and legislative measures will in and of themselves qualify the mass of Negro citizens to compete equally . . . is the most vicious type of chauvinism if espoused by Negroes, and blatant dishonesty or naïveté if argued by others." Despite the importance of the NAACP, SCLC, CORE, and other civil rights groups, only the League was equipped to help blacks in their social and economic aspirations. Young contended that League officials and supporters also should recognize that the organization's traditional role in addressing the health, housing, employment, and educational issues confronting blacks had to be pursued under different circumstances than in the past. There were other organizations whose structure, personnel, and financing made them better suited to fight for black rights. Social planning, an undeveloped League function, "is far more respectable than it was some years ago" and a service that "most communities are willing . . . to pay for." Finally, "human relations . . . has become a profession requiring appropriate knowledge, skills, and attitudes which can be tested." Young declared, "No longer shall kindness, personality, and racial identity be the main qualifications for practitioners. This is the day of specialists and specialized agencies."

Young prodded the League to realize its special role and specific function in the black community at a time of escalating social upheaval. While direct action groups fought over turf and argued tactics, Young wanted the League to carve out particular areas of black life that neither the NAACP, SCLC, and CORE nor white social agencies could effectively address. The League would not be a "civil rights or civil liberties organization, nor a political, legal, or social mass movement," and neither would its staff be "'race leaders' who automatically become experts in human relations because of their particular racial or religious identity." Rather, the League as a professional social work agency with formally trained staff would carry out a program focused on research and communication.

Young stressed research. He argued that the League "should be the one agency in the community where *all* facts regarding the health and welfare of the group or groups it serves should be found." He included information on population, education, employment, housing, and health. He stressed, "The day has long since passed when our facts secured from conversations on the street corner, or from observations at the railroad station will be accepted without question."

Communication was the League's other crucial service. "The value of the League," Young declared, "lies in its having the kind of respect and confidence which will encourage the policymaking bodies to consult regularly with them, if not actually include them in on their planning and decision-making activities." He referred to city planning commissions, labor organizations, chambers of commerce, boards of education, and various governmental agencies. While interaction with these influential groups would help produce expanded services and opportunities to various black communities, such vertical communication with these powerful elements was not enough. The League also needed to have backing from its clients. Whether a neighborhood organization, a ministerial group, a council of indigenous leaders, or a community newspaper, the League had to be certain that those served by the agency endorsed the programs, accepted the responses, and agreed with those issues that the organization communicated to the powers elite. Moreover, Young could have mentioned his own efforts to voice the integrationist aspirations of middle- and working-class blacks in the Twin Cities, Omaha, and Atlanta.

Actually, much of what Young said in his speech, while seemingly new, was conventional wisdom. In fact, Young cited numerous local Leagues that had already implemented some of these ideas. He pointed to the cooperative relationship between the Providence Urban League and the local Social Planning Council. He noted how a creative local executive persuaded the San Diego City Council to underwrite the League affiliate's budget for two years. He also cited the Chicago Urban League's "intensive and sound research program." Perhaps Young can be credited with effectively synthesizing an emerging consensus among local League executives for more cooperation with various social and governmental agencies for improved services to blacks.[1]

What was important about Young's speech was neither its creativity nor its intellectual depth but that Lindsley Kimball had heard him deliver it. Kimball was greatly impressed by Young's enthusiasm, his grasp of current issues confronting the League and blacks, and his personal magnetism. Kimball wanted to know more about Young and for good reason. He represented Rockefeller philanthropic interests of which the National Urban League was one. Whenever a promising talent emerged near or within League ranks, Kimball wanted to know that person.[2]

Born in Brooklyn in 1894, Lindsley Fiske Kimball was graduated from Columbia University and earned a Ph.D. at New York University. He accumulated vast experience in business, in the military, and in philanthropy. In 1947 he became an associate to John D. Rockefeller Jr. He served as treasurer at Rockefeller University, executive vice president of the Rockefeller Foundation, and vice president of the General Education Board. Kimball's involvement in race relations commenced in 1947 when he became a director and an executive committee member of the United Negro College Fund. From 1953 through 1955 he was the fund's national campaign chairman.[3]

Winthrop Rockefeller drew Kimball into League affairs. A board member of the National Urban League since the 1940s, Rockefeller developed a close relationship with Lester Granger, the executive director. Surreptitiously, Rockefeller assured Granger that whenever the League had a deficit at the close of any fiscal year, he would underwrite it.[4]

Rockefeller's commitment to Granger was part of his family's general support of the League. Between 1919 and 1931 the League received $121,500 from the Laura Spelman Rockefeller Memorial. Most of the funds came to the organization during Granger's tenure between 1941 and 1961. The General Education Board gave the group $132,500 for various programs in race relations between 1943 and 1948. Between 1941 and 1958 the Rockefeller Brothers Fund contributed $65,000 to the League. The biggest single contributions came in 1954 and 1957 when two $25,000 donations helped put on an annual convention and meet a general financial emergency.[5]

So Kimball's involvement with the League was another expression of Rockefeller interest in the group's affairs. First, Winthrop Rockefeller asked Kimball to join the board of the New York Urban League to help it with its financial crisis. The affiliate needed $200,000 and could not raise it. In 1958 Kimball came onto the board of the national organization, "which was in equal difficulty."[6] For the period between 1958 and 1961 Kimball noted that despite contributions from local affiliates, industry, community chests, and other public appeals, monies coming into the League treasury "has been reduced to a trickle." According to Kimball, the organization has "run down under the tottering administration" of Lester Granger. He met the payroll only by "hypothecating certain securities, by spending certain foundation grants a year in advance, by borrowing $17,000 as a personal loan from one of its trustees [and] finally by putting a mortgage on its National Headquarters building." The League was clearly in trouble, and with Granger's mandatory retirement imminent, both Kimball and the Rockefeller interests wanted to find a dynamic and competent successor to a tired sexagenarian.[7] Upon hearing Young's speech, Kimball knew he had found his man.

Kimball heard three major addresses at the League conference and concluded, "Whitney Young gave by far the best." While he was impressed with Young's "courageous vigor in dealing with difficult subjects before a mixed audience," Kimball was "even more struck" by the esteem which Young elicited from both blacks and whites. As a social work dean, Kimball observed, "Young has at a rather young age reached the top in his own field not in terms of his own ability, but in terms of opportunities open to him. No Negro could head a school of social work unless it were either Negro or second rate white." Kimball knew that Young "could expect a professorship, but his real strength lies in the arena of action and he ought to make a very valuable person to head a national social work agency or a college or university."[8]

While still in Washington, D.C., Kimball asked Young to meet with him. They spent a couple of hours together. Young later noted that he had monopolized the conversation. Actually, Kimball preferred it that way. He wanted to know Young better and discuss his immediate career plans. Young said he did not know. He knew that a deanship in social work at a first-rank institution like Columbia University would elude him. He had hit the ceiling of his advancement and was unsure where to go from there. Both agreed that they should meet again soon in New York City.

When Young arrived in New York "to make some crucial personal and professional decisions," he was "shocked" and pleasantly surprised when Kimball suggested that he pursue a grant from the General Education Board for graduate study in the social sciences. At that point Young stated unequivocally that he wanted to deepen his understanding of race relations. "With every fiber in me," he wrote, "I desire to see . . . segregation and discrimination become 'obsolete practices' in the history of this potentially great country of ours." He conceded, perhaps prematurely, that "virtually all legal segregation based on race has been eliminated." Although this was a necessary first step, it was not enough. Blacks had to attain economic and social opportunities commensurate with their newly won first-class legal and political rights.

Toward this end Young proposed to explore numerous issues that would help achieve a racially integrated society. For example, he wanted to develop incentives to encourage and reward integrated businesses, schools, neighborhoods, and professional and social organizations. He also wanted to devise strategies to prod and prepare blacks to be ready for fuller social and economic opportunities. To attain these objectives Young wanted to tackle advanced courses in social work, sociology, and social psychology. He also wanted to audit those education courses which dealt with curriculum teaching techniques for assisting the culturally deprived. Young did not desire a Ph.D., but he wanted to gain general knowledge from various subjects relevant to race relations.[9]

Initially, Young preferred the University of Minnesota, his graduate alma mater, as a first choice. It was soon replaced by Harvard and then the University of California at Berkeley and the University of Chicago as descending alternatives. In Harvard's Department of Social Relations, Young felt that he could also establish contacts in the School of Public Health and the School of Business Administration. Additionally, he would have access to relevant departments at Boston University and the Massachusetts Institute of Technology. Kimball had strongly urged Young to rule out Berkeley and narrow his choices to Columbia University and New York University and to the big three institutions in Boston/Cambridge. Young also visited the University of Chicago. By February 1960 Young had made his Boston trip and decided to make Harvard his base. The university granted him a special auditor's status with full faculty privileges there and at the neighboring institutions.[10]

When Young submitted his application to the General Education Board, he knew it would be accepted. Despite this pro forma procedure, Kimball solicited a recommendation from Lester Granger. Granger noted, "Mr. Young is one of the most capable men on the national scene carrying an executive responsibility in the field of social work." He added that Young was "one of the 'bright young men' of the Urban League movement." He further felt that Young's talents could be better utilized outside of academia "in the field of community organization rather than social work education." While he gave Young a glowing assessment, Granger stopped short of suggesting a national administrative post for his former subordinate. In any case, it made little difference because Kimball was already thinking in those terms. He observed in a confidential GEB memo that Young was the leading candidate to succeed Lester Granger as head of the National Urban League. In another internal foundation memo justifying Young's fellowship request, Kimball noted that Young would spend a year "preparing himself for more effective leadership in his own field, possibly in one of the national welfare agencies."[11]

While flattered by Kimball's unusual interest in him, Young remained unsure of his benefactor's ultimate goal. After submitting his application, Young told Kimball, "Other than very general encouragement you were never at all specific about what you would like for me to do. . . . You would not be making an investment of this type unless you had something in mind in terms of a substantial contribution which I might make." Young received formal notification around New Year's Day 1960 that a $15,000 GEB fellowship was his. The grant commenced on September 1, 1960, and would last for a year.

Although Young was uncertain about Kimball's ulterior motive, he was happy to receive the fellowship. First, it freed him from Atlanta. Unlike Martin Luther King Jr., who deliberately returned South from Boston University to participate in the fight for black rights, Young sought to escape the region. He had emphatically informed Kimball that he did not intend to return to Atlanta University after the year at Harvard. He was exhausted from his own involvement in civil rights activities, and he worried about the education his daughters received in segregated Atlanta. Young told the headmaster of the Cambridge School in Weston, Massachusetts, that he wanted his older daughter, Marcia, to enter the ninth grade. He felt that she could make the adjustment, although she had had "limited and restricted educational opportunities in the South."

The fellowship pleased Young for another reason. With Atlanta University behind him, he could use the year to prepare for his next position. Although Kimball probably had not mentioned it, Young indicated the NUL post as a possibility as well as potential opportunities with the Unitarian Service Committee, "professorships at one or two universities," and a possible college presidency. The GEB fellowship became Young's springboard out of the South toward a broader range of vocational choices.[12]

Having settled on Harvard and the Boston/Cambridge area, Young had to focus on particular subjects and programs he wished to pursue. Kimball tried to lend him a hand. He suggested that Young talk with Donald Young of the Russell Sage Foundation and James Perkins of the Carnegie Corporation, who would help him choose the best curriculum for the year. Donald Young wanted him to narrow his general social welfare focus to something more specific. Young also turned to his former colleague, Garnet Larson of the School of Social Work at the University of Nebraska. She urged him to forego Ph.D. preparations because the degree was neither essential for him nor an imaginative way to use the grant. Rather, Larson encouraged Young to combine his interest in race relations with "a realistic plan" of exploring specific problems and issues within the classroom and the surrounding area. Larson's advice proved quite helpful once Young arrived in Cambridge.[13]

Initially, Young preferred to establish a base in Harvard's Department of Social Relations of which Gordon W. Allport was a prominent part. Allport, a pioneer scholar on the nature of race prejudice, asked to be Young's major adviser. Because Allport planned a leave during Young's first semester, he directed him to another scholar of race relations, Thomas Pettigrew. However, Harold Isaacs, a research associate at MIT, and some other professors at the Boston/Cambridge institutions suggested that Young bypass Allport's Social Relations Department for the Joint Center for Urban Studies, which Harvard and MIT sponsored. Donald Young of the Russell Sage Foundation advised Young that the institute was more policy oriented than the Department of Social Relations, which stressed research. Moreover, the Center would narrow Young's focus onto urban affairs and augment his already solid background in race relations and community organization.[14]

When Young arrived in Boston/Cambridge for the fall semester, he registered for six courses. He enrolled in three at Harvard and one course each at Boston University, MIT, and Brandeis. These courses covered theories of social change, decision making and policy formation, social administration, and international relations. In the following semester he planned to take another four courses at Harvard and three during the summer of 1961. Kimball was pleased to learn that Young impressed his instructors at Harvard so much that they excused him from their courses and suggested that he randomly sit in on various classes according to his evolving interests.[15]

The advice of Donald Young, Harold Isaacs, and Max Milikan, an MIT economist and director of international relations, that Young focus on the Harvard/MIT Joint Center for Urban Studies allowed him to spend an unusually productive year in Boston/Cambridge. Established in the 1950s, the Center focused on "the tangled problems of big city growth." The institute drew on the expertise of engineers, architects, lawyers, urban planners, sociologists, economists, and numerous other professionals and scholars concerned with urban issues. At the time of Young's arrival, the Center supported scholars of local government, comparative development of French cities, philosophical perspectives on the city, urban traffic, the family, space utilization, and race relations.[16]

Martin Meyerson, an assertive and confident city planner, headed the Joint Center. Meyerson had been Frank Backus Williams Professor of City Planning and Urban Research and director of the Harvard Center of Urban Studies. Young had interacted with Meyerson in the early 1950s when the director taught at the University of Chicago and chaired a committee on planning and development for the Chicago Housing Authority. Young apparently shared some perspectives with Meyerson in this project, which put up 10,000 new dwelling units for the predominantly black South Side. As Young seriously considered studying at the Joint Center, he told Meyerson that he was interested "in the problems of assisting Negro citizens in the movement from . . . legal segregation to true and full integration."

Young was interested in social planning and wanted to be brought "up-to-date on the current trends and developments in the various social sciences as related to this problem." He also wrote to Harold Isaacs to inquire about the Urban Planning Center. Isaacs said that if Young wanted to study urban development, then the Urban Planning Center was where he should be. Meyerson, however, responded to Young and offered the facilities of the Joint Center to him. He suggested that he meet with MIT professor Lloyd Rodwin to explore possible research studies. That's what Young opted to do. The Joint Center became his link with inner-city problems in Boston, all of which helped to perfect his analytical skills in approaching race relations and the city.[17]

Young's affiliation with the Joint Center was probably pivotal to his involvement with the Boston Community Development Program. With a special foundation grant, the organization was given three months in 1961 to devise ways to examine the impact of Boston's urban renewal effort on a wide range of social issues. Charles W. Liddell, an official in the program, hired Young as a consultant and asked him to comment on the social planning and urban mobility aspects of the renewal proposal. Young believed that the ex-

clusion of blacks in the social planning initiative would lead to a continuation of racially segregated communities and various forms of social disorgani-
zation in crime, welfare, delinquency, and other behavior with costly social
and economic consequences. Since Young had been a local black leader who
voiced the views of his constituents, he urged grassroots involvement and the
identification of specific projects in health, recreation, and day care to help
the beneficiaries of these social planning initiatives.

On the issue of the urban mobility of blacks, Young condemned residential segregation and "the stigma of inferiority" it imposed. Moreover, segregated housing patterns locked blacks into areas with "a minimum of services from the city" in health, police and fire protection, street improvements,
and enforcement of housing codes. Mobility out of such areas, however, carried risks to blacks, including the fear of confronting higher living costs in
another community, fear of hostility from whites, and fear of isolation from
other blacks. Young was pragmatic on these issues. He noted that stabilization of existing black neighborhoods was one alternative. Improved housing
and upgraded city services would obviate the need for an exodus from black
enclaves. At the same time, he urged politicians, realtors, and mortgage bankers
to enforce open occupancy for those blacks who wished to move beyond the
ghetto community. He advised the Boston Community Development Program to enlist help from a wide range of antidiscrimination groups to aid in
the effort.[18]

Additionally, Young was invited to write a proposal for a social plan in
Roxbury, where the majority of Boston blacks lived. He worked with the
Community Organization Steering Group for Roxbury–North Dorchester, a
subcommittee of the Boston Community Development Program. Young's
task was to gather information that would help the agency prepare residents
for the physical renewal of their area. The subcommittee chairman directed
him to include in his recommendations provisions for neighborhood input
so that special needs would not be ignored. Young was also reminded that
"possibilities for implementation" should also influence his suggestions.[19]

No one needed to convince Young of the importance of consultations
with residents of affected neighborhoods. He suggested meetings in Roxbury–
North Dorchester with community representatives in which explanations
would be offered on the overall plans for urban renewal. As the same time,
Young wanted discussions and questions from residents to stay focused on
the social consequences of urban renewal, not the physical changes, although
he advised community input on the latter issues at an appropriate time. Young
also proposed that a special committee meet with the renewal agency to en-

sure continued consultations with resident representatives. Additionally, he successfully sought involvement from the Boston Urban League to provide assistance in getting relevant information about Roxbury for his report. Liddell approved Young's procedural suggestions and allocated a budget up to $2,000 for the project. He would also earn $100 per day for his consultant services.[20]

At the first community meeting Young urged neighborhood representatives to accept urban renewal as a fact of life. He invited them to indicate problems in the social realm that would likely result from urban renewal and the types of social services that would be needed to address the difficulties. Young stressed that now was the time to offer input into a new social plan for Roxbury–North Dorchester. The following week at another gathering Young said that Boston's effort to insert a social planning component in urban renewal was unprecedented. He noted that in bringing grassroots spokesmen together they had a chance to learn about other facets of their residential area. Perhaps Young hoped that these representatives would view the program as an opportunity to ponder a better future for Roxbury–North Dorchester now that they knew more about it. To another group Young specifically wanted feedback on social services in mental health, family and children's services, legal services, and other programs that needed improvements. Talking to a fourth gathering he said, "We are having urban renewal, but unless the people are frank [enough] to speak out forcibly and candidly about services needed, the job will not be satisfactory." Determined to get community perspectives to put in his written report, Young told Liddell that he would consult with delegates from the four sections of Roxbury–North Dorchester to elicit their final thoughts on the social plan.[21]

Young's report, while discussing a section of the city with a majority immigrant population, focused much attention on the plight of blacks. Although 45 percent of the area's population was black, 70 percent of all Boston blacks lived in Roxbury–North Dorchester. Hence much of the deficiencies in social services probably affected blacks more than others. Young noted a general breakdown in service delivery in this part of Boston. Poor rodent control, inadequate garbage collection, and dirty streets created unclean surroundings. Overcrowded medical facilities and ineffective public health clinics aggravated an already unhealthy environment. He suggested that municipal officials correct these inadequacies. In some instances, this section lacked important agencies that could enhance the quality of life. For example, the family service agency closed its Roxbury office, an action that Young recommended officials should reverse. Additionally, a reopened family service agency, he argued, would be helped by the establishment of a family or domestic relations court.

While he strongly urged physical improvements to school buildings, Young assertively advised that curricular innovations "to salvage talent" in the early grades would later keep black adolescents in school. He wanted more black principals to be hired and for teachers to take courses in intergroup relations. He further believed that policemen would also benefit from such training. Aside from suggesting better relations between the community and the police, Young urged law enforcement officers to crack down on the sale of liquor and narcotics to residents of Roxbury–North Dorchester. Furthermore, Young recommended more effort by municipal and private agencies to combat employment discrimination.

Prophetically, Young declared, "Boston's Negro population is now over 63,000, an increase of over 50 percent in the last ten years. . . . This trend will continue at the same rate for almost the next two decades. In the absence of making the Roxbury–North Dorchester area a stable community racially, and through failure to insist on open occupancy in all other parts of the city and suburbs, Boston will find itself by 1980 possessing the kind of ghetto, with all of the resultant social problems, economic cost and waste, and breeding grounds for tension and violence, which other communities are now desperately trying to correct. *It need not happen here.*" He added that the area had numerous competent agencies and organizations to help implement a social plan that would transform Roxbury–North Dorchester into a desirable residential community.[22]

With his participation in this urban renewal study, Young abandoned a principle that he inculcated to his Atlanta University students. Social workers, he taught, must change unpleasant and unjust realities rather than assist blacks to adjust to them. Thus, Young's role in this project was somewhat worrisome. He knowingly entered a situation where the basic decisions had been made without early input from black Bostonians. Always the pragmatist, Young believed that even tardy participation by blacks was better than none at all. Although Young fell far short of his own standard, he fulfilled an important objective of his "think" year in Boston/Cambridge. While Young was up to date on developments in social work education and race relations, he knew little about social planning and the problems related to urban renewal. Affiliation with the Joint Center and the Boston Community Development Program remedied that gap in his knowledge. He now saw firsthand how major decisions on urban issues developed without initial input from blacks and the difficulties which emanated from that. With these educational experiences Young was far more knowledgeable and sophisticated about urban issues that he had never explored before.

Young's report, however, did not satisfy all of those affiliated with the project. His principal critic thought that his stress on the "unrelieved misery and complaint" of Roxbury-North Dorchester residents gave "insufficient recognition of positives in certain services." For example, he criticized Young for not noting "the presence of good teachers here and there." The critic also said that he did not emphasize "the responsibility of citizens themselves." Although "trash and garbage collection," he wrote, "are handled by the city in a crummy way, how often did we also hear that some householders compound the problem by their own mishandling of trash? This is an area for citizen to citizen education as well as pressure on the city."[23] The critic missed the point of Young's report. Young stressed the consequences of institutional breakdown in social services in Roxbury-North Dorchester. No amount of voluntary effort could substitute for municipal failures to pick up trash, repair decaying school buildings, or establish a family or domestic relations court. What Young did not realize fully was the futility of eliciting grassroots perspectives on a process on which citizen views would have a marginal impact. Nonetheless, his participation in the project confirmed his long-held belief that effective leadership required the validation of rank-and-file residents of the black community.

Young's matriculation at Harvard, Brandeis, MIT, and Boston University, his participation in the Joint Center for Urban Studies, and consultant work with the Boston Community Development Program probably convinced Lindsley Kimball that his investment of foundation funds in Whitney Young had been a sound decision. The generous General Education Board fellowship also allowed Young to continue active participation in professional meetings and to venture beyond Boston/Cambridge to other metropolitan areas to study urban issues. He went off to Cincinnati to attend the National Association of Intergroup Relations and then to Minneapolis to deliver two papers at the National Conference of Social Welfare. Young's addresses were based on his experiences in Boston/Cambridge, and he looked forward to discussing what he had learned during his sabbatical year. Young also traveled to New York City and Chicago to observe groups involved in solving varied inner-city difficulties. The Horizons Unlimited Program in New York City tried "to increase the motivation and aspirations of children from lower socioeconomic families." He came to confer with officials of that organization. In addition, Young went to Chicago to speak with municipal and school officials and with social workers about correcting problems in education, housing, and among migrants. Young's sabbatical itinerary showed that the foundation funds were well spent.[24]

A crucial benefit that Young derived from his association with Lindsley Kimball was a broadened acquaintance with whites of national stature and influence. Although Young had become adept at dealing with elite whites whose principal sphere of activity was St. Paul, Omaha, or Atlanta, their importance was limited to these locales. He also knew persons of authority in national social work and social welfare groups, but their power seldom extended beyond their professional organizations. Kimball, however, gradually exposed Young to important whites who headed major foundations or who worked as brokers or liaisons for the nation's wealthiest families. Young advanced to another plateau of interaction with powerful whites he had never known before. Although his dealings with Donald Young of the Russell Sage Foundation had been brief and uneventful, his introduction to Dean Rusk was important and portended Young's eventual entry into the world of major national and international institutions of which foundations were a key part.

Dean Rusk, born in Georgia in 1909 and a graduate from Davidson College, had been a Rhodes scholar. After several years as a government professor and dean of the faculty at Mills College, Rusk served important stints in the State Department and at the United Nations. These experiences launched him into the presidency of the Rockefeller Foundation from 1952 to 1960. In the spring of 1960 Kimball thought it important that Young meet Rusk, whose retirement from the foundation was imminent. He urged Young to plan his next trip to New York City at a time when the future secretary of state could see him. At his meeting with Rusk, as in his initial encounter with Kimball, Young dominated the conversation. He told Rusk, "I fear that I spent more time talking than asking the many questions I would have liked to . . . someone of your great experience." It was just as well, since Kimball probably wanted Rusk to get to know more about Young. Young's garrulous nature actually helped to achieve that end.[25]

Young maintained contact with Rusk and asked for a second meeting. He also sent Rusk a paper he had written for another foundation. Young wrote on "The Status of the Negro Community" with some analysis on how race relations have been enhanced through foundation grants. There were also suggestions for the most effective use of funds to encourage improved intergroup relations. Young wanted Rusk to review the essay and offer his reaction. Rusk read the paper and suggested that Young strengthen it with a section on self-help. While he agreed with Young's discussion of white paternalism, he thought the phenomenon could be corrected by "a better under-

standing by both whites and negroes of the efforts made by the negroes themselves to deal with some of the problems you discuss." He added that there
may be "a better story than is generally known" about black self-help. Rusk's
comment echoed the criticism of Young's paper on Roxbury where his critic
decried Young's failure to point out ways that blacks could alleviate their own
problems. He wanted large institutions such as the Boston municipal government and the Rockefeller Foundation to play a greater role in addressing
issues that hindered black advancement. But this was not the time to debate
Dean Rusk about their differences. Besides, Rusk thought the essay important enough to share with several of his Rockefeller Foundation colleagues.
Young and Rusk, however, had the meeting that Young wanted. Afterwards,
he urged Rusk to issue a publicity release about Young's GEB grant to black
newspapers to acquaint their readers with the constructive efforts of the foundation.[26] He hoped that would broaden the relationship between the
Rockefeller philanthropies and the black community. Young could kill two
birds with one stone. The foundation would become a more familiar source
of assistance to blacks, and Whitney Young could become increasingly associated with this wealthy agency.

Although Lindsley Kimball secured the fellowship to prepare Young to
become the new NUL executive director, Young was not sure that he would
definitely succeed Lester Granger. While he stated emphatically that whatever happened, he would not return to Atlanta University, Young had neither
resigned his position as dean nor neglected minimal oversight of the School
of Social Work during his sabbatical. He entrusted his duties to Frankie V.
Adams, who had taught group work and community organization at the
school since 1931. She and Young developed a good relationship, with Adams
playing a crucial role in curriculum reform and in studying admissions policies during Young's tenure. They also coedited a student workbook, *Some
Pioneers in Social Work: Brief Sketches.*[27]

Frankie Adams kept Young abreast of the happenings at the School of
Social Work throughout the 1960-61 academic year. She shared with him her
failed effort to get more scholarship money from President Clement and news
about new faculty. Young planned to attend the 1961 Council on Social Work
Education meeting in Montreal in his capacity as Atlanta's social work dean,
but he could not persuade Adams to go along. "I called Dr. Clement . . .
saying in no uncertain terms that I did not want to compete with you,"
Adams said to Young. She added that whatever responsibilities needed to be
covered at the Council, Young could handle. Although Young may have been
mentally disengaged from Atlanta University, he still functioned as a dean.[28]

While dutiful in discharging occasional administrative duties for Atlanta University during his leave, Young kept his options open. The Unitarian Service Committee already had an interest in hiring him. Now that Young
was in the area, Frank Z. Glick, the executive director of the Boston-based
group, hoped to see more of his potential colleague.[29] The degree of Young's
interest in the denominational agency, however, was probably limited. Failed
effort to work with the United Nations a few years earlier did not diminish
his interest in foreign affairs. Two close friends, Arthur McCaw and Carl
Rowan from Omaha and Minneapolis, respectively, worked in the State Department at different times during the 1950s and 1960s and had broad contacts in that field. In fact, he helped a social work colleague promote a Freedom Road Foreign Service Exchange Program through his friendship with
Rowan. Additionally, Young told Dean Rusk, the nation's new secretary of
state, that he would consider a position in the department.[30]

Part of Young's interest in foreign affairs stemmed from the increased
attention that black American leaders gave to the emerging nations of Africa.
In 1959 Young joined with Martin Luther King Jr.'s Southern Christian Leadership Conference on an Africa freedom dinner committee, which planned to
bring Tom Mboya, the Kenya nationalist, to Atlanta. In 1960 Horace Mann
Bond, dean of the School of Education at Atlanta University and a noted expert on Africa, invited Young to join in a trip to the continent. He responded
enthusiastically and told Bond that he had been matriculating in the African
studies program at Boston University with his fellowship. Although all of these
options were exciting prospects, Kimball and other supporters of the League
reminded Young that his best work could be done in that organization.[31]

The competition to succeed Lester Granger seemed wide open. Despite
Whitney Young's formidable candidacy, he faced several tough rivals for the
League position. The board of directors chose four of its members, two blacks
and two whites, all New Yorkers, to constitute a search committee. They
included NUL president Henry Steeger, a publisher, Regina Andrews, a librarian, Mollie Moon, president of the NUL Guild, and Burns W. Roper, the
League treasurer and president of Elmo Roper and Associates, the public
opinion analysts.[32]

Several candidates from within the League wanted the job, including
local executive directors Edwin "Bill" Berry of Chicago, M. Leo Bohanon of
St. Louis, and Edward S. Lewis of New York. They believed in a more activist
League involved in direct action protests to enhance the organization's em-
ployment and housing programs. As an executive in both Baltimore and New
York, for example, Lewis became a noted labor organizer among black car-

penters, painters, and brewers. Berry, Bohanon, and Lewis wanted the League to identify with the emerging national civil rights movement. The search committee ultimately interviewed thirteen persons including some members of the NUL staff. Two educators, Alonzo G. Moron, president of Hampton Institute, and Whitney Young, also met with the committee.[33]

After the search committee interviewed the thirteen candidates, Steeger asked Andrews, Moon, and Roper to join him in indicating a first choice. Alonzo Moron received three votes, and Young drew his one vote from Burns Roper. Moron had been Roper's third choice. Steeger wanted to report a unanimous vote to the board of directors. Although Roper was willing to yield to the majority, the committee decided to put aside the 3:1 vote and invite Moron and Young back for second interviews.

Alonzo G. Moron, the fifty-two-year-old president of Hampton Institute, was born in the Virgin Islands. He held the Ph.D. from Brown University, the M.A. from the University of Pittsburgh, and a law degree from Harvard. His tenure at Hampton began in 1947 when he became the business manager, but culminated in the presidency two years later. He had extensive experience in social work administration. He had served as a commissioner of public welfare in the Virgin Islands, and he spent eight years as an official in the Atlanta Housing Authority. Moron was also a member of the executive committee of the National Conference on Social Work. With such stunning credentials, Moron was surprised that the committee required another interview. In fact, he was so visibly annoyed that his negative disposition harmed his candidacy. Moron was cool and reserved as he answered additional questions about his potential leadership of the National Urban League.

Young's first interview received mixed reviews from the search committee. While Steeger thought that his talk was too "pat" and lacked feeling, Roper believed that Young had been "enthusiastic" and "full of fire." In sharp contrast to Moron, Young was still enthusiastic during his second interview, according to Roper, and gave an excellent presentation. This time Steeger, Andrews, and Moon concurred with Roper and unanimously recommended Young to the full board of directors as their choice to succeed Lester Granger. Steeger told Young, "You've got it." The board agreed and elected Whitney Young the new executive director.[34]

Behind the scenes of these meetings of the search committee and the board of directors occurred a surreptitious tug-of-war between two sexagenarians, Lester Granger and Lindsley Kimball. Granger was well aware of Kimball's preference for Young. Just before the search process began, Granger told Henry Steeger that Whitney Young was interested in the post. He added,

"I consider him to be one of the better prospects. He is receiving a General Education Board fellowship—very handsome proportions—that will enable him to put in the next year . . . on study in the universities of Boston. . . . The fellowship was Lin Kimball's idea." At the same time, Granger encouraged the candidacy of Alonzo Moron. Granger belonged to Moron's trustee board at Hampton. His presidency was ending, and Granger tried to help him find another top-level position.[35]

Lindsley Kimball had a different agenda. Privately, he blamed Granger for the faltering financial conditions of the national League. As a board member and representative of the organization's principal benefactors, Kimball probably wanted to limit Granger's influence over the selection process. Although Granger had been Young's boss and adviser for more than a decade, it was Kimball who whetted Young's appetite for a position of national responsibility and provided him with the wherewithal to achieve it. Kimball persuaded him to apply for the job and muscled him in as the executive director. While Young also benefited from support given him by such board members as George O. Butler, a black official in the Labor Department, backing from Kimball was pivotal. Whether Granger had supported him or not proved unimportant. That Kimball was his staunch sponsor, however, made all the difference in the world.[36]

How vigorously Granger advanced Moron's candidacy once the competition yielded finalists is likewise unclear. He certainly had good reason to avoid a showdown with Lindsley Kimball because he simply could not win. Besides, Granger still had much to gain from continued favor from the Rockefeller philanthropies. As Granger retired from the National Urban League, he assumed the presidency of the International Conference of Social Work. To enable him to discharge his duties, the Rockefeller Brothers Fund gave him a $30,000 grant over two years. League president Henry Steeger consented to have his organization administer the funds to Granger. At the end of the period, Granger promised a publication discussing his travels and experiences. Steeger expected that Granger's new international perspectives would benefit the League. Kimball was more cynical. To help the League, Kimball stated, "The Rockefeller Brothers Fund has appropriated $30,000 to take Lester Granger off their hands for the next two years."[37]

Granger preferred Alonzo Moron, but he did not deeply oppose Young. Moreover, he was unwilling to let an open disagreement with Kimball end his continued dependence and deference to Rockefeller benefactors and their agents. To Dana S. Creel, director of the Rockefeller Brothers Fund, Granger wrote, "I shall never forget the personal interest that you have shown in the many problems which I have encountered during the years of my association, nor shall I ever forget the staunch support that the Rockefeller family has given to the Urban League almost from the first month of the League's establishment. It is no exaggeration to say that without the support of the Rockefeller family there may well have been an Urban League, but it could not have given anything like the extent and quality of service that we have been privileged to provide." Creel responded, "It is difficult to think of the Urban League movement without you in the picture." In preferring Moron, however, Granger did not recognize that the League required a more activist leader in tune with the emerging civil rights movement. Ironically, the other key sexagenarian, Lindsley Kimball, wisely noted the increased militancy of the black struggle and engineered a change in the League's leadership to accommodate these new racial realities.[38]

The most significant difference between Granger and Whitney Young was the latter's sophisticated critique of whites and their attitudes toward black advancement. From observing his father interact successfully with paternalistic whites in Kentucky to his own experiences drawing grudging support from conservative businessmen in Omaha, Young became adept at analyzing white perspectives and behavior toward blacks and their struggle for equality. His latest reflections on the subject enabled him to deliver a poignant speech to the Boston Urban League shortly after his election to succeed Lester Granger. In "I'm Liberal, But . . . ," Young frontally attacked the excuses and subterfuges that whites employed to justify opposition to black demands. For example, he noted that seemingly well-meaning whites often remarked, "You really can't change things overnight. The Negro has made a lot of progress and I am for him but if you go too fast it might antagonize even some of your friends." In his rejoinder Young pointed out that "after 300 years of slavery and almost 100 years of technical freedom he [the Negro] hardly feels qualified to be called a revolutionist." He expressed amazement "at how good, educated, and church-going Americans can tell a well-prepared Negro who has suffered all the indignities and pain of jobs, homes, and other normal needs being closed to him that he must be patient, be philosophical about these denials of civil and human rights."

He cited another of the "I'm Liberal, But . . ." syndrome. Whites sometimes said, "Prejudice begins in the hearts of men and it is there that it must be corrected. You just can't legislate attitudes and morality." Young observed, "We are talking about discrimination. Of all the laws proposed or passed, none has ever required that you like anybody. They have only asked that your dislike of another human being not deny to him such elementary rights as a job or a house. . . . In practically every case, attitude changes in a positive direction usually follow changes in practice or behavior." He added, "'The I'm Liberal, But Routine' is focused on the student sit-ins. The reaction usually being, well, I am for the ends but am not so sure about the means. They are after all breaking the law. Here I think all should know there were no laws in most southern cities. These were hastily passed after the sit-ins began and even here not a law against a Negro sitting at a counter but a trespass law." He contended that blacks were doing no more than the American colonists throwing tea overboard in Boston Harbor in 1773. "They sought a cup of untaxed tea," Young said. "The students seek a cup of unsegregated coffee."[39]

Perhaps taking a cue from an earlier criticism by Dean Rusk, Young also addressed the issue of "The Negro and Self-Help." He cited black-owned "banks, insurance companies, and other businesses which not only provide employment, but also make personal and home loans, provide . . . scholarships and give substantial support to social welfare and educational institutions." He included black churches as the principal purveyors of self-help. While the NAACP and the Urban League were important organizations, "less publicized but effective efforts" of the Elks, Masons, sororities, and fraternities impacted greatly on black self-help, especially in making scholarships available to needy students. He noted the Frontiers, a national service club, and numerous black professional groups and their programs to improve the social and economic condition of blacks. Young observed, "Hardly a week passes that Negroes are not solicited for funds needed as defense against some miscarriage of justice or infringement of property and personal rights."[40]

At the same time, Young contended that the major problems confronting blacks were too broad and deep to depend on black self-help to solve them. That's why he increasingly stressed the responsibility of powerful and influential whites to commit government, foundation, and corporate resources toward eliminating the incumbrances to black advancement. He was convinced that racial segregation, discrimination, and economic deprivation of blacks were issues that whites had to address. His speech, "I'm Liberal, But . . . ," was not meant as an exercise in sarcasm and satire. Rather, it was one of many attempts to emphasize the crucial impact of white attitudes and behavior in hindering black progress. Black self-help, while important, was not the answer. The development of genuine racial and economic liberalism, he believed, would go further to alleviate black social and economic distress than could the modest resources of black institutions. Perhaps Kimball and Rusk did not detect this streak of bold, independent thought in Whitney Young. So impressed were they with his wit and dynamism, they may have missed Young's message.

2

Retooling the League

Diverse elements of the civil rights struggle coalesced into a sustained and identifiable movement just as Whitney Young assumed his duties as executive director of the National Urban League. Starting with successful bus boycotts in 1953, 1955, and 1956 in Baton Rouge, Montgomery, and Tallahassee, respectively, southern blacks discovered the effectiveness of economic pressure and legal action as methods to destroy segregation in public transportation. Demonstrations and sit-ins to protest exclusion from department store lunch counters in numerous southern cities beginning in 1957 and culminating in 1960 in Greensboro drew black college students to the vanguard of civil rights activities. Black militancy was further buoyed by the Supreme Court's landmark Brown decision in 1954 and other federal initiatives including the 1957 and 1960 civil rights acts, the work of the newly established Civil Rights Commission, and the dramatic arrival of federal troops in Little Rock, Arkansas, to guard nine black students as they entered the formerly segregated Central High School.

As civil rights activism escalated and intensified, the venerable NAACP, a revived CORE, and the recently founded SCLC gained greater visibility as frontline organizations that articulated black demands and devised strategies to achieve integrationist objectives. The National Urban League, despite the militant involvement of some affiliates, acquired a reputation for conservatism. Lester Granger, an Eisenhower Republican, did not identify with the grassroots activism of such groups as CORE and SCLC, which mobilized blacks to attack segregation in a broad range of public facilities. Although the League had a special and indispensable social service function, Young wanted the organization to become an integral part of the increasingly militant civil rights movement and to influence its direction. Before that could be accomplished, however, Young tried to resuscitate the League and retool it for the changed environment of civil rights activism.

Unfortunately, Lester Granger passed on to his successor a nearly bankrupt organization. When Young replaced him, he inherited a deficit of $125,000.[1] Starting off with such financial difficulties made it hard for Young to meet even routine operating expenses. For example, the National Urban League sponsored an annual conference for two to three hundred persons from its sixty-two affiliates. The 1961 meeting, planned for Dayton, Ohio, however, faced possible postponement because the national office was in such desperate financial straits that its staff needed to pay their own expenses to the gathering. Young told Henry Steeger and Lindsley Kimball about the emergency. They in turn asked the president of the Rockefeller Foundation, J. George Harrar, for $5,000 to enable at least nineteen persons on the national staff to attend the Dayton meeting. Harrar approved the grant in order to ensure a better return on the investment that the Rockefeller Board had made in sending Whitney Young to Harvard. "It is understandably important," said foundation officials that as Young "takes the administrative reins of the agency . . . that he be able to count on the presence and active participation of his headquarters staff at this Conference."[2]

The Rockefeller donation was a small part of a larger effort that Lindsley Kimball spearheaded to restore financial integrity to the League's fiscal operations and to give Whitney Young a chance to succeed as the executive director. Kimball engineered a major rescue operation for the League assisted by the Carnegie Corporation, the Rockefeller Brothers Fund, the Taconic Foundation, and the Field Foundation. By March 1962, Kimball drew contributions totaling $168,000 from these foundations. Additionally, David Rockefeller of Chase Manhattan Bank and A.L. Nickerson, president of Socony Mobil Oil, hosted a gathering of businessmen to attract their support for the League bailout. That effort yielded $55,000 in pledges by February 1962 and eventually over $90,000 in contributions before the end of the fiscal year. With assistance initially given by Kimball and the Rockefellers, Young made valuable contacts with foundations and corporations, raising League income, mainly from these sources, from $284,000 in 1961 to $4,100,000 in 1968, an increase of 1,374 percent.[3]

As financial resources became increasingly available, the NUL staff grew from 30 to 110 between 1961 and 1965. Growth in personnel and programs severely taxed League facilities at 14 East 48th Street in New York City. The League rented two other premises to accommodate the additional staff. Lindsley Kimball, who had succeeded Henry Steeger as NUL president, found a solution. He proposed the purchase of the CBS building at 55-61 East 52d Street. Since the owner had recently put it on the market, numerous cash offers had been made already. Kimball moved quickly to put in a bid.

Although serving as league president, Kimball maintained a deep involvement with the United Negro College Fund. Like the NUL, the UNCF had outgrown its building and rented additional office space to house its expanded operations. Kimball proposed that the NUL and UNCF jointly purchase the CBS building. He figured that since the two groups often solicited funds from the same sources, it was cheaper to put them together under one roof. He added, "Neither organization is likely ever to need more space than this new building provides. . . . Urban League expansion will now take place in the field rather than in the national staff." Most important to Kimball was that "these two organizations should be more closely associated." He criticized the member colleges of UNCF for continuing "the old pattern of preparing young Negro men and women for teaching and for the ministry but *not* for the jobs that are open to them today." He believed that the National Urban League could help the UNCF to chart a new course. The League, Kimball observed, had a list of 37,000 jobs open to blacks, but they could not fill them because the blacks did not have the proper background education. If housed together the League could provide important services to the United Negro College Fund. In October 1965, Kimball and William Gossett, a former Ford Motor Company executive and chairman of UNCF, signed a purchase contract and paid a $20,000 deposit to hold the CBS building until other funds were raised.

Clearly, at this juncture, Young was not yet fully in charge of crucial fiscal matters pertaining to the League. Kimball played a visible role as liaison to the Rockefeller philanthropies and other foundations interested in supporting the League. John D. Rockefeller III told Harrar that he "might reasonably hope for financing by the family in an amount of $500,000." John III would contribute $200,000 and Laurence Rockefeller would give $300,000, "depending upon whether or not Winthrop 'chipped in.'" Kimball then asked Dana Creel of the Rockefeller Foundation to match the family money with a grant of $500,000. John III intervened again to urge J. George Harrar to put in $250,000 from the Rockefeller Brothers Fund. With the asking price for the building at $2 million, Kimball had gotten commitments for more than half of the amount.[4]

Kimball then approached Henry Heald and the Ford Foundation to contribute the remaining $500,000. His proposal called for joint ownership of the building on a two-thirds to one-third basis in favor of the League. Several Ford officials, however, for unrelated reasons had grown sour on the United Negro College Fund. One commented that Kimball's attempt to relate the programs of the two organizations was "overdrawn, unconvincing, and unnecessary to justify their joint use of the building." Points were also raised about the greater space needs of the League and the reluctance of the UNCF president to put the proceeds of his building sale "into the pot for the new building."[5]

Ultimately, Ford gave $600,000 to the League alone. Whitney Young had urged foundation officials "to proceed on a joint tenancy basis." Although Kimball agreed to cut out UNCF from its share of the Ford grant, he had put Whitney Young into a situation not of his making. In an attempt to draw together two unrelated organizations, he precluded protest from Whitney Young because the latter could not afford to alienate his important link to the Rockefeller philanthropies. In that Kimball drew the NUL and the UNCF together, Ford decoupled them, revised Kimball's proposal, and helped Young by recognizing his organization as deserving of full support.[6]

As with any new executive, Young had to deal with his predecessor and board members held over from the previous administration. Granger settled in New Orleans and became affiliated with Dillard University. He resumed his ties with the executive director of the New Orleans Urban League, a Young critic. On one occasion Granger explained to his New Orleans friend that a policy with which he disagreed actually had been in place before Young's arrival. Young thanked his predecessor for explaining matters to his critic. He interpreted Granger's intervention, however, as a plea for continued involvement in NUL affairs. Young apologized to Granger for not contacting him more often and promised "to sit down . . . for a talk" when Granger came to New York City again. Before two months elapsed, Young updated Granger on "how things are moving" in the national office. He told him about various staff matters, changes in personnel in regional offices, and efforts to increase League funds.[7]

Young had mixed results in dealing with holdovers from Granger's board of directors. Sophie Yarnall Jacobs, though devoted to Lester Granger, believed that Whitney Young was more forthright and courageous. She noted that Young was not one bit afraid of white people. Although Granger was also not intimidated by whites, he wanted them to be his friends.[8] Henry Steeger helped to facilitate acceptance of Whitney Young among some local League executives who were suspicious of his activism. Steeger himself had been unsure about Young's ability to step into Granger's shoes. Steeger and Young spent much time together, usually over evening cocktails. He tried to instruct Young, for example, on his diction. But he heard Young give a speech, and Steeger quickly noted that Young needed no advice either on speaking or on other important matters in the national office. Both Steeger and Jacobs became staunch Young supporters.[9]

Young and Burns Roper, however, had more to overcome in their developing relationship. Although he credited Young with giving the League a
new direction, Roper wanted him to acknowledge that Granger's successes
had been sharply limited by a less hospitable racial environment. Whenever
Roper told business associates that he was on his way to a League meeting,
they would taunt him about why he wanted to affiliate with a "nigger organization." With such attitudes rampant among monied whites during the 1950s,
Granger had formidable odds to overcome. Consequently, Roper grew annoyed with Young as he preached that things were going to change in the
League operation and no longer would it be a nickel-and-dime organization.
Roper interpreted such remarks as a putdown of Lester Granger and dispar-
aging of the previous board of directors. In fact, Roper contended that Young's
attitude created tension between board members elected during the Granger
period and those chosen during Young's tenure. Because the bylaws of the
National Urban League provided for the regular rotation of board members,
Young had numerous opportunities to influence the selection of sympathetic
new members. Moreover, Young was "able to shoot higher" for wealthier and
more influential board members.[10]

Young, like Lester Granger, gained board support for nearly all of his
major initiatives. The League's fifty-three elected board members and the six
honorary members met four times each year. Each member also served on
one of several committees that advised particular League departments on their
programs and monitored important administrative and financial matters. Usually board members supported initiatives that Young proposed or assisted
him in finding funds to implement them.[11]

The League attempted geographical, occupational, and racial balance
on the board. Labor leaders, corporate, government, and foundation officials
along with black educators, doctors, and fraternal leaders found places in this
influential body. Dr. Willa Player, president of Bennett College and a visible
supporter of student sit-ins in Greensboro, North Carolina, represented a
new breed of black southerners unafraid to challenge the racial status quo.
Hobson R. Reynolds, the grand exalted ruler of a half million black Elks, a
grassroots organization, helped the League identify with a broader constituency. At the same time, Young wanted more whites of greater wealth and
influence than those already on the board. So Dwight Zook of North American Aviation, James Linen of Time-Life, and Secretary of State Dean Rusk
joined the board.[12]

Normal attrition allowed Young to staff the national headquarters with
persons who shared his activist outlook for the League. His greatest impact

occurred, however, with choosing personnel for new departments that the changing environment of the 1960s required. In 1967, for example, he wanted to help blacks in the military, especially those returning from the Vietnam War, to get League assistance in training and finding employment in civilian life. Young secured board approval for an office of veterans' affairs. A few years later, to deal with various social pathologies in major League affiliated cities, Young proposed a new department to address crime, criminal justice, delinquency, and police relations. Moreover, the establishment of a Washington bureau under Cernoria D. Johnson allowed him to stay abreast of federal legislation and programs relevant to the national office and to local affiliates.[13]

Despite his administrative experience, Young disliked the day-to-day office demands placed on him. As the League's principal fund-raiser and spokesman, Young was frequently away from his desk. Moreover, as his involvement with the civil rights movement intensified and his consultations with Presidents Kennedy, Johnson, and Nixon became routine, Young's role in external affairs took up as much time as internal matters. Consequently, important administrative and personnel difficulties were left either unattended or ineffectively adjudicated. At his first staff conference, for example, he stressed the importance of the research department "as a basic program implementer." The departments of public relations, fund-raising, administration, programs, and field services would depend on it for "the kinds of facts and data useful for national program operations." Yet Young and the research director had problems that culminated in the latter's dismissal. Young performed this unpleasant task reluctantly and belatedly. His loose administrative style permeated his tenure at the National Urban League. After eight years in office, management consultants suggested extensive improvements to enhance the functioning of Young's office.[14]

Couched between the headquarters staff and the local affiliates were five regional offices, each with a director, divided among the eastern, mideastern, midwestern, southern, and western areas. Semiannually the regional directors monitored and evaluated the affiliates within their jurisdictions and kept the national office informed about problems occurring within them. Whitney Young appointed new regional directors to serve as liaisons between the national office and the affiliates. In 1967, for example, a year of unusual urban unrest, fourteen of the twenty-one League cities in the eastern region experienced racial violence. The regional director delivered background data on these occurrences to the National League's administration, public relations, and program departments. In cooperation with the national office, the regional director also cosponsored affiliate staff workshops. Moreover, these officials represented the region at various conferences on urban planning, social welfare, and urban tensions.[15]

While Young preferred to delegate responsibility to the headquarters staff, he could not always avoid direct involvement in the affairs of League affiliates. Problems with local programs and personnel often required Young's intervention to clarify the role of the League or discipline wayward local executives. Soon after Young succeeded Granger, program difficulties at the Urban League of Greater New York drew his attention. His administrative assistant briefed him on the perennial complaints directed to the national office from local employers and applicants about the industrial relations department of the New York affiliate. Persons seeking League services reported "indifference, rudeness, coldness, abruptness, and discourtesy." Employers observed similar unpleasantness in office staff. They also noted that applicant screening was "slipshoddy" and that follow-up on job referrals did not occur. The New York League gained "a very poor reputation in Harlem" and with such companies as CBS and Socony Mobil Oil. Furthermore, Julius A. Thomas, the national industrial relations secretary, told Young that the local League "is not interested in servicing business and industry . . . from whom [the] National receives contributions." He added, "It has taken a good many years of painstaking counsel and guidance to reach the point where we are regarded as 'experts' in the field." Consequently, Thomas did not want to see the expanded industrial relations program jeopardized by the New York affiliate. The problem was that the New York organization became exclusively interested in special job fields in executive and technical areas. Firms in search of stenographers, secretaries, and other lower-level office jobs, according to Thomas, received very little attention from the ULGNY office.[16]

Young noted a lack of consensus about the role of industrial relations in the national office and in the New York League. Young and his associate executive directors stressed to the affiliate that the national office was raising additional funds from numerous local corporations. They added that it was necessary to discuss with local officials what services those firms expected from the New York League. The local executive believed that his agency would prefer to work on job orders that called for employees with skills at the submanagerial or management training level. He thought that other agencies could help firms find people at the secretarial, clerical, and semiskilled levels. He flippantly observed that good secretaries were difficult to find, anyway. To resolve their problems, Young sent in his associate executive director, Mahlon T. Puryear, to teach the local League officials how to service the requests of all area businesses.[17]

Young also developed a new fund-raising agreement to end competition between the National Urban League and the New York affiliate,[18] and he brought in Alexander J. Allen to lead the affiliate and to restore its fiscal integrity. Allen hired new staff, which resolved many of the conflicts that originally caused Young's intervention.[19]

Young seldom hesitated to discipline affiliates that were financially delinquent or programmatically dysfunctional. He boasted wherever he spoke or solicited money that the League alone among black organizations had the actual capability and technical expertise to achieve the social and economic integration of blacks. If the League infrastructure faltered, then his argument lost credibility. The Buffalo Urban League, which Young deemed below standards, discovered how serious he had become about inefficient affiliates.

Buffalo had a recalcitrant local executive during the Granger era. When Granger ordered a review of its programs in 1958, a board member said, "Lester should run his office and let us run ours." When Young scheduled his first national conference, the Buffalo executive complained about the date. Moreover, from 1958 to 1961 the Buffalo League remitted only 4 percent of its national dues, and in 1962 it paid nothing at all. A national official investigating the affiliate found that mandated programs in employment and job development, housing, education and youth incentives, and health and welfare did not exist. The League functioned only as a job placement agency. Moreover, the affiliate's location, in the basement of a public housing project, was unacceptable.[20]

Upon receiving the report, Young told the president of the Buffalo affiliate that the national office would recommend probation for the local. He complained that the affiliate executive was well past retirement age and could not function effectively with his health problems. He insisted on a new leader for the Buffalo League. The industrial relations secretary worked as a paid consultant to some local firms and was also employed as an insurance salesman. These activities hinted at a possible conflict of interest and certainly denied the affiliate a full-time person in that important department. Actually, Young was ready to suspend the Buffalo League. These threats, however, produced the result that Young wanted. The local executive resigned, and soon Alexander Allen sent names of six League officials for the Buffalo affiliate to consider for the vacant position.[21]

On other occasions when internal dissension within local Leagues occurred, Young, when possible, arranged personal visits to ameliorate problems. That's what drew him to New Haven, Connecticut, in the spring of 1965. Richard S. Dowdy, the industrial relations secretary of the Pittsburgh

Urban League, came to work for the city of New Haven in 1959, but agreed to spearhead the founding of a League affiliate. Formal organization happened in 1962. A veteran executive from affiliates in the Midwest came to head the New Haven League. But trouble soon erupted. Two secretaries accused the executive of improper conduct toward them. Since their testimony did not convince the entire board of directors, disagreements occurred. Although the black executive acknowledged these indiscretions and agreed to seek professional help, he protested the way in which the divided board handled his termination. To his dismay, the board had voted two months of vacation and four months of severance pay.[22]

At this point, the heated impasse required Young's presence. The chairman of the personnel committee hosted the meeting. Young eased tensions between board members who supported the executive and those who did not. He promised that the National Urban League would employ the executive for the time remaining on his local League contract. If the affiliate could not pay him the extra remuneration, Young volunteered the national office to fulfill the rest of the salary commitments. With those issues resolved, Young urged the New Haven League to start interviews for a new executive director.[23]

The attention that Young devoted to the New York, Buffalo, and New Haven Urban Leagues typified a general problem he continuously confronted in numerous other affiliates. The executive directors of all of these locals were veteran League officials. All were Granger contemporaries whose effectiveness had been compromised by fatigue or burnout. Young wanted to replenish the ranks of both local executives and national staff with new blood. In some instances, Young's personal persuasion and example drew trained social service personnel into the League. More important, Young preferred the systematic recruitment of fresh talent into the organization.

Young's relationship with John W. Mack and Herman C. Ewing demonstrated his commitment to young, new executives and his vigorous promotion of their careers. Mack met Young while he was dean of the School of Social Work at Atlanta University. Young had come to North Carolina A&T in the spring of 1958 to draw students including Mack to social work careers. After Mack won a scholarship to Atlanta University, a solid relationship developed between the two men. When students at the Atlanta University Center participated in demonstrations to desegregate various public facilities in the city, Whitney Young and Martin Luther King Jr. served as advisers. Mack became one of the student leaders. Young encouraged him in this role and later hoped that he would bring that outlook to the League. A position in psychiatric social work in California following graduation preceded Mack's employment with the League. In 1964, through Young's influence, he became health, welfare, and housing secretary of the Flint affiliate. A year later, he became acting executive director. He served in the permanent position from 1965 to 1969. Young then assigned him to work in Washington on the national "New Thrust" initiative before urging the Los Angeles Urban League to hire him to revive that faltering affiliate.[24]

Although the executive director of the Little Rock Urban League drew Herman C. Ewing into the organization, Whitney Young introduced him to influential supporters and promoted his career. After his graduation from Lane College, Ewing worked in a federally funded program in Little Rock before he became head of the local League in 1965. Young put Ewing together with Winthrop Rockefeller, the governor of Arkansas and an active League supporter. Young helped Ewing get a $5,000 contribution from Jeannette Rockefeller, Winthrop's wife, for a Skills Bank. Young also helped him to persuade Mrs. Rockefeller to join the board of the Little Rock affiliate. In 1969 when Ewing wanted to become executive director of the Memphis Urban League, he secured the promotion with Young's influential endorsement.[25]

Young knew, however, that occasional opportunities to attract new and talented personnel to the League would not fully meet his organizational needs. Of the sixty-five local executive directors, Young estimated that one-third were good. Another third were adequate, but really needed to be much better. The rest were definitely below the standard, he said. He identified fifteen who were "not good enough to do their jobs, but not bad enough to be retired." Furthermore, broader opportunities for trained social service personnel in government, industry, and various other agencies siphoned off one-fifth of the League's professional staff.

In a proposal to the Rockefeller Foundation, Young requested funds to "crank up" ineffective executives and make them better leaders in their communities. He wanted to send them to a retreat in Maine for a summer session for training in more effective administration and in intergroup relations. Others needed to attend social work school to take additional courses, and some would enroll in special training seminars. Other monies would be used for fellowships to induce social work students to choose curricula relevant to careers in the League. The foundation, however, gave Young "a gentle no" because it appeared that Rockefeller was being asked to staff the League.[26]

Young took the same proposal to the Carnegie Corporation of New York. Although it mainly aimed to train graduate students for professional careers in the League, Young also wanted to target college sophomores who were making decisions about graduate training, southern youth who were attracted to the civil rights struggle, and Peace Corps personnel returning from service abroad. Of course, current staff who needed enrichment to enhance their competence were also included.

Young acknowledged that the concept was not new, since the League initiated such a program in 1910. Before financial difficulties forced an end to the effort in 1960, 136 blacks received graduate degrees in various social work specialties. Although employment with the League was not required, one-fourth of the recipients eventually worked for the organization. Nonetheless, Young wanted the reconstituted program specifically to channel recipients into League careers. He argued that recent successes in the civil rights movement increased the need for local leaders trained in positive programs of social planning in education and training, employment, housing, and health and welfare. He stressed that such efforts "are absolutely necessary for an orderly change from the Negro's present state [of inequality] to one in which he has the opportunity to become equal with other citizens." Carnegie's help in solving the League's manpower deficiencies would ensure the concrete achievement and maintenance of racial equality.[27]

The Carnegie Corporation granted the League $300,000 over three years to develop a fellowship program. The monies were paid to the organization in three $100,000 installments. Seventy-five graduate fellowships in intergroup relations at $3,000 each would be supported, and most fellows would complete their field assignments in various League affiliates across the country. The grant began on December 1, 1964.[28]

During the first two years of operation, thirty-eight students received fellowships for full-time study, and fourteen staff persons in the League secured support for part-time matriculation. In the third year, the organization wanted to award nineteen additional fellowships. The League reported that "virtually all those who completed their studies in the first year have been placed in NUL positions." Twelve fellows who were graduated in 1966, with one exception, did fieldwork with local Leagues in positions ranging from community organizer, job developer, to deputy executive director. Following graduation three of the twelve took League positions, one as associate executive director of the Richmond Urban League, another as director of health and welfare of the Essex County, New Jersey, affiliate, and a third as director of the summer fellowship program of the National Urban League.

Of the fifteen who graduated in 1967 with two years of fellowship assistance, eleven went on to full-time League employment. Three joined the national staff, and the others scattered among affiliates in Baltimore, Washington, Fort Wayne, Miami, Boston, Pittsburgh, and Atlanta. One became acting executive director of the Seattle Urban League. Another four fellowship recipients graduated in 1967, but held fellowships for only one year. Two of them took immediate League employment, one with the affiliate in Hartford and the other with the Urban League of Elkhart, Indiana.[29]

Furthermore, fellowship recipients during the 1966-67 academic year at Catholic University, Howard University, and the University of Maryland joined to lead an experimental program in mental health at the Washington Urban League. Another group at Western Reserve University conducted an experiment with the Cleveland Urban League. Staff who benefited from support during 1966-67 included two from the national office and twenty-two from affiliates.[30]

In 1967 Young proudly reported to the Carnegie Corporation that the fellowships program proved itself as a major source of personnel for the League. The executive committee of the board of directors voted in 1966 to continue the program after the grant expired. The committee directed Young, however, to request a two-year extension from Carnegie to allow time to develop the financial base necessary to incorporate the program into ongoing operations. Swayed by the success of the effort and the League's promise to fund it fully in the future, the Carnegie Corporation allocated $200,000 to support the fellowships for another two years. The program received two payments of $100,000 for the 1967-68 and 1968-69 academic years.[31]

As in previous years, the fellows interned at various League affiliates and locals in Atlanta, Cleveland, Jacksonville, and New York City benefited from other students whose graduate schools assigned them to work there for general study. The League continued to hire fellows in highly visible and responsible positions within the organization. Affiliates in Seattle, Nashville, Tallahassee, and New Orleans drew their executive directors from the program. Similarly, at least six affiliates attracted personnel from the 1969 fellows.[32]

Despite programs to upgrade the quality of local executives and to expand the pool of trained staff for the entire League, Young had accomplished only a part of his retooling effort. He also wanted local Leagues to be effective agencies of social change especially in areas like employment for blacks in trade, technical, and white-collar jobs and in housing. To overcome intractable problems in these fields, Young needed unprecedented sums of money to help his affiliates to break stubborn institutional practices that denied blacks equal access to jobs and housing.

Drawing blacks into trade occupations as workers and contractors had

long been an objective of the National Urban League and its numerous affiliates. Constitutional restrictions in union bylaws and decades of informal but
systematic racist practices, however, prevented blacks from becoming electri-
cians, plumbers, carpenters, and machinists and kept them from functioning
as contractors. Young envisaged the League spearheading a national effort to
draw together selected labor unions, federally supported apprenticeship programs, and League affiliates to increase the pool of skilled blacks, encourage
their acceptance into unions, and provide opportunities for those who wished
to try contracting. While some affiliates already operated the sort of programs that Young admired, they were confined to locals in Cleveland, New
York City, Atlanta, and Anderson, Indiana. Greater orientation to these issues required a broader implementation of these programs to many other
League affiliates. Young asked the Ford Foundation for a three-year grant of
$366,000 to staff and administer a nationwide program of projects to in-
crease black representation in special skill trades.

Young proposed to establish a National Urban League Trade Union
Advisory Council consisting of union leaders and some representatives from
business and government. The council's principal role would entail assistance
"in initiating working relationships between League staff and local labor union
officers where such contact has not previously existed." The program would
be coordinated from the League's five regional offices by special personnel.
Their primary duties would include community education efforts about
membership in labor unions and job opportunities in both business and blue-
collar fields. Most important, regional staffs would contact and persuade local union authorities to relax restrictive measures discouraging or barring
blacks. They would also advise those who operated job training centers, encourage black youth to pursue craft occupations, and help them find jobs
once their training was finished.[33]

Young involved fifteen cities in the Labor Education Advancement Program (LEAP). He pronounced "the acceptance of the program by both organized labor and the Negro community" as "excellent."[34] Among Young's principal achievements was strengthening some affiliates with funds and personnel
to address and implement a visible and crucial initiative in black employment and entrepreneurship. In Hartford, for example, the local League put
together black contractors and subcontractors with a downtown developer
who for the first time received bids from this once excluded group. The Jacksonville, Florida, affiliate sponsored a housing project that employed contractors organized by LEAP, and the affiliate in Colorado Springs planned
similar efforts using LEAP funds to bring together minority contractors.[35]

Other affiliates concentrated on educating blacks about organized labor. The St. Louis Urban League, the International Union of Electrical Workers, and the Amalgamated Clothing Workers Union sponsored twenty seminars in citizenship education. Moreover, the St. Louis affiliate reached 710 students at four predominantly black high schools and provided counseling and guidance on the organized labor movement. Convocation sessions were also held. National and regional LEAP representatives extended similar services to local Leagues in Milwaukee, Gary, Peoria, and Indianapolis.[36]

When Young drew to the National Urban League a Ford Foundation grant of $1,500,000 in 1966, he pushed the organization into one of its most ambitious projects ever. Young wished to involve various affiliates in "demonstration projects . . . to improve the availability of housing for non-white families." The four-year grant for "Operation Equality" put in $340,000 for national office expenses and $177,000 for a special project in Cleveland. The remaining $983,000 was divided among cities where project officials promised to raise matching funds to meet the Ford allocation. Although the National Urban League had been involved in housing issues long before Young assumed office, his new effort promised to pour into the organization major resources to enable local Leagues to effect significant reforms. Nine League cities mostly in New York state and New Jersey, but also including Pittsburgh, St. Louis, and Miami, participated. The grant embraced a few other affiliates as well.[37]

The Miami Urban League sponsored a housing conference and participated in efforts to get a fair housing ordinance passed in Dade County. The Bergen County, New Jersey, affiliate provided counselors to help clients find decent housing. In Philadelphia the local League put together black and white real estate brokers to encourage cooperation in promoting integrated housing. The Rochester Urban League advised clients on how to locate and purchase a house. The affiliate in Seattle formed a housing corporation to broaden availability for black buyers.[38]

While the League's grant application was under review by the Ford Foundation, one evaluator, a regional official in the federal Housing and Home Finance Agency was "extremely dubious about the validity of the request." Except for affiliates in New York City and Atlanta, neither the national office nor most of the local Leagues had appreciable experience in providing housing and stabilizing neighborhoods. Since these were local matters that required knowledge of land, materials, mortgage finance, site selection, and appraising, the reviewer was skeptical of NUL involvement and competence. He was equally doubtful of the expertise of one of the two affiliates with housing experience. He noted that the Atlanta Urban League shunned sponsorship of a housing project, citing threats to its tax-exempt status. Two NUL officers followed suit and expressed similar reservations about participation of the headquarters office. Yet a leading black Atlanta church and the local Prince Hall Masons became involved in federally funded housing without fears about their tax-exempt status. Ultimately, the reviewers believed that the League's impact would be negligible, since it would be "treating" only "the symptoms of what is wrong."[39]

Although Young could not completely dispute the objective assessment of the federal housing official, he could still credibly challenge the assumptions that underlay the unflattering evaluation of the League. Young's purpose in seeking the grant was to correct precisely what the observer viewed as a League weakness. Young wanted the organization to undertake bold initiatives to impact on the disadvantaged social conditions that afflicted urban blacks. The League had not been on the cutting edge of social activism. Young could only change that with the infusion of large sums of money to enable national and local officials to get the training and experience in housing issues to address more effectively these concerns in local communities. He was trying to transform and retool the personnel and procedures of the League on all levels, and he felt that the Ford grant would help achieve those objectives.

During his efforts to revamp the structure of the League, inaugurate expanded and better financed programs, and attract more trained personnel, Young also proved himself as an able bureaucratic strategist. With the founding of numerous Leagues, Young introduced a bold initiative. Thirty new affiliates significantly enlarged the League's national presence and drew its programs to many black communities where locals never existed before. Young announced in 1964 that he wanted to organize three new Leagues in each of the five regions by the end of 1965. That would bring the total of affiliates to eighty, nearly twenty more than he had inherited from Lester Granger. Young authorized the League's five regional directors and a special liaison, Charles E. Eason, to organize new Leagues. When information arrived about possibilities for a new affiliate, Young directed the regional director to visit the area and then help form a sponsoring committee. At that point, Eason would intervene to aid the committee to bring about affiliation with the national organization. That meant funding from the local community chest and identifying other fiscal resources.[40]

Bringing new affiliates into the fold demanded better analysis and strategy than most other innovations that Young attempted. The wise use of the regional directors, Charles Eason, and sometimes nearby local executives allowed the League to send in staffers to discover whether major community and fiscal support existed to sustain an affiliate. Often cities and metropolitan areas failed to meet the tough criteria for serious NUL backing.

Young dispatched Eason to Staten Island, one of the five boroughs of New York City, to determine whether a League was needed there. The primary issue was whether the borough could sustain an independent affiliate or if it needed to be a branch of the Urban League of Greater New York. Eason advised against an independent League on Staten Island. The community chest, the agency on which nearly all affiliates depended, was weak. Most of the social service organizations that the chest financed functioned on austere budgets. Moreover, Staten Island residents lacked an orientation toward support of social welfare efforts. Even the NAACP, the principal black group in that vicinity, was nonmilitant and specialized in holding public forums. At the same time, Eason believed that blacks in the borough needed a League. There were deficiencies in housing and little employment beyond the semiskilled level in the principal businesses. While there was no question that a League program was needed, Eason opposed an independent branch. Young adhered to the tough standard of substantive community and fiscal support for a local League. Because Staten Island failed those criteria, Young did not press for an affiliate there.[41]

League investigators discovered that branch status would also be appropriate for Olympia, Washington. Three hundred paid members constituted the Thurston County Urban League Committee. They wanted an affiliate because a new state college had been established there with strong efforts toward recruiting minority students. Additionally, the conservative white community became aroused over the influx of black students and faculty. Nonetheless, with a black population of only 300, League officials believed that $50,000 from the United Good Neighbors agency for full League status would be ill spent for such a small constituency. Instead, the Thurston County Committee was urged to gain official NUL status as a branch of the Tacoma Urban League, thirty-six miles away.

In Utah, a former League staff member attempted to interest local community and educational leaders in starting an affiliate to cover Salt Lake City, Ogden, and Provo. The director of the community chest in Salt Lake City, however, hesitated to offer support because the area's small black population did not "merit the kind of expenditure a UL affiliate would require." The presidents of five Utah universities cooperated in building a meaningful educational program. But the underrepresentation of top industries in Salt Lake City and vicinity with the affiliation effort and uncertain prospects in getting professional staffing caused the national and regional offices to withhold recognition from the Utah Urban League Committee.[42]

Requests to establish affiliates in Staten Island, Olympia, and Salt Lake City represented only a fraction of the inquiries flooding the League's national office. Charles Eason reported in February 1965 that organizing was already under way in eight cities, including Battle Creek and Saginaw, Michigan, Madison, Wisconsin, Colorado Springs, and Sacramento. Lindsley Kimball noted in September 1965 that twenty such requests were then pending before the national board of directors. In 1967 League representatives explored nearly three dozen communities where affiliates were desired. They had also identified thirty areas that they assigned secondary priority status.[43]

Sometimes it was a hard-hitting speech by Whitney Young to local business leaders that stirred them to form a League committee. On other occasions industry representatives made their own assessments of racial difficulties and invited League officials in to consult with them. Whatever the impetus, the escalation of the national civil rights movement and the League's centrist reputation drew local white leaders to Whitney Young to urge his organization to help ease racial tensions in their various communities.

In 1967 in Stamford, Connecticut, for example, Joseph J. Morrow Sr., the vice president of Pitney-Bowes, and former members of the National Urban League's Commerce and Industry Council "convened" local business leaders to form an affiliate to serve southern Fairfield County. The formal invitation to the national office came from Milton Hosack of the American Cyanamid Company. In nearby Bridgeport, Connecticut, corporate representatives and the director of the local United Fund laid the groundwork for a local League. They committed to a minimum budget of $50,000 annually and to hire two professional staff persons. Young also came to know M.R. Karrer, vice president of Electric Hose and Rubber Company, in Wilmington, Delaware. Karrer volunteered to form an affiliate in his city. The national office used this initiative to persuade DuPont officials, the United Fund, and local black spokesmen to cooperate. Also during this period, the director of the eastern region visited Poughkeepsie, New York, and Bucks County, Pennsylvania, at the request of local industry leaders.[44]

In the western region, Robert L. Jordan, the manager of a General Electric subsidiary in San Jose, California, expressed interest in bringing League services to his city. Henry A. Talbert, the regional director, informed Young that the stimulus came from the GE corporate offices in the East. Talbert and Percy Steele of the Bay Cities Urban League addressed thirty executives from Westinghouse, IBM, Lockheed, Continental Can, the United Fund, banks, and various government agencies. That initiative probably resulted from Young's contacts with GE headquarters officials. In Lake County, Illinois, a locale served modestly by the Chicago Urban League, a marathon effort culminated in an affiliate. The local group financed a study of conditions among the area's 15,000 blacks, set up an operating budget of $42,000 for a League, and secured a promise from the United Fund for inclusion in its annual allocations. The midwestern regional director urged Young to address a gathering sponsored by U.S. Steel, Sears, and Sara Lee Foods to bring the campaign for an affiliate to a successful conclusion.[45]

New affiliates in the North and West gained quick approval from the board of directors. The board received both the Lansing, Michigan, and Syracuse, New York, locals at the same October 20, 1964, meeting. Not long after this action, the Rochester, New York, affiliate, armed with an endorsement from the Council of Social Agencies and a $52,130 community chest budget, was put into operation. Within another year, the Indianapolis Urban League was admitted with $50,000 held in escrow pending the issuance of a charter.[46]

The growth of League affiliates in the North and West enabled the organization to play a leading role in addressing crucial issues in employment, housing, and education. While local chapters of the NAACP and CORE usually assumed leadership on the protest front, the nature of urban problems required the presence and participation of League officials. They developed strategy and cooperated on programs with government and business to end depressed social and economic conditions among blacks. A different challenge, however, faced the League in the South. The cutting edge of the black struggle concerned the exercise of basic civil rights in voting, public accommodations, and school desegregation. In these areas, the other civil rights organizations were better equipped than the League to deal effectively with these issues. Moreover, the near absence of League affiliates in southern locales where the struggle was most intense also contributed to the organization's marginal participation in the various grassroots efforts to desegregate the South.

Nonetheless, Young believed that the scarcity of local Leagues in several major southern cities boded ill for the black population. Urban blacks, whether in the North, the West, or the South, faced the same range of difficulties in housing, vocational training, education, and health. Despite functioning affiliates in Little Rock, Memphis, Atlanta, New Orleans, Tampa, and a few other southern cities, Young knew that they required more funding for expanded services. Moreover, he recognized that the national office needed to establish new affiliates in places where the League was notably absent.

Initially, Young had to sustain those affiliates already in existence. Increased pressures from the civil rights movement and higher expectations from the national office strained the modest budgets of these fragile organizations. Furthermore, as affiliate officials joined other blacks in supporting school desegregation, suffrage, and public accommodations for everyone, White Citizens Councils and a variety of other supremacist groups prevailed on nervous community chest boards to stop funding local Leagues. In Little Rock, Arkansas, in 1957, for example, George L. Henry, the executive director of the League, publicly endorsed the efforts of nine black students to desegregate Central High School. White resistance and the obstructionist tactics of Governor Orval Faubus persuaded President Eisenhower to dispatch federal troops to Little Rock to protect the students and enforce federally mandated desegregation. Although the Little Rock Urban League had been in the community chest since 1937, whites did not like the forthright stand of George Henry and threatened to withhold donations if the League was not ousted from the group. Rather than allow the record to show that the League had been thrown out, Henry and his board of directors voluntarily withdrew. The League did not return to the chest until the mid-1960s when Herman C. Ewing succeeded Henry. Probably for similar reasons, affiliates in Fort Worth, Jacksonville, New Orleans, and Richmond also lost their community chest funding. The Fort Worth Urban League ceased to function altogether. There were only twelve affiliates, including two in Oklahoma, in the entire South. With one defunct and another four subsisting on meager and irregular contributions, Young had to devise a major rescue operation for his southern affiliates.[47]

He drew help from the Taconic Foundation to sustain several southern Leagues. Shortly after Young took office, the Foundation responded quickly to an appeal for $10,000 for the Little Rock Urban League and $5,000 for the New Orleans Urban League. In 1964 Young requested $50,000 to bolster the southern Leagues. For the 1965-66 program year, Taconic gave the League two gifts of stock whose sale netted over $100,000. Grants ranging from $3,500 to $6,000 were extended to affiliates in New Orleans, Little Rock, Richmond, Tampa, Jacksonville, and Tulsa. The $6,000 grant to the New Orleans Urban League was used for a "program of family adjustment, health and welfare and youth development in areas of the city deprived of social service." The $5,000 grant to the Tampa Urban League paid the salary of an associate executive director, and the $3,500 grant to the Tulsa affiliate enabled the executive director to hire a job development and employment specialist. Similarly, Little Rock's $5,000 Taconic gift established an education and youth incentive program.[48]

Despite success in finding money to strengthen southern Leagues, Young was not content with only twelve affiliates in the region. When he succeeded Lester Granger, no locals existed in Alabama, Mississippi, or South Carolina. Only one affiliate had been established in a single city in North Carolina, Tennessee, and Texas. In most instances, Whitney Young and other officials initiated inquiries, but sometimes racially tense cities such as Selma, Alabama, requested a local affiliate.[49]

Young wanted to organize twenty new Urban Leagues in the South. Toward that end the national board of directors authorized the establishment of a southwide advisory committee of the League in 1963. Headed by Winthrop Rockefeller, now an Arkansas resident and later governor, and Leon Davis, president of the Tulsa Urban League, the committee aimed to persuade leading southern white businessmen, civic leaders, and professionals to help start local Leagues. In the letter of invitation to "carefully selected leaders of the South," Rockefeller said that the League had an unparalleled record "in organizing communities for orderly and stable interracial progress." He urged southern leaders to meet at his exclusive Winrock Farm in Morrilton, Arkansas, to explore the League's potential to facilitate social change in the region.[50]

The Southwide Advisory Committee was guided by Young's associate executive director, Nelson C. Jackson, and the southern regional director, Clarence D. Coleman. They solicited nominations from southern affiliates and from Coleman's staff for blacks and whites who "stand out as exceptional prospects" to help expand the League. While it was not difficult to get names of prominent southern black businessmen, educators, and professionals, identifying influential and sympathetic whites was much harder. In several instances, whites who already served on the boards of affiliates were nominated. The real task was to expand the League's base of support among persons in non-League cities and without connections to the League, the Southern Regional Council, or other groups involved in black advancement.

Coleman and Heman Sweatt, his associate director, noted some promising candidates. In a state where no League existed, they thought that Charles E. Daniel, who owned a construction company in Greenville, South Carolina, might assist. Daniel, who was "reported to be no liberal," was "a businessman of greatest possible influence" in his state. In 1963 he said, "The Negro manpower of South Carolina must be developed if the State is to develop to its fullest potential." Furthermore, in Tennessee, Alexander Heard, chancellor of Vanderbilt University in Nashville, was "reported to have been untried as a leader in the human relations field, but [was] an able and dedicated person." Also mentioned was David Vann, a white attorney in Birmingham, Alabama. He helped to settle the conflict between the Southern Christian Leadership Conference and municipal authorities after nonviolent black demonstrators were set upon by Police Commissioner Bull Connor's police dog and fire hoses. Winthrop Rockefeller, Ben S. Gilmer, president of the Atlanta-based Southern Bell Telephone Company, and one or two others were the only nominees of broad corporate influence. The other whites were local business men, educators, and civic leaders who possessed some potential to persuade their communities to consider support for new League affiliates.[51]

Generally, during the civil rights movement, some southern businessmen played moderating roles in cities where federal authorities clashed with local officeholders over school desegregation, suffrage, and public accommodations for blacks. When compelled to choose between economic advancements and racial segregation, many business owners preferred to swallow integration rather than risk embarrassment and ostracism from corporate leaders elsewhere in the nation. Although the Southwide Advisory Committee produced too few whites to spearhead the establishment of League affiliates, initiatives from Whitney Young and the growing intensity of the civil rights movement made numerous businessmen more receptive to a League presence rather than the continued agitation of the more militant SCLC, SNCC, and CORE organizations. Although Young noted in 1964 that many cities in the Deep South "are today begging for League affiliation," new locals came to fruition mainly because Young made the first move.[52]

Young wanted to hedge his bets. While local committees in southern cities often had good intentions, it was still difficult to get all the fiscal support necessary to start an affiliate. Although the League was the least visible and viewed as the least militant among black civil rights groups, it was by no means conservative or accommodationist. The League's forthright support of the general goals and tactics to achieve desegregation and enfranchisement of blacks was sufficient to cause alarm among whites wishing to maintain the racial status quo. Young knew he needed external funding to shore up local efforts to establish affiliates. Leon Davis, president of the Tulsa Urban League, understood the dilemma. Since he wanted twenty new affiliates in the South, he told Lindsley Kimball "that if sufficient funds were not immediately available locally to underwrite the establishment of these Leagues . . . such funds should be obtained from national firms through the National Urban League." Since the Southwide Advisory Committee to which Davis belonged produced "lots of conversation on this program, but no action," he probably endorsed

Young's effort to find other monies to organize new Leagues. Kimball tried to get the assistance of Jake Froelich Jr., president of the Charlotte-based Carolinas United Community Services. He told Froelich that the League could perform useful services in North and South Carolina "in this time of tension and stress." Ultimately, Young's solicitation of foundation, government, and corporate funds and contacts enabled the League to expand into several southern cities. Sympathetic southern white business leaders needed resources and vigorous prodding from Whitney Young to bring new Leagues into existence.[53]

In July 1965 Young appealed successfully to the Alfred P. Sloan Foundation for a $125,000 grant "for a crash program to organize Urban Leagues in ten high tension communities." Young noted that "the logjam of requests and inquiries for Urban League services that has poured in have been handled on a minimal level because of lack of funds to employ the necessary staff." Young went on to argue that "with industry expanding, especially in the South, and with demand for skilled manpower to meet the needs of this expansion, the necessity to assist in the development of human resources, especially within the Negro community, becomes increasingly important." Except for Wilmington, Delaware, Harrisburg, Pennsylvania, and the Youngstown-Toledo, Ohio, metropolitan area, the other seven communities in which Young wished to organize affiliates were located in the South. They included Birmingham, Huntsville, Knoxville, Nashville, Greensboro, and Corpus Christi. Young also targeted Fort Worth, where the White Citizens Council had caused the ouster of the affiliate from the community chest a few years earlier. Young wanted to reactivate this local League.

Young observed that a few of the cities had already shown interest and were in some stage of organization. Although he did not want to preempt "a community's initiative in seeking a League," he wanted to "speed up the organizing procedure by subsidizing the cost of full-time professional staff." With the regular procedure, bringing a new League into existence could take years. He told foundation officials that "the job can be done in six months to a year with subsidized professional staff." He asked for $12,500 for each of the ten potential affiliates. That money would pay full-time salaries for an executive director and secretary. Young urged Sloan Foundation officers to help the League in taking immediate advantage of the favorable climate in those ten communities.[54]

In establishing affiliates in Birmingham, Alabama, Columbia, South Carolina, and Jackson, Mississippi, Young did not rely entirely on local supporters. Efforts to start a Birmingham affiliate began between 1946 and 1950 when Nelson S. Jackson, then with the League's southern regional office, cooperated with white businessmen and a leading clergyman to raise $4,000 in seed money. The 1948 Dixiecrat revolt against the strong civil rights plank in the Democratic Party platform, however, convinced whites in Birmingham that a League would be a disruptive outside force. Thus, business backing for the affiliate disappeared. Young was heartened by the $5,000 that a local Birmingham committee raised for a League in 1966, but he knew that such an amount would hardly sustain the $47,000 annual budget needed for the affiliate. Consequently, Young pledged $25,000 from the national office to support the new Birmingham League during its first year. The new affiliate in Columbia, South Carolina, commenced in 1967 with more local support than its Birmingham counterpart. The $50,000 budget started with $25,000 from local sources and $25,000 from the National Urban League.[55]

The founding of an affiliate in Jackson, Mississippi, in 1966 had been a longtime objective of Whitney Young. He enlisted financial assistance from the Taconic Foundation. As in other southern cities, Jackson residents raised a token $2,500 and the national office provided $27,000 for the first annual budget. Although the community chest promised to take over the financing eventually, Young persuaded Mrs. Marshall Field III to induce the Field Foundation to allocate $25,000 to underwrite the Jackson Urban League. Within a year the affiliate provided various services in job registration and placement, adult enrichment, and agitation for a municipal youth and detention center and more day care facilities. The affiliate's salesmanship training program resulted in the hiring of five blacks in sales at downtown stores and as clerical workers at some local banks. These were unprecedented accomplishments in the capital city of Mississippi.[56]

Young received help from Hubert Crouch, an official in Frontiers International, to start an affiliate in Nashville, Tennessee. Young had been active in the black men's service organization in the Twin Cities. After Young visited Nashville in early 1965, Crouch and Stephen Wright, the president of Fisk University, presented the idea of founding an affiliate to the mayor and his human relations committee. The group included representatives from banks, large insurance companies, big merchandizing, big industry, and the chamber of commerce. Although they liked the idea of a League affiliate, Crouch became cautious and somewhat incredulous. He told Young, "We are faced with the job of selling these people on the matter of bringing another organization to Nashville which would expect assistance from the Council of Community Agencies for its on-going operations." Some Council members also served on the human relations committee. Whether Nashville got a

League depended almost entirely on them. He asked Young for "any information at hand which will aid in establishing that the League actually brings money into the community through its 'skills placement program.'" He added that he also needed proof that an affiliate would help in "upgrading the general economy of Negroes by creating better opportunities in housing, better jobs, and better training." Crouch advised Young, "These people with whom we are dealing are hard-nosed business executives who count progress almost entirely in terms of dollars and cents that come into the community."

Young responded quickly to Crouch's request. Although he had become modestly pessimistic, Crouch happily reported to Young that the reactions of the human relations committee "were quite favorable on inviting a League affiliate to Nashville." At that point they wanted "the names and occupations of national board members and some kind of documentation on how the work of the League has specifically benefited local communities where affiliates are located." Young sent the requested information to Crouch. His wise use of Crouch's advocacy paid off because soon the Nashville Urban League officially opened. Given that the city had been embroiled in downtown sit-ins and an escalating controversy over public school desegregation, support for a League affiliate seemingly gave the city's "power structure" the vain hope that they could channel black energies into moderate and nonconfrontational League programs. Although Young shared the same civil rights objectives of more militant black leaders, he gave Nashville businessmen an organization through which they could conservatively participate in the important social changes occurring in their region.[57]

Young must have been elated when in December 1964 an official of the Human Relations Commission of Lexington, Kentucky, expressed interest in establishing a local League in the city closest to his birthplace. Previous attempts to found an affiliate had failed, but Young's Brotherhood Week speech in Lexington apparently revived these efforts. To ensure strong backing for a potential affiliate, Young dispatched national staff persons to contact New York headquarters officials in IBM, Westinghouse, General Electric, and other firms with installations in Lexington. By December 1966, industry and business in Lexington were "favorable towards the Urban League." Although this economic elite promised support, it resisted a forefront role because "business does not wish to 'push its weight around.'" Nonetheless, a committee of three officials from IBM and Procter and Gamble agreed to contact other businesses to join the League's effort. Opposition mainly from the local newspaper editor was overcome, and the Lexington Urban League was finally launched.[58]

Young told Dana S. Creel of the Rockefeller Brothers Fund in 1965 that fourteen cities, mostly in the South, were seeking a League affiliate. Success in St. Petersburg, Knoxville, Greensboro, Newport News, Norfolk, Savannah, and others would go a long way toward expanding the League's presence in the South.[59] In several instances, however, skeptical businessmen and reluctant community chest officials ultimately feared that the League, like a Trojan horse, looked innocent, but once established in their cities could pursue as militant a posture as either SNCC or SCLC. Hence, some promising southern cities opted to avoid the League.

Failed attempts to organize affiliates in Norfolk, Virginia, and Greensboro, North Carolina, typified these difficulties. An influential speech by Whitney Young inspired moves toward League affiliation in Norfolk in 1965. An earlier effort by a staff person in the southern regional office did not succeed. To avoid previous pitfalls, Young was advised to cultivate Sidney S. Kellam of Virginia Beach, Virginia. According to one experienced observed, Kellam was "the greatest single force in the entire East Tidewater Area--financially, politically, civically, socially." Additionally, "he and his family and their multienterprises wield the greatest influence in that area. He was one of the first to move on the 'integration front'. . . and influenced others to move in that direction." Moreover, Kellam was impressed with Whitney Young and concluded that the Norfolk area needed a League. Young was urged to send additional information about the League to Kellam and to encourage the chairman of the Norfolk Friends of the NUL Committee. Support from the Norfolk Links, an elite black women's group, also materialized. To reduce municipal rivalry among Norfolk, Portsmouth, Virginia Beach, and other area communities, Young was advised to call the potential affiliate the Urban League of Eastern Tidewater. The second attempt to found a League, however, succumbed to stiff opposition from the same community chest executive who foiled the first effort. Moreover, gaining an ally in Sidney Kellam was not enough. Weak support among his peers in business and in the community chest left the Norfolk area without a League until 1978.[60]

The presence of a strong affiliate in Winston-Salem, North Carolina, emboldened efforts to start a League in neighboring Greensboro. Serious steps were taken by the southern regional office for fully exploring possibilities for an affiliate. Meetings occurred in 1963 with the Greensboro Community Relations Commission, the Community Fellowship, the Community Council, politicians, and faculty and students at North Carolina A&T College. Young and his colleagues hoped to transform the Greensboro Community Fellowship, a group sponsored by the Southern Regional Council, into a League affiliate. Like in Norfolk, the business and community chest support did not materialize to make this a viable proposal.[61]

Although Young's vigorous program to expand affiliates to major cities throughout the South met with mixed success, he still wanted those municipalities to receive various League services. When in 1969 the all-black town of Mound Bayou, Mississippi, needed funds and advice on its human and industrial development, Mayor Earl S. Lucas turned to Whitney Young. The town wanted monies especially to upgrade its water and sewage system. Young promised to raise funds to enable Mound Bayou to match a federal grant to finance the project. Young mailed checks to Lucas which totalled $11,926 to assist the municipality.[62] Furthermore, Young endorsed his southern regional office in accepting an invitation from the mayor of Augusta, Georgia, to conduct a socioeconomic study of that city's black population. Six blacks had been killed in recent racial disturbances, and the mayor wanted to explore programs to address housing, health, and criminal justice issues.[63]

As executive director of the National Urban League, Young constantly introduced initiatives, programs, personnel, and physical changes to the League's infrastructure. He argued that if the organization was to be relevant and on the cutting edge of social and racial reform, its affiliates needed to be strengthened and expanded to underserved areas. Moreover, he needed to place new people in the national, regional, and local offices who believed that activism was fully compatible with the steady and methodical administration of social welfare. With the League retooled, Young felt confident that more visible and militant civil rights organizations could exclude neither him nor his group in influencing directions in the civil rights movement and in articulating its objectives to powerful officials in government, business, and philanthropy. At the same time Young may not have realized that his growing identification with the national civil rights movement might have doomed efforts to start League affiliates in some southern cities.

8

Maintaining a
Middle Ground

When Bayard Rustin learned that Whitney Young would succeed Lester Granger as executive director of the National Urban League, he confided his utter astonishment to A. Philip Randolph. Randolph wondered, "What has happened to Whitney Young?" Was he out of his mind? He declared that the League would not be "on the cutting edge of any form of direct action," so why would Whitney affiliate with such a conservative organization? Rustin and Randolph, both veteran activists in civil rights, labor, and pacifist causes, admired Young for his work with student demonstrators in Atlanta and his advocacy of picketing, sit-ins, and boycotts as tactics to assault segregationist practices. They argued that Young was too militant to feel comfortable with a staid group like the National Urban League. Rustin, however, later conceded that Young had a workable perception about how to transform the League into a relevant and pivotal player in the evolving civil rights movement.[1]

Black journalist Louis E. Lomax understood Young's objectives much better than Rustin and Randolph. A decade earlier, while he served as executive director of the Omaha Urban League, Young learned that to achieve employment breakthroughs, improved housing, and better public education required more than exhortation and negotiation. When employers, public officials, and others in authority proved recalcitrant, Young knew that militant direct action groups would often help him win what skillful presentations could not. Young never forgot these instructive experiences, especially after he came to the National Urban League. Although the League disclaimed descriptions classifying it as a civil rights agency, it needed close affiliation with direct action groups to remind employers, politicians, federal bureaucrats, and other powerful officials that dealings with the moderate National Urban League were preferable to those with Young's more militant confrontational colleagues.

Lomax was perhaps the first observer of the civil rights movement to note this nuance in Young's leadership. In his insightful study, *The Negro Revolt* (1962), the journalist reported that Young "envisions close cooperation between the League and other Negro leadership organizations on the local level." Moreover, "implicit in Young's program is the intention that the League will work with white businessmen in the hope that they will see the rightness and wisdom of hiring Negroes." If these conferences failed, then Young and his colleagues would tell CORE and the NAACP. (Lomax could have added SCLC and SNCC.) In any case, the "failed efforts" would lead to picketing and demonstrations against the obdurate businessmen. In such circumstances the League would become the more reasonable and moderate organization with which to negotiate.[2]

Although black activism between 1954 and 1961 in several southern locations coalesced into a civil rights movement, national leadership of the black struggle was not yet in place. Scholars Clayborne Carson, Aldon Morris, John Dittmer, and Charles M. Payne correctly argue that the civil rights drive must be understood essentially as local grassroots movements,[3] but articulation of objectives and efforts to win allies for federal legislation and important economic initiatives required national black spokesmen. Martin Luther King Jr. increasingly personified the civil rights movement. His leadership of the successful Montgomery bus boycott won him international acclaim and put him on the cover of *Time*. Leadership of the black struggle, however, was not solely in his hands. With its founding in 1957, the Southern Christian Leadership Conference became one of five major groups in the national civil rights vanguard. King shared leadership with the heads of CORE, SNCC, the NAACP, and the NUL. Moreover, the national civil rights coalition had not coalesced until 1961. Because SCLC and SNCC were new organizations with fresh faces at the helm and the other three groups hired new executive directors between 1955 and 1961, it took awhile for the spokesmen to become comfortable with each other and with their respective followers. In this uncertain setting, Young grasped the opportunity to carve out a place for himself as a major black leader and for his organization as an important player in the civil rights movement.

Several discrete events that tested the 1954 Brown decision and other desegregation initiatives coalesced by the early 1960s to spearhead a coherent and carefully focused civil rights movement. The NAACP, adhering to its traditional legal tactics, and CORE, SNCC, and SCLC with their commitment to aggressive nonviolent direct action unwittingly combined to promote freedom rides. In this series of challenges to segregated interstate travel, the freedom rides fixed national attention on racial inequities in transportation. The NAACP supported Bruce Boynton of Richmond, Virginia, in 1958 in objecting to segregation in a local bus terminal. NAACP lawyers eventually argued the case before the Supreme Court and gained its endorsement for desegregated bus stations and other travel facilities. To test whether the high court decision meant what it said, James Farmer and CORE planned freedom rides from Washington, D.C., to New Orleans. A group of six whites and seven blacks in 1961 boarded buses in the nation's capital to travel to Richmond, Danville, Rock Hill, South Carolina, and beyond to integrate bus terminals. Violent reactions from segregationist whites in Anniston and Birmingham, Alabama, drew federal officials to the area to end the confrontations. The injuries suffered by the CORE contingent attracted SNCC, SCLC, and the Nashville Student Movement to the buses to bring the effort to its New Orleans destination. These actions, however, prompted Attorney General Robert F. Kennedy to seek a definitive ruling from the Interstate Commerce Commission, which ended segregation in bus terminals.[4]

Also during this period, in February 1960, four black students from North Carolina A&T in Greensboro, North Carolina, staged sit-ins at a local five-and-dime store to protest black exclusion from the lunch counter. These sit-ins mobilized the Greensboro black community in such an unprecedented way that they spread to numerous other southern cities and to Ohio, Illinois, and Nevada. The determination and dignity of the Greensboro students and their counterparts in other places attracted national notice and brought support to the civil rights cause.[5] Despite mixed results, the Albany, Georgia, campaign of 1961-62 became another important episode in the coalescing of the movement. First the youth chapter of the NAACP, then SNCC, and ultimately SCLC attempted to desegregate the bus terminal and other facilities in the south Georgia town. Although the presence of Martin Luther King Jr. brought some national attention to the events, the temperate response of Albany's police chief helped to maneuver the demonstrations and the economic boycott into a stalemate. Nonetheless, all of these incidents were increasingly associated as parts of a sustained movement for racial justice and put the NAACP, SNCC, CORE, and SCLC in the forefront of the black struggle.[6]

Sometimes by design, but at other times unplanned, Whitney Young and the National Urban League became involved in several major civil rights events. Although he regularly told audiences that the League was not a civil rights agency, he conceded that his organization pursued the same objectives as the NAACP and CORE. Young's group wanted "to eliminate racial segregation and discrimination in American life, and to give guidance and help to Negroes so that they may share equally the responsibilities and rewards of citizenship." Whatever distinctions Young drew between the League and the other activist groups, he wanted blacks and whites to associate his organization with the civil rights struggle.[7]

Within two years after the start of the Albany Movement, the direct action groups that participated in the campaign solicited advice from the National Urban League. Movement representatives wanted the League to investigate and make recommendations for action. Young did not move on this particular request, but he exploited another opportunity to involve the League in the south Georgia community. In the mid-1960s industrial development in Albany expanded faster than any city in Georgia. There was more need for educated and trained labor. Moreover, as J. Harvey Kerns of the League's southern regional office reported, "The climate of race relations has changed since 1963. Negroes and whites are working together in increasing numbers to give Albany the image of a united city of work."[8]

Black leaders in Albany invited the League to establish an affiliate. Kerns had also organized an Urban League Guild of fifty women. He urged Young to tell local white businessmen about leading monied and corporate white southerners already supporting the League, including Winthrop Rockefeller, James Haines, president of Haines Hosiery Mills and former president of the Winston-Salem Urban League, James Worthen, president of Worthen Bag and Textile Company and president of the Nashville Urban League. Kerns also reminded Young of the Albany Movement "in which SCLC and SNCC went into Albany and within a week or so tore the city asunder and left without any accomplishments. You may wish to *contrast their coming with the Urban League approach.*" Apparently that strategy worked because in 1967 the Albany, Georgia, Urban League came into being. Whites in Albany favored the League's stress on black self-help. The *Albany Herald* said, "Frankly we prefer the approach of the Urban League, as do many of the Negro leaders of Albany. By eschewing militantism, and stressing racial cooperation and harmony, the League opens the way for a racial dialogue in this community which the preferred preachings of the Reverend Martin Luther King, Junior could never achieve." Paradoxically, Young wanted League identification with the civil rights movement, but at the same time he contrasted the confrontational tactics of civil rights groups with the League's emphasis on biracial consensus on jobs, housing, and education. Young stated, "We are not competitive with nor rejecting of the legal and responsible methods of other organizations." But he surely wanted others to accept the legitimacy of League tactics as much as they did the techniques of CORE, SCLC, SNCC, and the NAACP.[9]

On other occasions Young spoke out as a civil rights leader in ways and in forums that Lester Granger may have avoided. In 1962 Young cooperated with Ella Baker, a founder of the Student Non-violent Coordinating Committee, in defending SNCC and CORE activists from criminal anarchy charges in Louisiana. When the civil rights committee of the New York City Central Labor Council in 1963 sponsored a mass rally "to protest the treatment of the Negro-Americans fighting for equal rights in Birmingham," Young served as a speaker along with CORE's James Farmer and SCLC's Reverend Fred Shuttlesworth. Young also addressed a 1963 memorial meeting to condemn the murder of Medgar Evers, the Mississippi field director of the NAACP. A New York City NAACP leader had invited Young to substitute for Roy Wilkins. "Your knowledge of the NAACP and your identification with us," she wrote, "all helped to bolster our pride as NAACP workers."[10]

Beyond speaking out publicly on civil rights matters, Young affiliated the National Urban League with the Leadership Conference on Civil Rights. The group functioned as a congressional lobbying organization to press for civil rights legislation and to urge compliance and enforcement of existing laws on desegregation and antidiscrimination. The League made annual contributions of $1,000 during the mid-1960s, but increased the donation to $1,500 in 1969. Young also served two terms on the executive committee. The League's legal counsel, Arthur Q. Funn, however, advised Young to withdraw from the Leadership Conference. He thought that the group was "purely and simply a lobbying adjunct to the 'civil rights' movement." He added that "quite aside from the questions of whether the National Urban League is a 'civil rights' organization, we are forbidden to engage in any substantial lobbying activities." Funn emphatically noted, "What we cannot do directly, we are equally unable to do indirectly." Young ignored Funn's advice and fostered the public perception that the League was just as involved in civil rights activism as the NAACP, CORE, SNCC, and SCLC.[11]

Young developed a dual identity for the Urban League. One image portrayed it as a professional social service agency with trained staff to bring to fruition the integration of blacks into the American mainstream. The other image projected the League as involved in the civil rights movement and in the vanguard of its leadership. Some staff believed that the League and its services should be distinguished from the groups more actively identified with civil rights in structure and methodology. Young often drew such distinctions when discussing how League programs uniquely helped blacks. At the same time, Young and others in the League knew and welcomed the fact that the League was grouped with the civil rights organizations in the minds of the general public. Young's pivotal and conspicuous involvement with the 1963 March on Washington established before a national audience his key role as a leader in the civil rights movement.[12]

A massive March on Washington had long been the dream of A. Philip Randolph. He attempted such a demonstration in 1941 to compel President Franklin D. Roosevelt to bar racial discrimination in the nation's defense industries. The threat of a march of thousands caused Roosevelt to issue Executive Order 8802, which established the Fair Employment Practices Committee. In 1963, with comprehensive civil rights legislation pending before Congress, Randolph again believed that dramatic yet peaceful public pressure was needed to convince President Kennedy and national legislators that many whites and blacks supported swift and definitive action to wipe out the vestiges of second-class citizenship.[13]

In the early spring of 1963 Randolph contacted the leaders of the major civil rights organizations to enlist their support for the march. When Randolph broached the issue with Whitney Young, he indicated interest but with "certain limitations." Young explained that the League was a tax-exempt group and could not engage in lobbying. If the march was to pressure for specific legislation, the League could not participate. As long as the effort focused on "a general expression of our concern about the problems of unemployment and infringement of uses of civil rights," then Randolph could expect Young's cooperation. Although subsequent planning meetings excluded Young, he ultimately involved his organization with the march when representatives from the NUL, the NAACP, SCLC, SNCC, CORE, and Randolph's Negro American Labor Council met in May 1963 to discuss the project.[14]

Randolph and Bayard Rustin, the march organizer, attached great importance to Young's agreement to participate. Rustin commended Young as the first among the civil rights leaders to back the march. Randolph and Rustin believed that Young's involvement would persuade Roy Wilkins of the NAACP to follow his lead. Both worried, however, about Martin Luther King Jr. of SCLC. King and Wilkins were intense rivals, with each believing that the other took credit for achievements that rightfully belonged to his counterpart. Nonetheless, with Young and Wilkins supporting the march, King could not risk embarrassment by remaining aloof from the effort. So he signed on SCLC. Rustin also credited Young as the first civil rights leader to disburse funds to finance the march. SCLC, despite constant entreaties from Rustin, never followed through with its fiscal commitment. Without League and NAACP funds, contended Rustin, he would not have been able to organize the march because other groups put in their monies either too late or not at all.[15]

Although Young encountered some doubtful board members at their 1963 Los Angeles meeting, he convinced a majority that the League's involvement in this cooperative civil rights endeavor was crucial to its credibility.[16] Young himself began to play an important role in defining and planning the March on Washington. First, there was the matter of Bayard Rustin as national coordinator. Roy Wilkins opposed Rustin's appointment. Young acknowledged "Bayard's vulnerabilities, also . . . his arrest, and some of his past problems." Nonetheless, Young thought that if his role were defined as a staff coordinator and organizer with the civil rights leaders making policy, Rustin's position would draw minimal criticism.[17]

Despite suggestions that "this ought to be a demonstration by black people," Young insisted that this would be a mistake. Since Young's view prevailed, Walter Reuther of the United Auto Workers, Eugene Carson Blake of the National Council of Churches, Matthew Ahmann of the National Catholic Conference for Interracial Justice, and Rabbi Joachim Printz of the American Jewish Congress had visible roles as spokesmen in the march. While Young hoped to boost his organization's civil rights credentials through his connection with the March on Washington, he also tried to shape the event into a moderate, interracial endeavor. In this way, League supporters, despite Young's more activist stance, ultimately would view the group in its traditional role as a broker between whites and blacks. Perhaps in sensing Young's strategy, officials in the more militant Student Non-Violent Coordinating Committee approached the march skeptically and doubted whether it would be the independent, protest demonstration that they wanted it to be. Subsequent events seemed to confirm their suspicions.[18]

Young supported the freedom rides, lunch counter sit-ins, and other nonviolent tactics to dramatize racial segregation, but he was not convinced that such methods would be appropriate in the march. So he opposed any efforts aimed at civil disobedience. "The chaining of oneself to the desk[s] of the Senate" or a "sit-in on the Capitol or the White House steps" Young believed to be foolish. Rather, he wanted the march to demonstrate "a forthright and militant, but dignified, legal, nonviolent manifestation of our concerns of the problem." Although Young vigorously argued for a march whose tone and objectives were quite moderate, he did not fear defections by CORE and SNCC, the most militant civil rights groups. Young concluded that they could choose to be on the outside of a very significant event and risk their credentials as bona fide civil rights leaders or they could participate in the march and try to project a militant posture in that context. Actually, that problem threatened to unravel the carefully constructed interracial and intergroup coalition that backed the march.

Young proposed three rules to govern participation in the march. First, no politicians would address the marchers. Some believed that Young endorsed this regulation to prevent the flamboyant black congressman, Adam Clayton Powell, from upstaging the civil rights leadership. Second, no speakers should make derogatory comments about Congress. The purpose of the march was to urge favorable consideration of civil rights legislation. Verbal barbs would undermine that objective. Third, no organization would attempt to speak for the entire movement. No one would try to use the march platform to advance particular organizational interests.

Fortuitously, this third rule developed into a problem for SNCC. Young insisted that speeches from each group representative would be discussed with the other leaders. Young noted, "We were not talking about censorship, but we were talking about the absolute necessity of having some basic similarity and objectives and goals so that the speeches would not be calling for different things." According to Rustin's mistaken assessment, John Lewis of the Student Non-violent Coordinating Committee had written a bland speech. Tom Kahn, a Rustin assistant and a white alumnus of Howard University, worked with Lewis to enliven his remarks. Forgetting Young's third rule, Kahn inserted into the speech a controversial metaphor about Civil War general William T. Sherman's deadly and destructive Atlanta "March to the Sea." Kahn urged Lewis to state that if the president and Congress did not effectively address the demands of the civil rights movement, then SNCC would "march through Dixie like Sherman, leaving a scorched earth with non-violence." This phrase merely amplified Lewis's general dissatisfaction with the federal government and its failure to protect SNCC workers in Georgia, Virginia, and Mississippi and its lackluster efforts to promote the voting rights and economic advancement of poor southern blacks.[19]

In violation of another march regulation, Rustin accused Stokely Carmichael, also of SNCC, of giving a copy of Lewis's revised speech to the press. An aide to Walter Reuther learned about the Sherman imagery, and the UAW president demanded that Lewis delete the offensive passage. At that point the Roman Catholic archbishop of Washington, D.C., Patrick O'Boyle, threatened to boycott the march in order to hold a news conference to denounce Lewis's speech if changes were not made. Randolph strongly admonished Lewis and indicated that he would not call on the SNCC leader to speak if he did not capitulate to his elders. James Forman, another SNCC official, and Lewis, with such unrelenting pressure from Reuther, O'Boyle, Randolph, and others, acquiesced and dropped the Sherman metaphor.[20] Ultimately, Whitney Young helped to fashion the sort of march that the League and its supporters could support.

Young also drew the League into funding the march and implementing plans to facilitate march operations. He noted that the League, the NAACP, and various labor unions were the key groups who financed the march. The League contributed $12,000. Of this amount, $9,000 was netted from the sale of *We Shall Overcome,* a portfolio of collages depicting the civil rights movement. Young gained the cooperation of two black Protestant Episcopal churches, St. Philip in New York City and St. Luke in Washington, D.C., to sell more than 10,000 copies. Even after the march was over, Young asked Martin Luther King Jr. and SCLC to help in selling the remaining 15,000 copies so "we can assure the March committee a sizeable additional contribution towards its expenses." Young also wrote a detailed appeal to "Friends of the Urban League" to donate money to the march "to insure the success of this historic event." He admitted that the League was a cosponsor "and as such we have been interested in a peaceful and orderly demonstration. To this end, we have provided the committee with professional help in planning and coordinating the many details." He noted numerous religious groups backing the march "financially and pledging participation." With these assurances that the march had the support of such mainstream organizations as the League and Roman Catholic Archdioceses in New York City, Chicago, and Washington, D.C., "I do ask you now to extend yourself a bit further and help finance this important event."[21]

As momentum and support coalesced for the march, meetings were held weekly at NUL headquarters. League officials Alexander Allen, Nelson C. Jackson, Guichard Parris, and Mahlon T. Puryear were involved in planning the march. Sterling Tucker, executive director of the Washington Urban League, functioned as Young's deputy. Tucker worked with SCLC's Walter Fauntroy and others. Young assigned Tucker to develop emergency shelter for stranded persons and lodging for League officers from various affiliates. At the League's 1963 delegate assembly in Los Angeles, Young urged local executives and other staff to mobilize their respective communities to participate in the march. He knew that some would face difficulty in justifying League involvement to local board members and contributors. So Young told them that the National YMCA, a United Fund agency, backed the march and encouraged "participation of each of its units." He also noted the endorsement of the National Council of Churches, which committed 40,000 marchers and whose World Service component promised to provide food to the participants. Furthermore, he cited the planned attendance of several congressmen as evidence that the march would be a moderate mainstream event.[22] Young also encouraged support from the New York State Association of the

Improved, Benevolent, and Protective Order of Elks of the World. The black Elks planned a civil rights rally at the Polo Grounds in New York City. The funds raised would go to the organizations, including the League, on the March on Washington committee. Earl Chapman, the Elks state financial secretary, invited Young to speak at the gathering in behalf of the League and the march committee.[23]

At the march itself on August 28, 1968, Young who typically delivered compelling addresses, spoke in a lackluster manner during his allotted six minutes. He stressed that the League, though different in methods from the other civil rights agencies, was nonetheless a major player in the march leadership. He castigated those who opposed black aspirations, especially members of Congress who tried to weaken pending civil rights legislation by pointing out technical flaws in the bill. Emphatically, Young declared that in 1963, black civil rights were not negotiable. He ended by urging march participants to continue the protest by marching blacks off relief rolls to full employment; marching them from the cemeteries where black infants died too often and black adults too early and to better health care facilities. He lauded other symbolic marches that challenged the nation to improve specific social and economic conditions for America's largest racial minority.[24]

Everyone was easily overshadowed by the last speaker on the program, Martin Luther King Jr. Tired and hot, the audience was suddenly and remarkably resuscitated by the gifted Baptist preacher and leader of SCLC. King's "I Have a Dream" oration captured the mood of the occasion and made the Atlanta cleric a compelling symbol of the historic march. Although his role in planning it and contributing funds to it had been peripheral, King eclipsed Young, Randolph, Rustin, and Wilkins as the leader who defined the march and gave it meaning.

When the march ended, President John F. Kennedy invited the leaders to the White House. Whitney Young, A. Philip Randolph and their colleagues from SCLC, SNCC, CORE, and the NAACP told a relieved Kennedy that his initial fear of a disorderly demonstration had been unfounded and his effort to get the march called off had been foolhardy. They also reminded him that the crowd of 250,000 exceeded their expectations and demonstrated widespread support for the civil rights movement. The presence of white labor and religious leaders showed that the civil rights coalition was thoroughly interracial. Later, at a televised news conference, Young emphasized the moderation of the march and that it showed the faith of blacks in the nonviolent method of redress for their historic grievances. "I would hope," he said, "that in America today, witnessing this and seeing Negroes still react with dignity and pride, still sing the 'Star-Spangled Banner' and 'My Country 'Tis of Thee,' would say now we do owe it to these citizens to let them get in the mainstream." Some criticized Young and other march leaders for their conservative, cautious characterization of the march. What these critics did not appreciate, however, was how far Young had pushed the National Urban League toward involvement in such uncharacteristic activism. The problem lay not with Young's own militancy. He had shown in the Midwest and in Atlanta his belief in direct action protest. Instead, he had to maneuver his conservative constituency toward greater identification with the vanguard of the black struggle.[25]

Neither Young nor anyone else in the League proposed that the organization abandon its function to find employment, job training, health, housing, and education for blacks. Nonetheless, many locals and their executives, challenged to join the NAACP or CORE in a boycott or picket line, had to ponder whether the League should participate in such activities. The group's usual tactics of negotiation and advocacy with facts and figures seemed to preclude protest and other tactics of direct action. Moreover, executives of some affiliates believed that recalcitrant employers, unions, and government agencies compelled the League to consider more militant methods to achieve its traditional objectives.

The experience of the New York Urban League illustrated the dilemma. In 1961 at the affiliate's board/staff institute, League officials "recommended that the National Urban League alter its general policy to the effect [that] after all milder methods of negotiations have been found to be of no avail, the Urban League should consider the use of economic and social sanctions." Cautiously, Young asked if the League should use boycotting as a tactic. Although he concluded that "a diversified approach" was best, he believed that Leagues should restrain themselves. He figured that when the "opposition . . . cannot deal directly with the people who are organizing and carrying out the boycotts," then it would turn to the League to resolve the matter.[26] Executive director Edward S. Lewis, while cognizant of League restrictions of direct action, tried to keep the New York affiliate abreast of direct action movements in his area. In 1962, in cooperation with Philip Randolph, Lewis became involved with a local hospital strike. He told Young, "We have to take a position with references to the sweatshop wages of Negroes and Puerto Ricans in the hospitals and we will not hesitate on this." At the same time, he assured Young that neither he nor the affiliate would associate with any strike action.[27] Ultimately, in 1966 the president of the New York Urban League vainly petitioned the national board to declare it an independent agency. He argued that the New York affiliate was a part of the mainstream of the city's civil rights movement and performed a valuable function in the Council of Harlem Organizations. Because the affiliate should associate itself with many direct action efforts that the national board eschewed, an independent status would best serve the New York group.[28]

Within the Chicago Urban League, board member N.O. Calloway, an influential black physician and civic leader, castigated the executive director, Edwin "Bill" Berry, for his activism. When Berry and his deputy were photographed while picketing, Calloway was outraged. "I do not doubt but what pickets, strikes and other types of more vigorous expressions of sociologic unrest are valuable," wrote the doctor. But he added, "I do not believe . . . they are a part of the program of the Urban League." Calloway's effort to induce Young and the national board to intervene and discipline Berry produced no results.[29]

Nonetheless, Young had to clarify League policy on demonstrations and picketing in a 1963 memorandum to executive directors of all affiliates. He recognized that "a number of our affiliates are under considerable pressure to participate in the current wave of demonstrations which are being used to dramatize racial inequities and press for corrective action." At the same time Young wanted local officials to understand the distinction he drew between demonstrations and picketing. A picket line affected a single employer or trade union by withholding manpower or purchasing power. A demonstration focused on the public in general by mobilizing public opinion. Young judged that "picketing is not an Urban League technique and would violate established agency policy." A public demonstration, however, "under responsible leadership, is an expression of broad community concern in which the [League] both can and should be represented."[30]

Young applied these principles to the Urban League in Portland, Oregon. E. Shelton Hill, the executive director, had written Young about whether the affiliate should publicly endorse a NAACP boycott against a grocery chain guilty of racial discrimination. Although the NAACP had not requested support, Hill wanted to know what the League's position should be "in the event that such a question is raised." Young clearly stated that the League did not engage in boycotts, although it was not critical of the method and sympathized with the goal. As always, Young viewed such circumstances as opportunities for the League to play its usual role of mediation. "I would always remind the concerned persons," said Young to his Oregon colleague, "that the alternative to this . . . method is for them to cooperate with the Urban League toward eliminating the injustice."[31] Such activities also bolstered

Young's claim that he and his NUL colleagues spoke for middle- and working-class blacks who wanted the League and other civil rights groups to fight hard for racial integration.

League participation in the March on Washington and the greater willingness of affiliates to endorse and at times promote direct action protest strengthened the group's identification with the civil rights movement. The Voter Education Project, however, drew the League even deeper into civil rights activism and unleashed a torrent of criticism that jeopardized some affiliates. In 1961 the Taconic and Field Foundations funded a major voter registration campaign among southern blacks. The NAACP, SCLC, CORE, SNCC, the Southern Regional Council, and the National Urban League signed on to implement individual efforts to increase the number of eligible black voters. Cognizant of proscriptions banning partisan advocacy, Young restricted League activity to voter education and citizenship training. In 1962 the League inaugurated successful programs administered by affiliates in Little Rock, Richmond, and Fort Worth. The Winston-Salem Urban League worked nearby in eleven rural communities to educate blacks about the suffrage. In 1963 the New Orleans affiliate cooperated with other community groups to encourage voter registration. A lackluster Florida campaign in 1962 by the NAACP prompted the Jacksonville Urban League to assume full responsibility for the effort in 1963.[32]

In 1964 the NUL launched a "March to the Ballot Box" campaign in sixty-eight League cities. After consulting with local executives, the NUL identified sixteen target areas. Although all sixty-eight of the affiliated cities participated, the special sixteen received funds for staff and other expenses from the League's national office. The voter registration phase included various modes of communication such as leaflets, bumper stickers, radio tapes, and television slides. Additionally, volunteers canvassed door-to-door and held rallies and parades. They also distributed recordings of Whitney Young urging blacks to register and vote. In one target city, Los Angeles, registration increased by 30 percent. The Pittsburgh Urban League reported a 100 percent increase in black voting. Similar results occurred in Atlanta, Cleveland, St. Louis, Chicago, Miami, and other target cities. Reports from twenty-four cities estimated that 250,000 blacks were either reinstated or added to the voters' lists. Of this number, 94 percent had never registered or voted before. In the twelve target cities, the League increased registration by 33 percent. The affiliates had deployed 57,414 volunteers and contacted 725,158 households.[33]

The League's growing activism worried some members of the national

board. Ramon Scruggs, manager of personnel relations at AT&T and the firm's
highest ranking black official, expressed some doubt about the voter education program. Scruggs preferred the League "to go on public record as supporting the principle of good citizenship" rather than direct involvement with
voter registration. He feared that the League's difference with the other civil
rights agencies would become blurred if the group continued in this activist
direction. While most board members backed Young, they favored participation in the voter project "with reservations."[32]

These minor instances of board discontent paled in comparison to opposition that Young and several affiliates encountered in southern and border
cities. Young's growing visibility as a civil rights spokesman and his vigorous
advocacy of racial equality convinced unsympathetic whites that no difference existed between the League director and the more militant SNCC and
CORE activists. Moreover, League involvement in the voter education project
and alleged partisanship against conservative Republicans subjected Young
and several affiliates to severe and sustained criticism that threatened funding
for NUL locals.

Dade County Republicans in 1965 accused the Miami Urban League
and its executive director, T. Willard Fair, of using Voter Education Project
funds to support political endeavors. A member of the board of both the
Miami Urban League and the local United Fund, Karl Bishopric, tried to
defend this activity in a meeting with local GOP representatives. He noted
that "encouragement to exercise citizenship rights, which include[s] the necessity for registration to vote, is and always has been an accepted Urban
League task." Still, Miami Republicans contended that the NUL Voter Education Project was "tantamount to a purchase of votes rather than an education
in citizenship." Clearly, they saw the effort as a benefit to the Democrats.[35]

Young told Bishopric that another Miami GOP charge--that Lester
Granger maintained communist connections--drew his "most dramatic refu-
tation." Young added that the League's financial support from the federal
government, major corporations, and leading foundations showed the "re-
spectability, loyalty, and soundness" of its programs. "At no time," Young
added, "has the Urban League ever been considered anything but a responsible patriotic organization by those in authority." Ultimately, Young agreed
with Bishopric that "it is practically impossible to satisfy a group of this type."
A few years later, in 1969, the Miami Urban League became embroiled in
controversy again because of its participation in Young's "New Thrust" program, which stressed empowering the poor through their own autonomous
groups and initiatives. Maud K. Reid, Fair's successor, reported that "many of

the big givers to the U.F. have threatened to withdraw their contributions to the U.F. as they do not wish to support the Urban League as a United Fund Agency."[36] These troubles at the Miami affiliate reminded Young that there was a price attached to League activism.

Similar circumstances drew attacks on the Wichita Urban League. In 1964, an official of the United Fund of Wichita and Sedgwick County, Paul Woods, asked Young to respond to local accusations that he and the NUL had entered the partisan political arena. At dispute were views printed in the *Congressional Record* that quoted Young as saying, "The ultra-conservative faction of the Republican Party has no consideration or sympathy for Negroes," and "The election of Senator Goldwater as President would open the door to rioting and disorder." In his reply Young told the United Fund official that the accusations were another in a series of attacks by the Ku Klux Klan, White Citizens Councils, the American Fascist Party, and the John Birch Society against "anybody who stands for civil rights and equality of opportunity for Negro citizens." He reminded the official that the League enjoyed firm support from the United Funds and Councils of America and from the National Budget and Consultation Committee, a group closely tied to United Fund–supported agencies. Woods, however, was not satisfied. He cited other statements attributed to Young that appeared in other newspapers and demanded to know "if the Urban League and/or its representatives have engaged in political activity."

An irritated Whitney Young told Woods that as the executive director of a tax-exempt nonpartisan agency he did not support any particular candidate or party. Nonetheless, he would respond to critics regardless of their party affiliation when attacks were "made upon me and other disadvantaged people." Specifically, Young contended, Barry Goldwater, the GOP 1964 presidential candidate, had been endorsed by an unlikely pair of extremists, Malcolm X of the Black Muslims and the Ku Klux Klan. He also condemned Goldwater's vote against the 1964 civil rights bill and "his sending of his son to Philadelphia, Mississippi to campaign, arm in arm, with the local Mayor who . . . has refused to urge indictment of the murderers of the young people fighting for the right to vote." Young did not mention Goldwater's party affiliation, but stressed that his racially insensitive actions were unacceptable. Nevertheless, Young believed he "showed great restraint" in the face of Goldwater's determined effort to inhibit civil rights progress.[37]

Hugh Jackson, executive director of the Wichita Urban League, was pleased and relieved that Young was willing to undergo this interrogation from the local United Fund. Jackson had been informed "that there was [a] general feeling [that] the local organization was without blame, but that probably there was something that could be criticized at the national level." Owen C. McEwen, president of the Wichita United Fund, thanked Young for his willingness to respond, but observed that his "opinion" on the boundaries within which he could express himself on political matters "differs from the standards we observe locally." McEwen also instructed the president of the Wichita Urban League to prevent NUL officials from issuing partisan statements. Young told McEwen that the Wichita affiliate could not "exert greater influence over their national executive," but instead urged the United Fund to "supplement your acquittal of the local League with . . . greater financial support" to close the social and economic gap between the town's white and black citizens. Hugh Jackson was never really concerned about the issue and believed that it would fizzle out.[38] Young was probably not as sanguine, since the Wichita incident had been a replay of the Miami controversy and another that brewed at the Tulsa Urban League.

Since the 1950s the White Citizens Council harassed the Tulsa Urban League and tried to blame it for a failed fund-raising drive in 1961. Moreover, Young's critical comments about Barry Goldwater fueled a campaign to oust the affiliate from the community chest.[39] Several ultra-rightist groups including the White Citizens Council, the Republic Minute Men, the John Birch chapter in Tulsa, and the Hargis group reiterated the charge that the League alienated potential donors to the community chest. Additionally, a retired oil company executive, probably a Goldwater supporter, resigned from the board of the Tulsa affiliate because "Whitney Young has put the Urban League in politics." Although Young promised emergency funds to the embattled affiliate, the fearful local executive wanted his boss to decline an invitation to visit the city to speak at a League function.[40]

Similar problems surfaced with affiliates in Cincinnati and Seattle.[41] Despite the troubles that these local Leagues suffered because of greater militancy and alleged partisan political involvement by the national executive director, Young remained convinced that his forthright stands against civil rights critics and his identification with King, Farmer, and his other activist colleagues helped the group to cement its claim to represent the integrationist objectives of a majority of the black population.

Although reactionary whites exerted intense financial pressure on the League and its affiliates, Young thought the price worth paying. Unprecedented outspokenness and visible activism on the national and local levels put Young's organization on the frontline of the civil rights movement. Additionally, as a facilitator and moderator Young was an important force in coordinating important activities and initiatives involving CORE, SNCC, the NAACP, and other groups.

Fiscal rather than fraternal concerns drew the major civil rights leaders together into a formal coalition called the Council for United Civil Rights Leadership. Although the initiative came from wealthy white supporters, Young played a large role in trying to use the organization to moderate the posture and pronouncements of his more militant colleagues. As long as money remained in CUCRL coffers, Young managed modestly to influence the activities of the other civil rights groups. Ultimately, he succeeded in ameliorating conflicts among the organizations on their various tactics and objectives.

Stephen Currier, a shy, young philanthropist, conceived of a formal coalition of civil rights leaders. He had been charted in this direction by his lawyer and adviser, Lloyd Garrison, a descendant of the famed nineteenth-century abolitionist. Wealthy in his own right, Currier married Audrey Bruce, a granddaughter and heir of multimillionaire Andrew W. Mellon. When he expressed his desire for involvement in meaningful social causes, Garrison had suggested in 1958 that he establish the Taconic Foundation. Garrison's longtime association with the National Urban League, though at times intermittent, had most recently placed him as president of the organization. Not surprisingly, Garrison advised Currier to deepen his understanding of blacks and their difficult struggle for racial equality.[42]

In 1961 Currier established the Potomac Institute in Washington, D.C. With a youthful and idealistic new president in the White House, Currier believed that the federal government would have a need for expert assistance in race relations issues. Currier brought Harold Fleming, director of the Southern Regional Council (SRC), to the capital to run the Potomac Institute. The Voter Education Project with interlocking support from Potomac, Taconic, and the SRC became a major recipient of Currier's philanthropy. These involvements drew Currier into closer contact with leading civil rights organizations and eventually made him a significant influence within the council of black leaders.[43]

In June 1963 when Currier learned of the assassination of Medgar Evers, the field secretary of the Mississippi NAACP, he concluded that wealthy whites needed to rally behind the civil rights movement with their financial support. With help from Garrison, Currier drew about one hundred "leading citizens" from the major corporations and foundations to a breakfast gathering, at Currier's expense, at the elegant Carlyle Hotel in New York City. There Currier's guests met King of SCLC, Wilkins of the NAACP, Farmer of CORE, Lewis of SNCC, and Young. These monied whites learned firsthand about the needs and objectives of the civil rights movement, and they were persuaded to contribute $100,000 for distribution among the major civil rights groups.[44]

To reduce competition for funds among the organizations and to promote cooperation on objectives, activities, and strategies, Currier proposed the creation of two separate but related groups. The Council for United Civil Rights Leadership would draw together King, Wilkins, Young, and others for regular discussions on the state and direction of the civil rights movement, and the Committee for Welfare, Education, and Legal Defense, a tax-exempt entity, would receive contributions to assist special civil rights projects and the organizations sponsoring them. CUCRL and WELD shared an interlocking board of directors. To serve as the executive director of the two organizations, Currier and the civil rights leaders chose Wiley Branton, a veteran civil rights attorney from Arkansas. Branton was already head of the Voter Education Project, and he had developed a good track record in working with Currier and civil rights leaders.[45]

Even before the Carlyle gathering, Currier had met Young, Wilkins, and others. When he initially heeded Garrison's suggestion that he learn more about blacks, Currier, through the Taconic Foundation, arranged a series of lunches with selected black spokesmen to increase his knowledge of race relations. Although Currier did not meet with Martin Luther King Jr., he dined with another six leaders including Whitney Young. Currier had become acquainted with Young when he consulted with the Potomac Institute on proposals to inaugurate the Voter Education Project. At first, Young expressed doubts about the Taconic/Potomac intention to establish a separate organization to function as a superstructure to spearhead voter registration programs with various civil rights groups. Young considered such an arrangement unnecessary. He preferred that the participating civil rights organizations receive funds directly.[46] In any case, Currier's genuine desire to draw together the civil rights leadership impressed the League leader. Perhaps Currier's emphasis on pecuniary support for the various groups gave Young, Farmer, King, Wilkins, and Lewis/Forman the impetus to commit valuable time and attention to this loose federation.

Currier honored his commitment to raise funds for the major civil rights groups to help them sustain existing programs and in some instances to inaugurate new projects to advance the cause. Within two months after the Carlyle gathering, CUCRL received $800,000. George D. Pratt Jr., a wealthy farmer in Connecticut, was probably the most generous single contributor to the Council. A 1921 graduate of Harvard University, Pratt had been affiliated with the American Friends Service Committee and had served on two important state commissions. Between 1963 and 1965 Pratt donated $200,000 to the civil rights consortium. Young took note of Pratt's "exemplary support" and personally commended him for helping "the cause of human rights."[47]

On September 11, 1963, Currier and Young appealed to foundations, wealthy individuals, and corporations to swell the $800,000 they had already collected to $1,500,000. The funds would be administered through WELD, the Council's tax-exempt arm. They fell far short of their goal, however. Between August 1963 and January 1964 CUCRL received a little over $123,500. Pratt's initial donation of $100,000 made up nearly all of the receipts. Currier gave $6,000, and the contributions of numerous other donors totaled over $17,500. An additional $26,000 boosted CUCRL income to $151,000, but those extra monies had come from the sale of March on Washington record albums, equality buttons, and various other projects.[48]

Despite Currier's conspicuous presence as a fiscal resource and liaison with wealthy whites, blacks also made major donations to sustain CUCRL. In 1964, for example, New York City's metropolitan chapter of Jack and Jill of America contributed $1,000 to WELD. When Martin Luther King Jr. won the Nobel Peace Prize in 1964, he gave all $54,000 to the civil rights movement. King's own Southern Christian Leadership Conference received $12,000, and $25,000 was put into a special fund for education in nonviolence. King donated the remaining $17,000 to CUCRL. Branton praised King as "extremely thoughtful and generous" and commended him for seeing "the necessity for continued unity." Whitney Young was "deeply impressed" with King and his willingness to decrease CUCRL's large dependence on monied whites.[49]

The assurance of monetary support for their organizations initially drew civil rights leaders to CUCRL and maintained their active participation as long as the funds lasted. At first, the monies were apportioned to the participating groups based on 10 percent of their respective operating budgets in 1962. Accordingly, $125,000 each went to the NAACP and the National Urban League, and CORE and the NAACP Legal Defense and Educational Fund each received $100,000. An unusually successful fund-raising drive by SCLC trimmed its request to $50,000. The same amount went to the National Council of Negro Women. SNCC's $15,000 share infuriated both John Lewis and James Forman, who believed that funds should be distributed on the basis of need. SNCC, however, was promised additional donations when its programs required urgent assistance.[50]

Friction over financial allotments was later allayed when specific grants to CUCRL stipulated equal distribution of funds. When a $50,000 installment from Pratt's continuing grants arrived in 1965, the seven participating organizations each received $6,000. Moreover, Dr. King's $17,000 donation was evenly apportioned to the six other civil rights groups excluding SCLC in the amounts of $2,833 each. The civil rights groups also received funds to underwrite special projects. Such requests required the approval of other Council leaders. Thus, in 1965 an emergency grant for $6,000 went to CORE. Another $6,000 went to an effort in Mississippi sponsored by SNCC to aid a write-in campaign to elect Aaron Henry governor. Although it was a mock election, it would dramatize that "there are thousands of Negroes in Mississippi who would vote except for discriminatory laws and customs which deny them this right." SNCC also received a grant to finance the Student Voice, Inc. CUCRL wanted to enhance the position of the group's civil rights fight.[51]

In 1963 and 1965 CUCRL expanded its membership to include Jack Greenberg, the director-counsel of the NAACP Legal Defense and Educational Fund, and A. Philip Randolph, president of the Brotherhood of Sleeping Car Porters. Greenberg's presence brought into the organization a major participant on the legal front of the southern civil rights struggle. Randolph, the venerable pioneer of nonviolent direct action, already knew about CUCRL. He asked Roy Wilkins in 1963 for an audience with the group to enlist its aid to develop a massive March on Washington. In 1966 Floyd McKissick, who succeeded James Farmer as executive director of CORE, replaced him as that organization's representative at CUCRL meetings.[52]

These leaders gathered to project unity among civil rights advocates, discuss pressing issues, and ameliorate tensions. In numerous instances CUCRL participants easily agreed on various approaches and actions to achieve civil rights objectives. Randolph, for example, speaking for CUCRL, noted that the major point of emphasis for the civil rights movement in 1965 would be the "maximum application of political power." He added, "It means pressing the issue of the right to vote and of Federal responsibility for guaranteeing that right where it is denied." This statement presaged demonstrations led by SNCC and SCLC to win passage of a federal voting rights act. Also in 1965, Jack Greenberg, in a letter to New York governor Nelson A. Rockefeller in behalf of CUCRL, urged him to sign a bill to abolish capital punishment. Since minority groups were disproportionately executed, civil rights leaders looked to the governor to lead in eliminating this "barbaric relic of the past."[53]

Consensus rather than election conferred CUCRL's "chairmanship" on Whitney Young. In that position Young, whom Farmer remembered as speaking more than anyone else and commenting on nearly every issue, played the needed role of mediator. Turf wars between Roy Wilkins of the NAACP and

James Forman of SNCC drew Young in to soothe bruised feelings. Also, Young sometimes overruled Wiley Branton's parsimony toward various civil rights groups when the former inclined toward greater generosity in the distribution of CUCRL funds. Such a stance, Young believed, was necessary for sustained unity among the organizations.[54]

Although he relished the role of moderator, compromiser, and mediator, Young still held to his cautious and conservative mien. Eschewing demonstrations except as a last resort, Young tried to persuade his equally strong-willed and able colleagues to appreciate the subtle methodologies of his National Urban League. Young felt more comfortable with Wilkins, whose NAACP painstakingly worked in the courts and in the Congress to win civil rights victories. Because they were skeptical of federal authority, King's SCLC, Farmer's CORE, and Lewis and Forman's SNCC relied on direct action methods, which made them unpredictable. The organizations that Young and Wilkins represented achieved social change because they cultivated establishment whites in the upper echelons of government, corporate, and foundation circles. These differences in strategies produced tension within CUCRL. As a facilitator of discussions Young had few equals. But as an opponent of insurgencies against friendly establishment benefactors, Young's militant colleagues parted ways with their "chairman." His interaction with SNCC was illustrative.[55]

James Forman recognized that Whitney Young's contacts in establishment institutions were greater than those of other civil rights leaders, so whenever SNCC wanted assistance in getting scholarships for civil rights workers, Forman approached Young. The higher education of several SNCC activists had been handicapped by various factors. Young agreed to intercede with the Rockefeller Foundation in SNCC's behalf. Whitney Young, who was at his best when dealing on this level of operation, interacted with an unusually solicitous SNCC. When that interaction involved basic approaches to social change, Young and his SNCC colleague behaved differently toward each other. SNCC, for example, relied a great deal on services provided to it by the National Lawyers Guild, a group of reputed radicals. Stephen Currier had warned SNCC about involvement with the Guild. Young echoed these sentiments when on two occasions he tried to prod CUCRL to bar communists from the civil rights movement and to repudiate any assistance that such persons wished to offer. Forman, sensing that these resolutions were aimed at the Guild, pronounced these statements as attempts at red-baiting and as violations of SNCC's civil liberties. While SNCC recognized and probably appreciated the value of Young's establishment contacts, Forman rejected his attempts to hinder militant civil rights advocacy with unwarranted caution.[56] Although the League reached into local black communities, SNCC's grassroots activities caused it to challenge the elites that Young tried to cultivate.

Obviously, Young exercised only limited influence over other civil rights organizations. Nonetheless, he tried to steer CUCRL support to activities consistent with NAACP and NUL approaches. Discussions on pending legislation in Congress and state legislatures and support for various social welfare and education initiatives crowded the agendas of CUCRL meetings. The same incentives, which brought together the civil rights leadership, however, also pulled them apart. When they met in February 1966, $67,000 remained in the treasury. After these funds were distributed to seven of the member groups and to some other organizations, no plans commenced to replenish CUCRL's dwindling resources. This fiscal reality reduced the already minimal opportunity that Young had to lead the Sanhedrin of civil rights leaders.[57]

As monies became scarce, it was increasingly difficult to get regular attendance at meetings. Jack Greenberg suggested to Whitney Young that CUCRL dissolve. With Young's assent, the General Counsel of the National Urban League inaugurated procedures for ending CUCRL's existence. The Council died in 1967.[58]

Young never denied his role as a mediator. He reveled in reconciling antagonists and their divergent points of view. The consensus that he expected to result seemingly justified his middle position. Such a stance, however, was almost always compromised by irreconcilable perspectives and his own deeply held beliefs. For example, he wanted the National Urban League and its affiliates to be identified with vanguard organizations of the civil rights movement. Yet, when the political right wing made no distinction between the negotiating League and its protesting counterparts in SNCC or SCLC, Young's middle position shifted to defenses of his militant colleagues and their direct action tactics. He could not negotiate with the right wing and reconcile their perspectives with those of the broad objectives of the civil rights crusade without undermining the movement. So he abandoned the middle ground and stood with the civil rights coalition.

Similarly, Young as a mediator among civil rights spokespersons tried to bring together the various elements within the coalition. He discovered that while he dispassionately attempted to referee and reconcile conflicts, it became harder to suppress his own particular views and predilections. Increasingly, CUCRL reflected his generally cautious and conservative posture in tactics and programmatic thrust. In both instances, with right-wing whites and with militant blacks, Young discovered the limits of his combined roles of an interracial and intraracial mediator. Although sometimes useful in defusing conflict and confrontation, such jockeying was ultimately unsatisfactory. Young was possessed of a point of view, and eventually he was compelled to state it and advance it. Whenever that happened, Young's advocacy of insider negotiation with powerful whites and their institutions as a major means to achieve significant social change became apparent. Also, when reactionary whites challenged civil rights leaders on their tactics of protest, Young was pressed to defend such militancy even though he preferred other methods.

Young's role as a mediator who often failed led to misunderstandings and groundless charges of "Uncle Tomism." A younger generation of black militants especially after 1966 cynically eclepted him "Whitey" Young. In 1970 the *New York Times Magazine* published a provocative article, "Whitney Young: Black Leader or 'Oreo Cookie?'" Written by reporter Tom Buckley, the article acknowledged that Young believed that all black leaders were "militants in different ways." The theme of the essay, however, stressed Young's interactions with white establishment leaders and their solid financial backing of the National Urban League. This reality, wrote Buckley, "puts Young in a difficult position with his own race." The article contended that younger black spokespersons considered Young and his organization the purchased property of their white backers. That Young dealt with President Richard Nixon seemed to prove that he would compromise the interests of blacks.[59]

Vernon Jordan, president of the United Negro College Fund, recalled that Whitney Young was quite hurt by the Buckley article. Randolph and other leading blacks jointly penned a biting letter of protest to the *New York Times*. Similarly, John A. Morsell, associate executive director of the NAACP, wrote to the *Times* and castigated Buckley on numerous factual errors. Moreover, Carl T. Rowan, the prominent black journalist, published a rebuttal essay on "White Liberals Who Pick Black Heroes."[60]

Although patronizing and simplistic, Buckley's perception of Whitney Young illustrated the perils of the middle ground that the League leader sought to occupy. Missing the complex forces with which Young had to deal, Buckley, like so many others, failed to see the essence of his leadership, that of negotiating and reconciling the perspectives of civil rights antagonists on the shifting sands of social change and social justice. Moreover, Buckley missed the impressive support that middle- and working-class blacks gave to Young's integrationist objectives. All that Buckley and others noted were the limits of Young's approach rather than his genuine attempts to bring harmony out of the chaos of conflicting objectives and tactics of civil rights activists and critics.

2

Humanizing the City

Whitney M. Young Jr., alone among the national leaders of the civil rights movement, focused his efforts on urban issues. Whereas successful assaults on legalized segregation in the South drew the attention of Young's colleagues in SCLC, SNCC, CORE, and the NAACP, only the National Urban League concerned itself exclusively with social and economic conditions among blacks in the nation's cities. Young addressed issues in housing, unemployment, welfare, educational inequality, and numerous other matters that defined the urban crisis of the 1960s. Because these ills disproportionately affected blacks, Whitney Young, an expert on urban affairs, joined with several public and private institutions to find solutions.

Young's position as NUL executive director and his reputation as a nationally acclaimed social work professional and administrator made him a major spokesman in urban affairs. As the only national black leader with such credentials, Young's views and recommendations became important to public and private officials worried about explosive conditions in the nation's ghettos.

Consequently, several urban-related groups and institutions involved Young in their deliberations and initiatives. They included such public groups as the Advisory Committee on Urban Development of the federal Department of Housing and Urban Development, the States Urban Action Center, and the Urban Design Council of New York City. Private organizations included the Urban Institute, the National Committee Against Discrimination in Housing, the National Welfare Rights Organization, and Urban America. In all of these organizations Young functioned either as a board or committee member or as a consultant. Therefore, his ability to influence the direction of these agencies was limited. Through his presidency of the National Association of Social Workers and the National Conference on Social Welfare, however, Young gained other platforms besides his NUL position to articulate his perspective on urban issues.

In most instances the groups with which Young affiliated were led by whites. Although he lauded such interest in urban issues from leaders in the majority population, he complained that the absence of experts from black communities would result in faulty strategies to improve ghetto areas. At the founding of the National Urban Coalition in 1967, he pressed vigorously and successfully for the appointment of a black official to head the new organization.

For Young the intersection of race relations and urban affairs made him singularly important among national black leaders. His perspectives on urban issues were taken as authoritative even when Martin Luther King Jr. led grassroots campaigns in northern cities. Until the establishment of the National Urban Coalition and the appointment of its first executive director, M. Carl Holman, only Young definitively spoke to major public and private institutions about the needs of black ghettos. That he mentored and sponsored Holman showed his desire for an additional spokesman for the nation's urban black population. Moreover, Young demonstrated a rare magnanimity in sharing leadership with a potential competitor who could argue eloquently for various proposals and programs in urban race relations.

During the 1960s Whitney Young delivered innumerable addresses about how the fate of urban America lay in the social and economic development of its black population. For him the bottom line was the elimination of black ghettos. Young's comprehensive domestic Marshall Plan outlined in his 1964 book, *To Be Equal*, noted the broad range of inequities that the black people bore and the programs required to solve them. Key for Young was positive action to destroy the racial ghetto. He declared, "Too long the cancerous sore of the ghetto has festered in our urban communities, spewing forth human wreckage and the major portion of criminal offenders; draining our body politic of treasure; robbing us of the meaningful contributions of hundreds of thousands of citizens whose lives and ambitions have been thwarted and truncated." The absence of decent housing, a productive welfare system, excellent education, and gainful employment were all characteristics of the ghetto. If the premises, proposals, and programs of powerful public and private officials could envisage the black population beyond the ghetto, then progress could be made in solving those problems which that environment produced.[1]

Young elaborated thoughtfully on this theme in response to a 1967 symposium paper about urban goals and urban action. "My central thesis is that the central cities of this increasingly urban nation are . . . collapsing . . . due to the fiscal drain of the ghetto." He added, "Such areas are utterly unable to make a satisfactory contribution to the city treasury in return for services." Concerning the racial dimension of this urban dilemma, Young predicted that by 1970 ten major cities would be 50 percent black and many others would be 25-35 percent black. One way to ameliorate the urban crisis,he said, would be public and private institutional building in the ghettos. Such an initiative would be "a nationwide program of locating new governmental, commercial, industrial, cultural, and educational buildings and developments in slum areas in order to spearhead the transformation of the ghettos into viable, integrated communities."

Young cited examples from New York City where various blighted areas were improved when major institutions were built in the ghetto communities. Several "tangential and eminently desirable effects" resulted, such as the creation of new jobs. This occurrence would bring about a mixed working population and mixed neighborhoods. Ultimately, Young wanted to disperse the ghetto and end its isolation. Such a development would improve the lot of blacks and create a healthier urban America.[2]

Young's visibility as NUL executive director drew him into numerous organizations and commissions related to urban issues. As he functioned as a board member, consultant, or adviser, Young seldom missed opportunities to tell those who served with him about the pivotal importance of race in understanding the problems of the cities. He thus influenced initiatives that groups, both public and private, devised to shape urban policies.

Officials in New York City and New York State took full advantage of Whitney Young's presence in their region. Plagued by a broad range of controversial issues Mayor John Lindsay, Governor Nelson A. Rockefeller, and other officeholders appointed Young to various committees to advise them about major urban initiatives. In 1967 Lindsay asked Young to join Mrs. W. Vincent Astor, CBS network head William S. Paley, and others on the Urban Design Council of New York. This advisory council aimed to develop urban renewal objectives for the area around the city's Lincoln Center and devise proposals for other parts of the metropolis.[3] Also in 1967, New York police commissioner H.R. Leary wanted Young on the board of a nonprofit corporation that tried to improve interactions between the police and the communities they served. Increased hostility toward the police from minorities, the poor, and some in the middle class prompted the commissioner to invite Young to participate in this endeavor. Young did not want to invade the turf of the executive director of the New York Urban League, Eugene Callender. If Callender could also attend the meetings, then Young promised to help in this determined effort to improve citizen-police relations. Commissioner Leary accepted this suggestion.[4]

In 1968, Mayor Lindsay drew Young into a tempestuous local dispute involving city schools. Two recent developments had plunged the New York City school system into unprecedented conflict: the unionization of teachers and the spread of decentralization or community governance of schools. A largely white corps of unionized teachers, many of them Jewish, were pitted against mainly minority parents who wanted more input in their children's education. In the Ocean Hill–Brownsville section of Brooklyn, a largely black and Puerto Rican school district, an experiment in community control resulted in the dismissal of thirteen teachers and administrators whom parents accused of sabotaging attempts at decentralization. Backing Brooklyn teachers in a strike was Albert Shanker, president of the United Federation of Teachers. Mayor Lindsay appointed a three-member panel that included Whitney Young to help resolve the strike. Later, Young, who was sympathetic to decentralization, resigned from the committee, accusing Shanker of exploiting the racial dimensions of the conflict. Later, he counselled blacks and Puerto Ricans to eschew anti-Semitic sentiments because they would "damage the cause of community control."[5]

Efforts by New York State to address problems in its various cities prompted Governor Nelson A. Rockefeller in 1967 to create an Urban Development Corporation. The purpose of the agency, Rockefeller told Young, was "to transform the blighted core areas of our urban centers." In 1968 Rockefeller asked Young to join the former president of the World Bank, George D. Woods, and other prestigious persons on UDC's board of directors. "I know of no more effective legal instrument anywhere in the United States than this new Corporation for dealing with the problems of housing and community development," observed Rockefeller in his appointment letter to Young.[6]

Relevant staff at the National Urban League monitored how the UDC dealt with racial issues. Since their boss was the only black on the board, Young's aides informed him when UDC policies lacked input from the grassroots. In 1969 the agency planned a community development project in the Buffalo-Amherst area. A League staff person, however, warned that UDC had not gotten any testimony from blacks in the vicinity. That the chosen sites were far from inner-city communities was one complaint, and the other concerned the absence of black participation in UDC's Buffalo deliberations. National and local League officials wanted Young to take a stand on activating a citizens' advisory group to advise UDC. The onetime general counsel to the League also served as UDC secretary. He urged Young to warn whites on the board of their racial myopia and to have them listen seriously to the NUL housing director. Otherwise, he said, "They're going to have a problem."[7]

Increasingly, Young discovered that whites with whom he served on various urban affairs boards did not understand how ghettos and their black inhabitants were integral to any solutions to city problems. Some staff within the NUL wanted Young to resign from UDC. On one occasion a League official who went to UDC to represent Young inexplicably was escorted out of the meeting room while fifteen white observers were allowed to remain. This action, while possibly "a comedy of errors," also could have been an insult to the NUL. Whatever Young decided to do, some staff pushed him to conclude that "UDC has failed to have any significant impact on the need for low- and moderate-income housing in New York State." Another aide to Young surmised that UDC prized amiable relations with municipal officials over those with grassroots blacks. That meant that Young's continued involvement could undermine League credibility with its low-income black constituents.[8]

Whatever hesitancy the League staff noted in their boss, Young always used a double entry ledger to determine what gains or losses would accrue to him if he forsook UDC. In the Ocean Hill–Brownsville case, Young was not vulnerable to retaliation from either Mayor Lindsay or Albert Shanker over his dramatic resignation from the teacher strike arbitration committee. A potential snub to Nelson A. Rockefeller was another matter altogether. Not only was he governor but he was a member of a wealthy family that made substantial contributions to the National Urban League. Additionally, Young believed that his participation on such commissions allowed him to influence, albeit in peripheral ways, important initiatives that would benefit blacks. While associated with UDC, for example, Young was impressed with a report about economic development in Harlem. Young urged the head of UDC to discuss the findings with the consultants who authored the study. Young endorsed their recommendations and gained a hearing for them within UDC.[9]

In 1967, during his involvement with the Urban Development Corporation, Young became a board member of the States Urban Action Center. The group, which mainly consisted of governors and mayors, chose several areas of emphasis and then agreed to send consultants to various states to advise officials on implementation. These issues included crime control, police and community relations, jobs for the underprivileged, improved educational opportunities, and reconstruction.[10] Although Young often missed meetings, executive director Stanley R. Tupper maintained contact and secured his advice by mail or telephone. When the Iowa state government proposed a model regional office in metropolitan Cedar Rapids, Young wrote

Tupper to express his approval. Clearly, Young encouraged efforts "to make State agencies dealing with urban problems more responsive to the people through more efficient regional operations."[11]

The range of Young's involvements steadily broadened as racial unrest in the nation's largest cities occurred with frightening frequency from 1964 through 1968. Moreover, the need to study and understand urban affairs and their racial dimensions also demanded the expertise of black leaders like himself. As Young moved among various public and private commissions, his judgment and advice became better known and greatly sought. Eventually, he became a part of an influential network of urban experts and a participant in interlocking directorates of various urban affairs organizations. His relationship to the States Urban Action Center and Urban America was illustrative. In 1968 Nelson Rockefeller in 1968 informed Young that the board had voted to merge with Urban America and continue its work within that group. Perhaps Rockefeller did not know that Young had already become involved with the larger and older organization and its programs to improve the urban environment.[12] Young's participation in one organization often drew him into others.

Young's involvement with Urban America allowed him to have a greater impact than in the other groups. The assassination of Martin Luther King Jr. precipitated massive rioting in large cities across the country. An alarmed James W. Rouse, president of Urban America, told Whitney Young that an ad campaign would inform the citizenry of the nature of the urban crisis and what they could do about it in their communities. He did not want to stop there. Rouse encouraged Urban America to become the lead organization in defining issues and solutions to the nation's urban problems. In this endeavor he thought that Young's participation would be crucial. Rouse invited him to join several other members of the board in devising policy directions for Urban America. He wanted Young's views about employment, housing, education, and community development. Rouse was certain that with Young's help this could become a major contribution by Urban America. As a part of this policy formation process, Young was also asked to respond in detail to Urban America proposals about family, welfare, youth initiatives, and other matters. An aide did the evaluations for Young. Additionally, William Slayton, executive vice president of the organization, impressed upon Young the importance of his visible participation in the group's 1968 meeting in Detroit. Slayton wanted him to chair a session about how the idea of community self-determined action was interpreted differently by inner-city residents and federal officials in Housing and Urban Development and in the Office of Economic Opportunity.[13]

Perhaps to Young's astonishment Slayton and others in Urban America increasingly realized the degree to which race relations and urban affairs were intricately intertwined. That realization meant that groups like Urban America needed more blacks to participate in organizations that affected urban policy and programs. Slayton asked Young to help the group find new black board members.[14]

Like the States Urban Action Center linked Young with Urban America, so did the latter organization enhance an already existing relationship that he had with HUD. While active in Urban America, Young served on the advisory committee of its nonprofit housing center. When Terry Sanford, former governor of North Carolina, succeeded to the presidency of the parent organization, he asked Young to continue his consultative role. Because the center offered technical assistance to nonprofit sponsors of lower-income housing, Sanford wanted to maintain Young's input in shaping program policy of the Center. An exacting schedule, however, ended his involvement with the agency in 1968.[15]

Young's consultations with federal officials about housing and other urban issues were the most fruitful of his organizational involvements. Always concerned about blacks making policy in urban affairs, Young was surely pleased that Robert C. Weaver served as administrator of the Housing and Home Finance Agency from 1961 to 1966, and then became the first secretary of Housing and Urban Development. Weaver and Young disagreed about the relationship that black betterment organizations should have with the federal government, with Weaver arguing that federal funding of any National Urban League projects would compromise the organization.[16] Nonetheless, Weaver and others involved in housing and urban issues called on Young to share his perspectives on programs they planned for the cities.

In 1965 as the Johnson administration was developing a Department of Housing and Urban Development, Young was tapped to serve on a secret task force to suggest an organizational structure. Officially known as the Task Force on Urban Problems, Young had an opportunity to shape the direction of this new cabinet department. He opposed proposals to put the Community Action Program into HUD. He also asked his national staff to review a broad range of recommendations for the federal agency, including comments on mass transit, suggestion for the Home Loan Bank Board, duties for the four undersecretaries, and functions for regional offices.[17]

HUD Secretary Weaver invited Young to serve on an advisory committee to help implement the recently enacted Demonstration Cities and Metropolitan Development Act. Particular communities would devise model projects on how "to attack both the human and physical problems that afflict many of our cities."[18]

At these meetings Young participated in broad discussions about HUD's relationship to the states, model cities, and the need for a HUD undersecretary for research. Aside from offering these perspectives, Young enhanced League involvement with HUD. Despite Weaver's distaste for fiscal entanglements between black advancement organizations and the federal government, Young reported that the HUD secretary would be receptive to any League requests to work with Federal Housing Authority officials in Washington, Baltimore, Philadelphia, St. Louis, and Milwaukee. In those cities the FHA assisted the poor in finding housing whether by renting, purchasing, or building. Since local Leagues existed in each of these five cities, Weaver welcomed their help in educating the public about the program and in getting someone at NUL headquarters to coordinate this activity.[19]

Young's extensive involvements in numerous urban affairs groups ultimately gave him the opportunity to clone himself. Fortuitously, an invitation from Andrew Heiskell of Urban America provided him with the chance for which he had been waiting. He valued his productive interaction with establishment whites who understood that urban and racial issues constituted a national emergency. Although their access to money and power proved crucial for many urban initiatives, these resources did not substitute for the paucity of blacks who influenced urban policies. Moreover, Young impacted national urban affairs in helping to found a major organization whose stress on inner cities enormously benefited the black population.

Widespread rioting in black communities from Rochester in 1964 to Newark in 1966 and Detroit in 1967 dramatically demonstrated that racial and urban issues had reached crisis proportions. Alarmed officers of Urban America resolved to respond in a major way to these dire events. During the fall of 1966, Stephen Currier, the group's president, expressed concern over an apparent trend of cutting back on programs to improve big cities. It was crucial to draw mayors and their various constituencies into a coalition to address these problems. In January 1967 an ad hoc group of mayors met twice with Urban America and then formed a prestigious steering committee consisting of Ivan Allen of Atlanta, Richard Daley of Chicago, John Lindsay of New York, Jerome Cavanagh of Detroit, and John Collins of Boston. In May 1967 Urban America and the mayors met with an influential group of corporate leaders including the heads of Litton Industries, ALCOA, General Electric, Allied Stores, and North Carolina Mutual Insurance Company, an important black business. At this point other national black leaders were asked to join. In July 1967 A. Philip Randolph and Whitney Young received invitations to affiliate with this emerging coalition.[20]

Although he was brought into the process late, Young had compelling reasons to associate with the group. First, he already had interacted with these men in other settings. He surely knew the recently deceased Stephen Currier and his Taconic Foundation. Andrew Heiskell, the chairman of the board of Urban America, had been involved with urban issues since 1953 in Chicago. There he was affiliated with the American Council to Improve Our Neighborhoods, an organization that developed into Urban America.

When the emergency convocation occurred in August 1967, Randolph, King, Wilkins, and Young joined the national steering committee. Randolph served with Heiskell as cochairman, and Young played a pivotal role in defining the National Urban Coalition's mission. In a speech before an assembly of politicians, corporate leaders, union officials, clergy, and civil rights advocates Young said, "Responsible leaders among the Negro community have not failed. We have been failed by responsible white leaders who have not responded to us." He cautioned whites against blaming racial rioting on militant Black Power spokespersons, such as the notorious H. Rap Brown. He said, "Rap Brown did not cause unemployment. . . . Rap Brown did not put Negroes in ghettos. Rap Brown did not perpetuate upon Negroes inferior education. This was done by other people in the society." Again, Young stressed the importance of jobs as a means to undermine the pathologies of the slums. "We got ten thousand jobs yesterday in Detroit," he exclaimed. "Those jobs were there before the riots. Are we going to have to wait for riots in other cities to find jobs?" Young endorsed a detailed document that articulated the Coalition's thrust. Government at all levels and the private sector were challenged to inaugurate massive efforts to bring good jobs to slum areas. Moreover, widespread endeavors to rehabilitate housing and education in ghetto communities were similarly endorsed. These objectives would be achieved through the collective and cooperative efforts of the political, economic, and social institutions represented at the convocation.[21]

Before the August 1967 emergency convocation, the Coalition had little visibility. Young had thought that the movement was only temporary, although it could develop into something more. Heiskell's involvement, however, changed his mind. As board chairman of Time and as brother-in-law to the publisher of the New York Times, Heiskell had an easy entry into circles beyond the reach of civil rights leaders. Heiskell simply called McGeorge Bundy, president of the Ford Foundation, for a meeting to discuss a grant to launch the National Urban Coalition. Bundy promised favorable action once

Heiskell secured an able administrator for the organization. In another instance, Heiskell went to the head of Morgan Guaranty Trust to solicit a donation. When the banker offered $5,000, Heiskell refused to accept anything below $100,000. His demand was heeded.[22]

At the same time, Heiskell's Time responsibilities interfered with his Coalition activities. So he asked the group to hire a full-time executive director. He consulted with McGeorge Bundy and James Reston, the influential New York Times columnist. Reston told Heiskell that John Gardner, HEW secretary in the Johnson administration, would soon resign his position. Reston called Gardner and learned of his interest in urban issues. The call had come at the right moment. The National Urban Coalition had found its man.[23]

Gardner had known Whitney Young since 1961. Lester Granger brought the two together because Gardner, who then headed the Carnegie Corporation, had been a League supporter.[24] Gardner valued Young's presence as a member of the Coalition's executive committee and his active participation. Often, he and others in the Coalition tapped Young's expertise to aid their various programs. In 1968 Lisle C. Carter Jr., the deputy director, solicited Young's input for a meeting designed to help the Coalition's Task Force on Equal Housing Opportunity, especially on how to respond to newly enacted federal fair housing legislation. Carter also wanted Young's opinion on possible cooperation between the Coalition and the National Committee Against Discrimination in Housing. Moreover, in 1969 Young chaired the Coalition's Advisory Committee on Income Maintenance. He endorsed efforts broadly to inform potential beneficiaries about welfare reform and other income programs.[25]

Legislative lobbying and other purely political activities became the agenda of the Urban Coalition Action Council. Young often cosigned letters that Gardner wrote to urge passage of federal laws that would help cities. One senator thanked the group for testimony at a hearing about public service employment. In another instance Gardner wanted Young to accompany him to Capitol Hill to lobby two senators on a welfare reform bill. He gradually separated such activities from the nonprofit coalition. In 1970 Gardner founded Common Cause to replace the action council. As this new group claimed Gardner's energies, a successor was needed to fill his position at the National Urban Coalition.[26]

A watchful Whitney Young was aware of this opportunity for increased black participation in the Coalition. In October 1969 Peter Libassi, executive vice president of the Coalition, informed Young that an influential officer at Urban America, William Slayton, had "precipitated very tentative conversations concerning a possible merger." A month later Libassi told Young that "conversations on the merger . . . have progressed to the point where consideration by the Executive Committee is now in order." Although problems of the cities would remain the principal priority of the merged organization, the lack of black participation at the highest policymaking level would be exacerbated with the addition of more staff and board members from the two groups. The absorption of Urban America into the National Urban Coalition in 1970 meant a larger organization and a greater necessity for black bureaucrats in the group. For Whitney Young, this matter had become urgent.[27]

Testimonies by blacks employed in the Coalition confirmed Young's analysis. John Gardner seemed sensitive to these matters. In 1968, for example, he solicited Young's reactions to the nominating committee and its attempt to maintain board representation from women, Mexican Americans, Puerto Rican Americans, governors, educators, youth, labor and, "additional black leadership." Andrew Young, an aide to Martin Luther King Jr., and recently elected black mayors from Cleveland, Washington, D.C., and Gary, Indiana, were among those considered. Moreover, Patricia Roberts Harris, whom President Johnson appointed as ambassador to Luxembourg, and Dr. Vivian Henderson, president of Clark College, were blacks suggested to fill respective slots for women and educators.[28]

These gestures, however, failed to allay frustrations felt by blacks in the organization. In February 1970 Young chaired an ad hoc meeting mostly of blacks to discuss "the continuing role to be played by blacks in shaping priorities and designing goals and purposes of the Coalition." Consensus emerged on several matters including the importance of communication with the non-white members of the group and the need for their active and effective participation in decision making. Concerning the merger with Urban America, the ad hoc conferees urged consideration of "the racial composition of the staff" and "reiteration of an earlier request that the number two man in the organizations be black." These proceedings clearly had an impact because Sol Linowitz, the new chairman, told Young in October 1970 that M. Carl Holman, a black, had been designated senior vice president for policy and program development and would continue to serve as chairman of the policy committee.[29]

Apparently, that change did not help matters very much. In November 1970 Holman kept Young "abreast of morale and staff problems relating particularly to black staff." Holman noted that four blacks had resigned simultaneously. The resignations occurred because "black professionals especially have

felt that arbitrary decisions regarding them have been made by whites without prior checking either with them or with black executives." Holman believed that his authority had been circumvented when two blacks on the
health staff were fired while he was out of the office. This action was particularly galling because Holman had recently circulated a memorandum lauding
the Coalition's health program.[30]

Young and Holman were very good friends. They had known each other
since their teaching days in the Atlanta University Center. When Young went
to the National Urban League, Holman came to Washington to work for the
U.S. Commission on Civil Rights. Young was on the board of the National
Urban Coalition when Holman joined the staff in 1968 and became vice
president in 1970. *JET,* an influential national weekly, credited Young with
Holman's rise in the organization. Similarly, he helped to catapult Holman
into the presidency of the Coalition in 1971.[31]

Young's intimate involvement with the National Urban Coalition posed
numerous challenges and problems for staff in the National Urban League
and its affiliates. From the outset Young offered League resources and personnel to launch the new organization. In 1967 he informed an aide that the
Coalition needed League staff members, national and local, to play an expanded role in its operation. Young appointed a subordinate to the Coalition's
Task Force on Private Employment. In 1968 John Gardner asked Young to
help in establishing strong local coalitions. Gardner shared with him a list of
twelve cities where the Coalition wanted to establish affiliates. He asked Young
to share with him the names of persons with whom he was well acquainted to
help expand the organization. With NUL affiliates in ninety-five cities, Gardner
knew that Young's long list of contacts would be very helpful. In a joint
communication in 1969 they told national and local staff in both groups that
in several cities a League board member served on the Coalition's steering
committee and that in some locales businessmen served on the boards of
both organizations. In fact, Young suggested to Gardner that they should to
promote interlocking directorships. Moreover, Gardner praised the Jacksonville, Florida, and Flint, Michigan, Urban Leagues for spearheading the founding of local coalitions.[32]

Some of Young's ablest advisers, however, did not share his zeal for helping
the Coalition. These staff believed that the Coalition was developing programs, local chapters, and funding sources that overlapped with the League,
duplicated many of its initiatives, and threatened to supplant it. By 1969 the
director of field operations noted that the Coalition operated in twenty-six of
the ninety-five League cities, and he wanted to know where else the group

would spread. Other League staff wondered why the Coalition pursued initiatives that the NUL had pioneered. For example, Young's domestic Marshall Plan had a counterpart in the Coalition's Alternative National Budget. The League's income maintenance, health manpower, housing, consumer education, and other proposals had their titles adopted verbatim by Coalition programs. The annoyed director of the League's Labor Education Advancement Program declared that the two organizations were embarking on a collision course. This official was especially angered when the Coalition submitted a proposal to the Ford Foundation to fund a program to organize black contractors and to increase minority apprentices and journeymen. He noted that the League was already working in this area. Moreover, this League staffer, while attending a black economic development conference, resented efforts by Coalition representatives to take exclusive control of the project nationwide. These persons gave the erroneous impression that the Coalition "was the only organization uniquely qualified to carry this responsibility." Another subordinate told Young that the Coalition was trying to take over NUL programs and was succeeding to a remarkable degree. Ultimately, this aide believed that continued duplication by the Coalition would lead to "the dissolution of the Urban League as a primary force in the civil rights and community service field."[33]

Perhaps John Gardner had sensed some hostility from League staff about the Coalition. Maybe that is what he had in mind when he spoke highly of Young and his group to a potential benefactor of the League. He observed that Young was "a great asset not only to the black community but to the whole nation. We must all support him." Gardner added that the National Urban Coalition and the National Urban League had similar names but that neither rivalry nor duplication existed between the two: "The Urban League has its own distinctive job to do and performs tasks that the Urban Coalition couldn't possibly tackle." At the same time Gardner agreed that the two staffs needed to meet. Both staffs felt an "urgency" for their bosses to talk. Gardner surely agreed.[34]

Although the League and the Coalition proposed to convene the senior staff of the two organizations in August 1970, aides to Whitney Young met a few months earlier to produce a brief report, "The National Urban Coalition: An Urban League View." League staff acknowledged the need for the Coalition, but they were not convinced that the organization had fulfilled its promise. Established in an atmosphere of widespread ghetto unrest, the group was meant to "mobilize and bring to bear new funds and resources" to solve urban problems. While the League eschewed direct involvement with politicians, the Coalition could cooperate openly with officeholders and draw in leaders from business, labor, and religion. League officials, however, concluded that the NUC had developed into "just another program operating agency, rather than a catalyst for joint community effort."

Riots in numerous large cities gave urban problems an urgency that the Coalition failed to sustain. Moreover, the waning of commitments from those with political and economic power rendered the organization increasingly ineffective. As a result, local chapters did not tackle difficult issues in employment, housing, and education. Instead, they operated limited programs, which did not achieve "the joint solution of community problems." Additionally, the similarity of the names of the two groups frequently confused their respective supporters. Coalition failures created difficulty for the NUL. Consequently, League staff endorsed efforts to meet with its counterpart for "positive mutual action to . . . clear up misunderstandings."[35]

Whitney Young and John Gardner made opening statements at the August meeting of the NUL and NUC. Young indicated that he thought the Coalition would complement the efforts of the League. While his organization did day-to-day programming, "the Coalition's main objective was to reinforce existing institutions, to lend what support [it] could to those that were effective and doing a job, and not be in the business of competing with . . . these institutions. . . . This we applauded and supported 100 percent." Young added, "We desperately need an Urban Coalition." He also observed that if the Coalition should make "modifications in the original objectives, we need to know about it." A defensive John Gardner said, "If we failed or if there is a better way to relate the two organizations, we ought to know about it." He declared that he came "solely to hear the various diagnoses" that will resolve the conflict between the League and the Coalition.

Detailed discussions occurred about programs that each organization pursued, competition for funds from similar sources, and how each group could clarify its national and local objectives. Most important, participants recommended ways to reduce friction. These suggestions included better intergroup communication, the recognition of possible duplication in national programming, and better coordination of local League and Coalition activities.[36]

Even after the August 1970 meeting, Young and Gardner backed continuing efforts to link their two organizations. Liaisons were named "to identify joint activities and possible duplication," and another team would "review specific cities where there seem to be problems and . . . develop strategies . . . at corrective action." Other League and Coalition staff were assigned to resolve conflicts. Three senior League officials—Cernoria D. Johnson, Dorothy K. Newman, and Betti S. Whaley—suggested ways to implement intergroup cooperation. They wanted a Coalition person to work full time at maintaining contact with the League and at designating NUC initiatives amenable to NUL participation. Furthermore, League staff should claim program initiatives in which the NUL would be singularly involved.

Johnson, Newman, and Whaley urged Young in a direction that he wanted to go. Although they and other staff had reservations about the programmatic thrust of the Coalition and its negative impact on the League, they endorsed Young's continued involvement with the maturing organization. They reminded him to emphasize the League's contributions to the Coalition.[37] None should forget that the development of the Coalition owed much to League magnanimity.

Young's encouragement of M. Carl Holman and the National Urban Coalition was repeated with George A. Wiley and the National Welfare Rights Organization. Wiley, a black Ph.D. in chemistry and a CORE activist, established the group in 1967. He designed NWRO to lobby government officials at every level to extend benefits to the needy, broaden programs, and prevent punitive measures against welfare recipients. Initially, Young criticized his objectives, arguing that getting jobs for people was better than improving the welfare system. Nonetheless, Young believed that NWRO was helpful to the urban poor, and he accepted Wiley's invitation for the NUL to be officially represented at the group's 1969 convention. Suggestions were also advanced concerning NWRO/NUL collaboration. In 1971 as Congress weighed passage of welfare legislation that Wiley deemed inimical to the interests of recipients, he conferred with Young about what could be done to stop that effort.[38]

Although he sometimes differed with the tactics of the federal Department of Housing and Urban Development, the National Urban Coalition, and the National Welfare Rights Organization, Young endorsed their efforts to improve urban life for the disadvantaged. Young was pleased when these institutions gained Robert C. Weaver, M. Carl Holman, and George A. Wiley as their executives. That he was not the only black of stature affecting how urban issues impacted on ghettos made his role in these groups worthwhile. His attempts to assist these spokesmen showed how much he cared about a broad presence of blacks making important decisions about American urban life. Moreover, his seeming lack of concern about the League sharing organizational turf with other groups demonstrated how deeply he cared about urban issues.

Whether he dealt with the States Urban Action Center, Urban America,

Above, Whitney M. Young Jr. with his parents and sisters. Left to right, Eleanor, Whitney Jr., Whitney Sr., Arnita, and Laura Ray. *Right,* With his wife and daughters. Left to right, Marcia, Whitney Jr., Lauren, and Margaret B. Young. Courtesy Margaret B. Young. *Below,* As dean of the Atlanta University's School of Social Work at a conference of field instructors. Next to Young (third from left) is John Kidneigh, who had been Young's social work professor at the University of Minnesota. Archives, Robert W. Woodruff Library, Atlanta University Center

Opposite above, Young and the Masonic Order. Whitney M. Young Jr. Collection, Rare Book and Manuscripts Library, Columbia University. *Opposite below,* Left to right, President John F. Kennedy, Whitney M. Young Jr., and Henry Steeger, president of the National Urban League, January 23, 1962. John F. Kennedy Library.

Right, Whitney M. Young Jr. at the White House, January 17, 1964. Yoichi R. Okamoto, Lyndon B. Johnson Presidential Library, Austin, Texas. *Below,* James Farmer, Roy Wilkins, Whitney M. Young Jr., and Martin Luther King Jr. at the White House, January 18, 1964. Yoichi R. Okamoto, Lyndon B. Johnson Library

Above, Martin Luther King Jr., President Lyndon B. Johnson, and Whitney M. Young Jr. January 18, 1964. *Below,* Young and Johnson, May 20, 1966. Both photos, Yoichi R. Okamoto, Lyndon B. Johnson Presidential Library

Above, Young and R. Sargent Shriver, director of the Office of Economic Opportunity, at the White House, March 16, 1967. *Below,* Young, Johnson, and Roy Wilkins at the White House, July 19, 1967. Both photos, Yoichi R. Okamoto, Lyndon B. Johnson Presidential Library

Opposite above left, Young and Johnson, November 19, 1968. Mike Geissinger, Lyndon B. Johnson Presidential Library. *Opposite above right,* Souvenir of 1966 reunion celebration of Lincoln Institute, where Whitney M. Young Sr. was president. *Opposite below,* Margaret B. Young (right) and Susan Scranton Linen at the 1968 Williams College commencement. Williams College Archives and Special Collections.

Right, Young at Williams College in Williamstown, Mass., in 1968. Williams College Archives and Special Collections. *Below,* Young with black GIs in Vietnam. Whitney M. Young Jr. Collection, Rare Book and Manuscripts Library, Butler Library, Columbia University

Left, N. Phillips Dodge, president of the Omaha League while Young was executive director. Courtesy N. Phillips Dodge. *Below left,* Lindsley F. Kimball, president of the National Urban League and liaison with the Rockefeller philanthropies. Courtesy Mrs. Maude Kimball. *Below right,* Stephen R. Currier of the Taconic Foundation, approved generous contributions to the National Urban League. Courtesy Jane Lee Eddy, Taconic Foundation

Right, McGeorge Bundy, president of the Ford Foundation, approved generous contributions to the National Urban League. Courtesy of the late McGeorge Bundy. *Below left,* Hobson R. Reynolds, Grand Exalted Ruler, Improved, Benevolent and Protective Order of the Elks of the World and National Urban League board member *Below right,* Alexander J. Allen, a longtime League associate of Whitney M. Young Jr. Professor Samuel W. Allen, Winthrop, Mass.

Above left, Rufus E. Clement, president of Atlanta University. The Archives, Robert W. Woodruff Library, Atlanta University Center. *Above right,* John W. Mack, executive director of the Los Angeles Urban League, who was recruited to Atlanta University School of Social Work and to the National Urban League by Young. Courtesy of John W. Mack. *Right,* Vernon Jordan, executive director of the United Negro College Fund and Young's confidant and League successor. Courtesy of Vernon Jordan

Above, Young with President John E. Sawyer at the 1968 Williams College commencement. Williams College Archives and Special Collections. *Below,* Young and Ellsworth Bunker, U.S. Ambassador to South Vietnam. Whitney M. Young Jr. Collection, Rare Book and Manuscripts Library, Butler Library, Columbia University

Above, Young and James Linen, president of Time-Life and of the National Urban League. *Below,* Young receiving award from Roy Wilkins, executive secretary of the NAACP. Both photos, Whitney M. Young Jr. Collection, Rare Book and Manuscripts Library, Butler Library, Columbia University

Above, Hubert H. Humphrey, Young, and Elliott Roosevelt. *Below,* Young and James Farmer, executive director of CORE. Both photos, Whitney M. Young Jr. Collection, Rare Book and Manuscripts Library, Butler Library, Columbia University

Above, Young with Floyd McKissick of CORE and Martin Luther King Jr. of SCLC. *Below,* Young in Hobson City Alabama. Both photos, Whitney M. Young Jr. Collection, Rare Book and Manuscripts Library, Butler Library, Columbia University

Above, Margaret B. and Lauren Young enter Riverside Church in New York City for the funeral of Whitney M. Young Jr. *Below,* President Richard M. Nixon delivering a eulogy at Young's graveside in Kentucky. Both photos, Whitney M. Young Jr. Collection, Rare Book and Manuscripts Library, Butler Library, Columbia University

Young at the White House, January 18, 1964. Yoichi R. Okamoto, Lyndon B. Johnson Presidential Library

the National Urban Coalition, or any other public or private institution devoted to urban affairs, Young's influence remained important but peripheral.
At times, he impacted these organizations in substantive ways, but he did not
affect them as much as groups that he headed. As executive director of the
National Urban League and simultaneously as president of the National Association of Social Workers and the National Conference on Social Welfare,
Young had direct opportunities to articulate and implement his vision of
urban America.

Mindful that widespread ghetto unrest posed new challenges to the
National Urban League, Whitney Young urged his national and local staff to
reevaluate their programs and decide whether they effectively served residents in the inner cities. He spent much time discussing these matters with
Sterling Tucker, the executive director of the Washington Urban League. They
had known each other since the late 1940s when both served as industrial
relations secretaries of midwestern affiliates. As the two discussed future directions for the League, the idea of "New Thrust" emerged. They agreed that
the urgency of grassroots grievances against slum conditions and their willingness to express their dissatisfaction pushed the black freedom struggle to
another plateau. These changed circumstances required a redefinition of the
role and function of the League. Since its founding, League officials represented blacks to the white power structure. In their behalf the organization
appealed to corporations, government, foundations, and other benefactors to
provide resources to ameliorate the social and economic condition of these
deprived persons. Young's conversations with Tucker convinced him that this
methodology had become obsolete.

Grassroots blacks in the southern civil rights movement and in northern ghetto rebellions showed that they wanted to articulate their grievances
and their demands without help or interpretation from such ambassadorial
groups as the National Urban League. This new reality required a New Thrust
from the League. It would now serve inner-city communities by helping to
empower people to act and speak for themselves. Although the League would
provide technical and organizational assistance, its goal would be to enable
grassroots organizations to converse with the power structure on their own.
The era of representing the inarticulate had come to an end.[39]

Extensive racial rioting in the aftermath of the assassination of Martin
Luther King Jr. in April 1968 moved Young to redefine the NUL mission. He
called an emergency conference of local League executives to discuss new
directions for the organization. Other meetings occurred and consensus
emerged about what Young and Tucker originally envisaged as a "New Thrust."

One foundation correctly understood it as the League's shift away from serving black bourgeois interests "to a concentration on the priority problems of ghetto areas." For Young, New Thrust was a quest for "ghetto power." He wanted the League to concentrate its resources and energies in the ghetto to improve it and to maintain its commitment to integration. Eliminating the ghetto remained Young's ultimate objective, but the empowerment of its residents had become an important prerequisite for their entry into the American mainstream.

Young projected a budget of $2 million for New Thrust. Approximately $1.5 million was designated for fifty affiliates, which would implement the program in their respective locales. He anticipated needing $500,000 for general administration. In 1968, however, Young actually drew $1,395,000 to fund this ambitious project. Support came from the Ford Foundation ($845,000), the Rockefeller Foundation ($300,000), and the Rockefeller Brothers Fund ($250,000).[40]

Young conceptualized New Thrust in three programmatic components. First, he noted that whenever business, government, and other elements of the elite dealt with spokespersons representing inner cities, the latter had to be authentic leaders ratified by ghetto residents. If these representatives lacked grassroots support, then whatever agreements they made with the establishment would be repudiated. Block organizations, Young contended, would remedy this problem. These neighborhood-based groups would "organize around an issue which motivates a community and on which relatively short-term results are possible." The local League would facilitate these efforts rather than lead them. The affiliate could provide data, reports, contacts with political and corporate leaders, and other assistance. But initiative and leadership would come from grassroots block organizations, not from the League.

A second aspect of Young's New Thrust thinking concerned the black middle class, "one of the most maligned groups in the United States." He argued that many of them wanted to address problems in the urban and race relations fields, but did not know how. He proposed to put more of them on local League boards of directors and in other positions where they could be useful. The development of grassroots leadership and expanded black middle-class involvement in inner-city affairs would become complementary aims of New Thrust.

Third, Young wanted the program to help in changing public opinion about integration. He believed that this well-known civil rights goal had become a casualty of the major race riots and the rise of black separatism. He wanted to rehabilitate integration as a societal objective and make it the "'in' rather than the 'out' thing to do" in housing and other social and economic spheres.[41]

Young's musings about middle- and working-class blacks and integrationism had been the League's foci during an earlier phase of the 1960s civil rights struggle. He knew, however, that his current emphasis on ghetto empowerment and the development of grassroots leadership had supplanted his organization's previous programs. Although racial integration remained his goal, New Thrust and the promised development of ghetto power would also bring grassroots blacks into the American mainstream. Like Young, officials throughout the League infrastructure realized that their relevance as a black organization lay in deeper involvement with inner-city inhabitants. With New Thrust, Young proved his mettle as a versatile and insightful leader.

Young articulated New Thrust to the Ford Foundation with greater clarity. He said that local League officials would establish "neighborhood outposts" in the inner city. These would be "community organization efforts providing service to people in the ghetto and mobilizing them for confrontation and change." He added that the "efforts would emanate from an Urban League outpost offering advice, service, and action." Consequently, the League would be identified "with the problems and population of the ghetto; developing and working with indigenous neighborhood leadership to build ghetto power; [and] forming ghetto-professional coalitions to work toward specific social change objectives defined in terms of priority community needs."[42]

New Thrust programs in Knoxville and San Diego fitted the model that Young identified in the Ford proposal. The League spearheaded a grassroots group in Knoxville's Lonsdale section which pressured the city council to establish a recreation commission responsible to the community. Moreover, the affiliate deployed community organizers to open "two ghetto offices to assist neighborhood residents in pressing for more frequent garbage pickups, regular street maintenance, the elimination of health hazards, and enforcement of laws pertaining to sewage." To fight employment discrimination, the League received complaints at one of its outpost offices and led a coalition of black organizations to press these grievances.

Similar emphasis on grassroots initiatives characterized the League's New Thrust in San Diego. The affiliate's main office moved into the heart of the community. Moreover, all professional staff members were considered community workers first and specialists second. The League also organized sixty-one block groups with more than one thousand members working on neighborhood problems that concerned them most. Its membership goal was 29,000. These efforts produced significant improvements in municipal services, and direct confrontations led to new hiring practices at San Diego hotels, motels, and restaurants.[43]

Young singled out the Boston Urban League for special attention. Mel King, a former teacher, settlement house worker, and community organizer, became the executive director of the Boston affiliate in 1967. King found the League office in downtown Boston without a full-time professional staff. Its principal function was providing industry with a pool of trained workers whom employers pledged to hire. King described League activities "as focused on institutions—schools, health services, interagency councils, [and] the United Community Services." He wanted to reorient the affiliate to a "philosophy of community development through community control." With Mel King at the helm, the Boston Urban League was ripe for Young's New Thrust. He supported King's effort to create a "New Urban League."[44] In proposals to the Ford and Rockefeller Foundations for New Thrust funding, Young made special financial appeals for the Boston affiliate.[45]

King proposed a partnership between the local League and Boston College called the Joint Community-University Center for Inner City Change. Roxbury residents would be in charge, and the College would offer technical assistance in planning and programming for economic development, jobs, and housing. With funding from Ford, Rockefeller, and Boston College, King's "New Urban League" established a Neighborhood Development Corporation, organized tenants to restore an apartment building, and formed an urban renewal committee. King also initiated a Survival Fund with contributions from League staff to strengthen special projects in inner-city Boston.[46]

Young drew from Ford, Rockefeller, Alfred Sloan, R.K. Mellon, and other foundations a total of $1.5 million for the 1969 fiscal year and $3 million for the 1970 fiscal year. He told the Rockefeller Brothers Fund in 1970 that he "hoped that by the end of the two-year period planned for the New Thrust, increases in local support, particularly from United Funds, would suffice to cover the expanded affiliate budgets." Although New Thrust would be phased out as a separate program, Young wanted to maintain funding for some projects at the reduced level of $1.75 million in fiscal 1971. That expectation, however, proved erroneous. Local United Funds did not respond by increasing their regular support of League affiliates. Young blamed the conservative political climate in some parts of the country for this unfortunate result. His disappointment was allayed somewhat by the continued support of the Rockefeller Brothers Fund albeit at the reduced level of $150,000.[47]

Originally a special project separate from the rest of National Urban League operations, New Thrust became for Whitney Young the principal means for his organization to address inner-city problems and interact with ghetto residents. In the future it was going to be "a day-to-day way of doing business." Because of New Thrust the League was "refining and institutionalizing its community action processes [and] changing its operational procedures in order to achieve new kinds of results from institutions which serve black and other minority Americans." The program's success convinced Young that change in urban America, especially for blacks, depended on grassroots action. The League's ambassadorial role, he contended, was obsolete. Unless the organization continued its thrust toward ghetto empowerment and providing to inner-city residents the technical assistance to compel action from political and economic elites, the League would become a peripheral presence in the nation's black communities.[48]

Young's visibility as the leader of the League and in urban affairs made him an attractive candidate to head two professional organizations in which he had been active. The National Conference on Social Welfare and the National Association of Social Workers dealt with a range of issues affecting the urban environment. NCSW functioned mainly as a forum on all aspects of health and welfare, whereas NASW addressed matters relevant to the professional interests of social workers. Despite the difference in emphasis, both bodies participated in the national discourse about cities and how they affected the disadvantaged. That such issues were intrinsically racial made Whitney Young an obvious choice to serve as president of the two organizations.

In 1966 Young became the second black ever to head the 8,000-member National Conference on Social Welfare. Quickly, he focused the organization on urban affairs and tried to affiliate it with government agencies working in that field. He tried to persuade HUD Secretary Robert C. Weaver to help fund a forum on social problems related to urban growth. Instead, Weaver suggested that Young and others in NCSW participate in HUD's Consultation on Urban Development and Social Welfare. He invited Young to designate persons from his group to consult with HUD representatives and offer their expertise on social welfare matters. Their involvement with the Consultation proved useful and seemingly presaged "a closer working relationship between HUD and the social welfare field."[49]

Although Weaver eschewed any financial ties with Young's organization, he permitted him to develop valuable contacts for NCSW within HUD. At the Consultation, for example, Young met Leonard Duhl, a special assistant to Weaver. He extended two significant invitations to Duhl, both of which the HUD official accepted. Duhl consented to serve on the U.S. Committee of the International Conference on Social Welfare, and he agreed to address Young's 1967 Dallas meeting on "Humanizing the City." He told Duhl that he was eminently qualified to address "Mental Health Aspects of Urbanization." Moreover, Young invited guidance on methods to produce more humane cities. Although Duhl preferred to speak on "The Shame of the Cities," Young had been successful in focusing his organization on urban issues and developing institutional settings in which the expertise of his members could be shared.[50]

His ultimate impact on the National Conference on Social Welfare, however, seemed mixed. While the organization benefited from Young's prominence and national influence, black members, especially those in the League, judged the group harshly. After Young relinquished the presidency, the League continued to send a program representative to the annual forum. In 1970 one League official noted that black participants "found the experience lacked meaning for them." Unfocused discussions, seeming mistreatment of the NCSW's Black Caucus and the National Welfare Rights Organization, and the use of the forum to maintain the status quo left blacks disappointed. Even some League personnel shunned involvement with the organization. Young's subordinate told him that if the NCSW was to continue, it should address relevant issues and become a force for "meaningful change."[51]

Young had similar experiences with the National Association of Social Workers. Like the NCSW, the NASW benefited from Young's national prominence. Predictably, when he assumed the presidency in 1969, congratulations poured in from influential institutions, including the White House.[52] At the same time, his presidency did not prevent disenchantment among black members who wanted influence in the association and attention drawn to inner-city concerns.

Those who hoped that Young's leadership would revive the NASW had their expectations fulfilled. One longtime participant had denigrated the group as "a sick, institutionalized organization in the terminal stages of development." Moreover, it "refused to address itself to the real world."[53] Many viewed Young's leadership as an antidote to these ills. Members counting on his establishment contacts to help resuscitate the group must have been greatly impressed. Immediately, he asked his friend Roger Wilkins, a program officer at the Ford Foundation, to aid in getting a $25,000 grant for this impecunious 50,000-member organization. Later, he invited Mitchell Sviridoff, a Ford Foundation vice president, to participate in a crucial NASW board of directors conference. Wilkins, who came in his place, won Young's praise for the key ideas he presented. He also solicited cooperation from HEW Secretary Elliott Richardson and his predecessor, John Gardner.[54]

Young succeeded in orienting the NASW toward numerous issues germane to ghetto residents. Police brutality, for example, became a concern for urban blacks. The NASW spoke out strongly against such practices and communicated this stand to its chapters. The president of the Philadelphia affiliate congratulated Young for a NASW statement that denounced police harassment aimed at the militant Black Panthers. This chapter then formed a committee to focus on police behavior as it affected the rights of minority groups. When Congress in 1970 debated the infamous D.C. Crime Bill, whose provisions included pretrial detention, no-knock entries, expanded wiretapping, and other controversial procedures, the Washington chapter rose to oppose it. A chapter official thanked Young for putting the issue before the NASW executive board to inaugurate action of its own.[55]

Forging relationships with other organizations interested in urban affairs was another way that Young fitted the NASW to address matters relevant to the nation's cities. For example, he urged the American Bar Association to endorse a statement by the National Conference of Lawyers and Social Workers on "The Urban Crisis: Roles of the Lawyer and Social Worker." Young had gotten NSAW approval and now wanted to attract greater ABA involvement in pressing urban issues. Also, he bolstered cooperative endeavors among the National Welfare Rights Organization, the NUL, and the NASW. The three groups appeared together on the *Today Show* to oppose a family assistance plan that the Nixon administration advanced. Heated but productive meetings also occurred between the NASW and NWRRO about possible contributions to various projects that the welfare rights group initiated.[56]

Despite Young's efforts, fellow blacks in the National Conference on Social Welfare and the National Association of Social Workers demanded that these organizations "repudiate the current welfare system which serves as a tool for oppression of black people as well as the social workers providing services." At a NASW meeting in April 1968 in Washington, blacks formed the National Association of Black Catalysts. A month later in San Francisco at the National Conference on Social Welfare, the Catalysts met with others and formed the National Association of Black Social Workers (NABSW). The new group challenged the National Conference on Social Welfare to grant membership to the National Welfare Rights Organization, denounced federal officials who supported laws that were racist, declared war on black AFDC mothers and their children, and requested greater involvement of black professionals on committees that addressed the needs of inner-city communities.[57]

Again, Young occupied the familiar middle ground. Some whites in the

NASW could fathom neither the discontent which the NABSW expressed nor the remedies it offered to correct the oversight of racial issues. One Illinois member disagreed with efforts to guarantee black representation at a delegate assembly. "I have always regarded NASW as a professional organization," she wrote, "and I cannot accept the implication that there are professional issues peculiar to black members which cannot be expressed by or negotiated by white members."[58] Although Young took account of such views, he validated the concerns of the NABSW. At the San Francisco meeting of the National Conference on Social Welfare, Young brought in a protesting group of black social workers to discuss their manifesto. He also endorsed the recommendation of the Black Caucus to designate racism as a priority item for the NASW. "Our major problem," he noted, "is to get sufficient funds . . . to make this resolution more than a statement of intent."[59]

With varying degrees of effectiveness, Young reoriented the National Urban League, the National Conference on Social Welfare, and the National Association of Social Workers toward greater relevance to the urgent needs of the nation's cities. Although militant elements in all three organizations challenged his caution and racial diplomacy, Young ultimately understood that blacks in inner cities and within the social work professions wished to be involved in identifying pressing urban issues and in fashioning solutions to them. So he proposed initiatives, mobilized resources, and developed programs to enable these groups to improve the urban environment for blacks and the poor.

10

Corporate Philanthropy and Civil Rights

During the 1960s Whitney M. Young Jr. drew from major corporations and foundations unprecedented financial support for black Americans. An atmosphere of urgency surrounding the civil rights movement surely played a pivotal role in opening corporation and foundation coffers, and the contacts that Young cultivated and the arguments he advanced for aiding the civil rights cause persuaded wealthy benefactors to fund the black freedom struggle.

When Young became executive director of the National Urban League in 1961, he inherited numerous corporate and philanthropic contributors from his predecessor, Lester Granger.[1] He increased donations from regular backers, and he solicited monies from previously untapped business and foundation sources. Grants to the National Urban League during Granger's tenure resulted from his gentle but persistent appeals to help blacks break social and economic barriers. Conversely, philanthropy for the League during the Young era occurred because blacks demanded massive programs to improve their status in American society. These circumstances emboldened Young to request and reach levels of funding that Granger may have considered unattainable.

The corporate and foundation officials from whom he solicited contributions generally liked Young and considered him a fellow bon vivant.[2] None of the other national civil rights leaders moved with such ease among the financial elite, and none mastered the rituals and etiquette of upper-class social and economic circles as effectively as Young. Consequently, the League leader gained unprecedented access to influential whites whom he vigorously pressed to release funds for an increasingly restive black population. Close friendships with Donald Kendall of Pepsico and Joseph Cullman III of Philip Morris also enhanced Young's entry into the corporate elite. For Young, a cocktail party at a Rockefeller residence or a luncheon at a downtown private club were comfortable opportunities to explain the urgency of the black struggle and to secure monies to bring the racially disadvantaged into the American mainstream.

Although Young thoroughly enjoyed these elite social interactions, grassroots activism kept him focused on movement goals. A decade earlier in Omaha, Young, as head of the League affiliate, positioned himself as both an activist and a mediator. In the latter role he sought out the middle ground to make himself the preferred negotiator when recalcitrant employers eschewed talks with more militant protesters. Young applied that successful tactic to his national dealings with corporate and foundation officials.

Young was an integrationist. He believed that the exclusion of blacks from mainstream institutions was their essential disadvantage. If legalized segregation ended and other racial barriers actually fell, then blacks could become productive citizens and consumers. He stressed neither the distinctiveness of the black experience nor the need for separate black communities when he sought improvements for this racial minority. Rather, he described blacks as just like other Americans with the same potential and aspirations. If only private resources would be mobilized to obliterate the ghettos and give blacks equal opportunities for education, employment, and housing, then the crippling legacies of slavery and segregation would disappear. Even as he appropriated the rhetoric of Black Power, he defined it in pluralist terms with integration as its ultimate objective.

Several reasons account for Young's success in gaining establishment financing. The development of national support for the civil rights cause compelled donors to take note of the growing influence of black protests. Sometimes subtly and at other times overtly, Young shrewdly observed that powerful whites would have to negotiate with black leaders. Either they would deal with leaders with integrationist views and establishment ties like the head of the National Urban League or they would arbitrate matters with the moralistic Martin Luther King Jr., unmanageable SNCC spokespersons, or black nationalist Malcolm X. Clearly, Young understood the establishment mind much better than other black leaders and believed that he could function as a better broker between philanthropic whites and grassroots blacks. Moreover, most of the major civil rights organizations were geared toward protest activities, grassroots organizing and litigation. Only the National Urban League had the experience, personnel, and structure to handle programs aimed at the social and economic improvement of the black population. So, as the marches, demonstrations, and riots dramatized these issues, Young convinced white benefactors that his organization was peculiarly and singularly suited to address these matters. Because donors found that his integrationist perspectives matched theirs, Young was able to draw large and unprecedented contributions to the National Urban League.

Once again Young had staked out a middle ground that was difficult to maintain. It was very important that he functioned as a broker for blacks to the nation's philanthropic elite. To become successful in that role, Young had to win the trust of some of American society's most influential persons and to be liked by these keepers of corporate and foundation coffers. That Young enjoyed these interactions is beyond question. At the same time he took his role as a mediator quite seriously, and he made no attempt to minimize or trivialize the seriousness of black discontent or the depth of black anger. Young assumed that blacks understood that he would represent their interests honestly and effectively, and all of the evidence suggests that he did. Sometimes, he failed to get ratification of his efforts from black constituencies beyond the League. His occasional oversight in this area allowed some militant and moderate blacks to dub him inaccurately as "Whitey" Young. His rubbing shoulders with Henry Ford II or David Rockefeller convinced some that he had "sold out" to the establishment. That unhappy perception gained some adherents as Young's fruitful work as a broker became wrongly characterized in pejorative terms.

Young's influence extended to institutions and issues in civil rights, urban affairs, and social welfare, but his most notable success came in corporate and foundation philanthropy. Two factors, however, limited his leverage with powerful whites in this field. First, these benefactors, though urgently responding to Young and the aggrieved black population, determined what initiatives would be funded and defined the parameters within which his leadership would be exercised. Second, Young naively believed that his access to these important institutions put him in line for a significant role or post in this upper stratum of American society. In both areas Young overrated his influence and ultimately discovered that blacks, whether they dealt in militant grassroots protest or in brokering their interests with the white establishment, possessed too little power to change their social and economic condition.

Young's introduction to the nation's corporate leaders came mainly through the National Urban League. He became acquainted with those who already contributed to the organization, and he met other executives through these original donors. Young also used various professional and social gatherings to educate potential benefactors about the League. Moreover, he invited

their participation on the boards of either the national body or a local affiliate. How Young came to know James Linen of Time-Life was illustrative.

When Young met Linen, the latter served as president of Time, Inc., a
post which he assumed in 1960. Linen had been the publisher of Time since
1945, a board member since 1959, and chairman of the executive committee
in 1969. Long active in various charitable organizations, the two men crossed
paths at meetings of the United Community Funds and Councils of America,
which Linen headed. As an agency which funded both the National Urban
League and its affiliates, Young made a special effort to get acquainted with
Linen.

Linen greatly admired Young. Moreover, he endorsed the League's emphasis upon employment, education, and community development as the
best means to improve the condition of blacks. As their friendship developed,
Linen played a pivotal role in introducing Young to other corporate leaders.
Annually, Time sponsored trips for leading business executives to important
international locations. In 1966 the Time-News tour went to Eastern Europe. Linen included Young on this junket.

The Time president put Young before a captive corporate audience.
They included chairmen of the board and presidents of such firms as Eli Lilly,
Honeywell, Armco Steel, Gillette Safety Razor, North American Aviation,
Caterpillar Tractor, and Pan American World Airways. On the plane Linen
deliberately seated Young next to Henry Ford II. Young was challenged to
convert Ford's disinterest in race relations to active advocacy and financial
support. Although the rhetorical sparring between Young and Ford produced
no agreement about the direction that the black struggle should take, it convinced the auto executive that the League deserved his personal backing. Ford
started with a $100,000 donation to the National Urban League.[3]

Upon his return from Eastern Europe, Young wrote to the business
executives whom he had accompanied on the trip. Several had never given
money to the National Urban League. What he wrote to Robert S. Oelman,
chairman of the board of the National Cash Register Company, was typical.
Jocularly, Young declared, "This letter comes to fulfill a promise: to stop
discriminating against your company by denying it an opportunity to contribute to the work of the National Urban League." He assured Oelman that
his firm's financial neglect of the League did not necessarily mean "a lack of
concern and respect for responsible leadership in the important field of civil
rights." Nonetheless, Young expected him to donate to the League and to
make "the most liberal contribution possible." With the letter Young enclosed various reports on League activities, which would help Oelman "un-

derstand the constructive role that we are playing in our effort to channel the understandable impatience of Negro citizens into productive, constructive activity, rather than permitting desperation and hopelessness to be reflected in disruptive violence." Young was giving the business community an opportunity to support the League. Similar correspondence went to Eugene S. Beesley of Eli Lilly, James H. Binger of Honeywell, William Blackie of Caterpillar Tractor, C. William Verity Jr. of Armco Steel, and others.[4]

With Linen's assistance Young was introduced to leading corporate executives. Moreover, in 1966, after he participated in President Johnson's Planning Council for the Civil Rights Conference, Linen addressed the League's commerce and industry meeting in Philadelphia. In 1968 he became president of the National Urban League. Linen's speeches across the nation gave credibility in corporate circles to Young and the League. Moreover, the perspectives and programs that Linen promoted suggested collaboration between him and Young. Linen continually stressed that corporations could not sit on the sidelines without offering solutions and substantive assistance in providing employment and job training to the disadvantaged. Both he and Young borrowed rhetoric from grassroots blacks and used it to emphasize the urgency of the racial crisis. For example, Linen lauded Black Power because "only black political power, black economic power, black social power and black educational power can insure progress toward a truer democracy." Corporate leaders, he contended, had special responsibilities. "It is clear that unless top management makes a full and complete commitment to the policy and practice of equal job opportunity, nothing much will happen." Young often made similar comments. Coming from Linen, these sentiments received a serious hearing from the nation's corporate elite.[5]

In speeches to business groups, Young stressed that corporate involvement would make the critical difference in resolving the nation's racial crisis. The observation that business executives should play a pivotal role was to some quite flattering and challenging. Others were convinced by Young's forceful arguments about how selfish corporate aims gave businesses an important stake in a well-trained and gainfully employed black population. He drew business backers because he articulated the needs and aspirations of blacks in ways that coincided with corporate interests. Moreover, the militancy of the civil rights movement and widespread ghetto rebellions caused corporate leaders to take notice of the peculiar and persistent problems of the black population. From their perspective only the National Urban League had in place an infrastructure and initiatives that allowed business executives to impact pressing racial issues.

In a 1968 speech to the American Iron and Steel Institute, Young reminded his listeners of a poignant point in the Kerner Commission report.
"White society is deeply implicated in the ghetto. White institutions created
it, white institutions maintain it, and white society condones it. . . . No one
institution in America is better equipped to exercise effective leadership and
turn America around than the business community." He told them that they
were "status symbols, the role models, the community leaders, the image
makers." Consequently, "You can't accept the plaudits for achievement without, at the same time, accepting responsibilities in those areas in which this
nation has failed." He blasted the iron and steel industry for its dismal record
in equal employment opportunity. The industry had a vested interest in el-
evating the black population because "if you ignore the crisis, the slums and
ghettos of this land will siphon off more and more of your profits. The erod-
ing tax base of the American city [will place] a larger and larger burden on the
business community."[6]

At the convention of the American Bankers Association Young told his
audience, "The bank has a greater stake in the promotion of a stable and
harmonious community than any other institution. . . . You as bankers have
the responsibility to lead the way in making the Negro citizen a producer of
goods and a consumer of products rather than a producer of violence and a
consumer of taxes. You have the choice of whether to spend monies on programs of apprenticeship training and rehabilitation or on programs of crime
and welfare." Young audaciously noted that in hiring blacks "particularly in
the managerial and policy making levels, banks have a long way to go. You
must not be afraid to use your imagination and to run some risks to raise
these figures." With federal pressure for the employment of blacks and dis-
comfort from recent urban rioting, the American Bankers Association welcomed Young's comments. A bankers' blue ribbon committee on urban problems was established. Plans commenced to work with government and private
agencies to help solve inner-city ills. Charles Walker, executive vice president
of the ABA, told Young, "We would hope to concentrate on . . . construction
loans in slum areas, and loans to small businesses in the ghetto." He added
that Young's appearance "made it a lot easier for us to get more banks active
in solving these problems."[7]

Similar reactions came from other business executives who heard Young
speak. The president of the Michigan State Chamber of Commerce told him,
"In all my years of experience in providing some leadership in the civil rights
area, I have never experienced a deeper impact that anyone has made on a
group than you did. . . . We are going to hold a series of meetings with our

industrial leaders to set up action programs to be certain that they become more active, by making special effort[s] for employment of minority workers." An officer in the Associated Merchandising Corporation wrote, "Your talk had great impact on our Directors. A great part of that impact . . . resulted from the number of positive programs which you enumerated for meeting the problems which face us." The executive director of the National Association of Mutual Savings Banks wrote to Young and observed, "I have never heard an address that had greater impact on [an] audience." He added that Young was correct. "Savings banks do have the capability to help black people, and this capability has not been applied to any where near the extent it should." The businessman concluded that Young's speech had given him "a genuine determination to do away with the indifference and insensitivity of the past, in order . . . to help black people." In agreement with the League leader, the banker declared that there was no problem in this nation more urgent.[8] Thus, Young's frank analysis of the issues facing the black population and how businesses could help in solving them won him applause from corporate audiences.

At the same time Young did not allow his commentaries to pull him toward positions that potential business benefactors deemed too "radical." Here again, he sought a middle ground that maintained his integrity as a black leader but preserved his credibility with corporate supporters. In 1968 Young traveled to Monticello, Mississippi, to participate in the opening of new facilities of the St. Regis Paper Company. He also spoke to supporters of the newly launched Jackson, Mississippi, Urban League. Since the Black Power ideology now dominated national discourse about race relations, Young focused his comments on this subject. Although many Black Power advocates emphasized separatism and sometimes racial chauvinism, the League leader vowed "to channel Black Power efforts into a constructive force." He wanted to "eliminate feelings of ill will and separatism." He added, "Black racism as opposed to white racism is a reaction to lynchings, discrimination, and the like, and we must be careful not to confuse the two. . . . If you truly believe in equality, however, you must realize that black people have the same right to a few crackpots as white people. It is rather strange, in fact, that there are not more black crackpots than there are. You hear very few instances of a gang of black men staging a lynching."[9] Young dismissed as racists and crackpots numerous Black Power advocates whose articulation of racial pride aroused in whites the specter of violence and racial militancy. Young wanted to dissociate himself and the League from such views. In that effort he met with some success among his business backers.

Young had expressed similar sentiments in Mississippi in 1966. At that time James Meredith, whose efforts in 1962 opened the University of Mississippi to black students, staged a one-man march against fear. After he was shot, numerous black leaders including Young agreed to finish the Meredith march. At a rally in LeFlore County, Mississippi, SNCC spokesman Stokely Carmichael introduced *Black Power* into the lexicon of the black struggle. Immediately, Young denounced the term and the separatist and violent connotations to which it referred. Business executives to whom Young sent a report applauded him for his responsible leadership. The vice president of the F&M Schaefer Brewing Company was so impressed with Young's statement "that I circulated it among my colleagues who were equally impressed." The vice president for industrial relations at the Garrett Corporation was encouraged "to know that America has a man like you, and an organization like 'our' Urban League to help us 'keep our heads' in troubled times." The senior vice president at the Newark-based Prudential Insurance Company understood Young's posture the best. To Young he wrote, "The civil rights movement . . . is taking a most unfortunate direction. The voices of sanity and wisdom are in danger of being drowned out by radicals preaching a doctrine that is going to do a lot of harm before it's discredited. This couldn't come at a worse time for me. I'm trying to get a group of Newark's business leaders organized to work on Newark's social problems, and this present trend, if it continues, isn't going to help any." He added that "the extremism that threatens to alienate so many people" had to be moderated. "If the negroes and whites get polarized into two hostile camps, we're in for serious trouble, and our efforts for real integration will be seriously set back."[10] Young wanted to retain support from corporate leaders like the Prudential executive, and clearly he had to eschew Black Power in order to do it.

Nonetheless, while he maintained business backing, Young found that this task was difficult. In 1968 the Shenango Valley Urban League, based in the Sharon-Farrell area of western Pennsylvania, sought support from the Westinghouse Electric Corporation. The vice president and general manager of the Sharon facility expressed skepticism about the League and refused sponsorship "without knowing more about it." A newspaper article about Young's speech at the convention of CORE simplistically noted that he espoused Black Power. In a clear reference to the League's "New Thrust," the article observed that Young's group was moving toward organizing blacks for political and social activity. The Westinghouse official wanted the executive director of the local United Fund to know that since "Mr. Young has embraced the concept of Black Power . . . I then consider the application of any United Fund money to foster that not only unwarranted but as undesirable." To eliminate the confusion Young forwarded a speech he gave in Denver to the United Community Funds and Councils of America. In it he said, "All Black Power is really saying is 'I want to participate in those decisions which affect the destiny of my family and my community.'" He explained that the aim of "New Thrust" was to facilitate communication between inner-city residents and "the man downtown."[11] Young's benign interpretation of Black Power made his adoption of the term palatable to the League's corporate benefactors and allowed for continued advocacy of business support of black aspirations.

Young used numerous strategies to solicit funds from major corporations. Interaction with executives at various civic and social gatherings, contacts with them at sites where he delivered speeches, and cultivation luncheons gave Young many opportunities to persuade potential contributors to donate money to the National Urban League. His relationship with Charles E. Spahr, president of Standard Oil of Ohio, for example, derived from their participation in the federally sponsored Plans for Progress, an initiative to encourage minority hiring. Young used the occasion to tell Spahr about the importance of business support for the League. Without corporate backing, he said, "We could not have developed the Skills Bank, which has been so helpful to corporations seeking non-white personnel." Although Spahr's company aided the Cleveland Urban League through its local United Fund donations, Young urged him also to consider the National Urban League and its constituency of 21 million blacks.[12] Young had also developed ties with Standard Oil of New Jersey. That firm's annual gift doubled from $25,000 in 1963 to $50,000 in 1966. He deepened that company's commitment to the League through his relationship with George M. Buckingham, executive secretary of Standard Oil's Contributions Committee, and M.M. Brisco, the company vice president. One executive noted that the League's increased funding from Standard Oil resulted from Young's personal contact with Brisco.[13]

Young's speaking engagements also provided him access to various corporate leaders whom he lobbied for contributions to the League. His interaction with a group of important insurance executives was illustrative. He addressed a meeting of theirs in 1966. His host introduced him to a vice president of the Continental Insurance Company. Both men believed that Young should also meet the chairman and chief executive officer of Continental, J. Victor Herd. At this point, an executive with Metropolitan Life Insurance Company suggested that Gilbert Fitzhugh, the firm's board chairman, should bring Young and Herd together. Fitzhugh consented. He arranged for Young to lunch with Herd and the new president of Metropolitan, Charles A. Siegfried.

Whitney Young thanked Fitzhugh for broadening his ties to other top executives in the insurance industry.[14] Similar procedures brought Young to the attention of other corporate leaders, many of whom became key contributors to the National Urban League.

Drawing business executives to the League's Corporate Support Committee was another way for Young to strengthen his financial appeals. At various times during the 1960s committee members included J.L. Atwood, president of North American Aviation, Kendrick R. Wilson Jr., chairman and chief executive officer of the Avco Corporation, Edgar M. Bronfman, president of Joseph Seagram and Son, and Russell DeYoung, chairman and chief executive officer of Goodyear Tire and Rubber. The firms over which they presided donated in 1966, for example, sums that ranged between $7,500 and $12,000.[15]

Moreover, these business leaders lent their names to the League's fund-raising letters, and they sponsored and hosted social gatherings at which Young solicited financial support from their industry colleagues. Sometimes Young drew influential business executives with the hope that exposure to League programs would deepen their commitment to the organization. That was probably his expectation in 1966 when the president of the powerful Bank of America joined the Corporate Support Committee, although that firm's annual donation had been a paltry $100.[16]

Crucial to Young's fund-raising efforts were cultivation luncheons held in Pittsburgh, Cincinnati, San Francisco, Los Angeles, Akron, Atlanta, Detroit, and numerous other cities. Either Young or William R. Simms, the head of the League's Fund Department, contacted a key business executive in the designated city. That person would host a luncheon to which colleagues from other major companies in the area would be invited. In some instances, letters to invitees would be sent over the signature of the host, whose affiliation with the League gave the luncheon credibility. Henry Ford II played a pivotal role in 1969 in putting together a cultivation luncheon for Detroit. He sent invitations to a prestigious roster of corporate leaders including the chairs or presidents of American Motors, Chrysler, General Motors, S.S. Kresge, McLouth Steel, Bendix, Burroughs, and Detroit Edison. He told them that Young, James Linen, and William M. Batten, board chairman of JC Penney and national chairman of the League's 1968-1969 campaign, would be there for "an informal presentation of some major new directions they are mapping out for the League."[17]

In 1969 Simms laid the groundwork for the League's second cultivation luncheon in St. Louis. Because William Batten played an important role behind the scenes, "a very top level group" came to meet Whitney Young. Batten persuaded Maurice Chambers, the chairman of Interco, Inc., to host the occasion. Chambers's company was one of the big suppliers to JC Penney, Batten's firm. Chambers invited an impressive group of St. Louis's corporate elite. They included the top executives from Ralston Purina, Southwestern Bell, Falstaff Brewing, Monsanto, and other major companies. Simms told Young that Batten's contact with Chambers produced an audience that was "much more imposing than the group that we spoke to . . . a couple of years ago."[188]

Young had high hopes for the League's Atlanta gathering. Coca-Cola seemed to be the linchpin in Young's fund-raising in the South. A relationship with J. Paul Austin, president of Coca-Cola, proved critical. He started to court Austin in 1968 when they met at an Equal Opportunity Day dinner sponsored by the Atlanta Urban League. A few months later Austin hosted a cultivation luncheon for the National Urban League. Although Coca-Cola had been a regular League contributor, Simms believed that the company "should be giving us more." He hoped that this involvement would nudge Austin to increase Coca-Cola's donations. Simms also wanted his boss to know about the Lette Pate Evans Foundation and the Emily and Ernest Woodruff Foundation, both of which grew out of fortunes made with the Coca-Cola Company. He thought that Young and James Linen "should seek Mr. Austin's advice on the best approach to these foundations and who the best person might be." Austin also agreed to solicit contributions from the excellent group of luncheon invitees.[19]

Young attached great importance to corporate solicitations. Throughout the 1960s contributions from major firms constituted a lion's share of League income. His persistence in raising money among business executives caused corporate donations to rise steadily. When Young became executive director of the national organization in 1961, business gave $70,000 to the League. Corporate funding doubled to $153,000 in 1962 and reached $1,500,000 in 1969.[20]

Corporate Donations to the National Urban League, 1961-1969

1961	$ 70,000	1965	$ 848,000
1962	$ 153,000	1966	$ 888,000
1963	$ 527,000	1968	$1,200,000
1964	$ 657,000	1969	$1,500,000

Nonetheless, these seemingly stunning amounts left Young dissatisfied. Although major corporations were making unprecedented financial commitments to aid the elevation of the black population, Young extended to them polite but restrained applause. Only seven companies in 1965, for example, contributed between $25,000 and $55,000. These included the Bell Systems, E.I. du Pont de Nemours, Ford, General Motors, IBM, Socony Mobil Oil, and Standard Oil of New Jersey. Another nineteen firms gave between $10,000 and $24,999, and thirty-two gave between $5,000 and $9,999. The other 119 corporations gave less than $5,000, with thirty-five giving less than $1,000.[21]

What irritated Young and Simms was the parsimony of some well-heeled companies. In discussing the League's Akron cultivation luncheon, for example, Simms reminded Young that $1,000 came from the General Tire Foundation and its parent company, Aerojet General Corporation in California. That amount, the two agreed, was far too small. When American Can cut its $5,000 donation in 1968 to $1,000, Young returned the check. Also, in 1968 Crown Zellerbach gave the League only $1,500, a small increase from an earlier contribution of $1,000. "When other companies recognized our increased needs," observed Simms, "this company did not."[22]

Far worse than parsimony was the failure to give at all. In 1968, for example, Young went to Chicago to address the American Paper Institute–Fibre Box Association Employee Relations Conference. This national group drew to its meeting 250 industrial relations officers from various pulp, paper, paperboard, and corrugated box companies. Although six important firms such as Scott Paper and St. Regis Paper regularly contributed, Young wanted to persuade another half dozen of the largest corporations to donate, including International Paper, Weyerhaeuser, and Kimberly Clark. He continued this campaign in 1969 in a speech to the Fibre Box Association where he impressed Charles S. Wolf of York Container Company with his "impassionate tone" and "good sense" about the need for business leaders to "involve themselves more in the problem of the races."[23]

Young's staff kept a careful tally on League donations by industries and cities. For example, he told the board chairman of the Dallas-based Dresser Industries that the NUL received very few contributions from the farm and construction machinery business. Moreover, other corporations in this Texas metropolis failed to follow Dresser in backing the League. Young urged the board chairman of the Hagger Company to consider a contribution and "join the Honor Roll of forward-looking companies that are supporting this work." He informed the head of Ling-Temco-Vought that the League already had nine benefactors from the electronics industry, and he urged this Dallas firm to become the tenth. On the other hand, Young was pleased that in 1969 Cincinnati yielded to the League a respectable $22,250 in contributions from Kroger, Federated Department Stores, Baldwin Piano and Organ, Western and Southern Life Insurance, and Procter and Gamble. Nonetheless, five contributing companies were too few for a city the size of Cincinnati. Young and Simms wanted to add numerous other corporations to its list of donors and increase support by at least $15,000.[24]

Young was correct in expecting greater support from the nation's Fortune 500. Whenever he encountered a company that either donated nothing or allowed a token contribution to be noted next to its corporate name, he loudly denounced it as short-sighted stinginess toward the black struggle. But even he understood that annual corporate gifts amounting to $1,000,000 were unprecedented. Such support argued for viewing the glass as half full rather than half empty.

Moreover, Young brought the civil rights movement into corporate boardrooms and caused executives to understand that their attitude toward the black struggle truly mattered. By ignoring it, they would intensify the problems. By engaging issues relevant to blacks, they had a chance to effect significant social and economic change. He provided business leaders with programs and an organization through which the black population could be helped. Young articulated issues in ways that conveyed the depth of black unrest and at the same time drew support from corporate executives. So impressive were his skills that the president of Standard Oil of Ohio offered Young a position in the company.[25]

Young's ability to win grants from foundations proved more successful than his solicitations from corporations. He developed remunerative relationships for the National Urban League with the Rockefeller philanthropies, the Ford Foundation, the Alfred P. Sloan Foundation, and the Carnegie Corporation of New York. Although smaller in size and resources, the Taconic Foundation also played a pivotal role. Special programs gained financial support from such sundry sources as the Richard King Mellon, Field, and Stern Foundations. These and other philanthropies contributed $62,000 to the National Urban League in 1961 and $707,000 in 1966. Various foundations donated $2,900,000 in 1969, nearly twice as much as corporate contributions during that year.[26]

Much of Young's success with foundation funding lay with the special ties between the League and the Rockefeller philanthropies. Although ongoing relationships with these important foundations predated Young, he ex-

tended them and drew to the League unprecedented financial support. Between 1941 and 1969 the Rockefeller Brothers Fund gave the NUL $1,518,184.
Only $73,850 came to the organization between 1941 and 1961. Approxi-
mately $1,444,334 flowed into League coffers from 1961 through 1969.[27]

A similarly productive relationship occurred with the Rockefeller Foundation. For example, between 1964 and 1971 the League received $1,850,000
for its Leadership Development Program and for New Thrust. Additional
support from the philanthropy benefited another program for black veterans
in 1969 in the amount of $500,000. The National Urban League received at
least $3,794,334 from the Rockefeller Brothers Fund and the Rockefeller
Foundation during the 1960s. While Young headed the National Urban
League, these two philanthropies gave more than any other foundation.[28]

Lindsley F. Kimball, who sponsored Young's candidacy to head the
National Urban League, remained an important liaison with the Rockefeller
Foundation. He served as a trustee of the foundation from 1947 through
1971 and its treasurer from 1959 through 1965. Kimball became a League
trustee in 1959 and its president in 1964. Both terms ended in 1968.[29]

At the same time Young's relationship with the Rockefeller Foundation
extended further. John D. Rockefeller III informed the League leader in 1968
that he had been elected to the Rockefeller Foundation board of trustees. In
urging Young's acceptance, Rockefeller added, "It would mean much to me."
He assured Young that "membership on the Board does not affect the financial relationship of the Trustee's institution with the Foundation." Whenever
the League presented a request, Young would simply excuse himself from that
part of the meeting. Surely, he was glad to have this new relationship with the
Foundation.[30]

The Rockefeller philanthropies made a major financial commitment to
the National Urban League. Moreover, with Young at the helm, it seemed
that the organization finally had a leader who acted in sync with the burgeoning civil rights movement. Nonetheless, Kimball took seriously the dual role
of NUL president and liaison with the Rockefeller philanthropies. In 1964
Young requested that the Rockefeller Foundation fund a leadership development program. At that point, Young, who sometimes disregarded bureaucratic procedures and unilaterally advanced League initiatives, met resistance
from Kimball.

Leland C. De Vinney, deputy director in the humanities and social
sciences at the Rockefeller Foundation, telephoned Kimball to determine
whether he knew about Young's submission of a leadership development proposal. Kimball noted that he had very limited information and thus was not

prepared to recommend it. According to De Vinney, Kimball criticized Young for becoming "foundation happy" and submitting large proposals to Ford, Carnegie, and Rockefeller without seeking approval from his own board or from Kimball. De Vinney learned that Kimball considered himself head of the national organization and Whitney Young merely head of the staff. Not surprisingly, De Vinney concluded that action would not proceed on a League proposal that its president opposed. Kimball replied that he was not opposing it. Rather, he expected to be consulted and allowed to approve Young's proposals.[31]

De Vinney contacted J. George Harrar, president of the Rockefeller Foundation, and he agreed that Kimball's reservations mandated a postponement. Young, who heard from both De Vinney and Kimball, learned that the foundation awaited a resolution of this bureaucratic matter before the grant request could be reconsidered. De Vinney wanted the assurance that the responsible officials of the National Urban League were in agreement. Young said that he understood, and he promised to "move promptly to clear up any internal confusion." That he did. Within days Kimball told De Vinney, "Whitney Young has been duly authorized to act for the League in this instance and I believe plans to resubmit the application. . . . It certainly has my blessing." The Rockefeller Foundation appropriated $450,000 to support the League initiative.[32]

This power play demonstrated that Young's importance as a black leader, while considerable, was nonetheless circumscribed. He proposed nothing radical in the leadership development program. Other than strengthening some of the specifics, Kimball asked for no major changes. In fact, he noted that the resubmitted proposal was substantially the same. What he wanted Young to know was that his access to the Rockefeller philanthropies depended on his assent.[33]

This incident probably explained why Young carefully cultivated and sustained these beneficial ties with the League's principal benefactors. In 1969, for example, Young denounced James Forman when the latter sharply criticized the Rockefeller family. Young knew the former spokesman for SNCC when Forman represented the organization on the Council for United Civil Rights Leadership (CUCRL). He was now involved with the Black Economic Development Conference, a group which demanded reparations for slavery and segregation. Toward this end Forman interrupted services at Riverside Church in New York City and declared to surprised worshippers that they bore responsibility for compensating blacks for their racial oppression. This congregation, an ecumenical venture which the Rockefellers started and supported, seemed to Forman an appropriate site to tell white churches what they owed to blacks. An irritated Young told John D. Rockefeller III, "Any time you want me to publicly explain to James Forman and his ilk . . . that the Rockefeller Family has in fact given to black people as much, if not more, than they are now asking, I am ready to do so." To Young the Rockefellers' contributions to the League surely qualified him to make such a declaration. Despite the constraints that foundation officials imposed upon him, Young defended these benefactors to seemingly ungrateful or uninformed black activists.[34] That Young positioned himself as sympathetic to Rockefeller perspectives certainly helped whenever the League required emergency donations. In 1970, for example, the Rockefeller Brothers Fund contributed $25,000 to the League during a financial crisis. Young told Dana Creel, the head of the Fund, and his staff, "Your confidence . . . lends much encouragement to me."[35]

The Rockefeller philanthropies also preferred Young's leadership for reasons similar to those of major corporations. He advocated ordered social change of the sort which allowed significant input from the foundations. Leland C. De Vinney, for example, proved to be an influential proponent of the League within the Rockefeller Foundation. Despite Young's bureaucratic blunder with Kimball over the League's chain of command, De Vinney believed that the League was peculiarly fitted to play a moderating role in the civil rights movement. That could be accomplished only with backing from the Rockefeller Foundation. De Vinney specifically referred to the leadership development proposal, which aimed "to identify and provide first rate education for talented Negro youth" so as "to build up intelligent and responsible Negro leadership."[36]

Another example was the Rockefeller Brothers' endorsement of the National Skills Bank. With $100,000 in grants in 1963 and 1964 and $50,000 in 1965, the Fund supported this practical program, which matched qualified blacks with available employment opportunities. In 1965 fifty-seven of the League's seventy-two affiliates participated with a record 5,300 placements. Kimball thought that the Fund had "bought the best eleemosynary bargain in the Skills Bank—no eyewash, good idea, capably carried out, and our money's worth in human betterment."[37]

While deference to officials in the Rockefeller philanthropies sometimes characterized Young's conduct, he tried the same methods that occasionally worked with corporate executives. Citing the militancy of other black leaders, Young appeared to coerce some foundation support for League proposals. In a 1964 proposal to the Rockefeller Foundation Young outlined an

Urban League fellowship program to improve staff training and performance. Additionally, Young wanted to finance the schooling of selected social work students to prepare them for careers with the League. One official did not want the Rockefeller Foundation to undertake the staffing of Young's organization. Apparently, Young contended that "beefing up" the League was "the only alternative to increased dominance of extremists in the civil rights conflict." Young's conclusion was soundly rejected. Moreover, the official noted in Young's rhetoric "a kind of threat implicit (and nearly explicit) in his presentation" which linked a failure to fund the project as tantamount to letting militants take over the black freedom struggle. Young's alleged ploy was characterized as "distasteful" and his proposal drew from the foundation "a gentle no"![38]

Although Young could claim much credit for the large sums he drew to the League from the Rockefeller philanthropies, other factors also accounted for his success. First, the League had been the recipient of Rockefeller generosity long before Young assumed national office. Second, he became the executive director because Kimball thought that he could revive the organization. Kimball instructed a sometimes impetuous Whitney Young on how to apply for foundation grants from the Rockefeller philanthropies.

A militant civil rights movement and a grassroots and seemingly hostile Black Power thrust alerted powerful white institutions to the depth of black discontent with discrimination and ghettoization. Officials in the Rockefeller charities supported proposals that stressed social and economic objectives in the hope that they would result in substantive racial progress. A well-equipped League, according to Rockefeller officials, seemed best suited to achieve such ends. As a result, Young had to say very little about the existence of a national racial crisis. Rather, the details of whatever proposal he advanced for funding became his primary emphasis in appealing for aid.

That Whitney Young bore Lindsley Kimball's imprimatur eased his entry into the Rockefeller philanthropies. This advantage was not applicable, however, to the Ford Foundation, the other important philanthropy with which Young had dealings. His initial encounters with the Ford Foundation did not produce any easy successes. Painstakingly, Young and his staff had to make their case for Ford funding.

Henry T. Heald, a civil engineer and former chancellor of New York University, served as president of the Ford Foundation from 1956 to 1966.[39] In October 1961 Lindsley Kimball reminded Heald that they had agreed to meet about a lifesaving operation for the National Urban League. Kimball wanted to include Young in a meeting with Heald and other Ford officials.

Young could be excluded if their need for candor required more privacy. Nonetheless, Heald received from Henry Steeger, then president of the National Urban League, a financial appeal for its 1962 program. Specifically, Steeger wanted funds to establish a Washington bureau "to provide our local affiliates with complete and current analyses of those federal programs which have a particular relevance to the needs and problems faced by Negro citizens." A potential Ford contribution would also "launch an effective action-oriented program of objective fact-finding and the use of such facts in constructive social change." Steeger called attention to proposals pertaining to the several areas in which the League was active including housing, health and welfare, youth guidance, and training and employment. "It is our sincere hope that funds can be provided for these programs," noted Steeger. These omnibus proposals, however, were not well received at Ford. The foundation "took the position," observed one staff member, "that we could not consider general support for them." Instead, Ford met with local and national League staff to "explore some specific program activities which would harmonize with our overall objectives in the Youth Development Program."[40]

The Ford Foundation solicited a League proposal on vocational guidance for black youth, and the League planned a youth program "to steer them toward realistic careers and employment and toward opening new opportunities." Six affiliates would share in a grant of $1.5 to $2 million over three years. The National Urban League would receive between 10 and 12 percent to administer the initiative. Young fashioned a proposal that reflected Ford preferences. For example, he was cognizant of foundation thinking concerning youth in public service jobs, apprenticeships, and preparation for middle-class leadership. Also, such consultants as Robert C. Weaver, then a federal housing official, and John Field of the President's Committee on Equal Employment Opportunities endorsed the capacity of the new National Urban League to implement this vocational program. Surprisingly, the Ford Foundation refused the grant.[41]

Henry Heald received a poignant letter from Young expressing his disappointment. He suggested that Winthrop Rockefeller, a board member of the National Urban League, arrange a conference with Heald on this matter. Ultimately, Young wanted Heald to allow a resubmission of the request so that Ford could give it favorable consideration. Heald, however, would not budge. He assured Young, "This is not something that my colleagues took lightly. A lot of time and attention were given to this proposal." Young could send additional information and meet about the matter if he wished. Heald acknowledged the importance of Winthrop Rockefeller in League affairs, but he pointedly told Young that a visit from him to Ford would have little significance in this case.[42]

Despite these disappointments, neither Kimball nor Young abandoned efforts to win Ford for the League. Subsequently, in 1965 there was funding for the League's business orientation program for black educators and the trade union occupations project. Moreover, Kimball met with Heald to solicit funds to help buy another headquarters for the League. Ford acquiesced with a $600,000 grant. As a result, Ford staff became better acquainted with the League and its national leader.

A memorandum that circulated within the Ford Foundation observed that the League, unlike other civil rights groups, had a singular capacity to deal with the social and economic issues confronting blacks. "It stands as the best example of a responsible organization with increasingly strong support throughout influential segments of the white community and excellent, up-to-date credentials in the Negro community," the memo stated. In the competition with more openly militant groups including the NAACP, CORE, and SNCC, "the League established anew its capacity to perform essential tasks in effecting social change." Because of the League's business and community chest funding, "its weapons therefore must be more subtle and professional than those of the civil rights organizations." To Young belonged much credit for ably leading the League. Ford officials who acknowledged that he was "an effective marcher when marching is called for" also liked his good sense in stating, "You can holler, protest, march, picket, demonstrate, but somebody must be able to sit in on the strategy conference and plot a course. There must be the strategists, the researchers and the professionals to carry out a program. That's our role." Ford staff liked these characteristics in a civil rights group and in its leader.[43]

Two major developments had occurred since Young's initial encounter with Henry Heald. First, the civil rights movement had gained widespread biracial support throughout the country and significant federal backing, especially from the White House. Also, as a major civil rights leader, Young made the League a visible and influential part of the movement coalition. Second, Ford officials in 1965, figuring that the League could be important "for access into the Negro community," wanted Whitney Young and the National Urban League to play this role. Moreover, the programmatic thrust of the League more easily fit Ford funding patterns, and less controversy would occur when foundation contributions poured into this business-backed organization.[44]

The impact of the civil rights movement on Ford officers is best seen in the growing influence of Paul N. Ylvisaker and Christopher F. Edley Sr. Ylvisaker, a Harvard Ph.D. and former professor, worked as assistant to the mayor of Philadelphia before he transferred to the Ford Foundation in 1955. He became the director of Ford's public affairs program. Already a racial liberal, Ylvisaker was greatly affected by the growing momentum of the civil rights movement, and he wanted the Ford Foundation to respond in some way. His hiring of Edley in 1963 derived in part from these sentiments.[45]

Edley and another staff member in the international affairs division were the first blacks to become program officers in the Ford Foundation. Prepared with a Harvard law degree, Edley served in Philadelphia as an assistant district attorney and as a federal counsel with the U.S. Commission of Civil Rights and the Federal Housing and Home Finance Agency. Once Ylvisaker hired him in his public affairs division, Edley shared his boss's zeal to change the Ford Foundation. A black Philadelphia pastor, the Reverend Leon H. Sullivan, asked for monies to launch vocational training centers for inner-city residents. When the proposal arrived on Edley's desk, it had already elicited negative comments from other program officials. Edley's persuasive rebuttal to his colleagues helped to get the grant for Sullivan's successful Opportunities Industrialization Centers (OIC).[46]

Ylvisaker and Edley brought this same altruism to the civil rights movement. Edley's first assignment was to write a report about whether Ford should do anything to help the various civil rights groups. Whitney Young and his National Urban League became his specific focus. He was particularly impressed with Young's leadership, noting that "a major criticism of the National Urban League has been its failure or inability to exercise central program direction." He credited Young with eliminating that problem.

In an intensive session Edley proposed two initiatives that he wanted Young to adopt for the League. First, Edley suggested an innovative way of strengthening the League infrastructure. He proposed that each division— education, housing, industrial relations, and others—have as its head a black who was the nation's foremost authority in that field. Young said, however, that he could not do it. Since League officials counted on promotion from within, such an initiative would undermine morale. Edley's second suggestion proposed the development of a nonprofit housing development corporation that Ford could help to fund through the League. Despite a prior approval from Edley's superiors, Young rejected the idea. Notwithstanding Young's negative responses, Edley remained committed to involving the Ford funds in League activities. In late 1965 he told Ylvisaker, "We must continue to give top priority to the substance of Urban League programming."[47]

Also, during this period other Ford officials grew impressed with the League and endorsed Young's leadership style. One officer said, "Young appears to hold his own effectively in the Wilkins-Farmer-King-Lewis circle." It was conceded that the League's popularity with corporate executives and conservative labor leaders occurred because it "looks safer than the alternatives." Young and his organization had to compete not only with other civil rights spokespersons and their groups but also with a younger generation of militants. They represented disillusioned inner-city blacks who recently rioted in Watts in Los Angeles and other ghetto communities. This Ford official liked the League because it was "increasingly professional in the way it does business." It resembled "those white community agencies with which any civic-minded businessman or labor leader has learned to work." Despite this visible white support, "the League is holding its own in the midst of the more militant groups." Consequently, "the Urban League is an organization that deserves our strong support." He added, "This support should take both the obvious financial form and the less obvious form of promoting individual leaders' growth" in the organization."[48]

When McGeorge Bundy succeeded Henry Heald in 1966, he inherited a foundation that already had important involvements with civil rights organizations. Bundy came to Ford with a distinguished background in academia and government. At Harvard University he was dean of the faculty of arts and sciences from 1953 through 1961. He then served as the president's special assistant for national security from 1961 through 1966.[49]

The year that Bundy assumed his duties at Ford was a critical year for the black freedom struggle. The civil rights movement with its focus on destroying legalized racial segregation with legislative and judicial remedies yielded to ghetto rebellions and the ugly social and economic inequities that they revealed. This shift in the black struggle challenged older establishment leaders and created angry, younger spokespersons who were cynical about the Lindsley Kimballs and McGeorge Bundys of the world. Whitney Young tried to stand in the breach. He believed that the League was well equipped to deal with the social and economic ills of inner cities. At the same time he had access to major foundations that could provide funding for such massive projects. Perhaps unwittingly Ylvisaker, Edley, and others had laid important groundwork for Young within the Ford Foundation. With extensive rioting in ghetto communities across the nation, Bundy wanted Ford to respond. Ironically, his predecessors had already prepared the way.[50]

Bundy announced a bold domestic initiative for the Ford Foundation on August 2, 1966. Speaking at a Philadelphia meeting of the National Ur-

ban League, he said, "Full equality for all American Negroes is now the most
urgent domestic concern of this country." The Ford Foundation, he observed,
would focus its funding in crucial efforts to improve the condition of blacks.
Bundy noted a "need for wider and stronger leadership, both among Negroes
and among whites." The nation needed white leaders squarely to face the
reality of racial issues while Negro leaders would be reinforced in their work
for "peaceful progress." He also wanted to make real the legal rights of blacks
"and all who are poor." Such talk of justice "calls for urgency, and priority,
and preference for what helps to end injustice." Moreover, he wanted the
Ford Foundation to be involved in that "special war on the special kind of
Negro poverty" that uniquely afflicted this segment of the population. In
keeping with his pledge to his League audience, Bundy received from his
board of trustees approval in December 1966 to allocate $4,270,000 "for
support of national organizations dedicated to the improvement of the status
of Negroes through positive action programs."[51]

The Ford Foundation pursued a multifaceted thrust into the nation's
black communities. The development of grassroots institutions, local leadership, and community rehabilitation like that in Brooklyn's Bedford Stuyvesant
Redevelopment Corporation became Ford's primary emphasis. The foundation also targeted its grants to legal groups who helped the disadvantaged.
The NAACP Legal Defense and Educational Fund, Inc., and the Lawyers' Committee on Civil Rights Under Law benefited from this initiative. Additionally, Ford officials supported national civil rights organizations and their leaders.
Hence, the NAACP, CORE, SCLC, and NUL received funding.[52]

McGeorge Bundy proved serious in his commitment to deeper Ford
involvement with civil rights groups. While all organizations were eligible for
Ford grants, foundation officials surely preferred some groups over others.
Consequently, the earliest deliberations about Ford funding resulted in "a
pecking order" that favored the NAACP and the NUL.[53]

Ford staff correctly contended that "the explosive 'Black Power' cry" in
1966 "effectively split the civil rights movement." While SNCC and CORE occupied one end of the spectrum, the NAACP, NUL, and to some extent SCLC
positioned themselves as less militant alternatives. This polarization caused
the black freedom struggle to lose "its former sense of direction" and to result
in Uncle Tom labels for the NAACP and the League. To the credit of these
organizations, believed the Ford staff, "they have not succumbed to pressures
for a recklessly militant posture." Although the foundation would not eschew
other groups, it was important to invest in a "centrist" leadership. Such support would encourage a "responsible, not conservative" direction for the black

freedom struggle. "Hold the center" was what Mitchell Sviridoff, the head of Ford's National Affairs Division, wished to do.[54]

The Ford Foundation also wanted to "invest" in Whitney Young. Bundy initially knew more about the NAACP. Once he had heard Walter White speak. He also became familiar with Roy Wilkins, whom he held in high regard. Upon meeting Young, however, Bundy came away very impressed. Whenever Wilkins came to the foundation offices, his staff would do the presentations. Young did his own presentations and often negotiated with Bundy for more funds. They dealt with each other with great ease, and Bundy apparently knew he was interacting with a peer! His respect for Young resulted in consideration of the League leader for the foundation's board of trustees. It was well known that Henry Ford "was very high on Young." Ultimately, Bundy abandoned the idea. First, Young was already on the board of the Rockefeller Foundation and was therefore unavailable to Ford. Second, some directors saw a conflict of interest as long as the League received Ford funds. That Bundy considered a Young nomination said much about his laudatory evaluation of the League leader.[55]

Sviridoff shared Bundy's high opinion of Young. Funding for the League, in Sviridoff's view, symbolized confidence in Young's leadership. He was seldom impressed with the League staff and their seemingly deficient presentations. According to Sviridoff, if League proposals had arrived at the foundation without the presence of Young as head of the organization they would not have been considered seriously. Young, while a centrist, was politically sophisticated and charismatic. Ford would be wise, according to Sviridoff, to uphold Young's leadership.[56]

In 1966, receptive Ford officials received a League proposal to finance several disparate projects. They included hiring additional staff, continuing education for League officials, improved public relations, "program-related research," and funds to establish new affiliates. In January 1967, Young learned that a $430,000 grant extending to January 1968 was approved. The League leader acknowledged that the Ford funds made a difference in League programming. For example, salary increases for staff occurred, expanded public relations allowed the organization to use radio and television, and League officials explored expansion possibilities in seven southern cities. An interim report showed that affiliates had opened already in Birmingham, Alabama, and in Columbia, South Carolina. The research area was the only initiative that awaited further development. Young cited "serious difficulties in recruiting a suitable director" as the main obstacle.[57]

Ford officials noted that except for research activities the League's intentions had been fulfilled. Consequently, foundation staff recommended a grant renewal of $400,000 "usable at their discretion." The Ford people recognized that the League "may seem conservative against today's racial background." Nonetheless, its centrist position remained important. These officials thought that the organization "commends itself because it has a large base of support and interest among those parts of the Negro and white communities which still seek amicable accommodation between the races." For this reason the Ford Foundation pledged funding to the League for another three years for a sum up to $800,000.[58] Young had clearly established himself as a spokesman for middle- and working-class blacks who remained committed to integrationism and those whites who shared this aspiration.

While McGeorge Bundy and Mitchell Sviridoff sustained Young's centrist leadership with major grants to the League, they and two black Ford officials wanted the group to stay "in step" with militant activists in the black freedom struggle. Christopher Edley did not abandon efforts to revamp the League and increase its effectiveness in inner cities. After Bundy announced bold initiatives to involve the Ford Foundation in the civil rights matters, Young submitted an omnibus proposal that included steps to upgrade the quality of League personnel. Edley commended Young for this capacity for self-criticism. Now that this subject was open for discussion, Edley frankly stated his worries about the professionalism of the League's national officers. "The Program division heads," he noted, "do not command the respect of the more experienced local directors and their staffs." Improvement in this sphere depended on whether the League wanted to respond to the challenges facing it. Edley also suggested placing two deputies under Young. The League leader was "obviously too busy to give personal attention" to every matter that came before him. Moreover, Young admitted and Edley concurred that "he has not significantly improved the performance of locals." The Ford official observed that "a limited financial base, conservatism, lack of aggressiveness . . . are the bane of the locals." Also, "many local executives remain conservative with impunity and NUL is powerless." To remedy this stagnation in the nation's dynamic racial environment, Edley invited discussion of affiliates's relationship to the national organization. Ultimately, he wanted the League "to set forth its strategy for change" and show how Ford funding would lead to greater effectiveness. That meant grants to strengthen infrastructure and to ensure a relevant League presence in the nation's inner cities.[59]

Roger Wilkins, nephew of NAACP leader Roy Wilkins, joined Edley at the Ford Foundation in 1969. Like Bundy and Sviridoff, Wilkins wanted to

strengthen centrist civil rights leadership. While he served in the Justice Department, he and other black Johnson administration officials sought the
cooperation of leading foundations to fortify black moderates in their competition with Black Power advocates. Moreover, they wanted civil rights leaders to be better informed when they entered meetings with Johnson administration cabinet and agency officers. Wilkins, M. Carl Holman, Ed Sylvester,
Lisle Carter, and a few others went to New York City to discuss with officials
from several foundations a proposal to establish a joint civil rights center in
Washington, D.C. As a headquarters for all the major civil rights groups, the
center would support lobbying and research activities. This consortium would
allow the organizations to learn firsthand about federal initiatives and would
enable them to use the information more effectively. Roger Wilkins was especially concerned about civil rights groups knowing where to target their protests, proposals, and requests. Young, Roy Wilkins, Martin Luther King Jr.,
and Kenneth B. Clark participated in the discussions. When the idea of the
civil rights headquarters was raised, Young, Roy Wilkins, and King turned
them down cold. Both Young and Roy Wilkins feared a compromised role
for Cernoria D. Johnson and Clarence Mitchell, their respective Washington, D.C. representatives. Roger Wilkins regretted the missed opportunity to
push issues within the federal government that would aid civil rights groups
and enhance their effectiveness and creativity as centrist organizations. At
Ford he had a better chance to influence and support Young and other moderate civil rights leaders.[60]

Wilkins served as a special assistant to Bundy, and he supervised experimental human-service programs in Sviridoff's national affairs division. Thus,
he had responsibility for some proposals that Young sent to the foundation.
Wilkins was bothered less than Edley about projects without detailed plans
of execution. What Wilkins stressed were innovative ideas that needed funding. Edley wanted some indication that proposals would work, whereas Wilkins
had fewer apprehensions about experimental endeavors. Consequently, Young's
"New Thrust" program gained Wilkins's support. He claimed credit for com-
mitting $3 million in Ford funds to the League initiative. While operating
differently from Edley, Wilkins, like his colleague, wanted for the League a
new direction and response to black urban violence and grassroots chants of
"Black Power." Surely, "New Thrust" would enable the League to remain
relevant to this important constituency. Edley and Wilkins apparently agreed
that the Ford Foundation could help Young and the League maintain their
credibility in the inner cities.[61]

Young desperately wanted a relevant League just as much as Edley and

Wilkins. He realized that his group needed strong ties with urban blacks and with restive black students on the nation's campuses. Young, for example, resolved to get student representation on the NUL board of trustees. Wendell Freeland, a black Pittsburgh attorney, nominated Charles J. Hamilton Jr., a native of the Smoky City and a black student leader at Harvard University. In 1968 he joined the board, where he was expected to share his activist perspectives with his older colleagues. Young secured from the Henry Luce Foundation a $35,000 grant to operate a summer program in 1968 that would draw members of the black student associations from black and white campuses to inner cities. To supplement the Luce grant, Young solicited $30,000 from the Ford Foundation.[62]

Young wanted to help "black student leaders . . . to move from the rhetoric of revolution to the relevance of constructive community effort." Thirty-six undergraduates from twenty-five institutions received assignments to various League affiliates to work with inner-city residents. Between June 1 and September 30, 1968, the students conducted black heritage classes, administered youth recreational programs, strengthened ties between the League and the Black Panthers, and discussed economic and political developments with the residents. Supervision by local League executives showed the "militant" students the depth of NUL interest and involvement in ghetto communities. Again, the Ford Foundation supported a reorientation of League programs and objectives and helped to enhance its credibility in inner cities.[63]

Young's relationship with Stephen Currier and the Taconic Foundation differed from his interactions with Lindsley Kimball of the Rockefeller philanthropies and McGeorge Bundy of the Ford Foundation. Kimball and Bundy represented established bureaucratic institutions in which numerous officials participated in grant decisions. The Taconic Foundation belonged to Stephen Currier, and he exercised direct control over its philanthropies.

Established in 1958, the foundation supported social causes important to Stephen and Audrey Currier. The National Urban League received contributions from both the Taconic Foundation and the Curriers themselves in the 1960s. Young regularly interacted with Stephen Currier, since they served as chairmen of the Council for United Civil Rights Leadership. Young also communicated frequently with Jane Lee J. Eddy, Taconic's executive director. Thus, he enjoyed an intimacy with the institution and its officials different from his dealings with the bureaucratic Rockefeller and Ford philanthropies. Moreover, Taconic's modest $7,770,397 assets, while small if compared with those of larger foundations, provided crucial funding to the National Urban League.[64]

Young's relationship with Lindsley Kimball resembled his interaction with Stephen Currier. While functioning as Young's liaison with the Rockefeller philanthropies, Kimball also served as an officer in the National Urban League. Similarly, Currier, an active League benefactor, shared involvement in CUCRL with Young. Each introduced Young to other powerful whites who donated to the League and to other black betterment groups. Kimball often represented Young to Rockefeller benefactors, and he tried to help him develop ties with Henry Heald of the Ford Foundation. Currier introduced Young and his civil rights colleagues to wealthy donors like George Pratt, a Connecticut businessman who gave large sums to CUCRL. In some respects, Kimball and Currier were different, and Young knew it. Kimball was almost thirty years older than Young, and he had as much experience with black organizations like the League and the United Negro College Fund as his younger protégé. Currier, however, lacked Kimball's sophisticated understanding about civil rights groups. Young's discussions with Kimball occurred between peers. His interaction with Currier, however, was educative.

While the Taconic Foundation contributed to general support programs of the National Urban League, Young argued that some monies should go to affiliates, especially in the South. Most of a $50,000 grant in 1962 went to the national organization, but $10,000 was earmarked for the Little Rock Urban League and $5,000 for the New Orleans Urban League. Taconic support helped with the founding of the Jackson, Mississippi, affiliate in 1966. Enid C. Baird, Young's office administrator, told a Taconic official, "It would have been impossible without the support (moral as well as financial) of persons such as yourself and the Curriers." Special interest also developed in the innovative but militant leadership of Edwin C. "Bill" Berry at the Chicago Urban League. In 1965 and 1966 the foundation transferred to the League stock whose sale yielded $100,882.90. The national organization kept over $34,000 and the Chicago affiliate gained nearly $36,000. Six southern affiliates shared the remainder, with most receiving $5,000 or $6,000. The $6,000 designated for the Jacksonville Urban League, for example, financed most of this affiliate's budget. The $3,500 for the Tulsa affiliate permitted the retention of an employment officer.[65]

Currier's involvement in CUCRL was unusual. Few benefactors became intimately involved with the routine fiscal affairs of the organizations they supported. Although he attended the meetings and for a time mailed out checks to the participating groups, Currier was unfamiliar with the civil rights movement. Currier was moved by his outrage over the 1963 Medgar Evers murder in Mississippi. He relied on Young to brief him on the broader meaning of the black struggle. Although Currier resigned from CUCRL in 1964, he maintained an active interest. Just before he died in an airplane crash in 1967, he gave the organization $43,500 for its national programs and for its Chicago affiliate. While the Rockefeller philanthropies and the Ford Foundation gave large sums to the League, the smaller donations of the Taconic Foundation strengthened several southern affiliates and supplemented the income of the national organization.[66]

The relationships that Young developed with John Gardner and Everett N. Case, the respective presidents of the Carnegie Corporation of New York and the Alfred P. Sloan Foundation, were unlike his close interactions with Kimball, Bundy, and Currier. Young would become Gardner's peer when the latter assumed leadership of the National Urban Coalition, but their contacts in the Carnegie context were formal and procedural.[67] Young could not as easily trade on his personal affability to produce funding for the League. Rather, the solid reputation of the League and objective evaluations of Young's leadership drew support from the two foundations. One Carnegie official noted that the League "is unquestionably one of the most effective agencies in the field of equal opportunity." Another Carnegie officer said that Young "has done much to give the NUL new life and [in making] it a powerful moderating influence in a period of controversy over civil rights."[68]

Young inherited ties with Carnegie that Lester B. Granger had established. When the foundation approved in 1962 a $215,000 grant for "educational motivation and guidance for Negro youth," Young was benefiting from Granger's groundwork. In 1964 Granger's track record helped Young again. He proposed "to reinstate a fellowship and training program which had been in operation prior to 1960." This program would assist students in intergroup relations, especially those wishing to work for the National Urban League." Carnegie authorized $300,000 to be paid in $100,000 installments over three years in 1964, 1965, and 1966. A $200,000 renewal came in 1967 for another two years in 1968 and 1969.[69]

Although the Carnegie Corporation remained impressed with the League as the strongest of the moderate civil rights organizations (along with the NAACP), badly planned and poorly implemented programs did not receive foundation support. Until 1969 the Carnegie Corporation put $500,000 in League initiatives that drew upon Granger precedents. Young thought his "New Thrust" effort would win similar support, so he proposed an executive development program to put in place better trained officials in the affiliates to reorient the League at the grassroots. The aim was to recruit and train twenty-five new executives and to retrain twenty-five current executives over two years. Young wanted $38,000 for planning and recruiting and $350,000 for the actual training. Carnegie granted the requested $38,000, but reduced the second request to $142,000.

Although Carnegie officials believed that the League deserved support, they were not impressed by the proposal. Funding had been approved, but Carnegie refused in 1970 to renew the grant. One officer noted that during the initial consideration of the appeal, "we were . . . simply trying to be responsive to the League." Once the funds had been disbursed, poor communications from the League official responsible for the program and limited results disappointed Carnegie officers. "They had been able to recruit only eight trainees," observed a Carnegie official, "of whom two dropped out." The foundation lost faith in the effort. "This was not an easy decision for us," wrote one official to Young.

The Carnegie Corporation, however, did not close the door on the League altogether. In the official letter of rejection, Young was invited to return to the foundation "to discuss the general question of leadership recruitment and training in the League and the group's role as a supplier of qualified black leadership for other organizations." Alan Pifer, Gardner's successor as president, told Young that Carnegie would continue funding the leadership program. Boldly, he asked Pifer for an immediate allocation of $30,000 to prevent discontinuity between the Executive Development Program and a future initiative aimed at similar goals.[70]

While Young benefited from Carnegie's previous relationship with Lester B. Granger, he had no such advantage in establishing ties with the Alfred P. Sloan Foundation. Sloan involvement with the League began in 1965 with a $10,000 grant to finance extension of NUL educational activities. Although another $10,000 in 1967 went for general support programs, Young's successful solicitations derived mainly from his emergency appeals. He told Everett N. Case, Sloan's president, in 1965 that he needed $125,000 for "a crash program to organize Urban Leagues in ten high tension communities" within a six-month period. A 1968 request for $10,000 followed the assassination of Martin Luther King Jr. This tragedy precipitated inner-city rioting across the nation, and that, noted Young, "has placed upon the Urban League unusual and fantastic demands." He added that "the non-violent approach has admittedly suffered a serious blow . . . necessitating an even greater effort by those of us who remain committed to constructive leadership." It was incumbent upon Sloan in view of these new pressures to continue its contributions to the League. Ultimately, Sloan's donation of $250,000 to the group's "New Thrust" brought its support to over $280,000 between 1965 and 1970.[71]

By 1970, when the National Urban League received $5,054,000 from foundations, it was clear that Young had outdistanced his civil rights colleagues in attracting philanthropic support. While the League attracted foundation funds during the early 1960s, these contributions rose sharply after 1966. At that time calls for "Black Power" and widespread rioting in numerous inner cities caused philanthropies to put more money into the League. These foundation funding patterns adhered to Mitchell Sviridoff's admonition to "hold the center." Since Whitney Young and the National Urban League occupied that terrain, major philanthropies disbursed large sums to the organization.[72]

While other black leaders were better known within the general public, Young was a familiar figure in foundation circles. That he became a trustee of the Rockefeller Foundation seemingly ratified his insider status. Nonetheless, Young inferred too much from his access to the foundation world. In 1961 he and J. George Harrar became executives of the National Urban League and the Rockefeller Foundation, respectively. After a decade, Harrar sought retirement and Young considered changing jobs. Casual comments from fellow Rockefeller trustees convinced Young that he could succeed Harrar as president of the foundation. Although Young was never seriously considered for the post, his name may have been mentioned at a preliminary stage of the presidential search. Surely, he wanted the position desperately. When he failed, Young was deeply disappointed. Never mind that the Rockefeller Foundation funded projects mainly in the sciences and medicine and that Harrar was a botanist and John Knowles, his successor, was a physician. The League's moderation in the midst of black militancy accounted for Young's growing influence among corporate philanthropists. He was a racial ambassador to powerful whites for the black population. Most elite whites viewed him as nothing more than that.[73]

11

Washington Insider

Young's easy access to the White House where he advised three successive presidential administrations had little to do with his savvy political skills. Rather, the enormous importance of the black freedom struggle put pressing issues before Presidents Kennedy, Johnson, and Nixon that required meetings with Young and his NAACP, CORE, SCLC, and SNCC colleagues. Although Kennedy usually conferred with groups of black spokespersons, which often included Young, Johnson and Nixon often preferred the League leader whenever they wanted intimate consultations about race relations. Moreover, Young accepted appointments to crucial federal commissions and drew contracts for the National Urban League with various governmental agencies. His pragmatic leadership of an organization singularly suited to address racial and urban issues enhanced his influence with these three presidents.

League officials in December 1960 sent Kennedy a document entitled "The Time Is Now." It dealt with urgent race relations problems. They wanted Kennedy to note crucial issues in "employment, housing, education and public welfare which are the areas in which the Urban League movement has . . . accumulated fifty years of seasoned experience." In a reminder to Kennedy about the report, League president Henry Steeger asked whether a small committee from his organization could come to the White House to discuss the memorandum with him.[1]

Louis E. Martin, a black journalist who served as deputy chairman of the Democratic National Committee, played a pivotal role in getting an audience for the League with Kennedy. Martin belonged to the NUL board of directors during the Granger years. Although Young became executive director during Martin's absence in Nigeria, the veteran reporter remained interested in the League. It was Martin's responsibility to introduce Kennedy to major black leaders. While Harris Wofford, a civil rights veteran, served as Kennedy's liaison with Martin Luther King Jr., Martin focused on interactions with Young and the League. On January 23, 1962, he helped to arrange a meeting for Steeger, Young, and Kennedy in the president's private living quarters in the White House.

Young used this opportunity to educate Kennedy about the League and to outline plans to retool the National Urban League with new programs. He also urged Kennedy to add to the cabinet a Department of Urban Affairs and to support voting rights legislation. That Kennedy already had appointed Robert C. Weaver as administrator of the Housing and Home Finance Agency showed his awareness of urban and housing issues. Moreover, this action moved the president toward his ultimate plan to upgrade HHFA into a cabinet department and to appoint Weaver as secretary. Young argued strongly for the protection of black suffrage and, later with Stephen R. Currier, persuaded the Kennedy administration to make the issue an important part of JFK's civil rights thrust.[2]

Young viewed the development of closer ties between the League and the federal government as the principal objective of this White House meeting. He asked Kennedy to allow his cabinet and agency administrators to meet with the League's national and affiliate officers to discuss how their cooperative efforts could benefit the black population. Specifically, Young wanted the president to order relevant departments and agencies "to make use of Urban League resources . . . and to invite League personnel to help in planning and implementing these programs." So, in May 1962 the federal government brought League officials from across the nation "to confer with staff leadership in the Departments of Labor, HEW and the Housing and Home Finance Agency to make certain what programs of these agencies are known and understood by the people who need them most." The meeting lasted three days. Moreover, the establishment of the NUL's Washington bureau gave Young an agency through which the League learned about federal programs and sought involvement in them.[3]

While Young knew various government officials, he realized that he needed someone in Washington to keep him apprised of federal programs and legislation. Initially, Sterling Tucker, the executive director of the Washington Urban League, functioned in that capacity. To sustain him in this assignment, the national office annually contributed $7,500 to the D.C. affiliate. During the fall of 1961, when Tucker declined an offer to become the full-time head of a Washington bureau, Young hired Cernoria D. Johnson, the executive director of the Oklahoma City Urban League and former head of the Fort Worth affiliate. Now the national office depended on a special Washington representative to keep "the entire League movement informed on developments important to us."[4]

Young assigned Johnson to follow up on President Kennedy's commitment to promote League participation in various federal programs. In January 1963, for example, Johnson solicited Louis E. Martin's assistance in getting government grants for the League to curb juvenile delinquency. Additionally, she and two NUL officials met in all-day conferences with several officials in the Department of Health, Education, and Welfare and in the U.S. Office of Education. The League staff learned about "the many facets of higher education that need improvement and expansion." One League officer discussed how his group could help combat adult illiteracy. Lisle Carter, a black lawyer who served as deputy assistant secretary of HEW, helped Johnson and her colleagues assess their various meetings within the department, advised them "regarding the development of proposals," and suggested meetings with additional HEW staff.[5]

Young also wanted Johnson to tell him about other HEW and Labor Department programs and whether involvement would be advantageous for the League. For example, Johnson told Young in May 1963, "We are beginning to develop the kind of relationship with Labor that can be of mutual benefit." As Congress considered a youth employment bill, Johnson informed Sam Merrick of the Labor Department of "the importance of Urban League inclusion at the program planning level." To Young she declared, "This has begun to pay off." Merrick "has called three times in the past ten days stressing that he is willing to meet with our Urban League personnel" to develop programs for the anticipated youth employment act. Young reviewed for HEW Secretary Anthony Celebrezze the League's "cooperative venture" with his cabinet department, and he lauded Lisle Carter for his assistance. Moreover, when the League convened a regional workshop in Chicago, several HEW officials attended and "offered advice and guidance" on family and children's services, welfare, and community health.[6]

The League's early contact with the Kennedy administration identified Young as a crucial consultant on race relations. While Martin Luther King Jr., James Farmer, John Lewis, and James Forman were busy with grassroots activism through mass marches, freedom rides, and sit-ins, Young engaged in the slow, methodical work of advising federal agencies about racial issues. His proficiency in bureaucratic and programmatic assessments gave Young a singular distinction among his civil rights colleagues. As a result, Young became involved with the Kennedy administration on these matters.

To the president's advisers, however, belonged substantial credit for developing contacts with black leaders and strengthening ties between them and the administration.[7] Young's relationship with the Department of Labor was illustrative. In November 1961 Secretary of Labor Arthur J. Goldberg told Young that he and the president were both "gratified" that he would attend a meeting of the Youth Employment Committee. W. Willard Wirtz, Goldberg's successor, asked Young in 1963 "to serve on an Implementation Subcommittee to plan follow-up action on the recommendations of the President's Committee on Youth Employment." Lack of time, however, compelled Young to say no. Assistant Labor Secretary Esther Peterson similarly drew upon Young's expertise. Since she was responsible for the minority rights aspects of labor standards, Peterson wanted Young's advice. At the same time, neither Young nor his staff were ever hesitant to criticize the Labor Department whenever racial discrimination appeared in its agencies and programs. Cernoria Johnson told officials in the U.S. Employment Service of bias within the bureau, and she offered to gather the documentation. Young expressed concern to Willard Wirtz about reports of a "segregated retraining program in Mississippi." He asked the secretary to "protect" the interests of blacks.[8]

Young also became an adviser to the surgeon general, Luther L. Terry. In 1961 Terry appointed him to the Consultant Group on Nursing. This HEW initiative dealt with "shortages of well-trained personnel for health care." Not surprisingly, Young contacted the American Nurses' Association to get an extensive list of Negro nurses. He wanted to choose three of them to represent fellow black nurses before this special committee. Additionally, as the Kennedy administration launched Volunteers in Service to America (VISTA), the attorney general, Robert F. Kennedy, asked Young to offer advice on what that agency should do "in addressing pressing human problems."[9]

In 1962 President Kennedy invited Young to serve on the Committee on Equality of Opportunity in the Armed Forces. This assignment provided him with a major chance to affect government policy in race relations. Since the Truman and Eisenhower administrations made only minimal progress toward racial integration in the military, Kennedy wanted to determine what further measures would be required to ensure full equality. He outlined to Young and other committee members what areas needed exploration. Specifically, Kennedy asked for information on whether military policy and procedures on equal opportunity required any improvements. His second concern focused on the treatment of black military families off base. The president wanted to know whether they had access to social amenities in neighboring civilian communities.[10]

Young participated fully in his committee assignments. In March 1963, for example, he toured Fort Gordon in Augusta, Georgia, and the Pensacola

Naval Air Station in Pensacola, Florida. At Fort Gordon he met with black officers, NCOs, and enlisted men. A meeting at Tabernacle Baptist Church in Augusta brought him together with local civil rights leaders, many of them affiliated with the NAACP. A similar group conferred with him in Pensacola. At both places he heard complaints from blacks in the military, and he was briefed by local leaders about race relations in the nearby cities.[11]

Young also served as a referee for racial complaints against the military. He received many letters chronicling instances of discrimination. When one complainant allowed his name to be used and provided documentation, Young told Gerhard Gesell, his chairman, that they should look into the army's nonofficer promotion practices. In another instance Young urged action by the committee's counsel, Laurence I. Hewes. The matter concerned a black in the air force. His grievance convinced Young that an examination was needed of the good faith of the air force in retaining and promoting black officers. Segregated off base housing caused Young to interact with the President's Committee on Equal Opportunity in Housing. Claude Organ Jr., a black surgeon and president of the Nebraska Urban League, called upon his longtime friendship with Young to adjudicate a housing matter. At the Strategic Air Command near Omaha, nonsegregated housing was not available near the base. After an unsatisfactory encounter with the base commander, Organ notified Young, whose contacts on the housing commission helped to end that discriminatory practice.[12]

Whenever Young was involved with the federal government, he perennially agitated for black hiring. His service with the President's Committee on Equal Opportunity in the Armed Forces was no exception. He pushed the air force, for example, to consider an acquaintance for a post as an intergroup relations specialist. Young believed that, as a manager of a large public housing project, this applicant was an obvious choice.[13]

These experiences influenced the initial report that the committee submitted to President Kennedy. A commitment was stressed by all officials in the Defense Department and armed forces to eliminate racial discrimination at military installations and at off base facilities. The committee recommended that job performance ratings for base commanders should include how well they dealt with issues of racial fairness. Commanders also would move against racial discrimination off base with such actions as litigation. Additionally, the committee believed that race relations officers should be employed throughout the Defense Department and armed forces.[14]

Apparently, Secretary of Defense Robert McNamara was impressed with Young's input on the committee. He invited the League leader to participate in a joint civilian orientation conference to get a firsthand view of U.S. armed forces. The invitation, while flattering, could tell Young little beyond what he already had seen on his Georgia and Florida tours. Besides, the daily pressures of the racial situation prevented his participation. Nonetheless, what was important for him and McNamara was that the League leader had become a familiar adviser to the Kennedy administration on civil rights and other related matters.[15]

These military matters drew at least a year's commitment from Young, but housing discrimination seemed a more urgent concern. During his 1960 campaign, Kennedy observed that this injustice could be ended "by the stroke of a presidential pen." Kennedy's commitment to handle this issue through an executive order buoyed civil rights advocates and motivated the National Urban League to push the president-elect in this direction. In "The Time Is Now" memorandum, League officials reminded Kennedy that blacks continued to face obstacles in federally sponsored housing. Moreover, Young told officers in the League's sixty-two affiliates to ask local groups to lobby the president for the promised executive order. In 1962 in meetings with Kennedy and the federal housing administrator Young, Steeger, and other League officials challenged the chief executive to act.[16]

President Kennedy issued the long-awaited edict on "Equal Opportunity in Housing" on November 20, 1962. A few days after signing it, he wrote Young to praise him and the League for their contributions in connection with the executive order. Such flattery, however, did not eliminate the doubts of many League officials. NUL president Henry Steeger recognized that the executive order did not "embrace all that might be desired," but he called it "an important first step." He also hoped for "corrective refinements to increase [the] effectiveness of the Order." Irritated League officials poignantly criticized those areas that the order did not cover. For example, it did not apply to housing, urban renewal, and other government actions that were signed and agreed on before Kennedy issued the regulation. Moreover, owners of single and duplex homes were exempt from the order. Also, Kennedy provided for no personnel to enforce this nondiscrimination statute.[17]

Young expressed his reservations to Robert C. Weaver, the administrator of the Housing and Home Finance Agency. Weaver believed that Young and the League exaggerated the ineffectiveness of the housing edict. For example, the ban on discrimination, despite Young's accusation, included "Federally assisted housing, regardless of whether the Federal aid was provided before or after the issuance of the Executive Order." Weaver also observed that the order allowed for sanctions against mortgagors who discriminated.

Additionally, he noted that urban renewal programs, while they displaced some blacks, still drew many of them into racially integrated developments.

Young maintained, however, that gaps in the administrative machinery of HHFA and vagueness in the executive order would allow discriminatory housing practices to continue. With respect to low rent housing subsidies, for example, the agency could only use its "good offices" to pursue nondiscrimination policies on units built before the Kennedy edict. Moreover, a loophole for such housing seemed unclear on whether the Public Housing Authority, an administrative component of HHFA, would still support projects that continued to segregate. Unless these uncertainties were clarified, argued Young, the executive order would be limited to selected sources of federal finance due to commitments negotiated before Kennedy issued the antidiscrimination ban.

While Weaver disagreed with Young, he assured him that the government would make every effort to implement all of the Executive Order's provisions. He wanted it to be "a forceful instrument for achieving true equality of housing opportunity." Always the pragmatist, Young suggested that Weaver nominate Reginald Johnson to Kennedy's White House Conference on Community Development. Young thought that Johnson would be an ideal appointee because he did national programming for the League in housing. "I can think of no better way," said Young to Weaver, "for you and the president to indicate your desire to effectively improve the housing situation . . . than to make this appointment."[18]

Participation on the National Committee Against Discrimination in Housing was another way Young expressed his views about Kennedy's executive order. With Roy Wilkins of the NAACP, James Farmer of CORE, and the committee's chairman, Algernon D. Black, the leaders contended that the decree was conceptualized too narrowly to end bias in housing. Five months after Kennedy signed the edict, the committee noted some "critical deficiencies" in the order. They included criticism of Kennedy for slowness in organizing the President's Committee on Equal Opportunity in Housing. Moreover, too little information had been directed either to the public or to those in housing construction and finance concerning specific provisions in the act. Also, those agencies charged with enforcement had not seriously explored ways for the edict to be used to fight discrimination. Finally, the Kennedy administration did not appoint any intergroup relations specialists to advise public and private institutions about housing bias and how to combat it. Some of these complaints echoed Young's earlier criticisms.[19]

The principal interaction between the Kennedy administration and the

League occurred in the programmatic sphere. Consequently, Young and other NUL officials pressed for League involvement in numerous federal initiatives. Additionally, Young's participation on various federal advisory committees extended the League's presence in the Kennedy administration. Although urban affairs, job training, and other social and economic matters claimed League energies, Young, in an unprecedented move, cooperated with a Kennedy-backed coalition on southern black voter registration.

Although President Kennedy dispatched U.S. marshals to Alabama to protect participants in the 1961 freedom rides, he and his aides preferred to avoid such displays of federal authority. Instead, a campaign to register southern black voters would yield political benefits for the Kennedy administration and shift civil rights activism to less controversial activities. Independently, Stephen R. Currier, benefactor of both the Taconic Foundation and the Potomac Institute, became interested in this initiative. Meetings that included Burke Marshall and Harris Wofford, both Kennedy officials, drew to the voter registration effort major foundation and federal support. Although the Southern Regional Council administered the Voter Education Project, the program involved the major civil rights organizations. As long as the initiative emphasized "voter education," Young believed that the League's tax-exempt status would not be jeopardized by NUL involvement.[20]

Soon after Wiley Branton became director of the Voter Education Project, he and Leslie Dunbar of the Southern Regional Council met in Young's office to discuss the participation of the National Urban League. Young appointed Heman Sweatt as coordinator of the League's Voter Education Program. A budget of $17,666 was approved as well as monies for involved local affiliates. The Jefferson County (Alabama) Voters Campaign learned of the League's civic education program and requested its assistance for a registration effort in October 1962. Such efforts drew the League into frontline activism that the group usually bypassed.[21]

The National Urban League and the Kennedy administration also interacted on social and economic issues. Moreover, Young served President Kennedy on various panels and as an adviser to several departments and agencies. The growing importance of the civil rights movement caused the White House to turn to the League leader for consultation. Although Young played a significant role as a race relations expert, he did not impact policy in a major way. He became closer to Lyndon B. Johnson than to Kennedy.

They met during the 1950s when Johnson was the Democratic majority leader in the Senate. Young occasionally came to Capitol Hill to testify about various bills, including the proposed Civil Rights Act of 1957. He spoke with Senator Johnson about these matters. Theodore W. Kheel, the League president during the Granger years, reintroduced Young to the new vice president in 1961. As chairman of the President's Committee on Equal Employment Opportunity, Johnson had come to New York City to discuss commission business with Kheel. Roy and Aminda Wilkins of the NAACP were sponsoring a reception that same day for Whitney and Margaret Young, and Kheel, still a member of the League's national board, invited Johnson to accompany him to the event. Although pressed for time, Johnson reluctantly agreed to go. What he intended as a brief appearance became a long discussion of race relations with the new NUL leader.[22]

When Kennedy chose Johnson as his running mate in 1960, some black leaders doubted the Texas politician on civil rights matters. Although surprised that Kennedy picked his major competitor in the Democratic primaries, Young kept an open mind about LBJ, saying, "Some of the best liberals I know are reconstructed southerners." Cooperation with Johnson through the PCEEO ultimately convinced Young that his assessment was correct.[23]

Young and Johnson followed through on plans to meet. Young recalled, "We visited on the phone at least once a week and in person at least once a month." In February 1962, for example, Young proposed that LBJ and other PCEEO officials explore with him how the NUL might cooperate with the committee. Johnson agreed, and a meeting was set up to discuss League perspectives on employment and job training for blacks. At an April 9, 1962, conference, League officials specifically outlined for Johnson "the bottlenecks and barriers to equal job opportunity." They included failures in the U.S. Employment Service, lack of scrutiny of various programs funded by the Manpower Development and Training Act of 1962, and the poor results from the President's Plans for Progress. This flawed effort meant that recalcitrant corporations could be trusted to pursue nondiscrimination policies. To avoid this serious lapse, Young suggested that the National Urban League through its experienced staff, its Commerce and Industry Council, and its Trade Union Advisory Council could provide the PCEEO with resources not available elsewhere. He wanted Johnson to use the League in a major way in the operation of this important federal panel.[24]

Young argued against voluntary compliance for corporations and urged Johnson to take strong action against discriminatory companies. Within two weeks after the League meeting with the vice president, Young congratulated Johnson and the PCEEO for rebukes of two firms guilty of biased hiring practices. Moreover, Young repeatedly told Johnson that policies aimed at ending employment discrimination should stress compulsory compliance for corporations rather than voluntary action. The vice president wanted to use any method that promised results. He believed that "a combination of the compliance program and a voluntary program holds forth the best hope for achieving our goal."[25]

The relationship between Young and Johnson solidified as the National Urban League participated in various PCEEO initiatives. When the Plans for Progress program gave federal contracts to several firms, Johnson's aide gave Young a list of these companies and urged him to inform his League affiliates that these corporations "will employ all without regard to race, creed or color." Moreover, Young was invited to join Johnson, Secretary of Labor Willard Wirtz, and executives from 150 firms at a Plans for Progress gathering.[26]

The close ties between Young and Johnson resulted in the vice president coming in 1962 to address the League's Equal Opportunity Day dinner. Johnson highlighted ten PCEEO achievements, including mandates for the building of a missile facility in the South on a basis of racial equality and tougher standards on employment equity for companies trying to get government contracts. Young lauded the vice president's speech and credited him with making the event "one of the very best we have ever had."[27]

The vice president liked Young because he seemed sensitive to LBJ's frustrations and limitations as a Kennedy subordinate. Young believed that Johnson possessed greater understanding and empathy for civil rights than the president and many of his advisers. Plans for a massive march on Washington in 1963 bothered President Kennedy. If violence occurred, JFK opined, civil rights legislation would never get through Congress. Johnson had similar reservations, but Young and others "convinced him before we did Mr. Kennedy—that this would be a very healthy sort of way of expressing the pent-up emotions" of black activists. Immediately after the march, Kennedy invited its leaders to the White House. Johnson, whom Young regarded as a close ally, spoke to the group about pending civil rights legislation. He noted, "No one can predict what Congress will do." He also observed that the Kennedy administration "has exercised all of the power that lies within its reach" to safeguard civil rights for blacks. At the same time LBJ privately advanced arguments in favor of stronger provisions that some Kennedy aides opposed. Young remembered that efforts to drop a section of public accommodations and a stipulation to withhold federal funds from discriminatory recipients met with Johnson's opposition. Thus, when he succeeded Kennedy, Johnson already had credibility with Whitney M. Young Jr.[28]

Although tragic circumstances thrust Johnson into the White House, he used his ebullient personality to charm black leaders and convince them of his serious commitment to the civil rights cause. LBJ was so quick to establish contact with black leaders right after the Kennedy assassination that they disagreed about whom the president called first. Roy Wilkins of the NAACP remembered that he was the first person with whom LBJ conferred, whereas James Farmer of CORE claimed that distinction for himself. Within a week after John F. Kennedy's funeral, Whitney Young met with the new president at the White House.[29]

James Farmer recalled that Lyndon B. Johnson adored Whitney Young. LBJ also respected Roy Wilkins. The independence and activism of Farmer and King, however, proved bothersome. Moreover, the uncontrollable young men and women at SNCC also produced for the president a low comfort level. He preferred to deal with Young.[30]

Clearly, Roy Wilkins became an important adviser as pending civil rights legislation lay before Congress in 1964 and 1965. His organization effectively lobbied the House and Senate to pass the Civil Rights Act of 1964 and the Voting Rights Act of 1965. Young joined Wilkins as a major consultant on White House civil rights initiatives.[31]

In numerous instances Young gave significant input on the handling of major civil rights matters. As northern students prepared for the Mississippi Freedom Summer of 1964, Young called White House aide Hobart Taylor Jr. to suggest a meeting between Johnson and civil rights leaders. Young believed that LBJ needed their advice and their cooperation in holding the situation in balance. Before Johnson delivered his 1965 State of the Union address, he asked Young for his thoughts on the proposed speech. The League leader criticized the administration for calling civil rights legislation "something revolutionary." He believed that such measures were neither extreme nor radical. Rather, "it calls for the elementary rights which all other Americans accept as routine."[32]

While the activism of Martin Luther King Jr. and the Southern Christian Leadership Conference focused the nation's attention on racial abuses in such southern locales as Selma, Alabama, less visible spokesmen such as Young, Wilkins, and Thurgood Marshall played important roles behind the scenes to advance the civil rights cause. For example, Young who participated in the Selma to Montgomery March, challenged John Doar, the acting assistant attorney general in the Civil Rights Division, to maintain pressure on officials in Selma and Dallas County, Alabama, who prevented blacks from voting. Doar informed Young about a successful suit against the Dallas County Board of Registrars that resulted in a court order in favor of black complainants. Doar also told the League leader that the Justice Department had filed a voting suit against all sixty-seven counties of Alabama. That suit charged that Alabama's very difficult voting test had the effect of discriminating against Negro voting applicants.[33]

When President Johnson signed the landmark Voting Rights Act on August 5, 1965 in a televised ceremony, he thought that Young's civil rights contributions were important enough to include him on the guest list with other movement activists. Others in the Johnson administration also believed that Young's counsel was key in implementing LBJ's civil rights agenda. Within five months after the Voting Rights Act was enacted, for example, Solicitor General Thurgood Marshall noted the need for a more intensive voter registration drive in the South. At LBJ's insistence, he traveled to NAACP headquarters to confer with Wilkins and Young. Marshall, a former NAACP attorney, wanted to find private monies to increase the number of southern black voters. Wilkins told Marshall, "The NAACP is just about broke." Young had already approached various foundations to aid this effort. In fact, Marshall had been sanguine about Young's probable success in getting funds to assist voter registration projects. "The Urban League," Marshall thought, "has always had a more direct line to foundations than the NAACP." Unfortunately, Young reported that he could not get any foundation money for this purpose. Marshall told President Johnson, "Whitney explained in detail the very excellent presentations which had been prepared, submitted and turned down." Although Young's attempt to find private funds to enfranchise southern blacks did not succeed, both Johnson and Marshall viewed him as one who could provide practical assistance to the civil rights cause.[34]

Although Young appreciated Johnson's racial liberalism, he monitored the effectiveness of administration civil rights efforts. The implementation of Title VI of the Civil Rights Act of 1964, for example, was a concern. This proviso denied or withdrew federal funding from any institution or program that practiced discrimination on the basis of race, color, religion, or national origin. Concerned that federal officials might miss or ignore violations of this statute, Young mobilized the entire League to determine what federally financed efforts in urban renewal, housing, vocational education, health care, and other initiatives discriminated against blacks.[35]

In 1964 Young backed LBJ on the need to enact the civil rights bill. On July 2, 1964, President Johnson signed it into law. On July 6 Young ordered executive directors of every League affiliate to investigate federal programs in their locales that violated Title VI of the new civil rights act. He noted, "The National Urban League has agreed to submit to the White House THIS WEEK a documented list of cities and their Federally supported or aided institutions and programs where Negroes are excluded, segregated or face other participation limitations." Concerning examples of racial discrimination in League communities, Young told his colleagues to "just name them and tell me what the practices are. THIS IS URGENT!"[36]

Speedily, local League leaders informed Young about racial discrimination in several federal programs including the Hill-Burton Act, programs in vocational training, apprenticeship and manpower retraining, various educational initiatives, and public housing. The Hill-Burton Act, for example, financed hospital construction. Approximately 6,810 hospitals received federal funding, but 104 facilities functioned on a segregated basis. Eighty-four hospitals served only whites and twenty admitted only blacks. Moreover, such facilities as Morton Plant Hospital in Clearwater, Florida, segregated black patients in the basement. Cleveland Clinic permitted no black physicians on its staff, and St. Vincent's Infirmary in Little Rock barred black nurses from assisting in births. League investigators found similar racial patterns in other federally funded programs.[37]

Young sent the report to the White House. He conceded that the Johnson administration was already working to put an end to Title VI violations. Young told the president that he hoped areas which may have been overlooked would receive needed attention. He added, "We must put an end to a situation in which the tax-dollars of some citizens are of little or no use to them because of segregation and discrimination." Lee White, a Johnson aide, forwarded the report to LeRoy Collins, director of the Community Relations Service in the Department of Commerce. Young met with Collins and his staff in "a most informative and productive exchange."[38]

That this crucial issue remained active among high-level Johnson appointees showed the significance of Young's civil rights advocacy. Two successive HEW secretaries, for example, interacted with Young on Title VI matters. In 1965 Anthony J. Celebrezze boasted of the progress made in relation to health and welfare programs, hospitals, and schools. He invited Young to meet with him and HEW officials. To sustain the momentum Young challenged Celebrezze's successor, John W. Gardner, to ponder with him some unforeseen consequences of Title VI enforcement. Young worried about the role of southern black hospitals after hospitals were fully integrated. Specifically, Young wondered, "If these Negro hospitals are allowed to remain open, there is a good chance that integration in the hospitals will not proceed quickly." The problem, Young believed, rested with some black physicians, who when rejected from hospital staffs would remain in black hospitals and push for their survival. Such issues, contended Young, were important enough for Gardner, selected League officials, and various experts to meet to formulate national guidelines by which HEW could address these difficulties.[39]

When Young learned that the U.S. Commission on Civil Rights found discriminatory practices within agencies of the Agriculture Department, he complained to President Johnson. As a result Secretary Orville Freeman assured Young that no effort would be spared to achieve equal services for black farmers. Freeman asked Young to help him bring the Agriculture Department into compliance with Title VI. He sent him newly developed rules and regulations that demonstrated Freeman's seriousness in ending racial discrimination. Various state programs that operated with federal monies were required to sign assurances that demonstrated their obedience to Title VI. Like Wilkins, King, and other black spokespersons, Young agitated for the passage of landmark civil rights laws. At the same time, he was one of the few leaders who monitored specific statues and determined whether they actually helped their intended beneficiaries.[40]

Although the enactment of the Civil Rights Act of 1964 gave Johnson a Lincolnesque reputation, he believed that his contributions to black advancement were incomplete. To the 1965 graduating class at Howard University Johnson declared that "the next and the more profound stage of the battle for civil rights" would require "equality as a fact and equality as a result." To achieve those goals LBJ announced a 1966 White House conference that would focus on the theme "To Fulfill These Rights." He envisaged for blacks a societal effort to bring them to actual social, political, and economic equality.[41]

In September 1965 Vice President Hubert Humphrey, Attorney General Nicholas Katzenbach, and several presidential aides discussed how to implement Johnson's pledge. They concluded that a planning conference of 400 persons should gather in November 1965. This group would propose topics for in-depth studies for presentation to a larger gathering of 4,000 in the spring of 1966. They chose A. Philip Randolph as the honorary chairman and two leading lawyers, Morris B. Abrams and William T. Coleman, as the cochairs of the November planning conference. They developed the agenda and polled several groups about their expectations for the proposed White House meetings. Those who attended the November planning sessions cited seven subjects on which to focus: welfare and health, the dynamics of the ghetto, administration of justice, legal guarantees, housing, employment, and education.[42]

Clifford Alexander Jr., a presidential aide, frequently reminded his White House superiors that they needed to keep civil rights leaders informed about

unfolding plans for the November planning session and the spring conference. Toward that end Roy Wilkins, Whitney Young, James Farmer, Dorothy
Height, and other representatives from the major civil rights organizations
came to the White House to meet with several high-ranking administration
officials. Alexander and his colleague, Joseph Califano, told Johnson that support for the conference from civil rights leaders was crucial. The two aides
were disturbed by reports of slow progress in southern black voter registration and lax enforcement of Title VI of the 1964 Civil Rights Act. It was
important that President Johnson deflect criticism through the full involvement of civil rights leaders in planning the conference.[43]

Actually, Johnson did not need to worry about the civil rights spokespersons. They neither criticized him nor tried to take control of the conference. Abrams and Coleman told the Council for United Civil Rights Leadership (CUCRL) that its recommendations for the planning conference had been
communicated to the president's advisers. CUCRL and other relevant groups
could suggest planning session participants and could discuss the unfinished
business of civil rights, including further implementation of the 1964 and 1965
Civil Rights Acts. CUCRL also agreed with the president on the importance of
jobs and economic security as a basis for black advancement. In a meeting with
presidential aides, Roy Wilkins "was of great assistance in establishing a total
atmosphere of cooperation and understanding." Bayard Rustin, who represented A. Philip Randolph, was "quite cooperative" despite his earlier criticisms
of Abrams, Coleman, and the spring conference agenda. Young was already
involved in the detailed planning of the two White House conferences.[44]

Not long after LBJ delivered his Howard University address, Young and
Lee C. White, the special assistant to the president, met to discuss the November planning conference. They agreed that Young should write a memorandum. While Young liked the theme, "To Fulfill These Rights," he wanted
it understood that the Negro problem was the white man's problem. He also
noted that "in no way should this conference suggest that the primary responsibility for the plight of the Negro American lies within the Negro community rather than at the feet of the majority community." Additionally, he
wanted the Johnson administration to recognize "the essential role which
Negro leadership and the Negro community must play" in efforts to advance
the black population. Young also wanted the participation of inner-city leaders like those involved in National Urban League Community Action Assembly and in various antipoverty groups. In other ways Young observed that the
League could be helpful by providing conference delegates with information
about particular black communities.[45]

Young had only modest success in determining how the White House conference would be conceptualized. Rather, his influence lay in two other spheres. He was named cochairman of the health and welfare section, which shaped an agenda for the spring 1966 plenary sessions on "To Fulfill These Rights." Lisle C. Carter, another black presidential aide, wrote the report, and it was sent to Young for his comments. Moreover, Young recommended Mahlon T. Puryear, his deputy executive director, and two national board members, John S. Hayes and Ramon S. Scruggs, to represent the League at this November planning meeting, and he persuaded LBJ's aides to include other League staff as consultants. Cernoria Johnson, director of the League's Washington bureau, for example, "carried a great responsibility for the development of the ideas" in Young's health and welfare group. Additionally, Sterling Tucker prepared a paper for the voting and citizen participation section. Young also tried to get invitations for two League workers, Isabel C. Clark, associate director of special programs, and Walter K. Dancy, president of the Youth Community.[46]

After the November gathering, M. Carl Holman announced a December meeting to review the findings and proposals from eight November workshops. His most important comments concerned participation in the spring conference. He especially wanted "some indigenous community representatives." Such persons "in their daily experience are in contact with the victims of poverty and discrimination." This suggestion was implemented. Young also thought that official government participation should be minimized, and for the most part invisible."[47]

Young wanted a cross section of American society to become involved in this conference. Although League participation mattered, Young believed that delegates ranging from grassroots black community leaders to corporate executives should talk about how the condition of blacks could be improved. Louis Martin, a DNC official, suggested that this idea should be tried if Young would agree to a prominent role for corporate executives. Clifford Alexander reported that Young appeared to be enthusiastic and had forwarded a list of names. Young figured that many of these corporate board chairmen and presidents of IBM, CBS, AT&T, Inland Steel, and other Fortune 500 firms already supported the National Urban League. Their involvement with the League could easily be parlayed toward direct identification with LBJ's broader civil rights agenda.[48]

With two friends, M. Carl Holman and Arthur C. McCaw, on the 1966 White House conference staff Young hoped to maximize League participation.[49] Berl I. Bernhard, a White House special counsel, projected 2,000 invitees apportioned among fourteen categories including labor, religion, education, foundations, and civil rights organizations. He asked Young for "a carefully evaluated list of individuals" for each of the categories. At the same time Bernhard reminded Young, "We have more names than could ever be invited." "Frankly, I am not happy with the allocation breakdown," replied the League leader. He repeated his objection to federal officeholders attending the conference as official delegates. "It is a serious mistake," he noted. For a "how-to-do conference," Young further asserted, too many "education people" were on the list. Also, the number of business and industry people whose presence he greatly favored as well as state and local officials were similarly too many. Young strongly objected to the allotment of 200 persons for the major civil rights organizations.

Although Young pressed for scores of League professionals and board members from the national, regional, and local levels, he knew that they would take practically all of the allotted 200 places for civil rights organizations. The Johnson administration permitted him to send forty-five League participants, which filled nearly one-fourth of the civil rights slots. Young succeeded in showing his League colleagues the extent of his influence in Johnson's White House.[50]

The League leader maintained a middle ground in an increasingly militant national black leadership. Disenchantment from SCLC, SNCC, and CORE spokespersons over growing American involvement in Vietnam War and criticism of poor federal enforcement of civil rights laws drew opposition to LBJ. To prevent these criticisms from embarrassing the Johnson administration, strict procedures were adopted for "To Fulfill These Rights." Presidential aides, for example, did not want any votes on prearranged resolutions by the 2,000-2,500 delegates in attendance at the June 1-2, 1966 conference. Only after the protests against this rule by Floyd McKissick, successor to James Farmer at CORE, did the Johnson administration reverse itself.[51]

Young's support of LBJ greatly aided the White House. In contrast to SNCC's boycott and the Vietnam War criticisms of King and McKissick, Young said that the Vietnam issue was not germane to the civil rights movement. Such sentiments helped LBJ to maintain credibility with blacks, and Johnson owed Young a large political debt. He and Roy Wilkins were credited with a "behind-the-scenes strategy . . . to keep the problem of Vietnam from sabotaging the potential of the White House Conference." Instead, recommendations to the federal government and the private sector to spend more money to improve the condition of blacks, home rule for the District of Columbia, federal prodding for civilian review boards to investigate police brutality, and other such measures dominated conference discussions. Young's involvement produced concrete benefits for him and the League. He introduced several League staff and officers to important federal officials, and he demonstrated to LBJ that he could be a valuable adviser and a trusted operative.[52]

The controversies that arose at the White House presaged further fractures in the national consensus on civil rights. Although Young remained an important adviser to President Johnson, both realized that Congress and the public had become uncertain about the future of the civil rights movement. Despite major legislative victories in 1964 and 1965, LBJ proposed in 1966 an omnibus civil rights bill to end racial discrimination in federal and state jury systems, strengthen federal intervention in school desegregation, and establish a national fair housing law. When Young and other civil rights leaders came to the White House to meet with the president, they received confirmation of what they already suspected. It would be difficult to move civil rights legislation through Congress. Rioters in Los Angeles's Watts section in August 1965 and attacks on Martin Luther King's open housing march through a Chicago suburb in July 1966 showed that the civil rights coalition was falling apart. Attorney General Nicholas Katzenbach reminded LBJ to tell Young and others that "even [congressional] supporters of civil rights are apathetic and none of the proposals have the sense of urgency which accompanied prior legislation." The fair housing section drew fatal opposition from Senate Minority Leader Everett M. Dirksen, an Illinois Republican. Additionally, Senate Majority Leader Mike Mansfield, a Montana Democrat, blamed Negro rioters in Watts and rock throwers in the Chicago area for creating an unfavorable atmosphere for the bill's passage. Young attributed the defeat to "northern liberals" who "weakened as the programs began to hit segregation" in the states they represented. Undaunted, LBJ made a second attempt in 1967 to push the bill through Congress. He brought Young and other civil rights leaders to the White House to discuss his plans. Young and Wilkins aided the effort by agreeing to a breakfast meeting with House Minority Leader Gerald R. Ford and twenty of his Republican colleagues. A GOP congressman from New York, Charles E. Goodell, told Young, "It was a pleasure to cooperate with the Urban League in this worthwhile endeavor." After the passage of this bill in the House of Representatives, there was a compromise with Senator Dirksen on gradual fair housing coverage of 80 percent of the nation's dwellings rather than 91 percent, which the Democrats had proposed. With GOP support the Civil Rights Act of 1968 became law. Young's efforts in both the Kennedy and Johnson administrations to elicit federal intervention against racial bias in housing finally reached fruition.[53]

Advice on civil rights was not the only major issue on which Young shared his views with President Johnson. LBJ's Great Society and its massive War on Poverty drew upon ideas and proposals that Young developed as executive director of the National Urban League. In his 1964 book, *To Be Equal,* Young called for an unprecedented domestic Marshall Plan to address a broad range of social and economic inequities that maintained black inequality with whites. "We urgently recommend," he wrote, "cooperative SPECIAL EFFORTS by private, public, and voluntary organizations in a massive 'crash' attack" on racial inequalities in employment, education, housing, and health. In his ten-point program to improve schools, provide job opportunities, "destroy the racial ghetto," "rehabilitate urban Negro families," and other efforts, Young argued, "This crash program should be seen as an investment rather than a give-away program. It constitutes an investment in human resources, and it will pay off just as the Marshall Plan paid off in a prosperous Western Europe of strong and friendly allies." His call for this "special effort" stimulated discussions about whether adherents of the American free enterprise system would support such massive expenditures. One observer hinted that Young's belief in capitalism could not be reconciled with this noncapitalist solution. Young's early support of a form of affirmative action anticipated later debates on the issue. In the 1960s, however, President Johnson saw merit in Young's ideas.[54]

Young discussed these ideas with LBJ. He shared with the president a memorandum that his board had worked on for several months before the announcement of the domestic Marshall Plan. As planning began on the War on Poverty, Young noted many similarities with his own plan. In Young's opinion, Johnson's War on Poverty derived from his League proposal.[55]

When Johnson told Congress in his 1964 State of the Union address that he would submit a billion dollar Economic Opportunity Act, Young already claimed ownership of this initiative. The League leader claimed, "I was involved in the Poverty Program, the planning of it, from the very start— even when John Kennedy was in, and more so when President Johnson came in." Thus, he announced his immediate support of the president's proposal and his group's cooperation. Andrew T. Hatcher, Johnson's associate press secretary, observed that the president was pleased to know that such organizations as the National Urban League were eager to participate in such a program. Moreover, Young went to Capitol Hill to support Johnson's proposal. A black presidential aide told him there had never been any finer testimony given before a congressional committee than Young's on the Poverty Bill.[56]

When Congress passed the Economic Opportunity Act of 1964 with an initial appropriation of $800 million, a national war on poverty officially began. Fearful that blacks would not play a crucial role in running the various programs that the act created, Young aggressively lobbied R. Sargent Shriver, the probable OEO director, to involve high-level black government officials. Young specifically mentioned black Johnson appointees in HEW, Commerce, Labor, Agriculture, and the President's Committee on Equal Employment Opportunity.[57]

Later, Young told Shriver, "The staffing of your program will be extremely critical in determining its success or failure. I am concerned not only about your top policy-makers and their experiences and attitudes with regard to race relations, but also with those persons who will play key roles in major cities." Young tried to show Shriver that his wide contacts could aid in staffing OEO. He knew persons both outside and within the League whose expertise would prove crucial to the fight against poverty. For example, Edwin C. Berry, executive director of the Chicago Urban League, told Young about Ray Hilliard, director of the Cook County Department of Public Aid. Cook was a "battler for civil rights and has never failed in his efforts to protect the poor," Berry declared. Young repeated Berry's high praise for Hilliard to Shriver. This public official, Young observed, "has the confidence of the people who stand to benefit most from the poverty program." A grateful Shriver invited the League leader to keep recommending participants in the antipoverty effort. "I am going to continue leaning on you," Shriver added.[58]

Aside from Hilliard and many others whom he recommended, Young wanted to be sure that his organization would be a major player in the federal antipoverty program. His regular correspondence with Shriver and a continuous flow of information from Cernoria Johnson of the League's Washington bureau kept Young well informed about the evolving poverty program. Johnson met with Hyman Bookbinder, Shriver's assistant, about League involvement with OEO. "Always we were pointing up the Urban League's unique qualifications and the contribution it could make," Johnson noted. Since fifty selected cities were rumored to be the inaugural sites of the antipoverty effort, Bookbinder and his associate promised that the League would be informed immediately about which municipalities would actually receive federal funds. She also obtained a commitment to hold a conference between League officials and OEO staff. Shriver asked Young to appoint a liaison committee of League members to assist the OEO as the situation might require.[59]

Young's persistent prodding about black involvement in the OEO bureaucracy and League participation in antipoverty programs yielded some positive results. Young became a member of the OEO advisory committee. Moreover, Cernoria Johnson kept Young informed about the employment of blacks in important OEO positions. She concluded, however, that these efforts were still not enough. Shriver, who was mindful of these criticisms, told Young about Samuel F. Yette, whom he appointed as special assistant to coordinate the civil rights matters to ensure fair employment and contract compliance. Also, in response to Young, Shriver hired Theodore A. Jones to direct the Chicago regional office. He thanked Young for his support of Theodore Brown, a consultant to VISTA, whom Shriver was considering for an OEO position.

Overall, Young's agitation produced only modest results. Cernoria Johnson happily reported that the Washington bureau helped OEO in promoting several state poverty workshops through the League's southern regional office. OEO provided speakers and literature to the program. On the other hand, Johnson complained that OEO hesitated to share with her the status of proposals submitted by League cities. Moreover, officials in the affiliates claimed that in their communities blacks were not included as representatives on the policymaking and program development level. Young learned from her about other examples of OEO's "failure to adequately involve the Negro."[60]

Young knew that Cernoria Johnson was right! Some presidential aides did not want the War on Poverty to be viewed as a program primarily for blacks. They believed that such an image would threaten congressional funding. Thus, it was possible that the paucity of blacks in OEO derived from these apprehensions. Moreover, Young's experience with OEO, despite his membership on its national advisory committee, showed that problems in getting OEO cooperation were real. The agency received in July 1966 an NUL proposal to train 500 home health aides through the League's western regional office. Six months had passed, and no action had been taken on the proposal.[61]

Nonetheless, the League remained the black betterment group that the Johnson administration trusted the most. In 1968 OEO and HEW reluctantly considered funding Youth Organizations United (YOU), a group that worked with gangs. Their support, however, was contingent upon a reputable organization such as the Urban League or the Urban Coalition overseeing YOU. When Young and Sterling Tucker offered the League as the grantee for YOU, Joseph Califano responded positively. Califano told the president that he and another aide agreed that "it is far easier" to entrust federal funds to the Urban League.[62]

Young's insider status during the Johnson years was manifested in several other ways. He interacted with numerous cabinet departments and agencies. He offered League expertise, sought the inclusion of himself and other League personnel on various commissions, and tried to affect the direction of policies that mainly impacted the black population. The Department of Defense, for example, confronted numerous racial equality issues that required Young's perspectives and assistance. The assistant secretary of defense for manpower in 1966 drew him to Washington as the principal speaker at its civil rights conference. The Navy Department needed his help to expand the number of black midshipmen at the Naval Academy. Young cooperated with Navy Secretary Paul Nitze and Defense Secretary Robert McNamara in promoting *The Navy Challenge: Future of the Negro in the United States Navy*, a publication aimed at the recruitment of black officers and noncommissioned personnel.[63] Some of the contacts that Young established with cabinet departments resulted in NUL contracts. In 1965, for example, the Labor Department disbursed $44,648 to the League for an on-the-job training and development program. Focused on eight cities, League affiliates were asked to cooperate with the local U.S. Employment Service and employers to expand job opportunities for inner-city blacks.[64]

President Johnson also appointed Young to several federal commissions dealing with urban affairs, education, and law enforcement. Young's presence on these panels sometimes yielded useful suggestions that impacted federal policy. Harry C. McPherson, Johnson's special assistant, thanked the League leader for his membership on LBJ's task force on urban problems. "The president," noted McPherson, "appreciates your assistance and your efforts to help us develop creative proposals for a better urban America." Mindful of the recent riots in Watts in August 1965, LBJ wanted Young's input on how to handle the nation's escalating urban crisis. On other occasions Young, as a moderate black leader, gave legitimacy to commissions that would otherwise consist only of whites. He consented to be on an advisory committee on the Vocational Education Act of 1963. Always interested in the involvement of other League officials, Young wanted Otis Finley to substitute for him whenever he failed to make a meeting. As a member of the President's Commission on Law Enforcement and Administration of Justice, Young persuaded the associate director of the panel to allow Arthur Q. Funn, the NUL general counsel, to represent him whenever he could not attend.[65]

Although Young believed that LBJ's civil rights achievements entitled him to a Lincolnesque reputation, the League leader would not accept a formal position in the Johnson administration. When the War on Poverty commenced in 1964, Young was offered the deputy directorship. One newspaper speculated that if Shriver, the OEO director, returned to the Peace Corps or

ran for the 1964 Democratic vice presidential nomination, Young could succeed him as head of the antipoverty agency. In January 1965 Johnson learned
from an aide that Young wanted to be a cabinet officer, preferably HEW, but
might be interested in an ambassadorial assignment. About a week later Martin Luther King Jr. asked President Johnson to appoint Young as HEW secretary. In September 1965 an Atlanta admirer in an unsolicited letter recommended Young as secretary of HUD.[66]

Robert C. Weaver, who actually obtained the HUD secretaryship, confirmed that Johnson had spoken to Young about HEW and HUD. Moreover,
Young himself acknowledged that he had been offered the OEO position and
several other positions by President Johnson. Some presidential aides, while
they noted that the OEO post had been offered to Young, criticized the League
leader for lobbying for membership in the cabinet. "Nobody in a position of
authority has indicated to Whitney," said one aide, "or to anyone else for that
matter that he is being considered for a Cabinet post. Obviously all who
know him have a high regard for his ability." The aide added, "We will continue to consider Whitney for any other vacancies for which he is qualified,
but his cause is not helped in the slightest by any efforts to mount a campaign."[67]

Apparently, some within the Johnson administration had less enthusiasm for Young as a high-level presidential appointee than LBJ himself. Clearly,
Johnson had spoken to Young about key positions that his aides apparently
knew little or nothing about. Whether LBJ seriously considered him for a
cabinet position is unclear. Surely, Young would not resign as NUL head to
serve as an assistant in a subcabinet agency such as OEO. Perhaps he would
have accepted a cabinet job if it had been offered. In any case, the aides were
wrong to conclude that the lobbying emanated from Young.

It seems that Young valued his access to the White House and liked to
be called to Washington to give advice. That he wanted to be LBJ's employee
seems doubtful. When rumors circulated in 1965 that an offer to serve in the
cabinet was forthcoming, Young told the NUL's board of directors executive
committee that he had received no official offer. He added that he would
have to do much soul-searching if such an offer was made. He noted that his
best service to the country and the cause of civil rights could be accomplished
best at the National Urban League. In a later recollection Young added that
his NUL position allowed him to exercise a maximum of influence and control, which a Johnson administration post would preclude. He added, "I
thought it would be unwise if all of the black leadership that had talent or

abilities were to leave and go with the administration. . . . Some of us needed to be outside."[68]

Although Young wanted to maintain his independence from LBJ, his admiration for the president's sincerity on civil rights made the League leader reluctant to criticize him. For example, widespread rioting in ghetto communities throughout the nation moved Johnson to establish the National Advisory Commission on Civil Disorders in 1967. Chaired by Illinois governor Otto Kerner, the panel concluded, "Our nation is moving toward two societies, one black, one separate and unequal. . . . Discrimination and segregation have long permeated much of American life; they now threaten the future of every American." Young quoted these excerpts from the Kerner Commission report in his second book, *Beyond Racism*. Yet, President Johnson embraced the panel's findings with only a tepid endorsement. "I think that was a mistake on the part of Mr. Johnson," Young remarked. LBJ was offended, he said, because the Kerner Report did not seem to acknowledge the many things that had been accomplished under his administration in the domestic area. Young contended that the president took the report as a personal criticism. While Young believed that the Kerner panel accurately diagnosed the nation's racial dilemma, Johnson had his doubts. Young commended the commission because "they listened to witnesses; they went into the ghettos; they climbed the broken stairways of decaying tenements; they saw the rat bites on children with bellies swollen with hunger; they heard the frustration of men who couldn't get jobs. They saw firsthand what America does to its poor." These realities Young recounted in *Beyond Racism*. Yet Johnson's reluctance to countenance these simple truths did not tear Young away from him. In his opinion, the president had accomplished too much for blacks and had changed their condition too dramatically to merit any harsh criticisms from the leader of the National Urban League.[69]

The esteem that Presidents Kennedy and Johnson held for Young probably shielded him from the same ruthless scrutiny that the Federal Bureau of Investigation imposed upon Martin Luther King Jr. Starting in 1961, FBI director J. Edgar Hoover authorized continuous surveillance of King because of alleged Communist connections. Hoover's disdain for King drove him to threaten the civil rights leader with incriminating personal material gotten from wiretaps and informants. Kennedy and Johnson acquiesced to Hoover's crusade to uncover King's suspected shortcomings. Except for routine background checks for clearance to serve on various presidential commissions, Hoover seemed uninterested in Young's personal or professional activities. Even when the FBI investigated him on its own, no damaging information seemed to surface.[70]

Young's sophistication in dealing with Hoover and the FBI partially explained why the bureau made no major attempt to discredit him. During the Kennedy administration Young signaled approval of the FBI when he "expressed a desire to maintain [a] close liaison" between the FBI and the National Urban League. Moreover, Young welcomed FBI interest in attracting black applicants for bureau positions, and he promised the cooperation of the League. When three slain civil rights workers—Schwerner, Goodman, and Chaney—were found near Philadelphia, Mississippi, Young commended Hoover and the FBI for their efforts in recovering and identifying the bodies. Hoover thanked Young for his "complimentary remarks" and called them "a source of encouragement." Additionally, Hoover in 1967 commended Young as "one stripe above Martin Luther King" and as "a very expedient person." A Hoover aide further observed that the League leader "has had a cooperative attitude toward the Bureau."[71]

Supposed missteps by Young were overlooked while similar suspicions may have been damaging to King. Although FBI officials remembered that Young had called Hoover's criticism of King "unfortunate," they still approved of the League as one of the more conservative civil rights groups and as one that opposed the black militants. When an informant saw Young on an airplane reading a letter from someone in the leftist W.E.B. DuBois Club, this seeming infraction required no action but was received at the FBI as "information."[72]

Despite Young's high regard for President Johnson, he maintained a political neutrality that freed him to cooperate with both Democrats and Republicans. That Young did not serve in the Johnson administration may have enhanced his credibility with Republicans in Congress and with Richard Nixon. Even before Johnson left office, Young endorsed the Human Renewal Fund proposed by the Urban Affairs Task Force of House Republicans. They wanted to put $6.6 billion of "non-essential Federal expenditures . . . into programs to meet urgent human needs." When these House Republicans asked Young for his "candid assessment," he agreed to come to Washington to consult with them. Young also appeared before both the 1968 platform committees of the Republican Party on July 29 and the Democratic Party on August 23. He told each group that better coordination of poverty programs was needed, that there should be major public and private construction in Negro ghettos to eliminate the slums, provide jobs, and act vigorously on Kerner Commission recommendations on race, housing, and social welfare. Finally, Young noted that presidential candidates should "abstain from appeals to the backlash vote through use of racial code terms such as 'crime in the streets' and 'neighborhood schools.'" Although addressed to all three presidential candidates, Young's admonitions mainly applied to the Republican nominee, Richard M. Nixon, and the American Independent Party candidate, George C. Wallace.[73]

The nonpartisan Whitney M. Young Jr. did not declare for the Democratic nominee, Hubert H. Humphrey. Maintaining such neutrality must have been hard for the League leader, who admired Humphrey as a longtime civil rights champion. Young's aloofness from party politics was a wise strategy, since Nixon won a narrow victory over Humphrey. Despite Young's private disappointment with the election results and notwithstanding Nixon's appeals to the backlash vote and rumors about a "southern strategy," he wanted to work with the new president on civil rights and poverty issues. Nixon also wanted to interact with Young. Right after the election, the two met to discuss whether Young would accept an appointment as secretary of HUD. In declining the position, Young repeated to Nixon what he had told President Johnson, that he could accomplish more outside government than inside. Despite his refusal, Young wanted to keep the lines of communication open between him and Nixon and between the new president and black leaders. Hence, he joined with other board members of the National Urban Coalition in meeting with President-elect Nixon about the urban crisis. Furthermore, Young urged James Farmer, the former executive director of CORE, to accept Nixon's offer to become an assistant secretary of Health, Education, and Welfare.[74]

On inauguration day, January 20, 1969, Young submitted to President Nixon "A Call to Action: Recommendations on the Urban and Racial Crisis." Young assumed that the new president would be responsive to the needs of the cities. The NUL document cited the rise in black unemployment as a pressing problem along with the other pathologies of ghetto life—overcrowded housing, poor education, and woefully inadequate social services. He urged Nixon to build on the recommendations of the Kerner Commission (the National Advisory Commission on Civil Disorders), the Kaiser Commission Report (the President's Committee on Urban Housing), and other panels that LBJ established to deal with urban issues. The report also reviewed a long list of federal programs that impacted the poor and assessed how well they helped the recipients. Young urged the Nixon administration to use existing volunteer agencies to supplement federal efforts in addressing poverty and discrimination. He also called for a White House conference on police and justice. Although most law enforcement officers were "decent, hard-working men," police lawlessness still needed to be curbed. Moreover, this White House initiative could encourage police to become more responsive to blacks. This League document signaled to Nixon that Young wanted to do business with the new GOP administration.[75]

Since Young wanted to give Nixon a chance to demonstrate friendship to blacks, he supported, whenever possible, presidential initiatives to address the plight of the disadvantaged. In 1969, for example, Young applauded Nixon's efforts to overhaul the welfare system. He told the president about particular aspects of his proposals that the League could endorse. Young agreed with Nixon's premise that "a simple declaration of need . . . which includes the working poor . . . and which would place a floor below which no one need fall" entitled such persons to welfare assistance. Young suggested that the Nixon initiative should assure federal administration of the entire welfare system, increased payments within five years, and deletion of compulsory work provisions. Young offered to Nixon the expertise of the League staff to help him draft the best possible measure for the Congress to consider.[76]

Nonetheless, Nixon's "southern strategy" distressed Young and other leaders. This agreement was a quid pro quo arrangement with Strom Thurmond, the GOP senator from South Carolina. Southerners would help Nixon to win the Republican presidential nomination and the election. If elected, Nixon would reduce federal pressure for school desegregation and appoint conservative southerners to the Supreme Court. Nixon kept his promises. His presidential predecessors pursued school desegregation by threatening to cut off HEW funds to offending school districts. The Nixon administration used the slower approach of individual lawsuits as the best strategy to achieve this objective. This policy shift, however, resulted in less emphasis on busing and a decline in the numbers of students who attended integrated schools.[77]

Moreover, in 1969 and 1970 Nixon successively nominated Clement F. Haynsworth of South Carolina and G. Harold Carswell of Florida to a Supreme Court vacancy created by the resignation of Associate Justice Abe Fortas. Both men were hostile to recent civil rights gains. Hence, the Leadership Conference on Civil Rights played a pivotal role in lobbying the Senate to defeat both nominations. Young, who belonged to the executive committee of the Leadership Conference, supported these efforts.[78]

Sharp criticism of the Nixon administration came from the NAACP board chairman, Bishop Stephen G. Spottswood of the African Methodist Episcopal Zion Church. Speaking at the organization's 1970 annual convention, Bishop Spottswood said, "This is the first time since Woodrow Wilson, we have a national administration that can be rightly characterized as anti-Ne-

gro." He added, "This is the first time since 1920 that the national administration has made it a matter of calculated policy to work against the needs
and aspirations of the largest minority of its citizens." Bishop Spottswood
cited the Haynsworth and Carswell Supreme Court nominations, "the pull-
back on school desegregation," federal contracts with racially discriminatory
defense companies, and attempts to weaken the voting rights act as evidence
of Nixon's hostility to blacks.[79]

   Bishop Spottswood's charge created a predicament for Whitney Young.
He shared these same concerns. At the same time Young did not want to close
the door to any possible cooperation between the National Urban League
and the Nixon administration. Concerning Spottswood's remarks, Young
noted at the 1970 annual NUL convention, "I don't think I would have used
just that language." He did not believe that there was a deliberate policy of
hating black people. Young admitted that the Nixon administration "faces a
credibility gap of enormous proportions. The record is sometimes muddled."
He also observed, "There are some signs that elements of this administration
are moving forward to bring about change." He cited the removal of tax
exemptions for segregated private academies, positive moves toward school
desegregation, action against job discrimination, and possible OEO and HEW
grants through black organizations to aid inner cities. Young's optimism had
been stirred by the presence of that other "element" within the Nixon administration who wanted a rapprochement with civil rights leaders.[80]

   Young preferred to believe that Nixon had repaid his debt to Senator
Thurmond and would abandon the racial insensitivity that the "southern
strategy" represented. Moreover, administration officials had also made over-
tures to him. For example, in early 1969 Young agreed to serve on the Economic Development Council to the Small Business Administration. The administrator, Howard J. Samuels, urged the League leader to advise him on
Project Own. This initiative aimed to increase black business ownership.
Moreover, Secretary of Commerce Maurice H. Stans in 1970 invited Young
to Atlanta to meet with federal officials and local leaders about minority businesses. Most important, the presence of Leonard Garment in the Nixon administration gave Young reasons to remain open-minded about Nixon. Garment, Nixon's law partner in New York City, came to Washington at the
president's invitation to open a branch of their firm. During Nixon's presidential campaign, Garment oversaw minority affairs that included blacks,
Jews, Hispanics, and Native Americans. He eventually joined the administration as a special consultant to the president with the same minority affairs
portfolio.[81]

Obviously, Garment cared a great deal about how blacks perceived the Nixon presidency. Stunned by Bishop Spottswood's NAACP speech, Garment wired the prelate and declared that his comments were "an unfair and disheartening attack." He cited the "Philadelphia Plan," an effort to put blacks in the construction trades, a $1.5 billion proposal for school desegregation, a family assistance plan, and other Nixon initiatives that would positively impact civil rights efforts. When Young said at the 1970 NUL convention that the Nixon administration was not anti-Negro, his comments apparently garnered grateful responses from Garment and other Nixon loyalists.[82]

In some ways, the Spottswood speech was a wake-up call for the Nixon administration. The bishop expressed what many believed about the president. Clearly, Garment and others had to develop closer ties with black leaders and publicize those Nixon initiatives which aided civil rights. Increasingly, Young and the National Urban League figured into Nixon administration plans to discredit Spottswood's accusations. While Nixon's treasury undersecretary commended Garment for his response to the bishop, he suggested that a developing relationship between the National Urban League's summer fellowship program and the federal government should be encouraged. A Treasury Department official had worked with the League to spearhead this program. Professors from black institutions pursued internships in various federal departments and agencies, which resulted in increasing the numbers of their students who chose majors in business administration, accounting, and economics. Garment's colleague suggested greater cooperation between this League program and the Nixon administration.[83]

Additionally, serious consideration was given to Young's appointment as civil rights consultant to the president. A GOP supporter in Indianapolis told John Ehrlichman, assistant to the president for domestic affairs, that Young's 1969 speech to the American Bar Association left "an indelible impression upon me." Although the appointment did not materialize, Young had become the black leader with whom the Nixon administration preferred to interact. Those who wanted to enhance President Nixon's reputation among blacks were sure that Young and the National Urban League were the best means to attain that end. If Garment and other Nixon Republicans wanted a special relationship with Young, then the League leader had no objection. What mattered most to Young was access to the administration. Strong ties with Garment and others could position the League to handle federal funds directed toward the nation's inner cities.[84]

Young asked Ehrlichman to schedule him for an appearance before the Domestic Affairs Council. He wanted to inform the Council about "the present status of black Americans, changing moods and attitudes, as well as what I feel to be some immediate and long-range steps which the administration and Federal Government can and must take." Both Ehrlichman and Garment responded with unusual enthusiasm to the proposal.[85]

Aside from letting the Nixon administration know about trends in the black community, Young's core concern related to the League. Nixon learned that the organization faced acute difficulties and needed assistance. An aide noted, "Young feels it will be to the Government's advantage not to let the Urban League go under." A meeting between the president and his cabinet with Young and his colleagues would be mutually beneficial. Young probably would commend the Nixon administration on its efforts in behalf of blacks, and the League would secure substantial federal funds, which would enhance its importance and visibility within the black population.[86]

On December 22, 1970, Whitney Young, Betti Whaley, and Sterling Tucker arrived at the White House to meet with President Nixon and the secretaries of Agriculture, Commerce, Labor, HEW, HUD, and Transportation. Also included were the deputy attorney general, the director-designate of the Office of Economic Opportunity, and the assistant secretary of defense for manpower. Sam Simmons, Sam Jackson, and Arthur Fletcher, three black appointees, also attended the session. Seated next to Nixon, Young told officials that human resources agencies in the federal government should "make more use of the unique capabilities of private, non-profit local organizations like the Urban League." His charts illustrated programs that totaled $70 million, which the League could administer and evaluate. Nixon agreed with Young and instructed the cabinet members to see what could be done. Specifically, Nixon wanted someone in each agency to "explore the ways in which the League and its network of local affiliates can, under contract, help the Departments carry out their human resources programs." Leonard Garment and George Shultz of the Office of Management and Budget served as liaisons with the League's Sterling Tucker. Nixon required a follow-up report about these efforts within a month after the December meeting.[87]

As a result, the Nixon administration extended to the League the largest package of federal funds ever offered to the organization. Young drew $21.24 million in contracts from eight departments for the 1971 and 1972 fiscal years. The Department of Commerce, for example, earmarked a $310,000 million contract plus another $140,000 for assistance in the census. Housing and Urban Development offered $1 million, "a promise" to give speedy attention to the applications of minority sponsors of Section 236 housing, and a commitment to persuade city governments to include the

League in urban renewal programs. The Department of Transportation found $1.25 million in its budget for partnership with League. Even the Department of Agriculture developed a $430,000 proposal for rural housing loans and guarantees for applicants whom the League identified.[88]

After the White House meeting, an elated Whitney Young quoted President Nixon to reporters at a press conference as saying, "What is good for the Urban League is good for the country." Young commended Nixon on his leadership, noting, "Before I could even get to make my appeal . . . he grabbed the ball and ran with it." The president "really called this meeting because he, first, respected the organization, he respected me, and that he really meant business about it." Moreover, Nixon reminded Young and his cabinet that he had gone to NUL headquarters right after the 1968 election to consult with the League leader. Then he "told every Cabinet member, the next time they are in New York to go visit the Urban League offices so they could get a firsthand look at the quality of this mechanism."[89]

Young and the Nixon administration gained what each had sought. The League obtained greater federal support for its programs than what either the Kennedy or Johnson administrations had offered. Nixon officials thought they now had a good chance to create a positive image of the president among blacks. Garment informed Nixon, "Whitney was so pleased with your favorable reaction that he went out and told the press . . . that this was 'a new start, a new day.'"[90]

Young generated such a good press for the Nixon administration that Garment and Ehrlichman revived efforts to attract him into the federal government. Garment advised President Nixon to "inquire—quite informally and privately—about his willingness to take an Ambassadorial appointment." In the meantime Ehrlichman would explore such possibilities with Secretary of State William P. Rogers. Sterling Tucker probably told Garment that Young had plans to retire from the League. Both men felt emboldened to spend an entire Saturday at Young's home in New Rochelle, New York, to discuss an appointment in the Nixon administration. While a significant ambassadorship was on the table, the three men had substantive exchanges about Young going to the White House as assistant to the president for civil rights. The daylong discussion explored the potential problems of how a person of Young's stature would handle a rebuff on a major policy matter. At the end of the Garment and Tucker visit, Young still had not decided whether he wanted to be considered.[91]

Young valued his deepening relationship with the Nixon administration. Although a White House position did not develop, he had already become a member of the Advisory Council on Social Security in May 1969. Robert Finch, the HEW secretary, gave Young the appointment and invited his views on several issues related to the trust fund, benefits policy, and public assistance programs. Young took the assignment so seriously that he asked Cernoria D. Johnson, his Washington bureau director, about NUL positions on social security issues. Young's service on the committee broadened his familiarity and influence with Nixon appointees and holdovers from the Kennedy/Johnson administrations. Additionally, in December 1970 President Nixon put Young on as a director of the Federal Reserve Bank in New York.[92]

Although Young realized that he and Nixon mutually benefited from their dealings with each other, he did not allow the president to exploit him politically or damage his credibility among blacks. An attempt to draw Young's support to an Honor America Day celebration on July 4, 1970, was illustrative. Headed by Nixon's close friends Billy Graham and Bob Hope, Honor America Day was planned as a patriotic event to respond to escalating criticism of Nixon's handling of the Vietnam War. J. Willard Marriott Sr., the hotel tycoon, invited Young to join the Honor America Day executive committee. Young, who objected to symbolic activities, told Marriott that he preferred "those movements that clearly focus on concrete issues or programs and lead to some constructive action." He added, "The most creditable way to honor America is to struggle daily in a sane, positive and constructive way to make its creed, its ideals and its traditional promise a reality for all citizens. . . . At this crucial time, given the high level of unemployment among the young and inner-city black residents, the serious housing crisis and the general unrest within our communities, my participation in Honor America Day might well detract from my efforts and abilities to provide leadership at a time when it is so badly needed." Young declined Marriott's invitation. He sent President Nixon a copy of his response to Marriott and noted that he hoped Nixon understood the validity of his position.[93]

Young's access to the Kennedy, Johnson, and Nixon administrations often resulted in his input into major policy initiatives, influence over the appointments of black officeholders, and federal involvement with the National Urban League. More than any other national black leader, Young consistently visited the White House over three presidencies to press for federal programs to benefit blacks. Richard Nixon recalled, "He was not a patient man, but he understood the uses of patience. And he was not a moderate man in terms of his goals, but he knew the uses of moderation in achieving those goals."[94]

12

On the War Front

When Congress overwhelmingly passed the Tonkin Gulf Resolution in 1964, U.S. military involvement in Vietnam sharply escalated from troop levels of 16,000 in 1963 to 184,000 in 1965, to 200,000 in 1966, and to 460,000 in 1967. Policies formulated by President Lyndon B. Johnson and the advisers he inherited from the Kennedy administration entangled the United States in a seemingly intractable war to help South Vietnam fight off invaders from communist North Vietnam. As a result, the Vietnam War deeply divided the nation's black leaders. Before 1965, James Forman, Robert Moses, and other members of the Student Nonviolent Coordinating Committee became the first civil rights activists to oppose the war. In 1966 SNCC officially denounced American foreign policy in Southeast Asia. Resentment over the military draft, distrust of the federal government, and sympathy for Third World liberation movements motivated SNCC's opposition. Members of the Black Panther Party developed a similar perspective on the war. Huey Newton, for example, criticized the United States as an "imperialistic" and "capitalistic" power that had no right to be in Vietnam. He added that the Black Panther Party supported "any people who are struggling to determine their destiny." He said, "The Vietnamese say Vietnam should be able to determine its own destiny. Power [to] the Vietnamese people." When Martin Luther King Jr. announced in 1967 at Riverside Church in New York City that he opposed the war, the Vietnam issue grew into a major concern that black leaders could not ignore. Speaking to Clergy and Laymen Concerned about Vietnam, King stated that when the United States deepened its involvement in Southeast Asia, he knew that resources required for ending American poverty would be siphoned off into military spending. Moreover, "We were taking the black young men who had been crippled by our society and sending them eight thousand miles away to guarantee liberties in Southeast Asia which they had not found in southwest Georgia and East Harlem." Repulsed by the violence of the war, King noted that his 1964 Nobel Peace Prize compelled him to seek peace. "This calling takes me beyond national allegiances," he said. His commitment to the ministry of Jesus Christ caused him to speak out for the victims of American violence in Vietnam. The views of Whitney M. Young Jr., however, sharply differed from other black leaders who opposed the war.[1]

Despite his initial neutrality, Young's relationship with President Johnson shaped his perspectives on the war and its impact on the black freedom struggle. His position on the Vietnam War moved through three overlapping phases. In 1966, while remaining noncommittal, he embarked on a League-funded trip to Vietnam to investigate the condition of blacks in the military. His friendship with Johnson, however, undermined his neutrality. LBJ was a civil rights champion whose racial liberalism Young greatly valued. Moreover, Young, himself a World War II veteran, believed that he and other black leaders should not criticize their presidential ally. Rather than taking sides in acrimonious debates concerning the war, Young established in the National Urban League an office of veterans' affairs to help black servicemen readjust to civilian life.

In 1967, Young could no longer maintain his neutrality. He accepted President Johnson's invitation to become an observer of the South Vietnamese elections. When he and others returned to the United States, they reported that the elections had been fair. This 1967 trip seemed to justify American involvement in the war against North Vietnam. The United States was fighting for an emergent democratic state in Southeast Asia, and the American military was required to protect South Vietnam from Communist aggressors. Young parlayed his enthusiasm for President Johnson's civil rights record into an endorsement of his controversial policies in Vietnam.

In 1968, after the Tet Offensive exposed the vulnerability of the American military, President Johnson decided against a reelection bid. Months later, Young announced his opposition to the Vietnam War. The wrongness of the war seemed a lesser motivation than the substantial pressure exerted upon the League leader by antiwar blacks and whites whom he could not ignore. Although he finally counseled an American withdrawal from Vietnam, Young did not explicitly criticize either President Johnson or his heir apparent, Hubert H. Humphrey.

Overall, Johnson's policies in Vietnam troubled Young less than the denunciations made against the president by other black leaders. They believed that the war harmed the black struggle and drew funds away from Great Society programs that benefited blacks. He contended that black leaders should not juxtapose civil rights issues with Vietnam War policies. These were mutually exclusive matters which should not have been linked. Johnson, he believed, deserved their support or at least their silence on the Vietnam War.

Maintaining a middle ground between Lyndon B. Johnson and antiwar black leaders became increasingly difficult for Young. Despite disagreement with Roy Wilkins and Young, SNCC counseled those in the civil rights movement to view their service as a "valid alternative to the draft." Clifford L. Alexander, a black official in the Johnson administration, told his boss that Roy Wilkins was distressed and planned to consult Young on this matter. Alexander further noted that some members of the Big Six would publicly dissociate themselves from the SNCC statement because of its negative consequences for the civil rights movement. Additionally, one militant black activist planned to picket the 1966 White House conference, "To Fulfill These Rights," and challenge the Johnson administration to spend as much money to relieve the problems of the ghettos as it was spending on the war. Despite these growing fissures among black leaders, Wilkins and Young tried to keep the problem of Vietnam from sabotaging the White House conference. Even though SNCC sent no representatives to the gathering, Young opposed efforts to bar the organization's participation in the meeting. King attended, but his antiwar posture put him in a marginal role in the proceedings. With SNCC, SCLC, and CORE's Floyd B. McKissick critical of the Vietnam War, Young had no more middle ground to occupy. When he observed that "the people are more concerned about the rat tonight and the job tomorrow than they are about Vietnam," he became an unwitting apologist for Johnson's foreign policy.[2]

It was Young's intention, however, to approach the Vietnam War pragmatically. There was no need to emulate Dr. King's moralism. Instead, Young would act responsibly by avoiding criticism of Johnson and at the same time he would gain administration support for helping blacks in the military. In 1966 he toured Vietnam on a mission financed by the National Urban League. The trip was an expression of the League's interest and concern for the 45,000 to 60,000 black troops. He boasted that he was the first civil rights leader to go to Vietnam to assess the welfare of black personnel. As a result he spent five days visiting black servicemen in all sectors and in many types of operations. He also observed them in Saigon restaurants, bars, the PX, and billets.

Although his trip was nongovernmental, Young told President Johnson that he enjoyed "the hearty cooperation of the civilian and military personnel who are there under your command." He extended special commendations to Ambassador Henry Cabot Lodge and General William Westmoreland.

Moreover, his presence drew the keen interest of the American and foreign press. Not surprisingly, American embassy officials telegrammed back to Washington, D.C., what Young told journalists about his findings. He testified that morale among black soldiers was high. Despite the complexity of the conflict, black servicemen understood why they were in Vietnam. Young also discovered a surprising amount of interracial teamwork. It seemed that color was irrelevant. "Heroes and cowards come in all colors," he said. He added that it was "a sad commentary on the life of the Negro in civilian life" that greater dignity was afforded to black servicemen in Vietnam than what they experienced in the United States. Young contended that this reality explained why blacks reenlisted in the armed forces in such large numbers.

Conversely, Young observed that the promotion of blacks into officer ranks remained rare. Although General Westmoreland populated his headquarters with black officers, there were no black generals and only one black navy pilot. Additionally, Young believed that field commanders had a responsibility to discourage soldiers from "this natural tendency to segregate." He regretted that in the bars during off-duty hours blacks engaged in a "voluntary and self-imposed" separation from their fellow servicemen. Moreover, white officers seemed "to go colorblind" when asked about the numbers of blacks under their command. To boost black representation in positions of authority, Young recommended "more color consciousness to overcome the years of limited opportunity."

Ultimately, Young emphasized to the press exactly why he had come to Southeast Asia. "We made it clear we would make no policy judgements." Rather, he wanted "to assist Negro veterans returning to the states." He added that the numerous affiliates of the National Urban League wanted to ensure a smooth transition from military to civilian life for thousands of black Vietnam vets.[3]

Johnson aides in Saigon and Washington believed that Young's findings reflected favorably on the president's conduct of the Vietnam War. Before Young returned to the United States, Ambassador Lodge cabled the White House about the press conference in which the League leader appeared. The ambassador liked his comment on the sense of pride of many Negroes serving in Vietnam. Young said that this sentiment was one "which he shared and hoped to convey to Negroes and other Americans back home." The fact that blacks received an equal break in military service also was a favorable commentary on today's armed forces. Lodge noted that in spite of Young's sharp questioning of General Westmoreland about the paucity of black officers, his "warts-and-all" observations "appeared to make [a] favorable impression on

Saigon's hard-boiled press corps." As a result, Ambassador Lodge "strongly recommended" that President Johnson and Deputy Secretary of Defense Cyrus Vance meet with Young as a "suitable capstone" to his "constructive and useful trip."[4]

Young did not need Lodge's intercession with the White House. Joseph Califano, a Johnson aide, reported that the League leader wanted to brief the president about his Vietnam trip. "From all indications" said Califano to Johnson, Young's "impressions should be quite positive." Before the meeting, Califano summarized for the president what Young had said at his Saigon news conference, including the references to high troop morale among blacks and interracial teamwork within the military. Johnson only needed to address Young's concerns about "why we have so few Negroes in the higher ranks."

Present in the meeting with Johnson and Young were Cyrus Vance, Walt Rostow, and Clifford Alexander. Young stressed the importance of getting black generals in high-level offices. Alexander recalled Young's observation that it was great that both Benjamin O. Davis Sr. and Benjamin O. Davis Jr. were generals. "Now, unfortunately," said Young to President Johnson, "B.O. Davis Jr. doesn't have any sons, so it looks like there aren't going to be any black generals unless you reach out and find one." Young hoped that Johnson would pay "careful attention" to this issue. Apparently, Young had not spoken in vain. He persuaded Johnson to push the Joint Chiefs of Staff on the matter of black generals. He also had in mind a new League program to help returning black Vietnam veterans to readjust to civilian life. Johnson endorsed that initiative as well. "I am happy you and the National Urban League undertook a mission to Vietnam," said Johnson to Young. He was pleased that his findings would be developed into positive programs for black servicemen.[5]

In the ensuing months after his trip to Vietnam, controversy stirred for Young. He noted that some in the press and public wondered why he shifted his focus away from civil rights matters to "some far-flung, war torn land." Additionally, blacks who opposed American involvement in Vietnam criticized Young for his support of President Johnson's controversial Southeast Asia policies. War expenditures, they argued, diminished resources that would have gone to fight poverty within black ghettoes. Cecil B. Moore, the militant president of the Philadelphia NAACP, claimed not to oppose the Vietnam War. Nonetheless, he accused Young of "being used as an instrument to whitewash discriminatory treatment in Vietnam." Although he apologized for wrongly calling Young a "draft dodger," Moore picketed the NUL convention and dubbed it an "Uncle Tom" meeting. Gloster Current, director of branches and field administration in the national NAACP, supported Young's visit to Vietnam. He denounced Moore for his "silly protest against a brother organization."[6]

The fissure between Young and King over Vietnam, however, was a far more serious matter. On one occasion their argument about the Vietnam War reached such intensity that King, an antiwar activist, hurled a hurtful comment at Young. "Whitney, what you're saying may get you a foundation grant, but it won't get you into the kingdom of truth." He later apologized to Young for this personal attack. Still, no agreement about the Vietnam War emerged between the two. In April 1967 Young further explained his perspectives. "The urgent domestic problem of civil rights and the issue of the war in Vietnam should remain separate. The masses of Negro citizens who are committed to serve and who have given Negro leaders . . . influence, have as their first priority the immediate problem of survival in this country." He added, "The limited resources and personnel available to civil rights agencies for work in their behalf should not be diverted into other channels." Young stated his disagreement with "the ultra-conservative who says that we must sacrifice domestic anti-poverty programs for the war effort." Without mentioning King by name, he dissented from "the opposite view that we cannot support massive domestic programs without an immediate cessation of the war in Vietnam. I am convinced that we do not have to face the choice between national security and internal chaos."[7]

In his syndicated column, "To Be Equal," Young observed that the belief of King and others that "the costs of war automatically stop further civil rights progress" was false. "Our nation can advance civil rights in some areas without spending money. Open housing legislation would not cost money. Whatever our personal feelings about the war in Vietnam, we have to recognize reality. It does no good to say to the nation: 'civil rights or international security—choose.' That's why civil rights should be kept separate and apart from questions like Vietnam."[8] Young suggested that he and other mainstream black leaders singlemindedly pursue a civil rights agenda and avoid entangling it with Vietnam issues because he viewed participation in the antiwar movement as a distraction. He was also wary of those who opposed American policies in Vietnam, because they stirred resentment in President Johnson, an important civil rights ally. Rather than alienate Johnson by associating with antiwar advocates, Young used the Vietnam War as a pressure point to maintain presidential support for black advancement. Young transformed the debate about black involvement in the Vietnam War into a civil rights issue. How were blacks being treated in the army? Were they dying in disproportionate numbers? How many blacks would be promoted, especially to general? How would civilian whites behave toward returning black servicemen? Whether the war was just or unjust was not the important issue. The issue was whether Vietnam would improve or undermine the condition of blacks. Although the war consumed more and more of Johnson's time, Young, who approached Vietnam as a civil rights matter, prevented the president and other powerful whites from neglecting the black struggle.

Young explained his perspective in a widely read *Harper's* article, "When the Negroes in Vietnam Come Home." The desegregation of the armed forces in 1948 set the context for his discussion of blacks in the Vietnam War. Integration as a matter of military policy created opportunities for blacks and discouraged discrimination from resentful whites. Demographic circumstances in the Vietnam War also encouraged interracialism in the military. White servicemen were in a nonwhite country. Their success depended on cooperation from Vietnamese civilians and fellow black soldiers. Although blacks seemed to die in larger proportions than whites, Young attributed this to higher black reenlistments. Even though the navy lagged behind the army in the numbers of black officers, "multiracial teamwork" still prevailed on the carriers that Young visited on his trip in 1966. Because the armed forces offered a better chance of meritorious advancement than the civilian sector, racial inequities in American society needed to be addressed. He reiterated that his purpose for going to Vietnam "was not to make any moral judgement, or any military or political analysis of the war. No sane man would champion the horrendous phenomenon of war, with its unspeakable atrocities, terrible human suffering, and tragic loss of life." Instead, his rationale was "to voice the concern of the Negro community for the men fighting and dying in Vietnam and to let Negroes know the fight was continuing at home to assure them equality for opportunity upon their return." Young drew support from President Johnson, the Department of Defense, and the Veterans' Administration to initiate a program to aid the return of black veterans to civilian life. The administration preferred that Young's interest in Vietnam focus on the status of blacks rather than their deployment with nearly a half million other soldiers to a distant war thousands of miles away from American shores.[9]

When Martin Luther King Jr. derisively told Young that he cared more about a foundation grant than whether the Vietnam War was right or wrong, he went to the core of their disagreement. King probably referred to a $150,000 grant that the League would receive over two years from the Rockefeller Brothers Fund. These funds along with donations from General Foods, Union Carbide, Johnson & Johnson, New York Community Trust, PPG Industries, and Joseph M. Kirchheimer launched an office of veterans' affairs in the National Urban League in September 1967. With 100,000 black veterans returning from Vietnam, the League planned to help them to find employment, to enroll in job training programs, and to locate adequate housing. The U.S. Department of Defense provided information on all black servicemen honorably discharged from the military. The charitable contributions allowed Young to hire a national veterans' affairs director with supporting staff. Moreover, foundation funds paid salaries for veterans' affairs coordinators at League affiliates in New York, Los Angeles, San Francisco, Chicago, Atlanta, New Orleans, Detroit, Washington, and Pittsburgh. NUL officials also sent information about black veterans to numerous other League affiliates.

From September 1967 through September 1968, Joseph F. Cannon, the League's national veterans' affairs director, reported that his office sent to the nine designated affiliates data on nearly 4,000 black servicemen. Eighty-three affiliates with limited services received information for over 7,000 black veterans. Leagues in Dallas, Richmond, and Philadelphia each logged over 500 referrals. Later, the General Foods Corporation funded for the Dallas, Richmond, Jacksonville, Winston-Salem, and Newark affiliates full-time veterans' affairs staff. Other corporate contributions enabled the Pittsburgh, New York, and Atlanta affiliates either to establish or to upgrade their Vietnam veterans' programs. These and other local Leagues provided employment, housing, job training, education, health and welfare, and legal counseling services to blacks recently discharged from the military. Approximately 9,143 received assistance. During the first year monies from individuals, corporations, and foundations totaled $195,015, and expenditures amounted to $192,074.[10]

On an annual budget of nearly $200,000, most of which the Rockefeller Brothers Fund provided, the veterans' affairs program continued its assistance to blacks honorably discharged from the military. Between 1967 and 1970, for example, the League received 42,293 requests and resolved 27,225. This promising start moved Young to approach the Rockefeller Foundation for funds to expand this effort. He had vowed not to ask the Rockefeller Brothers Fund for any more money because he wanted the program to become self-supporting. The increased numbers of black Vietnam veterans, however, caused Young to rethink this position. Moreover, J. George Harrar, president of the Rockefeller Foundation, agreed about expanding the project activities and he advocated recruiting in Vietnam even before veterans were released. So Young asked his staff to prepare a fresh three-year proposal for the Rockefeller Foundation to consider.[11]

Dealing with a new Defense Department estimate of 120,000 minority veterans becoming citizens again attached greater urgency to the veterans' affairs programs. Young told Harrar, "The increased unemployment—with its more serious impact on black people—and the increased rate of release of black servicemen are contributing to a more serious problem in the black community. The Veterans Affairs Program is more desperately needed now than ever before." Although the new proposal argued for an expanded outreach in the nine League affiliates, more cities could be included if the foundation allowed for some flexibility in the budget request. The League proposal raised several new concerns. Forty League affiliates rather than nine needed to have veterans' affairs coordinators. Moreover, the League had to be able to deal with Executive Order 11521, which addressed Vietnam Era Veterans Readjustment Appointments. The League also planned several initiatives to enhance employment, educational, and housing opportunities for black Vietnam servicemen. Young also hoped that disabled veterans would be helped and that more blacks would be encouraged to attend college. The League required $1,143,746, of which $387,935 would go to the national office for staff and other administrative expenses and $755,811 would be disbursed to the affiliates. With the understanding that Young would seek funding from other sources, the Rockefeller Foundation on December 17, 1970, gave a grant for $500,000 to support the program for three to five years.[12]

Young's embrace of the Vietnam War as an issue of fairness to blacks allowed him a veneer of neutrality on whether American involvement was right or wrong. Nevertheless, the League's veterans' affairs program, which Young launched with crucial cooperation from the Defense Department and the Veterans' Administration, implicated him and his organization in the president's Southeast Asia policies. Although Young preferred to avoid an unequivocal public stand on the war, Johnson made it increasingly difficult for him to adhere to this stance. When the president asked Young to become an observer at the 1967 South Vietnamese elections, he could not distance himself from the Johnson administration.

The United States sent nearly a half million troops to Southeast Asia to protect a developing democracy in South Vietnam. That justification was threatened when Buddhist critics mounted sustained opposition to the Nguyen Cao Ky military regime. Pressure from the Johnson administration compelled

Ky and his partner, Nguyen Van Thieu, to call for elections to the presidency and to the national assembly. To ensure fairness President Johnson convened a distinguished team of American observers to watch the election process throughout South Vietnam. He asked Young to join three U.S. senators, three governors, mayors, churchmen, businessmen, and labor leaders in this endeavor.[13]

When Young accepted Johnson's appointment, he became involved in a substantive policy matter. Pressure groups that wanted to influence his views on the South Vietnamese elections and ultimately his findings shared their unsolicited ideas with Young. A Quaker at the New York Center for War/ Peace Studies sent him a proposal to assist in the development of representative government in South Vietnam. An official from the General Board of Christian Concern of the Methodist Episcopal Church sent four documents to Young, "which we hope will help you in adding perspectives to your [election] observations." An interfaith group of clergy wanted Young to learn whether "the election process has already been distorted as to make a mockery of the goal of self-determination for which our young men are dying every day." They asked him to determine if antiwar candidates had been barred from the election and if the U.S. embassy had already stated a preference for the Ky/Thieu military regime. A representative of the Republican Vietnam Fair Elections Project mailed Young fifty questions on the course of the elections "which suggest at least as many possible ways in which the elections could be rigged." Now Young had become a significant participant in a major foreign policy matter. No longer could he restrict his involvement to military race relations. Whether the war was wise or not was an issue that Young had to face head-on.[14]

While in Vietnam, Young was impressed by Vietnamese enthusiasm for the electoral process. In Phanthiet, for example, rockets had just landed, yet there were people parading to the polls. He dismissed concerns about government pressure on the voters. Young observed that he was "more concerned about the fairness of the press than the fairness of the election." He became convinced that American reporters were not providing accurate coverage of the elections. At a reception at the ambassador's Saigon residence, Young blasted the press for bias in reporting on the campaign and on the election preparations. A telegram to Secretary of State Dean Rusk noted, "Young pointed out that from their reporting he had not been aware of all the campaign activity by opposition candidates. He had not realized the extent of the VC [Vietcong] pressures against the elections and thought that 'I would only see Thieu/Ky posters everywhere.'" According to another cable to Secretary

Rusk, "Whitney Young has said that unless he sees some indications of election rigging or pressure he is going to start asking reporters why they haven't
been reporting elections correctly." Walt Rostow seemed sufficiently impressed
with the criticism of the press by Young and other election observers that he
suggested to President Johnson that the *New York Times* and the Associated
Press should be told "that their representatives are not objective reporters but
political operatives."[15]

Although Thieu and Ky claimed victory with 35 percent of the votes,
they faced charges that their regime either prevented major opponents from
running or jailed them. Voter intimidation, repeat voting by soldiers, fraudu-
lent tallies, and stuffed ballot boxes were also alleged. Nonetheless, Young
and the other observers pronounced the elections as "reasonably efficient,
free, and honest." Young apparently agreed with another observer who commended the "progress" in Vietnam "as a result of the elections we were privileged to witness."[16]

Because of his participation on the team of election observers, Young's
views on the Vietnam War were now important to whites and blacks alike.
Moreover, he became identified with the Johnson administration and its Southeast Asia policies. A member of the National Association of Social Workers
criticized him for going to Vietnam, saying, "I am ashamed of your support
of the USA Vietnam War by participating in that 'white wash' commission."
Young's NASW colleague accused him and the team of "contributing to the
spurious and illegal election in South Vietnam." Moreover, "you and your
organization do not gain support from your giving in to Johnson and his
white power structure, and in my view, your trip to Vietnam betrayed your
stated principles. You certainly permitted yourself to be exploited through
pictures and words in press releases." Theodore E. Brown of the American
Negro Leadership Conference on Africa, however, agreed that Young's civil
rights angle concerning the war was defensible. In an NBC telecast, Young
commented on why he consented to serve on the team. Brown liked his
answer. "You are correct," he said. "American Negroes would have been most
vociferous in their complaints . . . if a distinguished Negro had not been
included in such a delegation." Brown congratulated him for undertaking
"that important and rather dangerous assignment." Whether Young pleased
or displeased supporters and critics of the Johnson administration, he was
now a major participant in the national debate about the Vietnam War.[17]

Those who suspected that Young was becoming cozier with Johnson's
Vietnam policy were proven correct. The *Chicago Sun-Times* published a pho-
tograph of Young and Henry Cabot Lodge, the former U.S. ambassador to

South Vietnam, swimming together on Waikiki in Hawaii during their return trip from the elections. Moreover, Young told General William C.
Westmoreland, "I came away . . . deeply impressed with the sterling role
which you are playing in this national effort." The State Department now
kept Young informed about administration policy in Vietnam. One official
updated him about tallies in South Vietnam's presidential and senatorial con-
tests. Another noted that in his upcoming speaking engagements Young might
refer to his recent experience in Vietnam. A speech written by a presidential
adviser was sent to help the League leader "in gaining a better understanding
of the Government's position and the steps that led to our present involvement in Vietnam."[18]

Although White House officials briefed Young on their nation-build-
ing efforts in Vietnam, they were aware of his ongoing concerns about black
servicemen. If they expected him to defend the president's foreign policy,
they had to provide him with information about blacks in Vietnam. Right
after his return from the South Vietnam elections, administration officials
prepared statistics for Young on blacks who were fighting in the war, those
who had reenlisted, and the disproportionate number of them who had been
killed. While in Vietnam, he met with black civilian personnel in the U.S.
Agency for International Development. After Young learned how one of them
faced difficulty in getting a promotion, he promised to look into the matter
when he returned to the United States.[19] White House officials understood
that Young preferred to talk about the Vietnam War in terms of its impact on
blacks. Since the president usually escaped Young's criticism on this matter,
Johnson could comfortably view him as an administration ally on the Vietnam issue.

Whatever doubts Young harbored about American involvement, he kept
them to himself. His loyalty to Lyndon B. Johnson, the second great emanci-
pator, prevented him from bolting administration policy in Southeast Asia.
Similar sentiments caused him to prefer, albeit tacitly, the presidential candidacy of Vice President Humphrey, another civil rights champion. After his
loss to Richard Nixon, Humphrey responded to Young's consoling telegram:
"It is good to know I have your friendship and support."[20]

Johnson's decision on March 31, 1968, to forego a reelection bid and
Humphrey's subsequent defeat in the general election freed Young to reassess
his position on the Vietnam War. When Nixon took the oath of office on
January 20, 1969, there were 536,000 troops in Vietnam and the war was
costing $30 billion annually. Although Nixon instituted a Vietnamization
effort whereby South Vietnamese troops replaced departing American sol-

diers, the war seemed far from over. The Vietnam Moratorium Committee, organized on June 30, 1969, planned nationwide demonstrations on October 15, 1969, to protest the continuation of the war. Endorsements from the Teamsters, the United Auto Workers, former Supreme Court justice Arthur Goldberg, former ambassador W. Averell Harriman, New York mayor John V. Lindsay, and members of Congress gave needed credibility to this antiwar effort. Millions across the United States participated in the Moratorium. In Boston, for example, 100,000 nonviolent antiwar demonstrators filled a downtown site.[21]

On October 7, 1969, Young told NUL trustees about the "terrific pressure from the black community, the youth community and the white liberal, intellectual community for the National Urban League to take some position on the war. This pressure has increased with the approaching October 15th Vietnam Moratorium." Although he would not commit the League, Young himself endorsed the demonstrations. To what extent Young actually backed the Moratorium is unclear. He surely wanted to explain publicly what meaning should be attached to his endorsement rather than allow Moratorium activists to interpret his stand. When Susan Werbe of the Moratorium received the news about his opposition to the Vietnam War, Young told her he would not speak at any rallies nor should she announce his statement of support. He would issue his own press release.[22]

Young declared, "I am totally convinced that Vietnam is tragically diverting America's attention from its primary problem—the urban and racial crisis—at the very time that crisis is at [a] flash point." He deplored the divisiveness that was caused within the military where "racial teamwork" once prevailed and within already tense black communities. The Vietnam War had "an extra dimension for black people." He said, "We are suffering doubly. We are dying for something abroad that we do not have at home." Moreover, blacks bore the brunt of white backlash growing out of frustration with the Vietnam problem. Despite high death rates for soldiers from the working class of whites and blacks, the two groups were locked in conflict. "Because of hunger, the wasteland in the black ghettos, and the revolt of young people both black and white," Young advised the American government to "turn away from Vietnam." He added that "we must terminate this war immediately" and "we must pour our vital resources back into our own land, our own cities, our own people." Now Young had joined the antiwar movement.[23]

Young's opposition to the Vietnam War produced some division within the National Urban League. The board of the Youngstown, Ohio, Urban League voted 16 to 3 in favor of Young's statement. One board member resigned in protest. One NUL supporter told Young that he understood the pressure Young was under to issue a statement. He agreed that the war was destructive, but Young's support for American withdrawal from Vietnam would cause repercussions. Young was a reluctant antiwar hero, and he declined invitations to speak at rallies.[24]

Young was less interested in activism against the nation's Vietnam involvement than in examining the war's impact on the black population. Although he changed positions on whether or not the war should be pursued, he remained consistent in his paramount concern about blacks and how they fared in military and civilian life. Because the Nixon administration promised an eventual withdrawal from Vietnam, talk about a "peace dividend" stimulated a national debate about how it would be spent. Savings from expenditures in Vietnam would yield $8 billion for social spending, argued Arthur F. Burns, a Nixon adviser. The president, however, thought that few funds would be available if the war ended soon. In September 1969 Young contended in his weekly column that Burns and Nixon missed the point. "Actually, the will to tackle poverty is all that's needed." Moreover, citizens should "tell their leaders that they're fed up with doubletalk about how poor the government is and demand that war savings become peace spending to build an open society."[25]

Young's vacillating positions on Vietnam derived from his primary commitment to black advancement. He believed that blacks would benefit from federal protection and programs if they withheld criticism of Johnson administration policies in Vietnam. After Johnson ended his term and Humphrey failed in his presidential bid, Young yielded to mounting pressure to oppose the Vietnam War. Because Nixon lacked Johnson's stature in civil rights, Young had few compelling reasons to resist whites and blacks who declared that the war was morally wrong and damaging to black people.

13

The Ties That Bind

Whitney M. Young Jr. recognized that his effectiveness with powerful whites depended on his credibility with the black population. Moderate blacks shared his integrationist ideology and lauded his success as executive director of the National Urban League. Invitations to address black churches, fraternities, women's clubs, civil rights organizations, and other mainstream groups continuously flowed into Young's New York City office. These requests reached such volume that the League leader vowed to "accept only those invitations extended by national groups—or at the most regional bodies with significant and influential participation."[1] These were the individuals and institutions who believed in his leadership and wanted to hear him speak. Similarly, Black Power advocates asked him to help with their projects and to address their gatherings. Despite their ideological disagreements, Young showed that he could interact and cooperate with the militant and sometimes separatist wing of the black freedom movement. Already, he had demonstrated that his moderate leadership would draw support from influential whites in the federal government, corporations, and foundations. That he played the same role within the black population validated lessons he learned as a local League official in St. Paul and in Omaha. In those communities Young's temperate posture and his skillful use of white allies persuaded midwestern elites to yield to black demands for jobs, education, and housing. At the same time blacks whom Young served through these League affiliates believed that he persistently advocated their cause and supported direct action tactics to win concessions from resistant white employers and politicians. As a national black leader Young successfully pursued these strategies in the civil rights movement. Powerful whites responded to his call to improve race relations because his support within the black population extended beyond the interracial National Urban League.

Thomas G. Shirreffs, vice president of the Standard Oil Company and a board member of the Cleveland Urban League, understood the relationship between Young and black institutions. In 1968 Young agreed to speak at the 75th anniversary banquet of the Antioch Baptist Church. Because the pastor, the Reverend Emanuel Branch Jr., presided over the Cleveland Urban League, both Young and Shirreffs agreed to come. Moreover, Shirreffs, an executive committee member of the Greater Cleveland Plans for Progress, wanted to discuss with Young a report on black employment. However, Shirreffs had to go to an inner city church to meet him. His Standard Oil connection was important to Young, but so was Branch's Antioch Baptist Church. Young's staff reminded him that this 2,700-member black congregation was one of the largest and most prestigious in the country. Antioch's promised contribution to the League's New Thrust and possibly to other programs also convinced Young that the congregation deserved to be cultivated like white institutions. Although Standard Oil gave far more money to the League than Antioch, Shirreffs knew that the support of Emanuel Branch was as important to Young as that of any corporate executive.[2]

The League leader had long recognized that black clergy and their congregations staunchly supported local Leagues. Many of them thought that Young was better acquainted than other national black leaders with the social and economic issues that confronted their communities. Reverend Wyatt Tee Walker, an aide to Martin Luther King Jr. and a special assistant on urban affairs to New York governor Nelson A. Rockefeller, invited Young to speak to his congregation, Canaan Baptist Church in Harlem in 1967. "I am convinced," he said, "that there is much good that can be realized from your public appearance in the ghetto community." Similarly, the Reverend Ulysses B. Blakeley, associate executive of the Synod of New Jersey of the Presbyterian Church, U.S.A., wrote to Young in behalf of the Caucus of Caucuses, an interdenominational group of black clergy. They wanted the League leader to participate in their "Emergency Meeting on Urban Distress." Francis A. Kornegay, executive director of the Detroit Urban League, reported anticipation among "people of the community" about Young's upcoming trip to address the General Conference of the African Methodist Episcopal Zion Church on its Human Relations Night. Young and Bishop Herbert Bell Shaw had agreed in 1967 that the National Urban League and the AME Zion Church would work together.[3]

Black clergy in the West also admired Young's leadership. The Reverend Joseph L. Griffin of Macedonia Baptist Church in Denver asked Sebastian C. Owens, executive director of the local League, to persuade Young to visit Colorado. "Because you have not been to Denver since you became Executive Director of the Urban League," said Griffin to Young, "it would be an opportunity for us to present you to the Denver community and for the community to hear from one of the National leaders in the Civil Rights struggle." The Reverend John Hurst Adams, pastor of First African Methodist Episcopal Church in Seattle, also invited Young to the Pacific Northwest. "National leadership is seldom in this area," Adams observed. He arranged for Young to meet the local press, employers who had signed equal opportunity pledges, and faculty and students on area campuses.[4]

Young believed that black middle-class and working-class congregations could spearhead concrete improvements in their communities. In fact, numerous preachers and parishioners drew Young to their churches because they knew he endorsed these objectives. After he consented to speak at Main Street Baptist Church of Aurora, Illinois, Frank L. Patterson, president of the Men's Club, informed the League leader that blacks, who constituted 6 percent of Aurora's 70,000 people, faced continued de facto housing segregation due to past patterns. A similar group within St. Catherine African Methodist Episcopal Zion Church in New Rochelle, New York, also drew Young's support. He spoke in 1966 at the congregation's business and professional night. Because Reverend Andrew E. Whitted and his members planned to build a community center and a middle-income apartment complex, they won Young's hearty commendation. When St. Philip Protestant Episcopal Church in Harlem pushed into the final phases of building a community center for day care, afterschool programs, and other services, Young, who gave a speech to the congregation, contributed his honorarium to this million-dollar undertaking.[5]

Young's appearance, especially at national religious gatherings, validated his leadership among blacks and strengthened his network of colleagues in the civil rights struggle. Numerous persons with whom Young cooperated in the "movement" also participated in black denominational affairs. Bishop Stephen G. Spottswood, chairman of the NAACP board of directors, extended to Young a formal invitation to speak to the 1968 General Conference of the African Methodist Episcopal Zion Church. "Looking forward to your coming to us with a large degree of pleasurable expectancy," said Spottswood to Young. The Reverend Sandy F. Ray, a colleague and confidant of Martin Luther King Jr. and his father, asked Young in 1969 to address for a second time the National Sunday School and Baptist Training Union Congress. These invitations were significant because Ray urged the National Baptist Convention, U.S.A., toward greater civil rights involvement. In 1970 Bishop Norris S. Curry invited Young to Memphis for the Centennial General Conference of the Christian Methodist Episcopal Church. Herman Ewing, executive director of the Memphis Urban League and a CME member, was pleased that Young agreed to come. He advised him to press the denomination to do more in the area of nonprofit housing.[6]

As Young sought ratification from black churches, he wrestled with his Unitarianism. Occasionally he and his wife, Margaret, accompanied their friends to St. Catherine African Methodist Episcopal Zion Church in New Rochelle. Young, however, remained a member of the White Plains Community Church, a Unitarian congregation which his wife attended but declined to join. Young, an active participant in congregational affairs, frequently delivered Sunday morning sermons, especially on social and civil rights concerns. Moreover, denominational officials involved him in the national Unitarian Service Committee, the Laymen's League, and the Commission on Religion and Race. Nonetheless, Young became increasingly dissatisfied with his congregation's aloofness from social activism. In December 1970, while maintaining his membership in the White Plains Church, Young decided that he and his wife should visit other churches, particularly in the black community. Such an act would be "an indication of our respect for them and [our] desire to support them." Young realized that his leadership required validation from black churches. Eventually, he concluded that his relationship with black congregations mandated a fuller commitment.[7]

Young, like Martin Luther King Jr., realized that when black clergy and congregations ratified his leadership, his claim to represent the African American population was strengthened. Surely, Young's influence with powerful whites derived from his persuasive arguments for social change and from his moderate leadership and integrationist ideology. But Young always spoke to influential whites as a leader of blacks.

Fraternal organizations drew extensively from the black professional and working classes. Young, a member of Alpha Phi Alpha, reflected that fraternity's integrationist beliefs, and he challenged his fraternity to contribute financially to the National Urban League. The Masons and the Elks also supported the interracialism of the civil rights movement and endorsed Young's eloquent espousal of this perspective.[8]

Alpha Phi Alpha's Gamma Iota Lambda chapter of Brooklyn and Long Island asked Young to speak at a 1963 public meeting at Reverend Sandy F. Ray's Cornerstone Baptist Church. Despite a successful scholarship program for high school students, Young was needed "to spur Alpha men to greater activity in the community." An Alpha official noted, "Our community has not heard you for a long time and would welcome any message you might give." So, in front of this integrationist fraternity crowd, Young strongly denounced racial separatism. According to this view, Young noted, "The answer to the problem of race discrimination . . . for the Negro is to separate and to withdraw from any association with non-Negro citizens. . . . This approach indicts all non-Negroes as evil, and implies honesty and virtue as qualities possessed only by Negroes." He blamed black Muslims and Representative Adam Clayton Powell of Harlem for promoting these ideas. Young defended the NAACP, CORE, SCLC, and his own "vilified" National Urban League against these black nationalist attacks. These groups were wrongly called "meaningless organizations controlled by evil white citizens and administered by 'Uncle Toms.'" To approving fellow Alphas, Young declared, "We are an integral part of the fabric of America. . . . Our blood, sweat and tears have gone into the wars to save this country, and into the business, educational and cultural life of this nation. We cannot give up what our forefathers helped to develop. . . . The Negro's destiny in this country is not to identify himself as a bloc against all white citizens. It is rather to ally himself with decent people of good will of every race, color and creed, in a coalition against evil and prejudiced people of whatever race."⁹

Agreement with Young's integrationist ideology and pride in his Alpha allegiance motivated fraternity members to support NUL initiatives. Frank W. Morris, eastern regional vice president, urged more than forty chapters in his jurisdiction to aid the League's program in "Strengthening Negro Family Life." Moreover, he asked Young to advise his public policy committee. "When you think Alpha should speak on something, just give me the word," he told Young.¹⁰

Although Young was pleased that Alpha members agreed with his integrationist perspectives, he also wanted their monetary support for NUL programs. "We would greatly appreciate some financial help," he declared to Alpha president T. Winston Cole in 1963. After he addressed the fraternity's 1967 annual convention in Los Angeles, Cole's successor, Lionel Newsom, told Young, "In private conversation with the brothers I wish you would sneak in a word for upping the allotment to the League." He sent Young his personal contribution and promised to enlist the help of the Alpha board of directors to persuade the general body to increase the fraternity's NUL donations.¹¹

Although the Masons existed in several autonomous groups, they were united in their commitment to interracialism. Young, who maintained his membership in Omaha's Prince Hall Rescue Lodge #4, pressed these Masonic groups to donate to the League. He also enlisted League subordinates to maintain contact with the Masons and remind them of the NUL's fiscal needs. Clarence Coleman, the League's southern regional director, interacted in Tulsa with Amos Hall, president of the Conference of Grand Masters of the Prince Hall Masons. Hall, who was already involved with the Tulsa Urban League, had recently gone to Europe to visit Masons in the American military. Hall noted that the servicemen had made a substantial contribution to the NAACP. He told Coleman that, "if convincingly approached," these Masonic members might do the same for the National Urban League. Coleman told Young's associate executive director, Nelson Jackson, to contact the Masons' military liaison in New York City to accomplish this goal. Hall also told Coleman that he hoped someone from the League's national headquarters would attend the Masons' 1962 meeting in Jackson, Mississippi. NUL contributions could be discussed at this meeting.[12]

That Young and other League officials belonged to the Masons ensured them a hearing before fraternity bursars. Moreover, John G. Lewis, the sovereign grand commander of the Prince Hall Masons, southern division, joined the NUL board. He then persuaded Young to attend the conference of Grand Masters where Lewis "received nothing but praise for having been the one to see that [the League leader] appeared." When Lewis challenged the Grand Masters to deepen their NUL involvement, he "found that about five of them claim[ed] to be the backbone of the League in their cities." He told Young that he hoped that the southern division Masons would "make a good showing on the national level" with their donations. He sent his own check to Young as a down payment. Similar support came to the League from the Prince Hall Masons in the northern division. In 1965 Young addressed the Most Excellent Prince Hall Grand Chapter Royal Arch Masons of the State of New York. Arthur Swaby, chairman of the national charity committee, informed Young that a financial contribution to the National Urban League would await him when he arrived at the event.[13] Similarly, the Ancient Egyptian Arabic Order Nobles of the Mystic Shrine of North and South America and Its Jurisdictions [Shriners] was another black Masonic group with which Young developed a relationship. Charles A. Dargan, the Imperial High Priest and Prophet, informed Young that his speech to the Shriners' 1963 awards banquet did a lot to create a new image for the League. Moreover, Young ingratiated himself with those who heard the address. Dargan suggested that Young also attend the group's Imperial Council meeting in Pittsburgh because "every conceivable effort" would be made to get a contribution for the League.[14]

Young also identified the Improved Benevolent and Protective Order of the Elks of the World as a potential NUL benefactor. The success of this undertaking depended on how well Young could cultivate Hobson R. Reynolds, the Grand Exalted Ruler of 500,000 black Elks. A Philadelphia mortician and a former housing appointee in the Eisenhower administration, Reynolds possessed exemplary civil rights credentials. During his 1934-38 term in the Pennsylvania legislature, he successfully pushed the passage of an equal rights bill. As the Elks grand director of civil liberties from 1938 through 1960, Reynolds brought such prominent black leaders as Walter White of the NAACP to speak to IBPOEW audiences. His department also supported the efforts of various civil rights groups to win legislative and judicial victories over racial segregation and discrimination. These Elks activities continued through Reynolds's tenure as Grand Exalted Ruler from 1960 until his retirement in 1982.[15]

Reynolds's reputation resulted in his nomination in 1962 to the NUL board of directors. Reynolds reminded Young that he already had served on the NUL board. "No one knows better than I the job the National Urban League has done," Reynolds noted. "Now that I am Grand Exalted Ruler," he continued, "I shall . . . strive zealously to help promote the great program that I am sure you will sponsor during your tenure of office." Toward that end Reynolds invited Young to Detroit to speak to the 1962 Elks Grand Lodge convention.[16]

Although Young's speech at the convention was well received, his request for a national roster of Elks lodges was not granted. "I am prohibited by our Grand Lodge law to send out these directories since this is a secret organization," said Grand Secretary Joseph F. Simmons to Young. Nonetheless, Young pressed Reynolds to acknowledge publicly his NUL affiliation. In an interview with the *Norfolk Journal and Guide*, a black newspaper, Reynolds, while lauding the NAACP, failed to mention the National Urban League. Young brought the omission to Reynold's attention. The Grand Exalted Ruler responded by offering the cooperation of the Elks Public Relations Department to promote League programs. Young was pleased because he believed that the Elks' support was vital.[17]

In 1965 he received the Elks' Lovejoy Award. Named for the martyred abolitionist Elijah Lovejoy, the award honored Americans who had made a great contribution toward the advancement of minority groups. The interracial roster of recipients included Eisenhower attorney general William P. Rogers, Ralph J. Bunche, Mary McLeod Bethune, Thurgood Marshall, Governor Alfred E. Driscoll, Martin Luther King Jr., A. Philip Randolph, and Young's predecessor, Lester B. Granger. Young was pleased that his interracialism had the endorsement of the nation's largest black fraternity.[18]

Within days after Young received the Lovejoy award, a race riot erupted in the Watts community of Los Angeles. Similar outbreaks of racial violence occurred in 1966, 1967, and 1968 in other black ghettoes across the nation. These riots, along with the growing visibility of Black Power advocates and the assassination of Martin Luther King Jr., fractured the civil rights movement and put integrationist leaders on the defensive. These circumstances increased Young's reliance on the Elks and other grassroots black organizations who espoused integrationist objectives. As a result, Reynolds's willingness to sign a joint proclamation with Young on cooperation between the Elks and the League gave a significant boost to Young's interracialism.

Addressed to the 1968 Elks Grand Lodge Convention, the open letter to the delegates acknowledged that blacks had not attained social and economic equality despite the passage of several civil rights laws. "At the present rate of improvement it will take black people until 1975 to catch up to where the average white person was in 1950 or 1960," Reynolds and Young asserted. They proposed that blacks respond in three ways. First, leaders of black organizations should denounce the race riots because they "accelerate racial polarization and unify the racists in opposition to progress by black people." Second, black organizations should maintain their financial commitment to ghetto communities even though such contributions "are grossly inadequate in light of the task we now face." Third, the Elks and other groups should support NUL's New Thrust plan by inviting League representatives to attend the Elks' local and district meetings.[19] The impact of these appeals was uncertain. That Young gained Elks endorsement of the League strengthened his credibility as an important black leader at a time when highly visible and publicized separatist spokesmen assailed him as an "Uncle Tom."

Reynolds's embrace of Young also translated into grassroots Elks backing for the League. The Ohio State Elks association, for example, selected Young as its 1966 man of the year "for your Liberal and Humane outlook on the problems of our times and your courage and ability to do something about them." Frank Huntley, a convention committee member, lived in Youngstown and belonged to the local Buckeye Elks Lodge #73. He included in his letter to Young "editorials on a need for an Urban League in Youngstown[,] a city of 200,000." Huntley hoped that "maybe we can work something out" to bring a League affiliate to the area.[20]

Whereas the Elks were largely working class, the Frontiers and the Links were service organizations that drew primarily from the educated and professional elite. The Frontiers identified with Yokefellow Whitney Young, a member, and shared his integrationist views. In 1963 he was invited to address the

annual meeting. Although Young could not attend, he suggested that Edwin
C. "Bill" Berry, the head of the Chicago affiliate, should substitute for him.
He hoped that Berry's presence would prod the Frontiers to give to the League
"strong moral support and a substantial financial contribution."[21]

As with the Frontiers, Young initiated an ongoing effort to attract funds
from the Links, an organization with 2,500 women in ninety chapters in
forty states. In 1962 Young addressed gatherings of the Links, including the
eastern area meeting in Williamsburg, Virginia, and a gathering of the Greater
New York chapter. A subsequent invitation to speak to the Links' thirteenth
national assembly in French Lick, Indiana, probably resulted from his previous two appearances. Although the organization could not pay his expenses
to the Indiana meeting, the national chairperson, Dr. Helen G. Edmonds,
hoped that Young could interpret his program to women community leaders.
Young's positive response must have surprised Edmonds. Although he wanted
to discuss NUL efforts to aid the black population, his larger objective was to
persuade the Links to contribute significantly to the League.[22]

Young's careful cultivation of the Links illustrated how much importance he attached to black organizations and the credibility they conferred on
his integrationist leadership. In 1966, for example, the group put him on the
program of its southern area meeting in New Orleans. Young told the national president, Vivian Beamon, that he hoped his remarks concerning financial support from the Links "made an impression." He added that funding of the League "would indicate that as an intelligent group of outstanding
Negro women, the Links recognize the true nature of the civil rights struggle
and the important role of the Urban League in that struggle."[23]

Ultimately, Young's appeals to the Links paid off. In 1969 the organization donated $50,000 to a League sponsored student summer program.
Moreover, President Beamon informed Young that on June 26, 1970 the
League would receive a second $50,000 contribution. A total of $100,000
from an influential black women's group legitimized Young's contention that
his leadership and integrationist perspectives enjoyed strong support within
the black population.[24]

Young's experience with the Links paralleled his interaction with the
National Urban League Guild. This group, which pharmacist and social worker
Mollie Moon founded in 1942, sponsored an annual Beaux-Arts Ball to raise
funds for the League. Moon, a NUL board member, also spearheaded local
guilds to support affiliates across the United States. As a result the Council of
Urban League Guilds was established and grew to eighty-three chapters.
Aleathia H. Mayo, who headed the council, worked with Moon during Young's

term as the NUL executive director. Over time Moon, Mayo, and other black women collected over $3.4 million for the League. Because Young was accustomed to working with educated black women who opted for supportive roles, he was stunned by the sharp criticism of Pauli Murray, who accused him and other civil rights leaders of sexism.[25] In 1963 Murray, a black lawyer and educator, challenged the claim of Young and his colleagues that they represented black women. She criticized A. Philip Randolph, the convener of the 1963 March on Washington, when he spoke at the all-male National Press Club, despite protests from female journalists. Moreover, she excoriated civil rights leaders for excluding women from their March meeting with President Kennedy. In a last-minute response, however, Dorothy Height of the National Council of Negro Women was included. When, in a speech to Height's organization, Murray repeated her denunciation of sexism among the civil rights leaders, Young responded. He saw nothing to inhibit "competent Negro women" from attaining leadership positions in civil rights organizations. He cited the League as an example. Four of the seven "top professionals" on his staff were black women. Young also reminded Murray of his personal efforts in behalf of Miss Dorothy Height's inclusion as a peer member of the Council of United Civil Rights Leadership. Additionally, Height's NCNW received funds and participated in CUCRL policymaking.

Although Young disavowed "any prejudice against women," he believed that "the goal of Negro women . . . should be somewhat different from that of white women." He said, "In the case of white women, whose men already occupy positions of high status, security and a much greater level of educational attainment than their women, just the reverse is true of Negroes." He noted, "For the purposes of improving the stability of our Negro family life, providing adequate role models for our sons and daughters, as well as increasing the number of available Negro women who can offer both economic security and intellectual compatibility, I would think that Negro women leaders . . . should make their primary goal the lifting of the social, economic, and educational status of their men."

Despite Young's traditional views on gender roles, he conceded that Murray validly criticized him and his colleagues for gender exclusion. He asked her "to identify . . . those Negro women whom other Negro women will generally accept as their official spokesmen such as now happens with Negro men through their civil rights leaders." He promised that black leaders would draw these persons into their ranks "as future opportunities come."[26]

Young defended himself against Murray's charge by citing gender equality within his own organization, but the League had a blemished record. Cernoria

D. Johnson, for example, appealed to Young when her authority as the Washington bureau chief was challenged by Sterling Tucker, the executive director of the local League. Before Johnson's arrival, Tucker usually represented Young at important meetings with federal officials. Johnson rightly believed that her appointment to the bureau position relieved Tucker of his previous role. Nonetheless, he represented Young at a crucial meeting with G. Mennen Williams, an adviser to President Kennedy. Tucker and other guests, including a representative from the National Women's Committee on Civil Rights, discussed with Williams what civil rights issues Kennedy should include in his legislative package. Although Tucker told Young that "any official follow-up" was in Johnson's domain, they had undercut her. Johnson fumed and expressed her "profound indignation" over her exclusion from the meeting. She told Young, "This is the way he has operated ever since I assumed this responsibility." Johnson asked Young to tell Tucker to inform her about these important invitations and to remind G. Mennen Williams that he should communicate with her. Young conferred major responsibility upon Johnson, but he was slow in signaling to other League officials that she was his designated spokesperson in the nation's capital. Although she and other female staff acknowledged Young as their leader on racial matters, they knew that gender issues still ranked a distant second to the fight for racial equality. The large infusion of funds that the Links and the Guilds poured into the National Urban League showed that thousands of black women esteemed Young's pursuit of interracialism.[27]

Black business and professional associations also ratified Young as a major spokesman. Some were all-black organizations, and others were subgroups within larger white associations. In any case these separate groups argued for their fuller inclusion in the American mainstream. In their opinion Whitney M. Young Jr. made that case better than any other civil rights leader. In 1961 Young urged black businessmen to revive the National Negro Business League. In 1969 the National Bankers Association, a group of twenty black financial institutions, cooperated with the Urban Affairs Committee of the American Bankers Association to sponsor a conference on inner-city problems and how banks should address them. Originally called the Black Bankers Conference, these black officials believed that a speech by Young on how the League viewed employment, lending, and housing would aid their cause.[28]

Blacks in the insurance industry drew special attention from Young and the League. Clarence Coleman, the NUL southern regional director, urged Young to deepen the League's relationship with Norris Herndon, president of the Atlanta Life Insurance Company and a potential benefactor. Herndon's

firm had given the NAACP $10,000 in 1962, and Young wanted similar sup-
port for the National Urban League. Jesse Hill, Young's friend from his Atlanta days, asked him to speak to the 1962 convention of the National Insurance Association. The organization consisted of fifty black-managed life and
disability companies. Young told Hill and Norman B. Houston, president of
the Los Angeles–based Golden State Mutual Life Insurance Company, that
he thought the NIA was "an important facet in community relations and a key
group to be brought into greater understanding of the work of the National
Urban League."[29]

Young was already mindful that black insurance leaders were involved
with the League. Asa T. Spaulding, president of the North Carolina Mutual
Life Insurance Company, served on the NUL board. In New Orleans where
racist detractors forced the local League affiliate out of the United Fund (community chest), black insurance officials helped to replace the withdrawn donations. Young challenged the NIA to redouble its tangible financial support.
"We not only need your money, but we also need to have these contributions
to show our present contributors—largely white and many of them insurance companies—that we as Negro citizens in general, and Negro business in
particular, have grown not only in wealth but also in the kind of maturity
that will reflect itself in support of its organizations."[30]

Carlton B. Goodlett, publisher of the *Sun-Reporter* in San Francisco,
wanted to broaden Young's involvement with black insurance companies. He
and Earl B. Dickerson wanted to put Young on the board of two of their
companies. The Supreme Life Insurance Company was organizing a New
York company as Supreme Life of New York. Goodlett said, "You are the type
of man who we must have on the team of younger men which Earl is select-
ing to give new vision, new impetus, and dynamic leadership as Supreme Life
attempts to become an integrated national insurance company." Young agreed
because involvement in the insurance field would enable him to promote
black business interests and to generate funding for the League.[31]

While the League leader welcomed contributions from black health
care organizations, he emphasized efforts to end the racial exclusion of black
hospitals, physicians, and administrators. That Young understood crucial issues which this constituency confronted gave him a wide following within
this important stratum of the black population. In 1962 the National Urban
League joined the NAACP and the National Medical Association (NMA) in sponsoring the Sixth Imhotep National Conference on Hospital Integration. Young
appeared on the program to discuss efforts to integrate formerly all-white
hospitals, to put black doctors on their staffs, and to prepare more blacks for

the nation's medical schools. He pledged the active participation of the League in attaining these objectives. In 1965 he agreed to be a part of the NMA's Council on Talent Recruitment. Moreover, when the American Hospital Association in 1968 invited Young to speak, Haynes Rice, the administrator of the all-black Norfolk Community Hospital, was enormously pleased. "This is, to my knowledge, the first opportunity a black man had . . . to address this group." Rice believed that integration threatened black medical institutions and personnel. He asked Young to encourage federal officials to allocate funds for facilities that served blacks and the poor. Whether affiliated with Imhotep, the NMA, or black hospitals, black professionals viewed Young as an advocate who would protect their interests as they integrated into the medical mainstream.[32]

Although Young was a fervent integrationist, his views fitted a pluralist perspective. He wanted blacks to participate fully in mainstream political, social, and economic affairs, but he had no quarrel with the continued existence of black institutions. As long as African American organizations rejected separatism and promoted broad involvement of blacks in American society, their racial identity was not worrisome to Young.

Young's conspicuous support of black colleges and universities stemmed from three principal sources. First, he was a loyal alumnus of Kentucky State College. Moreover, Rufus B. Atwood, president of Kentucky State, believed that Young's well-known advocacy of racial integration was a message that his students needed to hear. So he invited the League leader to deliver the commencement address to the 1962 graduates.[33] Second, as a dean at the School of Social Work at Atlanta University, Young joined with President Rufus E. Clement to build AU into a first-rate institution. He constantly pressed Clement to upgrade the school so that its graduates would be competitive participants in various social welfare occupations (see chapter 5).

Third, Young maintained close personal ties with two presidents of the United Negro College Fund, William J. Trent Jr. and Vernon Jordan. Through his friendship with both men Young recognized that the UNCF emphasized efforts to move black graduates into the American mainstream. Trent, who became head of UNCF in 1944, met Young at Atlanta University. After Young became the NUL executive director, he and Trent became neighbors in New Rochelle, New York. They were closely involved in each other's organization. Trent often invited Young to speak at UNCF institutions. Young pushed Trent to become the NUL treasurer. Their common integrationist perspectives were best expressed in a letter that Young wrote to Trent in 1963. He congratulated Trent on the role of the United Negro College Fund "in supplementing all of our efforts" in the National Urban League. Without black colleges, Young observed, "our goal of first class citizenship would be severely handicapped." Moreover, "the predominantly Negro college" referred to spokespersons who advocated integrationist objectives. Young's friendship with Vernon Jordan, Trent's UNCF successor, also was close. In 1965 they moved their respective organizations into the same New York City office building, and the proximity of their offices allowed Young and Jordan to advise and confide in each other.[34]

Similar relationships evolved between Young and various black college executives. Jerome Holland, the president of Hampton Institute in Virginia and a former NUL board member, invited his onetime colleague to address the 1967 graduates of his institution. Predictably, Young challenged the senior class to reject separatism. "Our forefathers have fought and died and given free labor in the building of this country. We have a claim to every inch of it." He emphasized their obligation to move into the mainstream, and he congratulated the Hampton faculty for teaching students how to compete in the modern world. Young also offered technical assistance to black college leaders. Rembert E. Stokes, the president of Wilberforce University in Ohio, hosted the League leader as a special lecturer in 1967. Young reciprocated with an invitation to Stokes to visit the League's national headquarters. Because this AME-supported institution operated a successful cooperative learning program in which students gained work experience, Stokes was eager to confer with Young and his staff and to benefit from their observations about Wilberforce.[35]

Young developed a formal commitment to Miles College in Birmingham, Alabama. He had become familiar with the CME-affiliated school because of Mahlon T. Puryear, a League official who had sponsored three jobs conferences on the Miles campus. This cooperative experience with the League caused Bishop E.P. Murchison, the Miles board chairman, to invite Young to become a trustee.[36]

Clearly, Bishop Murchison and President L.H. Pitts knew of Young's broad contacts with corporate and philanthropic leaders, and they hoped that he would help them with fund-raising. In 1964, for example, Pitts asked Young to solicit support from Roger Blough, chairman of the United States Steel Corporation, to help fund the construction of a new Miles science building. "A word from you to Roger Blough," said Pitts to Young, "might be the difference between Miles College's immediate acceptance in the Southern Association and another long year of struggle for us." Because a new science building was crucial to Pitts's accreditation effort, Young wrote to Blough and urged his "fullest consideration" of the Miles request. On another occasion Young spoke at some length with the chief education officer at the Ford Foundation in behalf of Miles College. "Arrange an appointment to explore this further," Young advised Pitts, and "do not mention my name in this connection."[37]

Through his extensive interactions with black churches, colleges, fraternities, professional associations, and other social groups, Young mobilized support for the integrationist objectives of the civil rights movement. In gaining the endorsement of the many institutions which formed the infrastructure of the black population, Young credibly claimed that his views mirrored those of most African Americans. Even when Black Power in the late 1960s seemingly displaced integrationism as the ascendant philosophy of the black freedom struggle, the Elks, Masons, Links, Alphas, Baptists and Methodists backed the interracialism that Young articulated. Clearly, he spoke for a large and significant segment of the nation's black communities.

Young must have been gratified in 1965 when an official in the activist Southern Christian Leadership Conference requested his picture to hang in the organization's main office "as one of a group of Distinguished Civil Rights Leaders."[38] The more militant leaders of CORE and SNCC and the more moderate spokespersons in the NAACP also acknowledged Young as a leader who articulated their perspectives about race in American society. Invitations to speak at national and local meetings of these civil rights groups and initiatives for cooperative activities with the League also strengthened Young's contention that he spoke for black people.

Speeches to various civil rights organizations demonstrated that Young and other officials formed a leadership vanguard in which each played distinct but complementary roles. Soon after Young became the NUL executive director, he invited Martin Luther King Jr. to speak at a League gathering. King reciprocated in 1962 when Young came to Birmingham to address SCLC's sixth annual convention. In fact, Wyatt Tee Walker, SCLC's executive director, referred to the League as a "buddy organization." Conceptually, Young accepted Walker's characterization, but he noted the groups' different tactics in pursuing racial equality. Young also observed that SCLC and the League needed to recognize that they confronted the same segregationist foes.[39]

Young thought the support that each civil rights leader extended to the organizations of his or her colleague was crucial to the success of the black struggle. In 1964, for example, he asked King to participate in the League's Community Action Assembly in Washington, D.C. "I am most anxious," said Young to King, "that this conference reflect the high degree of unity which exists within the civil rights movement." Although King's Nobel Peace Prize acceptance prevented his attendance, he promised that the Reverend Walter Fauntroy would come in his place.[40]

Participants in local affiliates of various civil rights organizations also viewed Young favorably. Both in 1963 and 1969, for example, the Far Rockaway–Inwood, New York, branch of the NAACP made vain attempts to commit Young to speaking engagements. These NAACP members thought that Young could best articulate their integrationist perspectives to a gathering of five hundred people of all races and religions. Similarly, the Stockton, California, branch of the NAACP, which recognized Young as "a prominent representative of our race," wanted him to praise its membership drive and honor the chapter's life members. The Las Vegas branch of the NAACP twice invited Young to speak. In 1969 he was needed for the Freedom Fund Banquet at which a pioneer civil rights lawyer and former associate of Lester Granger would be honored. Later in the year Charles L. Kellar, the branch president, asked Young to give a memorial address on Martin Luther King Jr.[41]

That national and local officers in the NAACP, CORE, and SCLC sought cooperation and assistance from the National Urban League and its affiliates testified to Young's broad appeal among civil rights leaders. Although Roy Wilkins, A. Philip Randolph, Martin Luther King Jr., and other leaders headed their own organizations, they often relied on Young for contacts, personnel, and resources. In 1966, for example, in a meeting with two Ford Foundation officials Young learned of their willingness to recommend grants to the National Urban League and the NAACP. Young informed Roy Wilkins about this possibility, and their two organizations submitted proposals to the foundation. Ultimately, the League and the NAACP received grants to underwrite staff salaries.[42] In 1967, at Young's suggestion, Wilkins agreed to a meeting between national officials of both organizations to discuss "ways in which we can supplement and complement each other." The two leaders agreed on an agenda that enunciated their positions on separatism vs. integration, looked at how to monitor progress in desegregation, and examined the Washington bureaus of both groups, among other issues.[43]

The Freedom Budget, which A. Philip Randolph and Bayard Rustin developed through the Randolph Institute, benefited from Young's endorsement and the critical evaluation that he compelled it to undergo. The Freedom Budget, which was similar to Young's domestic Marshall Plan, aimed to end poverty in the United States. Randolph and Rustin recommended the public expenditure of $180 billion over ten years to achieve this objective. They wanted to provide full employment, good wages, a minimum standard

of living for the unemployed, adequate medical care, and education. They
also wished to obliterate the nation's slums.[44]

Young's endorsement of the Randolph/Rustin Freedom Budget gave it
credibility to some prominent whites and blacks who would have otherwise
dismissed it. In 1966 in the wake of race riots in several cities Young praised
the Freedom Budget and said that it would help put the civil rights movement "back in perspective." Although he persuaded the board and staff at the
National Urban League to endorse the principle and the concept of the Budget, he worried about concerns that the idea was economically unsound. He
asked Andrew F. Brimmer, a black economist and a member of the board of
governors of the Federal Reserve System, William F. Butler, the vice president
of Chase Manhattan Bank, and other financial analysts to review the Randolph/
Rustin initiative.[45] Despite some criticisms, the initiative seemed promising.[46]

Although Martin Luther King Jr. seldom needed Young's advice and
assistance, his successor, Ralph D. Abernathy, sometimes depended on the
League to rescue SCLC's faltering programs. Young often appeared in SCLC-led
marches in the early 1960s, but he functioned in a supportive role far away
from King's inner circle of advisers.[47] These circumstances changed after King's
1968 assassination.

King planned to bring thousands of poor people to Washington to dramatize the scourge of poverty in the United States. His murder in Memphis
left Abernathy to carry out the Poor People's March. Bayard Rustin, the coordinator of the 1963 March on Washington, agreed to play the same role in
SCLC's Solidarity Day demonstration. Disagreements between Rustin and SCLC
officials on policy matters caused him to resign. Young allowed Sterling Tucker,
already the vice coordinator of the June 19, 1968, mobilization, to succeed
Rustin.[48]

That Young acquiesced to Tucker's participation in the Poor People's
campaign was one way that he helped SCLC. Tucker, the executive director of
the Washington Urban League, had recently become coordinator of the
League's ambitious New Thrust program. Although Young worried that the
SCLC assignment might distract Tucker from his NUL responsibilities, he viewed
the Poor People's mobilization as an example of what New Thrust was trying
to accomplish in inner cities throughout the nation.[49]

Young's authorization of other League personnel to participate in the
Poor People's project and his efforts to exclude critics of nonviolence from
any involvement with the march showed how much he had impacted
Abernathy's plans. Within a few weeks after Dr. King's death, Young defined

NUL involvement with the Poor People's campaign. He noted that it was the League's intention to cooperate where requested to ensure that it would be a "peaceful, nonviolent, and effective pilgrimage." He added that many League supporters would take part in the march. Two weeks later Young told Abernathy, "You need to know that I am available if you need me to keep this an effective nonviolent effort." He added that League staff in several affiliate cities would help to feed, house, and transport marchers on their way to Washington, D.C.[50]

Young's efforts helped to salvage the march. He encouraged Abernathy to stress nonviolence and integrationism. Some march supporters, especially some labor and Jewish group representatives, feared that the mobilization would be taken over by Stokely Carmichael or black militants. They believed that Black Power advocates would inject violence into the effort. At a meeting called by Rustin at NAACP headquarters in New York City, John Morsell, Roy Wilkins's assistant, a National Council of Churches representative, and Layhmond Robinson, Whitney Young's spokesman, "made clear that our groups would not be involved if we KNEW that violence was in the making." This stand enabled the labor and Jewish groups to remain in the coalition as long as the NAACP, the NCC, and the League kept Carmichael and others out. A reassured YWCA representative said, "There is no more danger of violence than there was at the beginning. If we pull out now, we will create the disaster we all seek to avert." "Your position carried the day," Robinson told Young.[51]

In his speech "The Power of the Poor," Young said, "Once again, blacks and whites together have come to Washington to ask for justice. . . . America is the richest country the world has ever known—but the spirits of children are crushed in the school systems of New York; they starve in the Mississippi Delta; they are bitten by rats in the ghettos of this, the nation's capital, and they waste away in the grape fields of California. . . . The poor know they don't have to starve; they don't have to live in shacks; they don't have to be shunted into a dark corner of the American conscience, unseen, unheard, unthought of. . . . Poverty is not God-given, but man-made. Poverty is created by discrimination and by blindness of our political and economic leaders. This nation is rich enough to end poverty today, and that's why we are here now." Again. Young, though quite comfortable mingling with powerful whites, spoke as a leader of grassroots blacks and the several organizations who articulated their desire for inclusion in the American mainstream.[52]

Young, a pragmatic integrationist and a proponent of ordered social change, believed that most African Americans preferred his leadership over what Black Power advocates offered. After 1964, however, sustained racial

violence in inner cities and the growing influence of black nationalists put
Young on the defensive. Although mainstream black organizations continually ratified his integrationism, Young reassured nervous and skeptical white
allies that his perspectives remained dominant among blacks. Despite his
criticisms of Black Power spokespersons, Young approved of some of their
efforts, and he offered resources and advice to his ideological adversaries.
Some militant blacks pejoratively called the League leader "Whitey" Young,
but he became a pivotal person upon whom other Black Power advocates
depended and openly acknowledged as a legitimate spokesman for black
people.

When Young became the executive director of the National Urban
League in 1961, he knew that issues of poverty, education, housing, and
police brutality stirred unrest and impatience, especially among blacks in
urban areas. Although he believed that pulling them into the mainstream of
American society was the ultimate solution, he acknowledged that the racially charged rhetoric of Malcolm X and his separatist successors appealed to
inhabitants of the nation's ghettos. In 1963 the black Muslim minister told
Young, "The present racial crisis in this country carries within it powerful
destructive ingredients that may soon erupt into an uncontrollable explo-
sion." He added that steps should be taken before "the racial powder keg
explodes." Although Young eschewed any public association with Malcolm
X, he surely agreed with his analysis. In a telegram to Robert F. Kennedy,
Young warned, "New York City is [a] racial tinderbox. We face [a] most haz-
ardous and difficult summer." He said that the New York Urban League was
making every effort to ameliorate the growing tension. Young understood
that these circumstances made it hard for many blacks to wait patiently for
nonviolent solutions offered by the civil rights movement. To provide instant
relief to the raw racial problems of the inner cities was a difficult challenge for
mainstream black leaders.[53]

Young never compromised his advocacy for ordered social change and
for racial integration. Overall, Black Power was a flawed plan for black advancement. But Young supported those elements of the doctrine which con-
formed to existing League practices and objectives. Those aspects of Black
Power which emphasized "violence or a retreat into separatism" drew Young's
strenuous denunciation. When it aimed toward development of pride and
self-respect and encouraged participation in community affairs and control
of one's own destiny, then Young enthusiastically endorsed it. He observed
that "the ghetto suffers from the results of white power." As a result, "positive,
constructive programs formulated and run by black people can help to undo

the damage." Nevertheless, "no responsible Negro leader wants to keep the ghetto a black reservation. . . . Our goal is a truly open society with all men benefitting from and participating in American democracy."[54]

Although the Black Power movement inherited Malcolm X's militant black nationalism, it also grew out of the disillusionment of former civil rights activists who rejected the interracial cooperation and the integrationist objectives of mainstream black leaders. The James Meredith March in Mississippi in 1966, for example, exposed the growing fissure between such "establishment" spokesmen as Roy Wilkins and Whitney M. Young Jr. and such SNCC officials as Stokely Carmichael. Meredith had been shot on June 4, 1966, during an attempted march through Mississippi to show blacks that they should be free from fear and should exercise their right to vote. Leaders of all the major civil rights organizations agreed that they should complete Meredith's march. Wilkins and Young, however, withdrew from the coalition when they learned that Carmichael wanted to bar whites from the march and invite the Deacons for Defense, an armed black organization from Louisiana, to guard the marchers. Although Carmichael previously had used the term *Black Power* at various rallies, his unnecessary arrest in Greenwood, Mississippi, for trespassing on public property provided a ripe setting for the angered SNCC leader to utter these provocative words. Out on bail Carmichael shouted at the Greenwood rally, "We want Black Power!" Repetitively, the crowd echoed, "We want Black Power!"[55]

The disenchantment that some black militants felt toward Young and Wilkins escalated to threats of violence. The most extreme belonged to the Revolutionary Action Movement (RAM), which was sympathetic to Red China and advocated the violent overthrow of the U.S. government. In 1967 twelve men and four women, all RAM members, were arrested for plotting the assassination of moderate black leaders. All but one were arraigned in New York City, where police confiscated 1,000 rounds of ammunition, rifles, shotguns, and carbines. Two were charged with planning to kill Young and Roy Wilkins. They said that any black spokesman who did not "believe" in machine guns was an "Uncle Tom."[56]

Black Power, this seemingly undefined term, clearly conveyed sentiments different from what the civil rights movement espoused. Solidarity with white allies, trust in the federal government to protect the rights of blacks, and a belief in racial integration now appeared to be foolish. Those who preached racial separatism, distrusted white liberalism, and moved to defend against white violence challenged the leadership of Young, Wilkins, and others.

Despite the rise of Black Power, Young seemed secure in his claim to speak for a majority of the black population. When a National Conference on Black Power was called in 1967, he said that it represented a black minority.[57] Nonetheless, he could not ignore the increased visibility of Stokely Carmichael, H. Rap Brown, Floyd B. McKissick, Imamu Amiri Baraka, Eldridge and Kathleen Cleaver, Bobby Seale, Huey Newton, Maulena Ron Karenga, and other Black Power advocates. They appeared on television, radio, and other media, they wrote books, they gave interviews to reporters, and they lectured widely. Whites paid attention to their views. They seemed to understand and interpret the feelings and perspectives of ghetto blacks, who turned to riots rather than to nonviolent protest to articulate their grievances. Although Young credibly claimed to represent the millions of blacks who populated the churches, fraternal groups, service organizations, and other institutions, he encountered the growing influence of Black Power proponents.

The media coverage that Carmichael, McKissick, the Cleavers, and others received greatly irritated Young. He was disappointed that "militant blacks got publicity while moderate blacks did not." He added, "Dissidents have managed to dominate public attention and draw it away from the quiet, constructive work of the Negro in his struggle for equality." Young was particularly irked that delegates were outnumbered by reporters at the 1966 CORE convention in Baltimore whereas the National Urban League convention had 1,500 delegates and less than thirty reporters.[58]

How did Young retain his relevance as a major black leader during the Black Power ascendancy? Although he denounced as "facetious" plans to divide the United States racially and to promote "paramilitary training of Negro youth," he endorsed those pragmatic Black Power proposals which could tangibly improve the social and economic condition of blacks.[59] Young also understood that the desire for self-determination and racial autonomy, while sometimes at odds with interracialism, were legitimate objectives that mainstream civil rights organizations could embrace. In fact, the League's 1967 New Thrust program was premised upon grassroots initiative and empowerment. Moreover, Young believed that his selective assistance to Black Power leaders and their organizations would encourage them to soften their rhetoric and move closer to his centrist posture. Unlike Roy Wilkins who castigated Carmichael, Cleaver, and others, Young left open the door to dialogue and cooperation with these potential antagonists. His evolving relationship with the Congress of Racial Equality, a group which moved from interracialism to racial nationalism, demonstrated how he tried to pull the group away from its separatist tendencies.

CORE started in 1942 as a pacifist, pro–civil rights fellowship. Its commitment to nonviolent direct action proved effective in opening public accommodations to blacks and in bringing national notice to segregation in interstate travel during freedom rides through the South.[60] Although CORE was far more confrontational than the League, their leader, James Farmer, like Young, believed strongly in integration and often cooperated to achieve this objective. In 1962, for example, Farmer initiated the Freedom Highways project to ensure service for black travelers at Howard Johnson's restaurants. Farmer solicited Young's advice on this campaign. He pledged to Farmer his "moral support and active cooperation wherever possible." In 1964 Farmer asked Young to address a CORE-sponsored pre–Republican Convention civil rights rally in San Francisco. Young could not attend, but he was confident that King, Wilkins, and Farmer would fairly present the League's view on the importance of civil rights legislation and the urgent need to remove any barriers to the full participation of blacks in American society. In 1965 Young was an organizer of the White House Conference on Education. He requested an invitation for Farmer for the session on "Skills Obsolescence and Retraining: Education's New Challenge." Even Farmer's subordinates requested Young's assistance on various projects despite occasional conflicts between League affiliates and CORE chapters. Clarence D.M. Funnye of New York CORE, for example, headed an urban fellows project and asked the League to help him. Inroads by separatists within CORE beginning in 1965, however, pulled the organization away from integrationism. Separatist Floyd McKissick, a North Carolina lawyer, was elected in 1966 as Farmer's successor. At a rally at the close of the Meredith March, McKissick declared that 1966 was "the year of the concept of Black Power" and "the year when black men realized their full worth in society." How much did CORE's embrace of Black Power change Young's relationship to the organization and its leader?[61]

Although McKissick and Young disagreed about Black Power, both were pragmatists. When the Ford Foundation in 1966 allocated major funds for black betterment organizations, McKissick felt slighted as the National Urban League and the NAACP received grants for $430,000 and $300,000, respectively. Although the foundation's legal department had advised against funding a CORE request, two program officers believed that McKissick should not be turned away. A project of Cleveland CORE that included a youth training institute, an adult training program, and a voter registration drive seemed promising. A Ford program officer spoke to Dr. Kenneth B. Clark, Jack Greenberg, and Whitney M. Young Jr.—all of whom were "very positive

about a grant to CORE." These endorsements reassured Ford officials that a
$175,000 grant to Cleveland CORE would be appropriate.

Young praised the Ford Foundation for funding CORE. To give money
to CORE, which recently had removed the word *multi-racial* from its constitution, required both intelligence and courage. Young assured McGeorge Bundy,
the foundation's new president, that the risk was worth taking. Young argued
that the grant would strengthen McKissick's leadership and temper the group's
antiestablishment tendencies. Young had confidence in Floyd McKissick's
sincerity and intentions and believed that "much of his difficulties could be
avoided if he had sufficient funds for meaningful programs."[62]

The strategy seemed to work. One Ford official noted that CORE "had a
role in the reapportionment [effort] that led to the emergence of the 21st
Congressional District, which is largely Negro." The Cleveland chapter helped
Mayor Carl Stokes "cool the ghetto" after the assassination of Martin Luther
King. Moreover, "it has served as a link between militant black groups, more
moderate Negro groups, City Hall and business groups" and "it has kept out
of trouble." The Ford Foundation gave another $300,000 in 1968 to fund
CORE's "Cleveland activities." Even before McKissick learned of the grant
renewal, he applauded the foundation for "having funded a Black Power Organization dedicated to bringing about an orderly change in the power im-
balance that exists between black and white America. Because of our joint
effort, that change is a step closer to becoming real."[63]

Despite CORE's nationalist rhetoric, Young helped to persuade its leaders to sponsor pragmatic programs. At the same time Young was himself affected by the Black Power perspectives and postures of CORE and other militant influences. Roy Innis, McKissick's successor, invited the League leader to
address CORE's 1968 convention in Columbus, Ohio, where he seemed to
abandon his hostility to Black Power. In an allusion to the growing militancy
of Black Power groups and grassroots residents of the inner cities Young declared that America "does not respond to people who beg on moral grounds."
The public is only moved by threats and pressure. As CORE delegates cheered
and some chanted, "The brother has come home," Young noted that the
change was painful, but added that an unwillingness to change was "fatal."
While the press proclaimed that Young had moved to the side of the black
nationalists, he finetuned his definition of Black Power to draw separatist
support.

Young said that blacks should develop "the power that America respects."
When blacks took political and economic control of their neighborhoods
and mobilized their resources for collective uplift, white Americans would

respect them. He supported "that interpretation of Black Power that emphasized self-determination, pride, self-respect and participation and control of
one's destiny and community affairs." Because other ethnic groups had attained influence in American society using these methods, Black Power could
be understood in a similar way. Moreover, blacks, rather than seeking integration, preferred "an open society where people have a choice." The pursuit
of black economic stability and the training of black doctors, black biolo-
gists, and black capitalists were all worthy goals and did not require extensive
interaction with whites. At the same time blacks needed to recognize that
"there can never be in America black capitalism, a black economy, a black
medicine, and black biology." Group identification and group objectives were
acceptable as long as they ultimately connected blacks to the broader American society. Although Young seemingly dropped the term *integration* from
his vocabulary, his use of the expression *open society* still argued against a
separatist strategy for black advancement.[64]

The July 7 *New York Times* noted in a front-page headline that "Young
Embraces Black Power Idea," and members of CORE concluded that he had
adopted their perspective, yet Young claimed that his speech signified no
change in his overall philosophy. A League intern congratulated Young on his
ability to reverse his past position. He added that in endorsing Black Power
Young decided "to walk among your people without fear and to be a true
leader rather than being a tool of the establishment." Young disagreed. "I
have not reversed my position," he said, "but have simply tried to give a
realistic and constructive interpretation to a phrase used so often." In fact,
W.H. Wheeler Jr., chairman of the board of Pitney-Bowes, told Young, "There
was absolutely nothing in what you said that I find myself in any disagreement with." A United Parcel Service official informed the League leader, "There
was nothing very startling about your position for I have heard you state our
beliefs on most of these issues on previous occasions." A White House fellow
in HUD echoed this sentiment: "Those of us who know you, know that you
have been saying this for a long time." Price M. Cobbs, the black psychiatrist,
was pleased by Young's "clear and forceful position on Black Power." William
R. Hudgins, president of the black Freedom National Bank of New York,
thought that the speech was "really great," and Floyd B. McKissick said that
Young's position showed that there was more unity in the black movement
than most people suspected. Additionally, Young assured a worried Millicent
Fenwick, a New Jersey Republican leader, that most of the mail "from big
industrialists and black people has been positive." They viewed the speech as
a "statement of responsible leadership."[65]

Young made common cause with McKissick and his successor, Roy Innis, on two projects. In 1969 McKissick founded Soul City, an all-black town in North Carolina. Although Young doubted its feasibility, he encouraged McKissick to adapt his plans to "one of the dozen or more all-black towns that already exist."[66] He also cooperated with Innis on an ambitious economic action proposal. In June 1969 Young, McKissick, and Innis met in Chicago with the black National Bankers Association and the Bankers Committee on Urban Affairs of the American Bankers Association. Innis demanded that the nation's bankers contribute $6 billion to a new black urban coalition to administer development funds for inner cities. Both Young and McKissick backed Innis, although the League leader noted that the requested amount was "'chicken feed' in terms of what the banks really should do." When Innis failed to follow through and both bankers groups reneged on their promised cooperation, Young and the League "stepped into the void."

Young authorized a survey of nearly 100 banks on their willingness to funnel resources through the League for a coordinated effort to address black urban issues. Encouraged by the response, Young with advice from Dunbar S. McLaurin, a founder of Freedom National Bank of New York, planned to raise $2 million and to form a coalition consisting of the League, CORE, the Black Economic Union, SCLC's Operation Breadbasket, the National Business League, the National Bankers Association, and other groups. He supported Innis's economic development initiative because this interpretation of Black Power was compatible with League objectives.[67]

Young approached cooperation with Imamu Amiri Baraka with the same realism that marked his relationship with McKissick and Innis. Baraka, who had changed his name from Leroi Jones, was a well-known writer and poet. As a Black Power theoretician he stressed cultural nationalism as an indispensable foundation for black nationhood. A native of Newark, New Jersey, Baraka joined with others on the Committee for Unified Newark to elect the city's first black mayor, Kenneth Gibson. To achieve this objective, he asked to meet Young to discuss League assistance on a voter education drive. Young advised Russell Bingham, the coordinator of Unified Newark, on where the committee should seek funding before the 1970 election.[68]

In 1970 Baraka brought Young to Newark to speak at a press conference. He also persuaded Young to attend a Black Power conference in Atlanta where the Newark project was explained. The press conference aimed to mobilize support for black and Puerto Rican voter registration and to solicit contributions to fund their candidates. In support of Baraka's initiative, Young said, "I am most emphatically in favor of the drive to get blacks and Puerto

Ricans elected to high office in Newark." He blamed the city's instability on
the absence of blacks and Puerto Ricans from the municipal government
despite their 65 percent majority in the population. He also endorsed the
idea of a black mayor who "could be effective in binding up the wounds of
racial antagonism," which the six-day riot in 1967 had stirred. For Young,
Black Power was inextricably linked to political power. He observed, "This
approach is a healthy and constructive alternative to violence and the chaos
that results from violence." Although Young and Baraka disagreed about
integrationism, they found common ground on Black Power and electoral
politics. As a result Newark's first black mayor was elected.[69]

Young worked closest with Black Power advocates in CORE and the Committee for Unified Newark. Although Percy Steele, the executive director of
the League's affiliate in Oakland, California, cooperated with the Black Panthers on various local projects, Young generally eschewed contacts with this
well-known socialist and self-defense organization. At the same time the League
leader strongly opposed "the undeclared war on radical groups like the Black
Panthers by the police." Because some Panthers had been killed as a result of
police repression, Young detected "a feeling of bitterness in the ghetto," and
he surely believed that a gross injustice had been done to the Panthers.[70]

Because some Johnson administration officials were unaware of Young's
extensive interaction with Black Power advocates, they advised the president
to broaden his contacts with militant black spokesmen. They seemed to articulate the views of inner-city blacks better than Young. Although one aide
preferred the "Randolph-Wilkins-Young type leadership," the rise of inner-
city rioting caused him to worry about the relevance of this triumvirate. Another said, "Even Whitney Young and Martin Luther King have been around
so long that they seem 'old school' to the young militants." This presidential
adviser regretted that "our lines of communication to the [civil rights] movement run generally (and from the White House, only) to the older Negro
establishment. We have very few contacts with younger Negro leaders. We
MUST develop those contacts."[71] Although he eschewed contact with Stokely
Carmichael and H. Rap Brown, a black presidential aide, Andrew Hatcher,
suggested that the president "establish some kind of dialogue with the leaders
of the [1967] Black Power Conference." He added that Johnson should "hear
for himself some of the fanaticism involved in this movement, to know the
enemy better, to listen and to warn against anarchy." However, Vice President Hubert H. Humphrey, Johnson's coordinator and chief adviser on civil
rights, adopted a more pragmatic perspective about which leaders the president should invite to the White House.[72]

Young was confident that Vice President Humphrey would protect the gains of the civil rights movement and rely on mainstream black leaders for advice. As the Johnson administration searched for ways to address racial unrest in the big cities, the League suggested to Humphrey, a program to prevent riots in twenty-one "high racial tension areas." Although he appreciated Young's input, the vice president concluded that exclusive contact with him and other traditional black leaders would end. Instead, Humphrey, who in 1966 belonged to a special summer task force on the riots, wanted to widen the spectrum of Negro activists with whom he interacted. His aides defined them as "the most aggressive Negro groups who do not advocate rioting or violence, except in self-defense." These groups included civil rights, Black Power, and black nationalist organizations. Although Young did not lose his coveted access to the president and vice president, Johnson and Humphrey aides pressed for other sources of advice about blacks.[73]

As the administration's ombudsman for civil rights, the vice president needed more information about black militants. His aides thought that "many young people, from college educated to dropout, have been adopting considerably more militant postures." It seemed that "the entire Negro community has been moving in this direction." Better communication and cooperation between militant blacks and federal officials would reduce the "anger" of the activists and turn it "toward constructive channels." A vice presidential aide observed, "Despite their strong statements, most militants are not dedicated to destroying American society. Instead, they appear essentially to want a meaningful part of the power within our society and especially within areas largely inhabited by Negroes. Many government programs are available to help Negroes, both militants and others, to achieve their fair share of economic and political power." It appeared to Humphrey's aides that Young and his mainstream colleagues lacked rapport with the activists and that the administration's effort to co-opt them would yield far more than what the League leader could deliver.[74]

Ultimately, President Johnson ignored the advice of several presidential and vice presidential aides who recommended improved communications with Black Power advocates. Since LBJ saw no reason to abandon Young and other mainstream leaders as his principal confidants on civil rights, militant black spokesmen remained strangers to the president. How Johnson orchestrated a response to the King assassination demonstrated how important Young and others remained to his administration. On April 4, 1968, James Earl Ray shot Martin Luther King Jr. in Memphis, Tennessee. News of the killing of this prominent practitioner of nonviolence unleashed widespread rioting in cities throughout the United States. President Johnson hurriedly assembled those black leaders whom he believed would help him quell this unexpected unrest. Floyd B. McKissick of CORE was the only Black Power proponent invited to a White House meeting on April 5, 1968. He had gone into hiding for fear of his life, and Roy Innis, his colleague, called the White House for McKissick and asked for a list of invitees. Specifically, he wanted to know whether Stokely Carmichael, H. Rap Brown, Elijah Muhammad, and Adam Clayton Powell had been invited. He received no answers to his inquiries. At this point, Harry McPherson and Joseph Califano, both senior aides to the president, nixed any further contacts with McKissick and Innis. McKissick decided to attend the White House meeting, but he arrived late. When a security guard prevented McKissick's two companions from accompanying him into the White House, the CORE leader left.[75]

To reassure the nation and to implore ghetto blacks to stop the riots, Johnson chose Young, Roy Wilkins, Dorothy Height, Walter Fauntroy, Bayard Rustin, two black mayors, and others to follow him onto a White House podium to deliver his televised message. Whether McKissick had come or not, LBJ probably would have forbidden him to make remarks. But Johnson allowed Young and the other mainstream leaders to express their thoughts. These were the persons whom he could trust, and for some like Young this presidential endorsement seemed to validate him as a preeminent black leader.[76]

Whitney M. Young Jr. derived his claim to speak for blacks from three principal sources. The majority of blacks who espoused integrationism and populated the thousands of churches, fraternal organizations, and service groups continuously ratified him as their spokesman. Moreover, Black Power advocates, although they criticized his interracialism, sought his advice and assistance with programs that transcended their ideological disagreement. And his close ties with three American presidents, especially Lyndon B. Johnson, validated for many blacks that Young was a man whom the White House regarded as a valued adviser and confidant.

14

Home to Africa

The staunch interracialism of Whitney M. Young Jr. never precluded broad concerns for Africa. Although he was not a black nationalist, racial pride stirred his interest in the progress and prosperity of the "mother" continent. His cooperation with integrationist blacks and whites aimed at economic development, the abolition of white minority rule, and the growth of political stability in newly independent nations. Unlike some Black Power advocates who viewed the continent with romantic attachment, Young believed that the modernization of sub-Saharan Africa would demonstrate the capacity of blacks to build productive and competitive economies in former colonial areas.

The Kennedy administration asked for Young's assistance in recruiting blacks for foreign policy positions. As a result of his interaction with Assistant Secretary of State G. Mennen Williams, Young nominated the executive director of the New York Urban League, a Ph.D., for a high-level position. Franklin H. Williams, the director of the Division of Private Organizations in the Peace Corps, wanted the National Urban League to cosponsor a rural development project in the Camerouns. Afraid that the League might "overextend itself," Young rejected this proposal. Despite this setback, he maintained contact with Williams and later supported his appointment as U.S. ambassador to Ghana.[1]

Young congratulated the president when he ordered three American transport aircraft and crews to help the black-led Democratic Republic of the Congo to resist a rebellion led by white mercenaries. In Young's view Johnson was right "to avert serious internal conflict and chaos in this critical region." Johnson replied that his actions were consistent with United Nations resolutions on the territorial integrity of the Congo and with his concern for the safety of Americans who were present in the area. Although the Congo matter only marginally impacted the African American condition, it showed how important African issues were to Young.[2]

He mainly dealt with Africa through his affiliation with several institutes and committees organized to aid Africans and to broaden the discourse
about African issues among academic, corporate, government, and civil rights
leaders. Although Young had traveled to the continent only a few times, many
blacks and whites interested in Africa believed that his League experiences
gave him special insights about developing nations, especially in the sub-
Saharan region. Young's earliest and longest association occurred with the
American Negro Leadership Conference on Africa. Organized in 1962 by
the American Committee on Africa, the ANLCA initially drew together the six
major civil rights leaders: A. Philip Randolph, Martin Luther King Jr., Roy
Wilkins, Dorothy Height, James Farmer, and Whitney M. Young Jr. A former
Randolph protégé in the Brotherhood of Sleeping Car Porters, Theodore E.
Brown, became the executive director, and an interracial group of religious,
labor, and cultural organizations, fraternities, and sororities signed on as supporters. Young and the other five civil rights leaders served as a permanent
"call committee." This position obligated them to give regularly to ANLCA. In
1967, for example, Young's National Urban League contributed $1,500.[3]

ANLCA tried to influence American government policies toward Africa
and to ameliorate crisis situations on the continent. After identifying crucial
issues that demanded the immediate attention of the six civil rights leaders,
Brown convened at least three biennial conferences and occasional meetings.
In 1966, for example, Roy Wilkins, chairman of the call committee, asked
Young and other supporters to meet in Washington to prepare the ANLCA
structure for issues it needed to tackle. He cited the efforts of the white minority government of Rhodesia to thwart black majority rule and recent coups
in several African nations as matters for a strengthened ANLCA to handle. Brown
informed Young that he and the other call committee members would host
President Kenneth Kaunda of Zambia at their 1966 biennial conference.
Conflicting schedules, however, prevented both Kaunda and Young from going
to the meeting.[4]

More important, Brown involved Young, Wilkins, Randolph, and the
other civil leaders in confronting South Africa's interference in South West
Africa and in dealing with the civil war in Nigeria. Because the apartheid
regime in South Africa administered South West Africa with the acquiescence of the United Nations. Brown invited Young to meet with several African ambassadors to discuss this matter. Although Young missed the meeting,
he agreed that this "critical issue" should be raised in a special United Nations
session. Moreover, the six civil rights leaders endorsed a telegram sent to President Johnson which stated that the "apartheid policy of South Africa dis-

qualifies that country morally and democratically from ruling South West Africa." Because the territory had a black majority, South Africa's white supremacist government should withdraw from the region. The American Negro Leadership Conference urged LBJ to instruct the United States delegation to the United Nations to ask that body to supervise South West Africa as it moved toward self-determination and independence. The Johnson administration agreed to review its policy on South West Africa, but Brown, after a White House meeting with two presidential aides, concluded that the ANLCA request was not viewed as an urgent matter.[5]

Also in 1967 the ANLCA tried to prevent a civil war in Nigeria. Brown invited the six civil rights leaders to authorize a cable to Nigerian officials to urge a peaceful resolution of tribal conflicts. The ANLCA offered its services to preserve unity in the "largest, richest and . . . most promising nation in Black Africa." Brown informed Young that this message seemed to draw "favorable interest and reaction" from the nation's federal and regional leaders. Ultimately, with endorsements from the U.S. State Department, the Nigerian embassy, and the ANLCA leadership, Brown traveled to Nigeria as an emissary for peace. Young, Wilkins, Randolph, and King aided his efforts by agreeing to raise $15,000 to finance ANLCA's peace mission. Young suggested that the appeals should go toward "those American concerns with investments in Nigeria and other parts of Africa." Although a destructive civil war still occurred, ANLCA initiatives showed how the "ethnic relationship between 56 million Nigerians and 22 million Afro-Americans" motivated Young and other civil rights leaders to tie together the concerns of blacks on both continents.[6]

Although Young applauded ANLCA efforts on the South West Africa and Nigeria issues, he had doubts about the organization's effectiveness. George M. Houser, a founder of CORE and head of the American Committee on Africa, shared with Young an evaluation of ANLCA. Although Houser worried most about areas of overlap between the two groups, he also noted its structural weaknesses. He believed that it would be a stronger organization if policy positions were well developed, especially on southern Africa and American assistance programs. Moreover, there should have been greater contact between the ANLCA and federal officials. Young agreed with Houser's analysis and admitted to a certain degree of frustration about the conference. But he thought that the ANLCA remained an important venue for his concerns for an "improved and strengthened American policy in Africa." Young hoped that money and full-time leadership would realize this objective.[7]

Other groups that dealt with African affairs discovered that Young's involvement with their efforts enhanced their objectives. The Reverend James

H. Robinson, pastor of the Presbyterian Church of the Master in Harlem, knew that Young had traveled to Africa. Robinson's Operation Crossroads Africa recruited volunteers to help Africans build roads, dig wells, operate schools, and initiate other practical projects. In 1965 he believed that his contingent of 220 should hear Young speak on some aspect of race relations. Although Young could not fulfill his commitment, he endorsed Robinson's approach to African development.[8]

A. Philip Randolph introduced Young to African issues far more controversial than Robinson's Crossroads program. In 1966 Randolph became chairman of the Committee of Conscience Against Apartheid. Earlier Young joined Randolph and other civil rights leaders in asking President Kennedy to put economic pressure on South Africa. Young shared Randolph's disgust with the ruthless system of racial oppression that the South African government imposed on blacks and other nonwhites. "There is no question in my mind," said Young, "concerning the viciousness of the South African policy of apartheid or the need for a change in the attitude [of] the government." What Randolph proposed, however, proved problematic for the League leader. He suggested that Young join him in persuading depositors at First National City and Chase Manhattan to withdraw their accounts because the two banks did business with the apartheid regime. Young declined because the project illegally would implicate the National Urban League, and he believed that the effort would fail. In another instance, Randolph was successful in getting Young's support. He invited the League leader to sign an advertisement in support of the state of Israel for several major newspapers. The ad affirmed "Israel's right to exist because it is by far the most democratic country" in the Middle East. Moreover, Randolph told Young, "Israel has established remarkably effective technical assistance programs in Black Africa." In fact, it had "done more in this area than any of the countries that are aligned against it," Randolph observed. The ad commended Israel for drawing many of its immigrants from Africa, and it denounced the Arab-dominated government of Sudan for its "brutal persecution of black Africans." Young readily signed this petition.

Charles Hightower, the Washington director of the American Committee on Africa, criticized all of the signatories to the pro-Israel ad because they seemed to ignore the relationship between Israel and the apartheid regime in South Africa. He claimed that ties were close enough that in 1968 a South Africa–Israel committee had been formed. Young told Hightower, "Israel has never publicly supported South Africa in her oppression of black people, and if she trades with that country, so, too, does most of Black Africa." Concerning the alleged South Africa–Israel committee, Young said that its "mere formation" was "hardly evidence of joint interest with a racist nation whose leaders have been openly anti-Semitic." Young also commended Israel's aid to black Africa. Its record was superior to oil-rich Arab countries, which contributed too few funds to sub-Saharan nations.[9]

The African American Institute, based at the United Nations in New York City, was another group that drew Young's involvement. Concerned with creating dialogue between American government and corporate leaders and their counterparts in Africa, the Institute called on Young to speak and participate in its various programs. In 1968, for example, the State Department asked Institute officials to arrange an orientation at Princeton University for fifty-nine African students from English- and French-speaking areas of Africa. Young was asked to address both groups on urban issues or civil rights. The Institute vice president, Frank E. Ferrari, commended Young on his speech and observed that "it meant a great deal to the Africans who were there." In 1969 the Institute brought the League leader to Tunis, Tunisia, to participate in an American/African dialogue. Young noted that top officials from seventeen African countries attended. His grasp of the issues apparently impressed Institute officials because they invited him to attend a future dialogue elsewhere on the continent.[10]

The timing of the Institute's 1971 dialogue in Lagos, Nigeria, could not have been worse for Young. Frank Buckner, his father-in-law, had recently died in Aurora, Illinois, and Young's Lagos trip took him away from his grieving wife, Margaret. "I hope you are making gains in recovery from the terrible strain and ordeal of your father's passing," said Young in a letter from Lagos. "My travel I can't help, but so much," he observed, "but maybe you can go more with me." There was one consolation for Young in being so far away from home. The quality of discussion at the Lagos meeting was very high.

The Institute drew from the United States several prominent politicians and corporate executives, including Senator Edmund S. Muskie, former attorney general Ramsey Clark, W.W. Broom, Washington bureau chief of Ridder Publications, Thomas Wyman, senior vice president of Polaroid, and black congressmen. Young noted, "This is a far better meeting than Tunis. The caliber of the delegates both from Africa and America are far superior. The Africans are young, intense, highly intelligent, and beautifully articulate. The discussion is more candid and specific." Wyman and Young sat next to each other in the sessions and continued their interaction during the free periods. Polaroid recently had been accused of collaborating with the apartheid regime of South Africa, so Wyman came to the meeting to deepen his company's understanding of Africa. Moreover, Institute officials believed that Polaroid's experience in South Africa would enhance discussions. Wyman talked with Young about how Polaroid ended its sales to the South African government. Polaroid identification equipment was used to put together pass-books, which nonwhites were compelled to carry and display whenever the police demanded to see them. Young commended company efforts to repair its image through full-page ads in leading American and South African news-papers that denounced apartheid. Polaroid endorsed the Sullivan principles, aided antiapartheid activists, and funded exchange programs. Young, who promoted constructive engagement, agreed that Polaroid should remain in South Africa and champion Sullivan standards for responsible corporate be-havior. Although Young applauded corporate stands against racial injustice in America and Africa, he reminded Wyman and others that they still had many more miles to travel to aid black progress.[11]

The Institute meetings ended on March 11, 1971. Young, Wyman, Broom, Ramsey and Georgia Clark, and a few others decided to skip the final reception to go to the beach to swim. Because the surf was choppy, everyone agreed to stay close together. When most in the party decided to leave the unclean waters, Young and two translators opted to remain. Notwithstand-ing his swimming skills, Young apparently was caught in a heavy surf. Mis-takenly, one of the translators commented, "He's playing fish." Ramsey Clark thought otherwise. He saw Young's arm go up twice as if to signal that he was in trouble. Both Clarks rushed into the water to rescue him. After Ramsey Clark pulled the League leader onto the beach, he and Broom tried mouth-to-mouth resuscitation. Their efforts were in vain. A Nigerian pathologist performed an autopsy and concluded that Young died of a subarachnoid hem-orrhage. A second autopsy in New York City produced no evidence of brain damage, and he was pronounced a victim of drowning.[12]

President Richard M. Nixon dispatched an air force transport plane to bring his body back from Africa. He sent his personal emissaries, General Daniel "Chappie" James and William Rumsfeld. Young's funeral service at Riverside Church in New York City featured the Reverend Dr. Benjamin E. Mays, the retired president of Morehouse College, and the Reverend Dr. Howard Thurman, the famed mystic and Dean of Marsh Chapel at Boston University. Young's father and sisters arranged for his burial in the all-black Greenwood Cemetery in Lexington, Kentucky, not far from his boyhood home. President Nixon delivered a brief eulogy in which he praised Young as a quintessential American. Young "loved America with all its faults," Nixon said, "loved it because he realized that this was a country in which we had the power to change what was wrong and change it peacefully."[13]

New York City and Westchester County had been the center of Young's activities and the place where his widow planned to reside. Margaret's wishes had not been fully considered when the Kentucky burial site was chosen, and she authorized the reinterment of her husband in a Hartsdale, New York, cemetery. Support from various family members and consultation with Howard Thurman readied her to move on this matter.[14]

Epilogue

Whitney M. Young Jr. believed that racial equality was an attainable goal if powerful and influential whites joined with civil rights leaders to tear down social and economic barriers to black advancement. He inherited this perspective from his father, a black leader in Kentucky during the pre–civil rights era. Although different racial realities shaped the leadership of the two Youngs, the father strongly influenced how the son interpreted to privileged and monied whites the grievances of restless and disadvantaged blacks. To reconcile the seemingly disparate interests of whites and blacks, a diplomatic spokesperson was needed to mediate their differences. Whitney M. Young Sr. served that role in the limited setting of a private Kentucky secondary school to which he drew both public and private support. He developed Lincoln Institute into an educational venture that simultaneously addressed white expectations and black aspirations. As a National Urban League executive in the broader arena of local and national race relations, his son persuaded powerful whites to finance unprecedented social and economic programs to benefit the black population.

Specifically, how did Young's leadership impact the black freedom struggle? Young's interracialism posited to influential whites in government, business, and the foundations that de jure and de facto equality for blacks were constitutional and socioeconomic necessities. Moreover, the elimination of ghettoes, Young contended, would pull blacks into mainstream participation in every facet of American society. As a result, powerful whites gave the National Urban League large sums of money to achieve integrationist objectives. While his ambitious domestic Marshall Plan never received ample support, aspects of important League programs and President Johnson's Great Society initiatives drew from Young's blueprint and helped blacks who would have never benefited from federal, corporate, and philanthropic largesse. What ultimately disappointed Young was the realization that the billions which were needed to elevate the black population were not forthcoming to the

League and other social service organizations.

How effective was the leadership paradigm that Young pursued? He sought support for black advancement from elite whites while credibly representing the interracialism that most middle- and working-class African Americans espoused. Throughout his career, whether as head of the Omaha Urban League or as the NUL executive director, Young recognized that whatever favor he gained from influential whites also required ratification from fellow blacks. Moreover, he understood that whites preferred to deal with him rather than with moderate and militant integrationists or with impatient Black Power advocates. Young also knew that their seeming radicalism made him a more palatable negotiator than some of the other black leaders.

At the same time Young sometimes failed to maintain the delicate balance between acceptability to powerful whites and credibility with grassroots blacks. Moreover, he occasionally mistook his access to elite whites for inclusion as their peer. His profound disappointment at missing the presidency of the wealthy Rockefeller Foundation and his unusual loyalty to Lyndon B. Johnson despite the deepening tragedy of the Vietnam War are examples of Young caring more for the approval of influential whites than endorsements from grassroots blacks. Young was most effective when he balanced his relationship between whites and blacks. Whenever he appeared to identify with important whites, he exposed himself to the pejorative and unfair appellation—"whitey" Young.

What is too often overlooked about Young's leadership was the extent to which he cultivated the favor of blacks and their many institutions and organizations. While he pitched his appeal primarily to the interracialism of middle- and working-class African Americans, Young cooperated with separatists on practical programs consistent with League objectives. Also, through New Thrust and other League initiatives Young spearheaded efforts to empower blacks in ghetto communities. In so doing he challenged the claims of Black Power proponents that they rather than Young and the League understood their condition and articulated their aspirations. As much as he valued and pursued access to powerful whites, Young also sought the approval of blacks to justify his claim to be their spokesman. Ultimately, Young discovered that the racial equality that he desperately desired for blacks carried for whites too high a price in private funds and public expenditures.

Notes

Introduction

1. James Farmer, *Lay Bare the Heart: An Autobiography of the Civil Rights Movement* (New York: Arbor House, 1985), 214-20.

2. Tom Buckley, "Whitney Young: Black Leader or 'Oreo Cookie'?" *New York Times Magazine,* 20 September 1970, 32-33, 74-77, 80-85; Nancy Weiss, *Whitney M. Young Jr. and the Struggle for Civil Rights* (Princeton: Princeton University Press, 1989).

3. Harvard Sitkoff, *The Struggle for Black Equality, 1954-1980* (New York: Hill and Wang, 1981), 23.

1. "As the Twig Is Bent"

1. Steven A. Channing, *Kentucky: A Bicentennial History* (New York: W.W. Norton, 1977), 94-136; see also Victor B. Howard, *Black Liberation in Kentucky: Emancipation and Freedom, 1862-1884* (Lexington: University Press of Kentucky, 1983); George C. Wright, *Life behind a Veil: Blacks in Louisville, Kentucky, 1865-1920* (Baton Rouge: Louisiana State University Press, 1985), 28, 52, 78-87; *Racial Violence in Kentucky, 1865-1940: Lynchings, Mob Rule, and "Legal Lynchings"* (Baton Rouge: Louisiana State University Press, 1990); *A History of Blacks in Kentucky, 1890-1980* (Frankfort: Kentucky Historical Society, 1992).

2. John Benjamin Horton, *Not without Struggle* (New York: Vantage Press, 1979), 6-14, 18-19.

3. George C. Wright, "The Founding of Lincoln Institute," *Filson Club History Quarterly* 49 (January 1975): 57-60.

4. Obsequies for the late Mrs. Laura Ray Young, 6 October 1962 (courtesy of Dr. Eleanor Young Love, Louisville, Ky.); Twelfth Census of the United States, 1900, Schedule 1—Population, Kentucky—Marion County, vol. 54, E.D. 73, sheet 11, line 69; *Who's Who in Colored America, 1933-37,* 4th ed. (New York: Who's Who in Colored America Corp., 1937), 597.

5. Joseph and Kathleen Carroll, interviewed by author, Indianapolis, 23 April 1982.

6. Dr. Eleanor Young Love, interviewed by author, Louisville, 19 July 1982; Lauren Young Casteel, interviewed by author, Denver, 19 June 1982; obsequies of Laura Ray Young.

7. Twelfth Census of the United States, 1900, Schedule 1—Population, Kentucky—Woodford County, vol. 76, E.D. 78, sheet 2, line 32; Dr. Eleanor Young Love, interviewed by Kenneth Chumbley, University of Louisville, 2 October 1978. The birthdates of Whitney M. Young Sr. and Laura Ray Young are confused. The 1900 federal census is cited in the text of this chapter. Whitney M. Young Jr., however, gave his parents' birthdates as 25 August 1898 and 22 September 1902. The obsequies of both parents also indicate these dates.

8. Twelfth Census, 1900, Kentucky—Woodford County; Family History Statement, box 2, scrapbook 21, and résumé of Dr. Whitney M. Young Sr., WMY Sr. Papers, box 1, album

12, Blazer Library, Kentucky State University, Frankfort; Love, Chumbley interview.

9. George C. Wright, "The Faith Plan: A Black Institution Grows during the Depression," *Filson Club History Quarterly* 51 (October 1977): 336, 340.

10. Young Sr., enlistment record; honorable discharge from the U.S. army, WMY Sr. Papers, box 9, letters and cards, maroon scrapbook, Letters to WMY Sr. scrapbook.

11. Young Jr. to Ralph Edwards, 10 January 1957, WMY Jr. Papers, box 1, personal correspondence, 1958-60, Columbia University Libraries, New York.

12. Love, author interview; *Lincoln Institute Worker* 20 (April 1928) and 22 (April 1930).

13. Lincoln Institute of Kentucky, microfilm, *Scrapbooks and Photographs, 1904-1971,* University of Louisville Archives and Record Center, Louisville.

14. Wright, "Faith Plan," 337-44, 348.

15. L.N. Taylor to J. Mansir Tydings, 9 November 1938, WMY Sr. Papers, box 1, album 6; Charles W. Anderson to Young Sr., 7 April 1937, WMY Sr. Papers, box 2, scrapbook 16; contract (between Kentucky State Board of Education . . . and Lincoln Institute of Kentucky), WMY Sr. Papers, box 1, album 12.

16. Young Sr. résumé; L.N. Taylor to Young Sr., 5 July 1938, 11 July 1938, WMY Sr. Papers, box 1; Young Jr. to Ralph Edwards, 10 January 1957, WMY Jr. Papers; report to board of regents, April 1954, by Young Sr., Lincoln Institute, 2, in Charles Henry Parrish Jr. Papers, box 15, file 7, University Archives and Records Center, William Ekstrom Library, University of Louisville.

17. C.H. Parrish to Young Sr., 21 May 1966, Parrish Papers, box 24, outgoing professional correspondence, 1964-69; Young Sr. résumé; John Fred Williams to Young Sr., 10 September 1945, WMY Sr. Papers, box 1; Watson Cormstrong to Young Sr., 12 March 1952, WMY Sr. Papers, box 2, scrapbook 16; Justine Tandy Campbell to Young Sr., 22 June 1947, WMY Sr. Papers.

18. Parrish to Young, 21 May 1966, Parrish Papers; J.W. Whitehouse to Young Sr., 17 April 1948, WMY Sr. Papers, box 1; Young Sr. to Frank L. Stanley, 3 January 1950, WMY Sr. Papers, box 2, scrapbook 16; J. Mansir Tydings, memorandum, 13 May 1954, Parrish Papers, box 23, incoming professional correspondence, 1954-55, file 1.

19. "Education in Kentucky," by Whitney M. Young Sr., WMY Sr. Papers, box 1, album 11; Gladys O'Bannon to Young Sr., 28 October 1941, WMY Sr. Papers, box 1; Young Sr. to Horace Mann Bond, 10 July 1959, correspondence 10 July–15 September 1959, series 2, box 13, file 374, Horace Mann Bond Papers, Archives, University of Massachusetts, Amherst.

20. Newspaper clipping, "Blacks Merge with KEA," WMY Sr. Papers, box 1, album 12; "Long Live the KTA" by Whitney Young, 5 April 1955, WMY Sr. Papers, box 9, letters and cards, maroon scrapbook.

21. "The Role of Lincoln Institute in a Desegregated Pattern," and Young Sr. to Joseph R. Ray, 22 February 1955, WMY Sr. Papers, box 2, scrapbook 16.

22. "State Department Advocates Integration," by Whitney Young, 4 January 1954, WMY Sr. Papers, box 8, scrapbook 97.

23. Dr. Samuel Robinson, interviewed by author, Lincoln Ridge, Ky., 20 July 1982; minutes, board of trustees, Lincoln Foundation, Louisville, 10 April 1970, WMY Jr. Papers, box 107, Lincoln Foundation file.

24. For examples of southern black leadership in the generation before the civil rights movement see David M. Tucker, *Lieutenant Lee of Beale Street* (Nashville: Vanderbilt University Press, 1971); Raymond Gavins, *The Perils and Prospects of Southern Black Leadership: Gordon Blaine Hancock, 1884-1970* (Durham, N.C.: Duke University Press, 1977).

25. S. Vincent Owens to Young Sr., 13 October 1947, WMY Sr. papers, box 2, scrapbook 17; Young Sr. to Rufus E. Clement, 9 December 1953, Rufus E. Clement Papers, Y file, Atlanta University (hereafter AU) 1953-54, U-Z, Robert W. Woodruff Library, Atlanta University Center.

26. Young Sr. to Young Jr., 28 January 1954, WMY Jr. Papers, box 263, file 195 (correspondence).

27. Allison Davis, *Leadership, Love, and Aggression: The Psychological Factors in the Making of Four Black Leaders* (New York: Harcourt Brace Jovanovich, 1983), 193-94, 201.

28. Martin Luther King Sr. with Clayton Riley, *Daddy King: An Autobiography* (New York: William Morrow, 1980), 98-102. For a useful discussion of the influence of the black church tradition on King see James H. Cone, "Martin Luther King Jr., Black Theology— Black Church," *Theology Today* 40 (January 1984): 409-20.

29. Young Sr. to Young Jr., 10 June 1948, WMY Jr. Papers, box 1A, personal correspondence, 1943-60.

30. Young Jr. to Young Sr., 14 October 1955, WMY Sr. Papers, box 2, scrapbook 17.

31. Young Jr. to Ralph Edwards, 10 January 1957, WMY Jr. Papers, box 1, personal correspondence, 1958-60.

32. Young Sr. to Young Jr., 11 June 1964, WMY Sr. Papers, box 1.

33. Robinson, interview.

34. "Application for Financial Aid to Organize and Develop a Program and to Promote the Establishment of Intergroup Relations Study Centers in American Universities," submitted by the Lincoln Foundation, February 1970; J. Mansir Tydings to Rockefeller Foundation, 19 March 1970; Tydings to Young Sr., March 1970; Tydings to Young Jr., 16 April 1970, WMY Jr. Papers, box 107, Lincoln Foundation file.

35. Val Habjan to Joseph E. Black, 8 June 1970; Marvin J. Gold to Black, 30 July 1970, WMY Jr. Papers, box 107, Lincoln Foundation file.

2. Growing Up with Jim Crow

1. Carter G. Woodson, *The Negro Professional Men and the Community* (Washington, D.C.: Association for the Study of Negro Life and History, 1934), 81-116; also see Dennis C. Dickerson, "Eugene Percy Roberts: Black Physician and Leader," *New York State Journal of Medicine* 85 (April 1985): 143-44.

2. Peggy Mann, "Whitney M. Young Jr.: Bridge Builder between Two Worlds," unpublished MS, 4, 9-10, WMY Jr. Papers, box 11A, Peggy Mann–Whitney Young file; Love, author interview.

3. Love, interview; Richard Bruner, *Whitney M. Young Jr.: The Story of a Pragmatic Humanist* (New York: David McKay, 1972), 11.

4. Love, interview.

5. Joseph and Kathleen Carroll, interview; Lincoln Institute of Kentucky, *Lincoln Log* 2, no. 1 (1937-38), courtesy of Professor George C. Wright, University of Texas, Austin. Joseph A. Carroll and Kathleen A. McClain married in 1939 while teaching at Lincoln Institute.

6. Mann, "Bridge Builder," 13; Love, interview; Young to Ralph Edwards, 10 January 1957, WMY Jr. Papers, box 1, personal correspondence, 1958-60.

7. Judge Benjamin Shobe, interviewed by author, Louisville, 20 July 1982; Harvey C. Russell Jr., interviewed by author, New York, 16 January 1984.

8. Bruner, *Young*, 18; "Kentucky State University," in *Encyclopedia of Black America*, ed. W. Augustus Low and Virgil A. Clift (New York: McGraw-Hill, 1981), 484-85; Shobe, interview.

9. D.W. Lyons to Dennis C. Dickerson, 20 December 1984; Alice A. Dunigan, *The Fascinating Story of Black Kentuckians: Their Heritage and Tradition*, 180 (courtesy of D.W. Lyons, Blazer Library, Kentucky State University, Frankfort); Charles H. Wesley, *The History of Sigma Pi Phi* (Washington, D.C.: Association for the Study of Negro Life and History, 1969), 26, 252-53; Shobe, interview; "Rufus Ballard Atwood," in *Who's Who in Colored America, 1928-1929* (New York: Who's Who in Colored America Corp., 1929), 17; Gerald L. Smith, *A Black Educator in the Segregated South: Kentucky's Rufus B. Atwood* (Lexington: University Press of Kentucky, 1994).

10. *Kentucky Thorobred*, December 1939, December 1940, February 1941; Mann, "Bridge Builder," 15; Shobe, interview.

11. Margaret Young, interviewed by author, New Rochelle, N.Y., 5 November 1982; Fourteenth Census of the United States, 1920: Population, 2:62.

12. Margaret Young, 1982 interview; Margaret Young, interviewed by Betty Barnes, New Rochelle, N.Y., 13 November 1975, Oral History Research Office, Columbia University, New York, 5.

13. Mrs. Ersa Hines Poston, interviewed by author, Washington, D.C., 24 September 1982; Margaret Young, 1982 interview.

14. *Kentucky Thorobred,* April-May 1942; Poston, interview.

15. *Kentucky Thorobred,* December 1940, February 1941, October 1941, November-December 1941.

16. *Kentucky Thorobred,* April-May 1942.

17. Poston, interview; Mann, "Bridge Builder," 15-16; Margaret Young, 1982 interview.

18. Kentucky State College, *Commencement Programs, 1930-1947,* vol. 1, *The Fifty-Third Annual Commencement,* 10 June 1941, Blazer Library, Kentucky State University, Frankfort; Margaret Young, 1975 interview, 9.

19. Mann, "Bridge Builder," 17. The competition among black students to gain admittance to the Howard and Meharry medical schools was intense. Young's name was placed on waiting lists.

20. Mann, "Bridge Builder," 17-19; Margaret Young, 1975 interview, 10-11; Paul L. Stagg to Mrs. Whitney Young Sr., 26 July 1943, WMY Sr. Papers, box 1, album 4; Whitney Moore Young Jr.—Special Inquiry, 30 December 1964, St. Louis Office, and Whitney Moore Young Jr.—Special Inquiry, 25 January 1965, Boston Office, both in Whitney M. Young Jr. FBI files, J. Edgar Hoover Building, Washington, D.C.

21. Mann, "Bridge Builder," 19-20; Margaret Young, 1982 interview; Margaret Young, 1975 interview, 6.

22. A. Russell Buchanan, *Black Americans in World War II* (Santa Barbara, Calif.: Clio Books, 1977), 71-101.

23. Bruner, *Young,* 26-27; Margaret Young, 1975 interview, 10; Mann, "Bridge Builder," 20.

24. Bruner, *Young,* 27-28.

25. Shobe, interview.

26. Buchanan, *Black Americans in World War II,* 29-57; Dennis C. Dickerson, *Out of the Crucible: Black Steelworkers in Western Pennsylvania, 1875-1980* (Albany: State University of New York Press, 1986), 151-81; Young to Margaret Young, 24 December 1945, Margaret Buckner Young Personal Papers, New Rochelle, N.Y.

27. Young to Margaret Young, 16 December 1945, Margaret Buckner Young Personal Papers.

28. Young Jr.—Special Inquiry, 30 December 1964, FBI files.

3. Maturing in Minnesota

1. Howard Jacob Karger, "Phyllis Wheatley House: A History of the Minneapolis Black Settlement House, 1924-1940," *Phylon* 47 (March 1986): 79-90; Margaret Young, 1975 interview, 25-26.

2. Mr. and Mrs. Ashby Gaskins, interviewed by author, Minneapolis, 4 August 1982.

3. W.E.B. Dubois and Augustus G. Dill, eds., *The College Bred Negro American,* AU Publication no. 15 (Atlanta: Atlanta University Press, 1910), 48; Roy Wilkins with Tom Matthews, *Standing Fast: The Autobiography of Roy Wilkins* (New York: Viking Press, 1982), 46; Wesley, *Sigma Pi Phi,* 155-56; John C. Kidneigh, interviewed by author, St. Paul, 3 August 1982.

4. Kidneigh, interview; Gisela P. Konopka, interviewed by author, Minneapolis, 5 August 1982; "John Christopher Kidneigh," in *Who's Who in America, 1964-65,* vol. 33 (Chicago: A.N. Marquis, 1964), 1091; "Gisela Peiper Konopka," in *Who's Who in America, 1984-85,* 43d ed., vol. 1 (Chicago: A.N. Marquis, 1984), 1828.

5. Kidneigh, interview; Konopka, interview; James T. Wardlaw Sr., interviewed by author, Minneapolis, 4 August 1982.

6. Academic transcript, WMY Jr., Admissions and Records, University of Minnesota, Minneapolis; *Bulletin,* UM School of Social Work, 1947-48, Social Welfare History Archives, University Libraries, University of Minnesota.

7. John C. Kidneigh to Ann Tanneyhill, 13 January 1947, WMY Jr. Papers, box 259, personal correspondence, 1947-70.

8. Nancy J. Weiss, *The National Urban League, 1910-1940* (New York: Oxford University Press, 1974), 43-44, 81-82, 163-64; Jesse T. Moore Jr., *A Search for Equality: The National Urban League, 1910-1961* (University Park: Pennsylvania State University Press, 1981), 47, 95; *New York Times,* 10 January 1976.

9. Earl Spangler, *The Negro in Minnesota* (Minneapolis: T.S. Denison, 1961), 105; Whitney M. Young Jr., "History of the St. Paul Urban League," M.A. thesis, University of Minnesota, 1947, 30-31; *Bulletin,* UM School of Social Work, 1947-48, 4.

10. Guichard Parris and Lester Brooks, *Blacks in the City: A History of the National Urban League* (Boston: Little, Brown, 1971), 395-96; Margaret Young, 1982 interview.

11. Kidneigh, interview; Wardlaw, interview; James T. Wardlaw, intermediate report on WMY Jr.'s field assignment, 18 March 1947; Wardlaw to Ann Tanneyhill, 1 April 1947, WMY Jr. Papers, box 259, personal correspondence, 1947-70.

12. Wardlaw, interview.

13. Young, "St. Paul Urban League," 4-5, 51-54.

14. Ibid., 22-27, 66-68.

15. Academic transcript, WMY Jr.; S. Vincent Owens to Ann Tanneyhill, 26 May 1949, WMY Jr. Papers, box 259, personal correspondence, 1947-70; Wardlaw, interview; Charles F. Rogers, interviewed by author, St. Paul, 3 August 1982; *St. Paul Recorder,* 22 August 1947.

16. *St. Paul Pioneer Press,* 4 October 1952; Young, "St. Paul Urban League," 32.

17. Estyr B. Peake, interviewed by author, St. Paul, 12 October 1983; James S. Griffin, interviewed by author, St. Paul, 11 October 1983.

18. Neil A. Wynn, *The Afro-American and the Second World War* (New York: Holmes and Meier, 1975), 60-78; Harvard Sitkoff, "The Detroit Race Riot of 1943," *Michigan History* (fall 1969): 183-206; Harvard Sitkoff, "Racial Militancy and Interracial Violence in the Second World War," *Journal of American History* (December 1971): 661-81.

19. Clifford E. Rucker, "The Governor's Interracial Commission of Minnesota: An Administrative History," M.A. thesis, University of Minnesota, 1955, 2-3, 6, 8, 10; "The Negro Worker in Minnesota," a report to Governor Edward J. Thye by the Governor's Interracial Commission of Minnesota, 10 March 1945, i, 16-20, 25-35, 51; Luther Youngdahl to Lester B. Granger, 1 December 1949, Governor Luther Youngdahl Records, Minnesota Historical Society, St. Paul; Rogers, interview.

20. *St. Paul Recorder,* 22 August 1947; Palmer Sather to Ed Gehrke, 26 August 1947, WMY Jr. Papers, box 1A, personal correspondence, 1943-60.

21. Adolph Reed Jr., *The Jesse Jackson Phenomena: The Crisis of Purpose in Afro-American Politics* (New Haven: Yale University Press, 1986), 9. Reed addressed himself specifically to black politicians, but this analysis applies also to black leadership in other fields, especially to such social service spheres as the Urban League.

22. Robert Esbjornson, *A Christian in Politics: Luther W. Youngdahl* (Minneapolis: T.S. Denison, 1955), 182-84; Addie C. Few to Youngdahl, 7 June 1949; Youngdahl to L.B. Benson, 7 November 1949; Benson to Youngdahl, 14 November 1949, Governor Luther Youngdahl Records.

23. Carl Solberg, *Hubert Humphrey: A Biography* (New York: W.W. Norton, 1984), 105-6; William Seabron to Humphrey, 22 February 1947, correspondence—FEPC file, and Humphrey to James T. Wardlaw, 7 April 1948, Hubert H. Humphrey Papers, mayoralty files, 1945-48, Minneapolis Committees, Commissions, Minnesota Historical Society, St. Paul. At the Democratic National Convention 1948, on the eve of a Dixiecrat walkout, Humphrey

gave a stirring speech that persuaded delegates to include a strong civil rights plank in the party platform. This speech made Humphrey a national spokesman for the civil rights cause.

24. Young, "St. Paul Urban League," 31, 49; *Twenty-Sixth Annual Report, 1949,* and *Twenty-Seventh Annual Report, 1950,* National Urban League Records (hereafter cited as NUL Records), series 13, box 27, St. Paul Urban League, 1938-58 annual and semiannual reports file, Manuscript Division, Library of Congress.

25. Walter Rock, interviewed by author, North St. Paul, 4 August 1982; Bruner, *Young,* 33-34.

26. *Twenty-Sixth Annual Report, 1949,* and *Twenty-Seventh Annual Report, 1950,* St. Paul Urban League, NUL Records.

27. "The Negro Worker's Progress in Minnesota," a report to Governor Luther W. Youngdahl by the Governor's Interracial Commission of Minnesota, 30 June 1949, 20-29, 30-32, 42-45.

28. Youngdahl to Young, 20 May 1949, WMY Jr. Papers, box 1A, personal correspondence, 1943-60.

29. Bernhard W. LeVander to Richard Hansen, 29 November 1949; Hansen to R.A. Trovatten, 16 December 1949, Governor Luther Youngdahl Records.

30. Esbjornson, *A Christian in Politics,* 182-84; Malcolm G. Dade Jr. to Young, 11 February 1949, and Jessica Page and Wayne Wattman to Young, 21 February 1949, WMY Jr. Papers, box 1A, personal correspondence, 1943-60; *Twenty-Sixth Annual Report, 1949,* St. Paul Urban League, NUL Records.

31. Weiss, *National Urban League,* 257; *Twenty-Sixth Annual Report, 1949,* St. Paul Urban League, NUL Records; *St. Paul Recorder,* 12 March 1948, 13 May 1949.

32. Rogers, interview; Charles H. Wesley, *The History of Alpha Phi Alpha* (Chicago: Foundation, 1961), 112-13, 627; Sue Williams, interviewed by author, St. Paul, 3 August 1982.

33. Frank L. Stanley to Young, 23 November 1949, and Young to Stanley, 29 November 1949, WMY Jr. Papers, box 1A, personal correspondence, 1943-60.

34. Arthur McWatt, interviewed by author, St. Paul, 12 October 1983.

35. Williams, interview; Rogers, interview.

36. *St. Paul Recorder,* 12 November 1948; Lucille Black to Beatrice Boyd, 6 October 1947, NAACP Records, branch file, St. Paul, 1946-50 file, group 2, box 86.

37. Griffin, interview; *St. Paul Recorder,* 25 November 1949; "Nimrod Allen," in *Encyclopedia of African Methodism,* ed. Richard R. Wright Jr. (Philadelphia: AME Church, 1947), 27-28.

38. *St. Paul Recorder,* 11 March 1949; Margaret Young, 1982 interview; S. Vincent Owens to Ann Tanneyhill, 26 May 1949, WMY Jr. Papers, box 259, personal correspondence, 1947-70; "Benjamin N. Moore," "James W. Crump," "Lillian Parks Balenger," and "Floyd Massey, Jr.," all in Who's Who, St. Paul, Minnesota, in the Urban League, NUL Records, Public Relations Dept., biographical file, series 5, box 28.

39. Williams, interview.

40. *St. Paul Recorder,* 25 February 1949. See Jon H. Butler, "Communities and Congregations: The Black Church in St. Paul, 1860-1900," *Journal of Negro History* 56 (April 1971): 118-34. Butler's essay discusses class differences among St. Paul blacks as reflected in religious institutions. Although he examines an earlier period, his observations are applicable to St. Paul's black community after World War II.

41. Seventeenth Census of the United States, 1950: Population, pt. 23: Minnesota, 2:23-65.

42. Anna K. Schwartz to Young, 17 March 1948; Young to Vernon P. Bodein, 6 February 1948; Arthur K. Krueger to Young, 7 January 1949, WMY Jr. Papers, box 1A, personal correspondence, 1943-60.

43. Frank S. Mead and Samuel S. Hill, *Handbook of Denominations in the United States,* 8th ed. (Nashville: Abingdon Press, 1985), 240.

44. Mark D. Morrison-Reed, *Black Pioneers in a White Denomination* (Boston: Beacon Press, 1980), 143.

45. "Benjamin N. Moore" and "Floyd Massey Jr.," in Who's Who, St. Paul, NUL Records.
46. "Arthur Foote," in Who's Who, St. Paul, NUL Records; Margaret Young, 1982 interview; Margaret Young, 1975 interview, 35.
47. Harvard Sitkoff, *A New Deal for Blacks* (New York: Oxford University Press, 1978); Richard Dalfiume, "The 'Forgotten Years' of the Negro Revolution," *Journal of American History* 55 (June 1968): 90-106; Harvard Sitkoff, "Harry Truman and the Election of 1948: The Coming of Age of Civil Rights in American Politics," *Journal of Southern History* 37 (November 1971): 597-616.
48. Young Jr. to Young Sr., 30 April 1948, WMY Jr. Papers, box 1A, personal correspondence, 1943-60.
49. *St. Paul Recorder*, 21 May 1948.
50. S. Vincent Owens to Ann Tanneyhill, 26 May 1949, WMY Jr. Papers, box 259, personal correspondence, 1947-70.
51. Young to Lester B. Granger, 28 November 1949, NUL Records, Admin. Dept., affiliates file, series 1, box 116, 1950 Omaha file.

4. Becoming a Leader

1. William Ramsey, interviewed by author, Omaha, 6 July 1982; Eugene Skinner, interviewed by author, Omaha, 6 July 1982; Alyce Wilson, interviewed by author, Omaha, 8 July 1982; Jeffrey H. Smith, "The Omaha De Porres Club," *Negro History Bulletin* 33 (December 1970): 197.
2. Sixteenth Census of the United States, 1940: Population, pt. 4: Minnesota–New Mexico, 2:705; Seventeenth Census of the United States, 1950: Population, pt. 27: Nebraska, 2:27-47; Dennis N. Mihelich, "World War II and the Transformation of the Omaha Urban League," *Nebraska History* 60 (fall 1979): 406-8, 410-14, 416-18.
3. R. Maurice Moss to James Paxson, 9 December 1949; Young to Lester B. Granger, 28 November 1949; Young to Moss, 23 December 1949, all in NUL Records, Admin. Dept., affiliates file, series 1, box 116, 1950 Omaha file; Skinner, interview.
4. "Otto W. Swanson," in Who's Who, Omaha, in the Urban League, NUL Records, Public Relations Dept., biographical file, series 5, box 28; *Omaha World-Herald*, 15 May 1973; Ramsey, interview; N. Phillips Dodge Sr., interviewed by author, Omaha, 7 July 1982; Margaret Fischer, interviewed by author, Omaha, 8 July 1982.
5. Ramsey, interview; Dodge, interview; Fischer, interview.
6. Skinner, interview; Judge Elizabeth Pittman, interviewed by author, Omaha, 9 July 1982.
7. Ramsey, interview; Dodge, interview.
8. *Omaha Star*, 13 November 1953.
9. Marion M. Taylor to R. Maurice Moss, 30 December 1949, 22 June 1950, NUL Records, Admin. Dept., affiliates file, series 1, box 116, 1950 Omaha file; memorandum, Lester B. Granger to Community Services, 13 February 1953, NUL Records, Admin. Dept., affiliates file, series 1, box 116, 1953-54 Omaha file; 1953 annual report of the Omaha Urban League, NUL Records, Housing Activities Dept., affiliates file, series 3, box 59, 1948-59 Omaha Urban League file (hereafter OUL); *Omaha Star*, 19 and 28 June 1953.
10. *Omaha Evening World Herald*, 1 and 15 February 1950.
11. "Does State FEPC Hamper You?" *Business Week*, 25 February 1950, 114-16; McCaw, interview; Theodore Sorensen, interviewed by author, New York, 12 January 1984; *Omaha Star*, 12 May 1950.
12. Sorensen, interview; *Lincoln (Nebraska) Star*, 17 October 1950; *Omaha Star*, 16 January 1953; Judge Elizabeth Pittman, interview; Dennis C. Dickerson, "John Adams: An AME Preacher in Nebraska Politics," in *Religion, Race, and Region: Research Notes on AME Church History* (Nashville: AME Sunday School Union, 1995), 109-10.
13. *Omaha Star*, 10 and 31 March 1950, 16 June 1950, 21 July 1950, 17 August 1951;

OUL executive secretary's report, 9 May 1950, NUL Records, Admin. Dept., affiliates file, series 1, box 116, 1950 Omaha file.

14. *Omaha Star,* 6 April 1951.

15. Dodge, interview.

16. Ramsey, interview.

17. Arthur C. McCaw, interviewed by author, Kissimmee, Fla., 29 July 1982; Lillian Dorsey, interviewed by author, Omaha, 9 July 1982.

18. Smith, "The Omaha De Porres Club," 194-95; Dr. Claude Organ, interviewed by author, Oklahoma City, 7 February 1987; John P. Markoe, S.J., "Omaha De Porres Center," *Interracial Review* 21 (February 1950): 24; Young to John Markoe, S.J., 17 March 1965, WMY Jr. Papers, box 128, speaking engagements (not accepted), January-April 1965 file.

19. Organ, interview. For a time the De Porres Club also boycotted the transit company: *Omaha Star,* 18 April 1952.

20. Organ, interview; McCaw, interview.

21. Smith, "The Omaha De Porres Club," 197; *Omaha Star,* 7 and 15 June 1951.

22. Betty Corbin, interviewed by author, Omaha, 6 July 1982; John F. Daly to Young, 12 November 1953, WMY Jr. Papers, box 1A, personal correspondence, 1943-60; Smith, "The Omaha De Porres Club," 197; John P. Markoe, S.J., to Young, 6 March 1954, WMY Jr. Papers, box 263, file 195 (correspondence).

23. *Omaha Star,* 15 August 1950; OUL executive secretary's report, 9 May 1950, NUL Records.

24. Annual report, OUL, 1950, NUL Records, Admin. Dept., affiliates file, series 13, box 21, 1928-60 annual and semiannual reports file; Young to R. Maurice Moss, 31 December 1952; additional personnel data on Whitney M. Young Jr., WMY Jr. Papers, box 259, personal correspondence, 1947-70; *Omaha Star,* 16 June 1950.

25. Dodge, interview; Ramsey, interview; Fischer, interview; Bertha Calloway, interviewed by author, Omaha, 5 July 1982.

26. Alfred C. Kennedy, "Good Homes Make Good Citizens," Lincoln Urban League annual dinner, 28 January 1953, NUL Records, Admin. Dept., affiliates file, series 1, box 102, 1952-53 Lincoln, Nebraska, file; remarks by Young Jr., Housing Panel, September 1953, NUL Records, Public Relations Dept., speeches file, series 15, box 1, WMY Jr. 1953.

27. Donna Mays Polk, "Dr. A.B. Pittman," *Black Men and Women of Nebraska* (Lincoln: Nebraska Black History Preservation Society, 1981), 35; Dr. A.B. Pittman, interviewed by author, Omaha, 7 July 1982; Fischer, interview.

28. Lavonne Curtis, interviewed by author, Omaha, 9 July 1982; Skinner, interview; Smith, "The Omaha De Porres Club," 195-96.

29. Dorsey, interview; Dodge, interview; Wilson, interview; Kennedy, "Good Homes Make Good Citizens"; Dr. A.B. Pittman, interview.

30. *Omaha Star,* 19 May 1950; memorandum, Lester B. Granger to Community Services, 13 February 1953, NUL Records; Corbin, interview.

31. Dodge, interview.

32. *Omaha Star,* 30 June 1950; *Omaha Evening World Herald,* 15 February 1950.

33. *Omaha Evening World Herald,* 7 June 1953, 23 October 1953; additional personnel data; Young to Reginald Johnson, 15 December 1952, NUL Records, Housing Activities Dept., affiliates file, series 3, box 59, 1948-59 OUL file.

34. Remarks by WMY Jr., Housing Panel, September 1953, NUL Records; Young to Johnson, 15 December 1952, NUL Records, Housing Activities Dept., affiliates file, series 3, box 59, 1948-59 OUL file; Kennedy, "Good Homes Make Good Neighbors."

35. Memorandum, Young to NUL, 23 November 1951, NUL Records, Housing Activities Dept., affiliates file, series 3, box 59, 1948-59 OUL file; McCaw, interview; *Omaha Star,* 23 November 1951.

36. Young to Lester B. Granger, 15 July 1952; Young to Negro Ministers of Omaha, n.d., NUL Records, Housing Activities Dept., affiliates file, series 3, box 59, 1948-59 OUL file.

37. Frank S. Horne to Reginald A. Johnson, 9 October 1952; "Review of Omaha, Nebraska, Urban League's Letters, re the Omaha City Council's Rejection of Title I Study Areas," NUL Records, Housing Activities Dept., affiliates file, series 3, box 59, 1948-59 OUL file.

38. OUL report, September 1952, NUL Records, Public Relations Dept., affiliates file, series 5, box 46, 1952 Omaha monthly reports; "Eugene Skinner," in Polk, *Black Men and Women of Nebraska*, 45; 1953 OUL board of directors, NUL Records, Public Relations Dept., series 5, box 15, 1941-59 OUL file; "Wanasebe Fletcher," "Zell R. Sahn," Who's Who, Omaha, in Urban League, NUL Records, Public Relations Dept., biographical file, series 5, box 28; *Omaha Star*, 9 June 1950.

39. *Omaha Evening World Herald*, 15 February 1950; telegram, G. Aneita Hayes to Lester B. Granger, 1 February 1950, and Young to Granger, 6 February 1950, NUL Records, Admin. Dept., affiliates file, series 1, box 116, 1950 Omaha file; additional personnel data."

40. Wilson, interview; Skinner, interview; Judge Elizabeth Pittman, interview; Claude Organ, interviewed by author, Oklahoma City, 7 February 1987.

41. Fischer, interview; Dodge, interview; additional personnel data.

42. Bess Pollak to Young, 30 December 1950; Steve C. Brace to Young, 17 November 1953, WMY Jr. Papers, box 1A, personal correspondence, 1943-60.

43. *Omaha Star*, 16 January 1953; Robert B. Crosby to Young, 6 October 1953, WMY Jr. Papers, box 1A, personal correspondence, 1943-60.

44. 1950 OUL annual report, in NUL Records, annual and semiannual reports, series 13, box 21, 1928-60 OUL file; Fischer, interview.

45. *Omaha Star*, 24 August 1951; Ramsey, interview.

46. Alfred C. Kennedy to Young Sr., 14 November 1953, WMY Sr. Papers, box 2, scrapbook 16.

47. McCaw, interview; Dr. A.B. Pittman, interview.

48. Dodge, interview; "Nathan Phillips Dodge," in Who's Who, Omaha, in the Urban League, NUL Records, Public Relations Dept., biographical file, series 5, box 28; Ramsey, interview.

49. John P. Markoe, S.J., to Young, 5 December 1953, 6 March 1953, WMY Jr. Papers, box 263, file 195 (correspondence); Organ, interview.

50. *Omaha Star*, 9 August 1952; Smith, "The Omaha De Porres Club," 195.

51. *Omaha Star*, 9 February 1951, 24 August 1951.

52. Wilson, interview; Mrs. Ralph Adams, interviewed by author, Omaha, 7 July 1982.

53. *Omaha Star*, 24 and 31 March 1950; Adams, interview; Eva Hanna to Lucille Black, 7 November 1953, NAACP Records, branch file, Omaha, 1953-55 file, group 2, series C, box 95, Manuscript Division, Library of Congress.

54. John G. Lewis Jr. to Young, 25 January 1963, NUL Records, Administrative Department affiliates file, series 1, part 2, box 86, WMY Jr. correspondence, 1963-65, A-Y unidentified; *Omaha Star*, 7 April 1950, 9 and 16 June 1950; Adams, interview.

55. McCaw, interview; Young to Arthur B. McCaw, 24 November 1953, WMY Jr. Papers, box 1A, personal correspondence, 1943-60.

56. McCaw, interview; Adams, interview; Young to Arthur McCaw, n.d., Arthur B. McCaw Personal Papers, Kissimmee, Fla.; "Charles F. Davis," in Who's Who, Omaha, in Urban League, NUL Records, Public Relations Dept., biographical file, series 5, box 28.

57. Wright, *Encyclopedia of African Methodism*, 460; Young to Reverend S.H. Lewis, 24 September 1953, WMY Jr. Papers, box 1A, personal correspondence, 1943-60; Reverend Noah W. Lewis to Dennis C. Dickerson, 1 September 1982.

58. Additional personnel data; McCaw, interview; Adams, interview; Calloway, interview.

59. Dodge, interview; Dorsey, interview.

60. Monthly reports, NUL Records, Public Relations Dept., affiliates file, series 5, box 46, 1952 Omaha monthly reports file; Skinner, interview; Dorsey, interview.

61. Young to Lester Granger, 24 November 1950, NUL Records, Admin. Dept., affili-

ates file, series 1, box 116, 1950 Omaha file; Granger to Community Services, 13 February 1953, NUL Records.

62. Obsequies, Clyde Wilbur Malone, WMY memorandum, 6 March 1951; remarks by Whitney Young at the funeral of Clyde Malone, NUL Records, Research Dept., affiliates file, series 6, box 93, Omaha, 1943, 1948-49, 1951; George Randol to Lester B. Granger, 15 September 1952; Randol to N.P. Dotson, 12 August 1953; Sidney H. Alexander to Reginald A. Johnson, 21 December 1953, NUL Records, Housing Activities, affiliates file, series 3, box 56, 1952-54 Lincoln Urban League file; Kennedy, "Good Homes Make Good Citizens."

63. Moore, *Search for Equality*, 98-101, 144, 155-56; Parris and Brooks, *Blacks in the City*, 387; Wilson, interview.

64. Young to Lester B. Granger, 16 October 1950, 24 November 1950, NUL Records, Admin. Dept., affiliates file, series 1, box 116, 1950 Omaha file.

65. Moore, *Search for Equality*, 157-63.

66. Young to Granger, 29 May 1950, 24 November 1950, NUL Records, Admin. Dept., affiliates file, series 1, box 116, 1950 Omaha file; McCaw, interview.

67. *Omaha Star*, 19 January 1951; Bruner, *Young*, 40-41; Frank Z. Glick to Alfred C. Kennedy, 3 January 1951, WMY Jr. Papers, box 1A, personal correspondence, 1943-60; additional personnel data.

68. Young to Granger, 9 October 1953, WMY Jr. Papers, box 1A, personal correspondence, 1943-60; *Omaha Evening World Herald*, 11 November 1953.

5. An Activist Educator

1. Harvard Sitkoff, "Harry Truman and the Election of 1948: The Coming of Age of Civil Rights in American Politics," *Journal of Southern History* 37 (November 1971): 597-616; William C. Berman, *The Politics of Civil Rights in the Truman Administration* (Columbus: Ohio State University Press, 1970); Barton J. Bernstein, "The Ambiguous Legacy: The Truman Administration and Civil Rights," in *Politics and Policies of the Truman Administration*, ed. Barton J. Bernstein (Chicago: Quadrangle Books, 1972).

2. Robert F. Burk, *The Eisenhower Administration and Black Civil Rights* (Knoxville: University of Tennessee Press, 1984); Michael Mayer, "With Much Deliberation and Some Speed: Eisenhower and the Brown Decision," *Journal of Southern History* 52 (February 1986): 43-76.

3. Aldon D. Morris, *The Origins of the Civil Rights Movement: Black Communities Organizing for Change* (New York: Free Press, 1984).

4. Clarence A. Bacote, *The Story of Atlanta University: A Century of Service, 1865-1965* (Atlanta: Atlanta University, 1969), 328-30, 353-56; Forrester B. Washington to Rufus E. Clement, 20 June 1953, "Successor to F.B. Washington as Director of School of Social Work," Rufus E. Clement Papers, School of Social Work file (hereafter SSW file), AU general correspondence, 1953-54, box 1.

5. Dr. Thomas D. Jarrett, interviewed by author, Atlanta, 29 July 1982; Young to Nelson C. Jackson, 12 January 1954, WMY Jr. Papers, box 1A, personal correspondence, 1943-60; Ersa Hines Clinton to Young, 4 January 1954, WMY Jr. Papers, box 263, file 195 (correspondence).

6. Genevieve Hill, interviewed by author, Atlanta, 27 July 1982.

7. Young to Rufus E. Clement, 14 April 1954, "Requested Changes in Budget for 1954-55"; Young to Clement, 4 December 1954; Elizabeth Wisner to Young, 3 May 1955; Young to Benjamin Youngdahl, 6 April 1955; Youngdahl to Young, 11 April 1955; Young to Clement, 13 May 1955, Clement Papers, SSW file, AU 1954-55, A-C, box 1; Young to Clement, 14 October 1955, Clement Papers, SSW file, AU Archives, 1955-56, A.

8. Forrester B. Washington to Young, 11 December 1953, "Recommendations Regarding Operation of the Atlanta University School of Social Work," 8, 27; Young to Clement, 27 April 1954, Clement Papers, SSW file, AU general correspondence, 1953-54, box 1; Young to

Clement, 14 April 1954, "Requested Changes in Budget," Clement Papers, SSW file, AU 1954-55, A-C, box 1; Young to Clement, 14 April 1954, "Attendance at National Conference of Social Work"; Young to Clement, 21 July 1955, Clement Papers, SSW file, AU Archives, 1955-56, A.

9. Young to Clement, 12 January 1954, 6 November 1954; Mary E. Switzer to Young, 28 October 1954, Clement Papers, SSW file, AU general correspondence, 1953-54, box 1; Young to Clement, 12 and 26 May 1955, and Clement to Young, 30 May 1955, Clement Papers, SSW file, AU 1954-55, A-C, box 1.

10. "Statement of Training Grant under the National Health Act," Clement Papers, Grant for Psychiatric Social Work file, July 1954, AU 1954-55, A-C, box 1; Young to Clement, 11 February 1954, Clement Papers, SSW file, AU general correspondence, 1953-54, box 1; Young to Clement, 6 February 1956, report of the school year 1955-56, Clement Papers, general correspondence, 1955-56, AU Archives, G-S; Young to Clement, 16 August 1955, Clement Papers, SSW file, AU Archives 1955-56, A.

11. Young to Clement, 14 April 1954, "Requested Changes in Budget," Clement Papers.

12. Memo to Rufus E. Clement, 1 February 1955; program, eighth annual out-of-town supervisors' conference, 2-4 November 1954, Clement Papers, AU 1954-55, C-F, box 2; Young to Clement, 6 February 1956, report of the social year, 1955-56, Clement Papers, general correspondence, 1955-56, AU Archives, G-S; Young to Clement, 30 August 1954; Administrative Assistant to Young Jr., 31 August 1954; Young to Clement, 28 September 1954, Clement Papers, SSW file, AU 1954-55, A-C, box 1; *Atlanta University Bulletin*, 1954-55, 1958-59, Woodruff Library, Atlanta University Center.

13. Young to Clement, 13 May 1955, 30 August 1954, Clement Papers, SSW file, AU 1954-55, A-C, box 1.

14. Hill, interview; Young to Clement, 1 February 1955, Clement Papers, AU 1954-55, C-F, box 2; "Objectives of the Atlanta University School of Social Work," 11 October 1955; Young to Clement, 15 October 1955, Clement Papers, SSW file, AU Archives, 1955-56, A.

15. Young to Clement, 18 November 1953, Clement Papers, SSW file, AU general correspondence, 1953-54, box 1; Young to Clement, 1 February 1955, Clement Papers, AU 1954-55, C-F, box 2.

16. Katharine A. Kendall to Young, 23 December 1955, WMY Jr. Papers, box 1A, personal correspondence, 1943-60.

17. Ernest F. Witte to Young, 22 November 1955, WMY Jr. Papers, box 1A, personal correspondence, 1943-60.

18. Young to Clement, 1 February 1955, Clement Papers, AU 1954-55, C-F, box 2; Young to Clement, 9 May 1955, and Clement to Hortense E. Lilly, 11 May 1955, Clement Papers, SSW file, AU 1954-55, A-C, box 1.

19. "Dynamic Young Dean Chose Social Work Aboard Warship," WMY Jr. Papers, box 259, miscellaneous file.

20. Forrester Washington to Board of Trustees, 18 February 1952, Clement Papers, SSW file, AU general correspondence, 1951-52, A-G, box 1; Washington to Young, 11 December 1953, "Recommendations," Clement Papers, SSW file, AU general correspondence, 1953-54, box 1; Young to Clement, 1 February 1955, Clement Papers, AU 1954-55, C-F, box 2; Young to Clement, 6 February 1956, Clement Papers, general correspondence, 1955-56, AU Archives, G-S.

21. Young to Nelson C. Jackson, 3 May 1958, NUL Records, Community Services Dept., general department file, series 2, box 15, WMY Jr. file, 1957-60.

22. Washington to Young, 11 December 1953, Clement Papers, SSW file, AU general correspondence, 1953-54, box 1; Mrs. A.D. King to Miss Florence M. Read, 7 December 1954, 7 March 1955, Clement Papers, SSW file, AU 1954-55, A-C, box 1.

23. Young to Clement, 14 April 1954, "Requested Changes in Budget," Clement Papers.

24. Young to Clement, 6 February 1956, Clement Papers, general correspondence, 1955-56, AU Archives, G-S.

25. Young to Clement, 1 February 1955, Clement Papers, AU 1954-55, C-F, box 2; Young to Jackson, 3 May 1958, NUL Records.

26. Young to Clement, 17 September 1953, WMY Jr. Papers, box 1A, personal correspondence, 1943-60; Hill, interview; Washington to Young, "Recommendations," 11 December 1953, Clement Papers; Young to Jackson, 3 May 1958, NUL Records.

27. "Minutes of Meeting of Local Agency Executives with Representatives of Faculty," 25 May 1955, Clement Papers, SSW file, AU Archives 1955-56, A.

28. Young to Clement, 1 and 6 February 1955, Clement Papers.

29. Young to Clement, 11 October 1955, faculty teaching load 1st semester 1955-56, President's Office 1955-56, AU Archives, B-F; organization and committee chart, Clement Papers, AU 1954-55, C-F, box 2.

30. Rufus E. Clement to Ernest Vandiver, 5 May 1959, WMY Jr. Papers, box 1A, personal correspondence, 1943-60; *Atlanta University Bulletin*, July 1955, July 1956, July 1957, December 1957; Young to Clement, 11 January 1956, personal data, Clement Papers.

31. Robert C. Anderson to Young, 19 June 1957, WMY Jr. Papers, box 1, personal correspondence, 1943-60; Young to Clement, 20 June 1955, Clement Papers, SSW file, AU 1954-55, A-C, box 1; *Atlanta University Bulletin*, July 1955, July 1960; Whitney Moore Young Jr., "Loyalty of Employees of United Nations," 24 July 1956, Atlanta, Results of Investigation, FBI files.

32. Young to Clement, 11 January 1956, personal data, Clement Papers; *Atlanta University Bulletin*, July 1955, December 1955, July 1956, August 1956, July 1957, December 1957, July 1958, December 1958, December 1959, July 1960.

33. *Atlanta University Bulletin*, December 1953; Joseph Golden to Clara A. Kaiser, 2 January 1959, WMY Jr. Papers, box 1A, personal correspondence, 1943-60; Young, "Review of Social Work Today," *Phylon* 15, no. 2 (1954): 219; Young, "Participation of Citizens," *Phylon* 19, no. 1 (1958): 96; Young, "Attitude Survey on Desegregation," *Phylon* 19, no. 4 (1958): 425-26.

34. Golden to Kaiser, 2 January 1959, WMY Jr. Papers; *Atlanta University Bulletin*, July 1959. In 1959 *Ebony* did a feature article on Young and the AU School of Social Work. See Young to John Johnson, 23 September 1959, WMY Jr. Papers, box 1, personal correspondence, 1958-60.

35. Rufus E. Clement to Young, 14 December 1956, 17 July 1957, 15 January 1958, 6 August 1958, 11 August 1959, WMY Jr. Papers, box 7, SSW file.

36. Young to John Kidneigh, 28 October 1959, 15 December 1959, WMY Jr. Papers, box 1, personal correspondence, 1958-60; Sam B. Taylor to Young, 27 June 1956; C.B. Nuckolls to Young, 3 July 1956; Nuckolls to Taylor, 3 July 1956; Young to Nuckolls, 7 July 1956; WMY Jr. Papers, box 1A, personal correspondence, 1943-60.

37. Donald B. Kennedy to Young, 5 April 1956; Young to Kennedy, 9 April 1956; Martha Branscombe to Young, 16 January 1957; Young to Branscombe, 21 January 1957; Kennedy to Young, 14 February 1957; Young to Branscombe, 25 February 1957, WMY Jr. Papers, box 2, miscellaneous 1961.

38. Young to Clement, 22 April 1958; Young to Donald S. Howard, 22 April 1958, WMY Jr. Papers, box 1A, personal correspondence, 1943-60.

39. Young to Howard, 25 February 1958, WMY Jr. Papers, box 1A, personal correspondence, 1943-60; Margaret Young, 1982 interview.

40. Young to Howard, 22 April 1958, WMY Jr. Papers, box 1A, personal correspondence, 1943-60. Young was not granted tenure at Atlanta University until 12 November 1959. See Clement to Young, 30 November 1959, WMY Jr. Papers, box 7, SSW file.

41. *Atlanta University Bulletin*, July 1959; Hill, interview.

42. Young, "New Dimensions in Intergroup Relations—Implications for Social Welfare," Intergroup Relations Committee of the National Social Welfare Assembly, 12 December 1960; "Intergroup Relations as a Challenge to Social Work Practice," National Conference on Social Welfare, 9 June 1960, WMY Jr. Papers, box 121A, speeches, 1954-60.

43. Joseph Golden to Clara A. Kaiser, 2 January 1959, WMY Jr. Papers; Young, "Attitude Survey on Desegregation," *Phylon* 19, no. 4 (1958): 425-26.

44. Young, "The Role of the Community Organizer in Desegregation," *Journal of Orthopsychiatry* (June 1956): 452-55.

45. Carlton B. Goodlett to Horace Mann Bond, 19 June 1959, Bond Papers, 27 May 1959–23 June 1959, correspondence, series 2, box 13, file 360; Bayard Rustin, interviewed by author, New York, 11 January 1984.

46. Young Jr. "Your Community and You," annual meeting, Malone Community Centers, Lincoln, Nebraska, 30 January 1957, WMY Jr. Papers, box 121A, speeches, 1954-60; Reverend Ralph D. Abernathy, interviewed by author, Atlanta, 26 October 1983; Dr. Kenneth B. Clark, interviewed by author, New York, 13 September 1984.

47. Atlanta Branch, NAACP Officers and Executive Committee—1955, NAACP Records, branch file, Atlanta, 1954-55, group 2, series C, box 35, Manuscript Division, Library of Congress; Walter L. Wallace to Rufus E. Clement, 9 May 1955, Clement Papers, SSW file, AU 1954-55, A-C, box 1; Young to Roy Wilkins, 18 July 1958, WMY Jr. Papers, box 1, personal correspondence, 1958-60; Young to Wilkins, 11 February 1959, WMY Jr. Papers, box 2, miscellaneous 1961; *Atlanta Daily World*, 13 February 1955, 18 May 1955.

48. F.H. Wenderoth to Young, 20 September 1958; Young to Wenderoth, 29 September 1958, WMY Jr. Papers, box 1, personal correspondence, 1958-60. In this instance Young was asked to assess Milton Lewis, a candidate for the top post at the Massillon, Ohio, Urban League. Lewis had been on Young's OUL staff. Young recommended Lewis highly. *Atlanta University Bulletin*, July 1959, December 1955, December 1958, July 1960.

49. M.T. Puryear to Young, 30 March 1954; Puryear to Rufus E. Clement, 10 February 1955; Puryear to Young, 10 February 1955, Clement Papers, SSW file, AU general correspondence, 1953-54, box 1.

50. John C. Dancy to Young, 18 September 1958, WMY Jr. Papers, box 1, personal correspondence, 1958-60; William E. Hill to Lester B. Granger, 29 September 1958, WMY Jr. Papers, box 1, personal correspondence-general ca. 1958-68.

51. Granger to Young, 26 January 1954, WMY Jr. Papers, box 1A, personal correspondence, 1943-60.

52. Young to Granger, 9 June 1958, WMY Jr. Papers, box 1, personal correspondence, 1958-60.

53. Lester to Young, 24 June 1959, WMY Jr. Papers, box 1, personal correspondence, 1958-60.

54. Young to Warren Banner, 11 February 1959, WMY Jr. Papers, box 2, miscellaneous 1961.

55. Young to Granger, 18 July 1960, WMY Jr. Papers, box 259, personal correspondence, 1947-70.

56. Samuel Z. Westerfield to Young, 15 December 1958, WMY Jr. Papers, box 2, miscellaneous 1961; Young to Hylan Lewis, 24 December 1959, WMY Jr. Papers, box 1A, personal correspondence, 1943-60.

57. Young to Boyd Wilson, 8 March 1960, WMY Jr. Papers, box 32, United Steelworkers of America file.

58. Young, "Integration: The Role of Labor Education," WMY Jr. Papers, box 32, United Steelworkers of America file.

59. Young to Emery F. Bacon, 8 March 1960; Bacon to Young, 9 March 1960; Young to David McDonald, 8 March 1960, WMY Jr. Papers, box 32, United Steelworkers of America file.

60. Young, "Youth and Adults in Creative Community Living," Montclair State Teachers College, Montclair, N.J., 4 June 1960, WMY Jr. Papers, box 121A, speeches, 1954-60.

61. Young, speech, sixth annual meeting, San Diego Urban League, 21 February 1960, WMY Jr. Papers, box 121A, speeches, 1954-60.

62. Young, "Status of the Negro Community: Problems—Proposals—Projection," Spring-

field College, Springfield, Mass., 15 June 1960, WMY Jr. Papers, box 121A, speeches, 1954-60; Young to John C. Dancy, 22 September 1958, WMY Jr. Papers, box 1, personal correspondence, 1958-60.

63. Young, speech, San Diego Urban League, 21 February 1960, WMY Jr. Papers.

64. King, *Daddy King,* 121-26, 132-38, 152-61; Atlton Hornsby Jr., "A City That Was Too Busy to Hate: Atlanta Businessmen and Desegregation," in *Southern Businessmen and Desegregation,* ed. Elizabeth Jacoway and David Colburn (Baton Rouge: Louisiana State University Press, 1982), 120-36.

65. Morris, *Origins of the Civil Rights Movement,* 4-76.

66. King, *Daddy King,* 154-57; Clarence Coleman, interviewed by author, Atlanta, 28 July 1982; James W. English, *Handyman of the Lord: The Life and Ministry of the Reverend William Holmes Borders* (New York: Meredith Press, 1967), 88-99.

67. M. Carl Holman, interviewed by author, Washington, D.C., 24 September 1982; King, *Daddy King,* 154.

68. Young to Dorothea Spellman, 3 February 1959, WMY Jr. Papers, box 1, personal correspondence, 1958-60.

69. Morris, *Origins of the Civil Rights Movement,* 30-35; Holman, interview.

70. Young to John Chapman, 2 November 1959, WMY Jr. Papers, box 1, personal correspondence, 1958-60; letter to Walter O'Malley, 16 December 1959; Atlanta Committee for Cooperative Action, minutes, 7 April 1960, WMY Jr. Papers, box 32, WMY Committee Affiliation, ACCA, 1961.

71. Holman, interview; ACCA letter, n.d., *The King Cole Show,* WMY Jr. Papers, box 32, WMY Committee Affiliation, ACCA, 1961.

72. Memorandum, Young to Executive Committee, Greater Atlanta Council on Human Relations, n.d., WMY Jr. Papers, box 32, WMY Committee Affiliation, ACCA, 1961.

73. Holman, interview.

74. *A Second Look: The Negro Citizen in Atlanta,* Atlanta Committee for Cooperative Action, January 1960, WMY Jr. Papers, box 259, miscellaneous file.

75. Young to Norris B. Herndon, 6 December 1959, WMY Jr. Papers, box 32, WMY Committee Affiliation, ACCA, 1961.

76. Holman, interview; James P. Brawley to Young, 9 March 1960; M.T. Puryear to members, Atlanta Committee for Cooperative Action, n.d., WMY Jr. Papers, box 32, WMY Committee Affiliation, ACCA, 1961.

77. Young to Albert E. Manley, 27 February 1958, WMY Jr. Papers, box 1, personal correspondence, 1958-60; Holman, interview; *Atlanta University Bulletin,* July 1960.

78. Frank S. Jones to Young, 12 May 1960, WMY Jr. Papers, box 1, personal correspondence, 1958-60.

79. Young to Jacob M. Rothchild, 17 October 1958; Rothchild to Young, 27 October 1958, WMY Jr. Papers, box 1, personal correspondence, 1958-60.

80. Harolyn Miller to Young, 29 September 1958, WMY Jr. Papers, box, 1, personal correspondence, 1958-60; *Atlanta University Bulletin,* July 1955.

81. On a General Education Board application, Young cited the Reverend Edward Cahill as a reference. See GEB application, 30 December 1959, GEB Papers, 950 Whitney M. Young Jr., 1959-62, box 529, file 5663, Rockefeller Archive Center, North Tarrytown, N.Y.

82. Young to the editor, *Atlanta Constitution,* 26 June 1956; Young to Charles L. Allen, 6 January 1959, WMY Jr. Papers, box 1, personal correspondence, 1958-60. Also see Andrew M. Manis, *Southern Civil Religions in Conflict: Black and White Baptists and Civil Rights, 1947-1957* (Athens: University of Georgia Press, 1987).

83. See Tinsley E. Yarbrough, *A Passion for Justice: J. Waites Waring and Civil Rights* (New York: Oxford University Press, 1987); Anne C. Loveland, *Lillian Smith: A Southerner Confronting the South* (Baton Rouge: Louisiana State University Press, 1986).

84. Young to William B. Hartsfield, 17 October 1958, WMY Jr. Papers, box 1, personal correspondence, 1958-60.

85. Young to Ralph McGill, 27 June 1957, WMY Jr. Papers, box 1, personal correspondence, 1958-60; Young to McGill, 7 May 1959, Ralph E. McGill Papers, box 8, file 7, WMY Jr. file, Robert W. Woodruff Library, Special Collections, Emory University, Atlanta.

86. Young to Mrs. Dudley H. Mills, 17 April 1959, WMY Jr. Papers, box 1, personal correspondence, 1958-60.

87. Young to James L. Cox, 22 March 1958; Young to Alfred Kennedy, 5 June 1959, WMY Jr. Papers, box 1, personal correspondence, 1958-60; Margaret Young, 1982 interview; Margaret Young to A.E. Manley, 9 February 1960, WMY Jr. Papers, box 1A, personal correspondence, 1943-60.

88. Young to Rufus E. Clement, 12 February 1960; Clement to Young, 13 April 1960, WMY Jr. Papers, box 263, correspondence, 1960.

6. Crossroads

1. Young, "The Role of the Urban League in the Current American Scene," WMY Jr. Papers, box 121A, speeches, 1954-60.

2. Dr. Lindsley F. Kimball, interviewed by author, Newtown, Pa., 19 June 1984.

3. "Lindsley Fiske Kimball," in *The National Cyclopaedia of American Biography,* vol. 1, *1953-1959* (New York: James T. White, 1960), 137-38.

4. Burns Roper, interviewed by author, New York, 14 December 1983.

5. Grant-in-Aid to the NUL, 5 September 1961, GEB Papers, 628 NUL Conf. 1961, box 276, file 2878; RBF Contributions—National Urban League, Rockefeller Brothers Fund Papers, RBF project files, NUL 1970, Rockefeller Archive Center, North Tarrytown, N.Y.

6. Kimball, interview; "Lindsley Fiske Kimball," in *The National Cyclopaedia,* 137.

7. Lindsley F. Kimball to J. George Harrar, 28 August 1961, GEB Papers, 628 NUL Conf. 1961, box 276, file 2878.

8. Memorandum, Lindsley F. Kimball to Flora M. Rhind, 16 December 1959, GEB Papers, 950 WMY Jr., 1959-62, box 529, file 5663.

9. Kimball, interview; Young to Kimball, 23 October 1959, 23 November 1959, GEB Papers, 950 WMY Jr., 1959-62, box 529, file 5663.

10. Young to Kimball, 7 December 1959, 5 February 1960, GEB Papers, 950 WMY Jr., 1959-62, box 529, file 5663; Young to Kimball, 6 January 1960; Kimball to Young, 12 January 1960, WMY Jr. Papers, box 263, correspondence, 1960.

11. Young to Flora A. Rhind, 11 December 1959, WMY Jr. Papers, box 263, correspondence, 1960; Lester B. Granger to Lindsley F. Kimball, 15 December 1959; Kimball to Rhind, 16 December 1959; Grant-in-Aid—WMY Jr., 23 December 1959; GEB Papers, 950 WMY Jr., 1959-62, box 529, file 5663.

12. Young to Lindsley F. Kimball, 17 December 1959, GEB Papers, 950 WMY Jr., 1959-62, box 529, file 5663; Flora M. Rhind to Young, 28 December 1959; Young to M. Adolphus Cheek Jr., 5 July 1960, WMY Jr. Papers, box 263, correspondence, 1959, 1960.

13. Kimball to Young, 26 January 1960; Garnet Larson to Young, 26 January 1960, WMY Jr. Papers, box 263, correspondence, 1960.

14. Young to Gordon W. Allport, 13 May 1960; Allport to Young, 1 June 1960; Young to Harold Isaacs, 10 February 1960, WMY Jr. Papers, box 263, correspondence, 1960.

15. Young to Dean Rusk, 29 September 1960, GEB Papers, 950 WMY Jr., 1959-62, box 529, file 5663; Young to Rowe S. Steel, n.d., WMY Jr. Papers, box 263, correspondence, 1960; Kimball, interview.

16. Young to Martin Meyerson, 8 February 1960; press release: MIT and Harvard, morning papers of Wednesday, 4 March 1959, WMY Jr. Papers, box 263, correspondence, 1960.

17. Résumé, Martin Meyerson; Meyerson, interviewed by author, Philadelphia, 29 June 1985; Young to Meyerson, 8 February 1960; Young to Harold Isaacs, 15 February 1960; Meyerson to Young, 10 March 1960, WMY Jr. Papers, box 263, correspondence, 1960.

18. Charles W. Liddell to Young, 17 March 1961; Young, "Comments on *Social Plan-*

ning Aspects of Urban Renewal" and "Comments on *Urban Mobility*," WMY Jr. Papers, box 32A, loose material.

19. Albert F. Mitchell to Young, 6 April 1961; Lloyd to Young, 20 April 1961, WMY Jr. Papers, box 32A, loose material.

20. Young to Charles W. Liddell, 7 April 1961; Charles W. Liddell to Young, 2 May 1961, WMY Jr. Papers, box 32A, WMY Jr. file.

21. Boston Community Development Program, WMY Jr. Task Force, minutes, 4 May 1961, 8 May 1961, 22 May 1961, 23 May 1961; Young to Charles W. Liddell, 30 May 1961, WMY Jr. Papers, box 32A, WMY Jr. file.

22. Young, "An Exploration of Community Development in the Roxbury–North Dorchester GNRP Area," WMY Jr. Papers, box 32A, untitled file, 7, 18-22, 26-38, 40, 42, 45-46.

23. R. Perlman, "Comments on Whitney Young's Report," WMY Jr. Papers, box 32A, untitled file.

24. Young to Rowe S. Steel, n.d., WMY Jr. Papers; Young to Steel, 21 April 1961, GEB Papers, 950 WMY Jr., 1959-62, box 529, file 5663.

25. "Dean Rusk," in *Who's Who in America, 1968-1969*, vol. 35 (Chicago: A.N. Marquis, 1968), 1890; Lindsley F. Kimball to Young, 25 April 1960, WMY Jr. Papers, box 263, correspondence, 1960; Young to Rusk, 6 May 1960, WMY Jr. Papers, box 1, personal correspondence, 1958-60.

26. Young to Dean Rusk, 20 July 1960; Rusk to Young, 26 July 1960; Young to Rusk, 29 September 1960, GEB Papers, 950 WMY Jr., 1959-62, box 529, file 5663.

27. Barbara Baskerville to Young, 24 October 1960, WMY Jr. Papers, box 7, School of Social Work file; Frankie V. Adams to Rufus E. Clement, 9 August 1961; Young to Adams, 13 January 1958; "Biographical Sketch—Frankie V. Adams," June 1967; Young and Adams, comps., *Some Pioneers in Social Work: Brief Sketches* (Atlanta: Atlanta University Press, 1958), Frankie V. Adams Papers, Robert W. Woodruff Library, Atlanta University Center.

28. Frankie V. Adams to Young, 1 November 1960, 18 January 1961, WMY Jr. Papers, box 7, School of Social Work file.

29. Young to Kimball, 17 December 1959; Frank Z. Glick to Young, 15 February 1960, WMY Jr. Papers, box 263, correspondence, 1960.

30. Albert F. Mitchell to Young, 6 April 1961, box 32A, loose material; Archie Albright to Young, 4 January 1961, WMY Jr. Papers, box 263, correspondence, 1961.

31. Ella J. Baker to Young, 27 May 1959, WMY Jr. Papers, box 1, personal correspondence, 1958-60; Young to Horace Mann Bond, 24 December 1960, Bond Papers, series 2, box 13, file 40, correspondence, 5 October 1960.

32. Roper, interview; Parris and Brooks, *Blacks in the City*, 395.

33. Edward S. Lewis, interviewed by author, New York, 11 January 1984; George O. Butler, interviewed by author, Washington, D.C., 1 February 1985; Roper, interview; Lester B. Granger to Young, 3 June 1960, WMY Jr. Papers, box 12, Urban League job application, 1960-62 file.

34. Roper, interview; "Alonzo Grasenno Moron," in *Who's Who in America, 1956-1957*, vol. 29 (Chicago: A.N. Marquis, 1956), 1829; Henry Steeger, interviewed by author, New York, 17 January 1984.

35. Granger to Steeger, 7 March 1960, WMY Jr. Papers, box 2, Administration: WMY Jr., Personal 1961; Butler, interview.

36. Kimball, interview; Butler, interview.

37. Steeger to Dana S. Creel, 20 June 1962; Creel to Steeger, 26 June 1962, Rockefeller Brothers Fund Papers, project files, NUL 1962, box 75; Kimball to Harrar, 28 August 1961, GEB Papers, 628 NUL Conf. 1961, box 276, file 2878.

38. Granger to Creel, 2 June 1961; Creel to Granger, 13 June 1961, Rockefeller Brothers Fund Papers, project files, NUL 1961, box 95.

39. Young, "I'm Liberal, But . . . ," 8 April 1961, Ralph E. McGill Papers, series 8 (Vine City to Youth March), WMY Jr. file.

40. Young, "The Negro and Self-Help," McGill Papers, series 8, WMY Jr. file.

7. Retooling the League

1. David R. Hunter, public affairs staff, "Second Discussion on National Urban League Proposal," 30 March 1962, Ford Foundation Grant, PA 61-1417, Ford Foundation Archives, New York.

2. Lindsley F. Kimball to J. George Harrar, 28 August 1961; Henry Steeger to Harrar, 29 August 1961; Grant-in-Aid to the NUL, 15 September 1961, GEB Papers, 628 NUL Conf. 1961, box 276, folder 2878.

3. Hunter, "Second Discussion"; Kimball to Harrar, 28 August 1961, GEB Papers, 628 NUL Conf. 1961, box 276, folder 2878; Young to Jane Lee Eddy, 26 December 1961; Young to Stephen Currier, 23 February 1962, NUL folder, 1962-67, Taconic Foundation, New York; "National Urban League: Study of Organizations and Management Practices," March 1969, II-3, Ford Foundation Grant, PA 68-470.

4. Memorandum, Lindsley F. Kimball to Rockefeller Foundation, "Purchase of Building. . . on Behalf of the National Urban League, Inc. and United Negro College Fund," 4 October 1965; Rockefeller Foundation Motion 65058, National Urban League, Inc., United Negro College Fund, Inc.—Headquarters Building, 22 October 1965; John D. Rockefeller III to J. George Harrar, 26 October 1965, Rockefeller Foundation Papers, 200 NUL, National Headquarters 1965-66, RG 1.2, box 71, folder 603, Rockefeller Archive Center, North Tarrytown, N.Y.

5. Kimball to Henry T. Heald, 22 October 1965; Kimball to John R. Coleman, 8 March 1966; Christopher F. Edley to Paul Ylvisaker, 2 November 1965; Coleman to Marshall A. Robinson, 28 March 1966, Ford Foundation Grant, PA 66-139.

6. Young to Joseph M. McDaniel Jr., 7 April 1966; John R. Coleman to file, 20 January 1966; Kimball to Coleman, 8 March 1966, Ford Foundation Grant, PA 66-139.

7. Lester B. Granger to Young, 5 February 1962; Young to Granger, 28 February 1962, 18 April 1962, National Urban League (NUL) Records, series 1, part 2, box 86, Young correspondence 1962, A-M folder, Manuscript Division, Library of Congress.

8. Sophie Yarnall Jacobs, interviewed by author, New York, 27 December 1983.

9. Henry Steeger, interviewed by author, New York, 17 January 1984; Jacobs, interview.

10. Burns Roper, interviewed by author, New York, 14 December 1983.

11. "NUL: A Study of Organization and Management Practices," March 1969, III-1, III-2, Ford Foundation Grant, PA 68-470.

12. William H. Chafe, *Civilities and Civil Rights: Greensboro, North Carolina, and the Black Struggle for Freedom* (New York: Oxford University Press, 1980), 134-35; *New York Times,* 3 February 1988; NUL Executive Committee, WMY Jr. Papers, 11 January 1962, box 12; NUL Executive Committee, 20 October 1970, box 24; NUL Executive Committee, 16 January 1964, box 14.

13. Minutes of NUL Executive Committee, 23 October 1967, 5; NUL Executive Committee, 23 October 1967, WMY Jr. Papers, box 17; NUL Executive Committee, 16 June 1970, box 24; "NUL: A Study of Organization and Management Practices," Ford Foundation Grant, III-5, PA 68-470.

14. Enid Baird, interviewed by author, Brooklyn, 11 January 1984; "NUL: A Study of Organization and Management Practices," Ford Foundation Grant, III-2, IV-2-5, PA 68-470; Altamont staff conference, 26-28 October 1961, Millbrook, N.Y., p. 5, NUL Records, box A-215, southern regional office, WMY Jr. November-December 1961.

15. Young to Granger, 18 April 1962, NUL Records, series 1, part 2, box 86, WMY Jr. correspondence 1962, A-M folder; National Urban League, eastern region report, 15 November 1967, WMY Jr. Papers, box 17, eastern regional office.

16. Ruth Allen King to Young, 24 November 1961; Julius A. Thomas to Young, 4 January 1962; Thomas to Young, 4 January 1962 (correspondence with Ramon Rivera), NUL Records, series 4, part 2, box 31, Job Development and Employment: Program Discussions, 1961-62.

17. Minutes of NUL/ULGNY meeting, 1 March 1962, 1-3, 5, NUL Records, series 4, part 2, box 31, Job Development and Employment: Program Discussions, 1961-62; M.T. Puryear to Edward S. Lewis, 22 March 1962, NUL Records, Admin. Dept., affiliates file, series 1, part 2, box 74, ULGNY January-June 1962.

18. Young to Edward S. Lewis, 11 March 1962, series 1, part 2, box 74, ULGNY January-June 1962; Fund-raising agreement between the National and New York Urban Leagues, NUL Records, series 1, part 2, box 74, ULGNY May-December 1961.

19. Young to Mrs. McAdams, 23 June 1964; Young to Stephen R. Currier, 8 December 1964; Alexander J. Allen to David Freeman, 22 June 1964; Nelson C. Jackson to ULGNY, 4 May 1964, NUL Records, Admin. Dept., affiliates file, series 1, part 2, box 74, ULGNY 1963-64.

20. Otis E. Finley to Young, 28 August 1962; Young and Henry Steeger to Clarence M. Maloney, 3 August 1962; Nelson C. Jackson to Young, 18 July 1962, NUL Records, Admin. Dept., affiliates file, series 1, part 2, box 63, 1962 Buffalo Urban League.

21. Young and Steeger to Maloney, 3 August 1962; Young to Nelson C. Jackson, n.d.; Alexander J. Allen to Reverend William Horner, 31 December 1962, NUL Records, Admin. Dept., affiliates file, series 1, part 2, box 63, 1962 Buffalo Urban League.

22. Richard S. Dowdy, interviewed by author, Hamden, Conn., 13 February 1984; Nelson C. Jackson to Urban League files, 2 March 1965; S.H.A. to Edwin R. Edmonds, 7 July 1965, NUL Records, Admin. Dept., affiliates file, series 1, part 2, box 73, 1965 New Haven Urban League.

23. Dowdy, interview; Young to Edwin R. Edmonds, 10 June 1965, NUL Records, Admin. Dept., affiliates file, series 1, part 2, box 73, 1965 New Haven Urban League.

24. John H. Mack, interviewed by author, Los Angeles, 29 February 1988.

25. Herman C. Ewing, interviewed by author, Memphis, 23 August 1985.

26. Leland C. DeVinney interview with Young, 18 March 1964; "Appeal to the Rockefeller Foundation for a Grant to Establish an Urban League Fellowship Program," 28 January 1964, 5, and J.K.S. to Leland DeVinney, 5 February 1964, Rockefeller Foundation Papers, 200 NUL, NUL Fellowship, U-Z 1964, box 482, general correspondence.

27. Young to John W. Gardner, 7 July 1964, "Appeal to the Carnegie Corporation for a Grant to Establish an Urban League Fellowship Program," Carnegie Corporation of New York Grant Files, NUL Fund, Graduate Fellowships Program folder, 2, 5-7, New York.

28. Letter to Young, 18 November 1964, agenda sheet, Carnegie Grant Files, NUL Fund, Graduate Fellowships Program folder.

29. Memorandum: S.H.S. to A.P., L.M., 23 March 1967, National Urban League: Two-Year Renewal of Graduate Fellowship Program, NUL report to Carnegie Corporation of New York, 1 December 1967 through 30 November 1968, Carnegie Papers, NUL Fund, Graduate Fellowships Program folder.

30. NUL report to Carnegie Corporation of New York for 1 December 1965–30 November 1966, Carnegie Grant Files, NUL Fund, Graduate Fellowships Program folder.

31. Young to Steven Stackpole, 12 January 1967; letter to Young, 20 April 1967, Carnegie Papers, NUL Fund, Graduate Fellowships Program folder.

32. NUL report on the Urban League Fellowship Program submitted to Carnegie Corporation of New York, December 1, 1968–November 30, 1969, NUL Fund, Carnegie Grant Files, Graduate Fellowships Program folder.

33. "National Urban League–Trade Union Program," 4, 6-7; Young to William P. Gormbley, 28 September 1965, Ford Foundation Grant, PA 65-374.

34. "NUL–Trade Union Program," 1-2; Joseph M. McDaniel to Lindsley F. Kimball, 15 October 1965, Ford Foundation Grant, PA 65-374.

35. Young to Joseph M. McDaniel, 18 November 1966; "Yearly Progress Report: Labor Affairs Program," March 1971, 6, 8, Ford Foundation Grant, PA 65-374.

36. Report, midwestern regional office, WMY Jr. Papers, box 18, midwestern regional office 1967.

37. Young to Howard R. Dressner, 12 December 1968, Ford Foundation Grant, PA 66-153.

38. Tom Gale to Operation Equality Offices, 5 March 1969, Ford Foundation Grant, PA 66-153.

39. R.A. Thompson to Christopher F. Edley, 6 October 1965, Ford Foundation Grant, PA 66-153.

40. Young to regional directors, NUL Records, series 1, part 2, box 49, Southern Regional Council 1964.

41. Charles E. Eason to Alexander J. Allen, 31 January 1964, NUL Records, Admin. Dept., affiliates file, series 1, part 2, box 74, ULGNY 1963-64.

42. Juanita C. Dudley to Henry A. Talbert, 13 October 1970; Joseph W. Walker to Urban League Committee of Utah, 10 June 1970; Walker to Harold Sims, 12 June 1970, WMY Jr. Papers, box 27, western regional office folder.

43. Charles E. Eason to Young, 18 February 1965; Lindsley F. Kimball to Jake Froelich Jr., 21 September 1965, NUL Records, Admin. Dept., general files, series 1, part 2, box 40, Organization of New Leagues 1965; list of potential League cities, WHY Jr. Papers, box 8, WMY 1967—Luncheon with Mrs. Marshall Field.

44. Alexander J. Allen to Young, 20 February 1967; Charles E. Eason to Young, 21 December 1967; Allen to M.R. Karrer, 2 January 1967, WMY Jr. Papers, box 18, regional offices—eastern, adm. 1967; "Organization of New Affiliates," eastern region report, 15 November 1967, WMY Jr. Papers, box 17.

45. Henry A. Talbert to Young, 15 March 1965; M. Leo Bohanon to Enid Baird, 22 April 1965, NUL Records, Admin. Dept., general files, series 2, part 1, box 40, Organization of New Leagues 1965.

46. Minutes of NUL Executive Committee, 20 October 1964, box 14; minutes of NUL Executive Committee, 13 April 1965, Adm. 1965, box 15; minutes of NUL Executive Committee, 19 April 1966, WMY Jr. Papers, Adm. 1966, Exec. Comm. Meeting, box 16.

47. Ewing, interview; Baird, interview; Howard L. Love, interviewed by author, Little Rock, Ark., 21 July 1984; "Urban League Operations in the South Today and Suggestions for Expanded Services in the Future," NUL Records, box A-215, southern regional office, WMY Jr. February-October 1961.

48. Young to Stephen R. Currier, 31 October 1961, NUL Records, box A-215, southern regional office, WMY Jr. February-October 1961; Young to Currier, 2 January 1962, 25 June 1964; report to the Taconic Foundation, 8 July 1966, NUL folder, 1962-67.

49. "Urban League Operations in the South," NUL Records, box A-215, southern regional office, WMY Jr. February-October 1961; Kimball to Froelich, 21 September 1965, NUL Records, Admin. Dept., general files, series 1, part 2, box 40, Organization of New Leagues 1965.

50. Leon Davis to Lindsley F. Kimball, 11 May 1965, NUL Records, Admin. Dept., affiliates file, series 1, part 2, box 80, Tulsa Urban League 1965; letter from Winthrop Rockefeller, NUL Records, series 1, part 2, box 49, Southwide Advisory Committee, correspondence 1963.

51. Clarence D. Coleman to Nelson C. Jackson, 12 June 1963; Coleman and Heman Sweatt to Jackson, 12 June 1963, NUL Records, series 1, part 2, box 49, Southwide Advisory Committee, correspondence 1963.

52. Jacoway and Colburn, *Southern Businessmen and Desegregation*, 5-11; Young to Marion M. Taylor, 30 October 1964, NUL Records, Admin. Dept., affiliates file, series 1, part 2, box 80, Tulsa Urban League 1964.

53. Davis to Kimball, 11 May 1965, NUL Records, Admin. Dept., affiliates file, series 1, part 2, box 80, Tulsa Urban League 1965; Kimball to Froelich, 21 September 1965, NUL

Records, Admin. Dept., general files, series 1, part 2, box 40, Organization of New Leagues 1965.

54. Young to Everett N. Case, 1 July 1965, NUL grant-in-aid, Alfred P. Sloan Foundation file, New York.

55. Robert Corley, "In Search of Racial Harmony: Birmingham Business Leaders and Desegregation, 1950-63," in Jacoway and Colburn, *Southern Businessmen and Desegregation,* 173-74; NUL Executive Committee, 17 January and 18 April 1967, WMY Jr. Papers, box 17, Executive Committee Adm. 1967 folder.

56. Enid Baird to Jane Lee Eddy, 28 October 1966, Taconic Foundation files, NUL folder, 1962-67; NUL Executive Committee, 18 October 1966, WMY Jr. Papers, box 16; Gary M. Bloom to Young, 23 October 1967, WMY Jr. Papers, box 8, WMY 1967 luncheons with Mrs. Marshall Field.

57. Hubert B. Crouch to Young, 22 March 1965, 12 April 1965; Young to Crouch, 26 April 1965, NUL Records, Admin. Dept., general files, series 2, part 1, box 40, Organization of New Leagues 1965. See Richard A. Pride and J. David Woodard, *The Burden of Busing: The Politics of Desegregation in Nashville, Tennessee* (Knoxville: University of Tennessee Press, 1985).

58. Sequence of contacts, minutes, Urban League meeting of the board of directors, 6 September 1966, WMY Jr. Papers, box 152, Urban League Organizing Committee, Lexington, Ky., folder.

59. Young to Dana S. Creel, 1 July 1965; "New League Project—Selected Target Cities," Rockefeller Brothers Fund, project files, NUL, 1965-66 folder, box 75.

60. Isobel C. Clark to Young, 4 June 1965, NUL Records, Admin. Dept., general files, series 1, part 2, box 40, Organization of New Leagues 1965.

61. Heman M. Sweatt to Clarence D. Coleman, 20 February 1964, NUL Records, Admin. Dept., affiliates file, series 1, part 2, box 82, Winston-Salem Urban League 1964; Coleman to Nelson C. Jackson, 9 January 1964, NUL Records, series 1, part 2, box 58, southern regional office, correspondence 1964.

62. Earl S. Lucas to Young, 13 August 1969; letter from Young, draft, 14 August 1969; Young to Lucas, 27 August 1969; Young to Lucas, 30 January 1970, WMY Jr. Papers, box 30, NUL-Mound Bayou folder.

63. Charles O. Phillips to Clarence D. Coleman, 21 July 1970; J. Thomas Swines to Coleman, 23 July 1970; Coleman to Harold Sims, 31 July 1970; Dorothy K. Newman to Coleman, 12 August 1970, WMY Jr. Papers, box 27, southern regional office 1970.

8. Maintaining a Middle Ground

1. Bayard Rustin, interviewed by author, New York, 11 January 1984.

2. Louis E. Lomax, *The Negro Revolt* (New York: Harper and Row, 1962), 235.

3. Clayborne Carson, *In Struggle: SNCC and the Black Awakening of the 1960s* (Cambridge: Harvard University Press, 1981); Aldon D. Morris, *Origins of the Civil Rights Movement* (New York: Free Press, 1984); John Dittmer, *Local People: The Struggle for Civil Rights in Mississippi* (Urbana: University of Illinois Press, 1994); Charles M. Payne, *I've Got the Light of Freedom: The Organizing Tradition and the Mississippi Freedom Struggle* (Berkeley: University of California Press, 1995).

4. Lomax, *The Negro Revolt,* 146-56; Carson, *In Struggle,* 31-44; Farmer, *Lay Bare the Heart,* 195-214.

5. Lomax, *The Negro Revolt,* 136; Chafe, *Civilities and Civil Rights,* 71-101.

6. Lomax, *The Negro Revolt,* 107-11; Carson, *In Struggle,* 56-65; David J. Garrow, *Bearing the Cross: Martin Luther King Jr. and the Southern Christian Leadership Conference* (New York: William Morrow, 1986), 173-230.

7. Young, "Civil Rights Action and the Urban League," February Symposium of Wayne State University, Detroit, 13 February 1963, WMY Jr. Papers, box 127, Wayne State folder.

8. Clarence D. Coleman to Nelson C. Jackson, 9 January 1964, NUL Records, series 1,

part 2, box 58, southern regional office, correspondence 1964; J. Harvey Kerns to Young, "Facts on Albany, Georgia," WMY Jr. Papers, box 176, Albany, Ga., Urban League folder.

9. "Facts on Albany, Georgia"; *Albany Herald,* 2 April 1967, WMY Jr. Papers, box 176, Albany Urban League folder; Young, "Civil Rights Action," Wayne State University, WMY Jr. Papers, box 127, Wayne State folder.

10. Ella J. Baker to Young, 15 March 1962, NUL Records, series 1, part 2, box 49, SNCC 1962-63; Louis Simon and William Bowe to Young, 7 May 1963; Mary Lefson to Young, 28 June 1963, WMY Jr. Papers, box 125, Speaking Engagements 1963.

11. Arthur Q. Funn to Guichard Parris, 1 February 1967; Arnold Aronson to Young, 1 August 1967; Roy Wilkins to Young, 30 October 1969, Leadership Conference on Civil Rights folder, box 29A; Wilkins to Young, 10 February 1969, WMY Jr. Papers, box 21, Leadership Conference on Civil Rights folder.

12. NUL Executive Committee, 23 October 1967, WMY Jr. Papers, box 17.

13. Jervis Anderson, *A. Philip Randolph: A Biographical Portrait* (New York: Harcourt Brace Jovanovich, 1972), 323-32.

14. Young, interview, 26 July 1967, WMY Jr. Papers, box 9, Interview on March on Washington folder. Andrew Young of SCLC claimed that Young and Wilkins opposed the march until a skeptical JFK gave his support. See Andrew Young, *An Easy Burden: The Civil Rights Movement and the Transformation of America* (New York: HarperCollins, 1996), 270.

15. Rustin, interview. Jervis Anderson, in *Bayard Rustin: Troubles I've Seen, A Biography* (New York: Harper Collins, 1997), contends that Farmer, Lewis, and King agreed to participate before both Young and Wilkins. See pp. 240-41.

16. Sterling Tucker, interviewed by author, Washington, D.C., 7 March 1984.

17. Young, interview, March on Washington, 26 July 1967; Rustin, interview.

18. Young, interview, March on Washington, 26 July 1967; James Forman, *The Making of Black Revolutionaries* (Washington, D.C.: Open Hand, 1972, 1985), 331-37.

19. Young, interview, March on Washington, 26 July 1967; Rustin interview; Forman, *Black Revolutionaries,* 332, 334, 336-37.

20. Rustin, interview.

21. Young, interview, March on Washington, 26 July 1967; Young to Martin Luther King Jr., 24 September 1963, Martin Luther King Jr. Papers, box 18:4, NUL file #4, July 1963–April 1964, King Library and Archives, Martin Luther King Jr. Center for Nonviolent Social Change, Atlanta; Young to Friends of the Urban League, 21 August 1963, NUL Records, series 5, part 2, box 12, March on Washington Speeches and Press Releases 1963.

22. Young, interview, March on Washington, 26 July 1967; Tucker, interview; Young to executive directors of Urban League affiliates, 12 August 1963, NUL Records, Washington bureau, box 16, WMY Jr. correspondence, January-December 1963.

23. Earl Chapman to Young, 18 July 1963; Young to Chapman, 30 July 1963; Chapman to Young, 20 August 1963, WMY Jr. Papers, box 125, Speaking Engagements 1963 folder.

24. "Whitney M. Young Jr. Speech," *The Great March on Washington,* sound recording, Gordy: A Division of Motown Record Corp., 1963.

25. Transcript of "March on Washington . . . Report by the Leaders," Metropolitan Broadcasting Television, 28 August 1963, King Papers, MLK Speeches.

26. Minutes of NUL/ULGNY meeting, 1 March 1962, NUL Records, series 4, part 2, box 31, Job Development and Employment: Program Discussions, 1961-62.

27. Edward S. Lewis to Young, 11 July 1962, NUL Records, Admin. Dept., affiliates file, series 1, part 2, box 74, ULGNY July-December 1962.

28. Minutes, executive committee meeting, 18 January 1966, WMY Jr. Papers, box 16.

29. Letter from N.O. Calloway, 31 January 1962; Calloway to board of directors, Chicago Urban League, April 3, 1962, NUL Records, Admin. Dept., affiliates file, box 64, Chicago Urban League.

30. Young to executive directors of Urban League affiliates, 3 July 1963, NUL Records, Washington bureau, box 16, WMY Jr. correspondence, January-December 1963.

31. E. Shelton Hill to Young, 14 June 1963; Young to Hill, 5 July 1962, NUL Records, Admin. Dept., affiliates file, series 1, part 2, box 77, Portland Urban League.

32. Minutes, Executive Committee Meeting, 11 January 1962, WMY Jr. Papers, box 12; Heman W. Sweatt to Alexander J. Allen, 21 May 1963, NUL Records, series 1, part 2, box 58, southern regional office, correspondence 1963.

33. Summary, NUL voter education report, 1964, NUL Records, series 1, part 2, box 18, Dept. of State 1965; report on first month's activities, 30 September 1964, NUL Records, series 5, part 2, box 12, March to the Ballot Box 1964.

34. Minutes, Executive Committee Meeting, 11 January 1962, WMY Jr. Papers, box 12.

35. T. Willard Fair to Young, 3 March 1965; Karl Bishopric to M.M. Brisco, 5 March 1965, NUL Records, Admin. Dept., affiliates file, series 1, part 2, box 72, Miami Urban League 1965.

36. Young to Karl Bishopric, 2 April 1965; Confidential Memo, Lester B. Granger; Bishopric to Young, 5 March 1965, NUL Records, Admin. Dept., affiliates file, series 1, part 2, box 72, Miami Urban League 1965; Maude K. Reid to Young, 15 July 1969, WMY Jr. Papers, box 179, Miami Urban League folder.

37. Paul Woods to Young, 25 November 1964; Young to Woods, 4 December 1964; Woods to Young, 6 January 1965; Young to Woods, 13 January 1965, NUL Records, Admin. Dept., affiliates file, series 1, part 2, box 82, Wichita Urban League 1965.

38. Hugh Jackson to Young, 25 January 1965; Owen C. McEwen to Young, 17 February 1965; McEwen to Robert Watson, 17 February 1965; Young to Owen C. McEwen, 26 February 1965, NUL Records, Admin. Dept., affiliates file, series 1, part 2, box 82, Wichita Urban League 1965.

39. Marion M. Taylor to Young, 31 October 1961, NUL Records, series 1, part 2, box 80, Tulsa Urban League 1961; Taylor to Young, 2 March 1964, NUL Records, Admin. Dept., affiliates file, series 1, part 2, box 80, Tulsa Urban League 1964.

40. Taylor to Young, 19 October 1964; Young to Taylor, 30 October 1964; Taylor to Young, 27 November 1964; Young to Taylor, 3 December 1964, NUL Records, Admin. Dept., affiliates file, series 1, part 2, box 80, Tulsa Urban League 1964.

41. Joseph A. Hall to Young, 13 October 1961, NUL Records, Admin. Dept., affiliates file, series 1, part 2, box 65, Cincinnati Urban League 1961; Edwin T. Pratt to Young, 2 June 1965; Young to Pratt, 24 May 1965, NUL Records, Admin. Dept., affiliates file, series 1, part 2, box 79, Seattle Urban League 1965 folder file.

42. Lloyd Garrison, interviewed by author, New York, 12 January 1984.

43. Harold Fleming, interviewed by author, Washington, D.C., 6 March 1984.

44. Garrison, interview.

45. Wiley Branton, interviewed by author, Washington, D.C., 8 February 1984; Reese Cleghorn, "The Angels Are White: Who Pays the Bills for Civil Rights," New Republic, 17 August 1963, 12-13.

46. Garrison, interview; Fleming, interview.

47. Cleghorn, "Angels," 12; New York Times, 13 December 1975; Young to George D. Pratt Jr., 28 June 1965, NUL Records, series 1, part 2, box 13.

48. Letter from Stephen R. Currier and Young, 11 September 1963, WMY Jr. Papers, box 38, Council on Civil Rights Leadership folder; Council for United Civil Rights Leadership cash transactions, 12 August 1963 to 27 January 1964, Martin Luther King Jr. Papers, box 7, folder 29.

49. Wiley Branton to LaValla Simmons, 22 June 1964, WMY Jr. Papers, box 38, CUCRL; Martin Luther King Jr. to Branton, 13 January 1965; Branton to King, 15 January 1965; Young to King, 4 February 1965, NUL Records, series 1, part 2, box 13, CUCRL 1965.

50. Cleghorn, "Angels," 13; Forman, Black Revolutionaries, 366.

51. Wiley A. Branton to James Forman, 7 July 1964; Branton to Nathantiel Hoffman, 29 April 1965; CUCRL minutes, 28 April 1965, WMY Jr. Papers, box 38, CUCRL; Jay Goodlette-Bass to Al Lowenstein, 29 October 1963, Martin Luther King Jr. Papers, box 7, folder 29.

52. Jack Greenberg, interviewed by author, New York, 27 January 1984; Wiley A. Branton to A. Philip Randolph, 4 March 1965, Martin Luther King Jr. Papers, box 7, folder 30; Minutes, Meeting of Council of United Civil Rights Leadership, 23 March 1966, WMY Jr. Papers, box 54, United Civil Rights folder.

53. Statement by A. Philip Randolph on behalf of Negro Leaders Conference, 30-31 January 1965; Jack Greenberg to Nelson Rockefeller, 21 May 1965, NUL Records, series 1, part 2, box 13, CUCRL 1965.

54. Farmer, *Lay Bare the Heart*, 216-17; James Farmer, interviewed by author, Washington, D.C., 8 March 1984; Branton, interview.

55. Farmer, *Lay Bare the Heart*, 217; Forman, *Black Revolutionaries*, 367.

56. Carole E. Merritt to Young, 20 June 1965, NUL Records, series 1, part 2, box 49, SNCC 1965; Forman, *Black Revolutionaries*, 367.

57. Minutes, Council of United Civil Rights Leadership, 25 February 1966, Martin Luther King Jr. Papers, box 7, folder 31.

58. Jack Greenberg, interviewed by author, New York, 27 January 1984; Arthur Funn to Roy Wilkins, 30 January 1967, NAACP Records, General Office file, series B, box 455, Urban League folder, 1964-67, Manuscript Division, Library of Congress, Washington, D.C.

59. Buckley, "Black Leader or 'Oreo Cookie?'" 32-33, 74.

60. Vernon Jordan, interviewed by author, Washington, D.C., 10 February 1984; A. Philip Randolph to the Editor, 25 September 1970; John A. Morrell to the Editor, 23, September 1970; Young to Carl T. Rowan, 7 October 1970, WMY Jr. Papers, box 11, *New York Times* article on WMY 1970 folder.

9. Humanizing the City

1. Young, *To Be Equal* (New York: McGraw-Hill, 1964), 28-31.

2. Young, "Commentary on Urban Goals and Urban Action," in *Governing Urban Society*, Monograph no. 7 (Philadelphia: American Academy of Political and Social Science, May 1967), 19-20, 24, WMY Jr. Papers, box 71, loose material.

3. Edgar B. Young to Young, 11 October 1967, WMY Jr. Papers, box 75, Urban Design Council of the City of New York folder.

4. H.R. Leary to Young, 8 February 1967; Young to Leary, 20 February 1967; Leary to Young, 24 February 1967, WMY Jr. Papers, box 70, New York Policy Commission folder.

5. *New York Times*, 14 May 1968, 6 October 1968, 17 October 1968, 2 November 1968. "Negroes Warned on Anti-Semitism," undated newspaper clipping; Adm. 1969 Anti-Semitism Articles folder, box 19, WMY Jr. Papers.

6. Nelson A. Rockefeller to Young, 30 September 1967; Rockefeller to Young, 25 June 1968, WMY Jr. Papers, box 86, Urban Development Corporation folder.

7. Walter N. South to Enid Baird, n.d., Arthur Funn to Young, WMY Jr. Papers, box 100, Urban Development Corporation, correspondence.

8. Glenn A. Claytor to Young, 6 February 1970; Tom Gale to Glenn Claytor, 15 December 1969, WMY Jr. Papers, box 118, Urban Development Corporation, correspondence.

9. Leyland R. Hazelwood to Young, 19 February 1969, WMY Jr. Papers, box 100, Urban Development Corporation, correspondence.

10. Stanley R. Tupper to Young, 17 November 1967, WMY Jr. Papers, box 73, States Urban Action Center folder.

11. Stanley R. Tupper to Young, 6 September 1968; Young to Tupper, 2 October 1968, WMY Jr. Papers, box 83, States Urban Action Center folder.

12. Nelson A. Rockefeller to Young, 27 December 1968, WMY Jr. Papers, box 83, States Urban Action Center.

13. James W. Rouse to Young, 17 April 1968; Enid C. Baird to William L. Slayton, 10 May 1968, WMY Jr. Papers, box 84, Urban America Paper on the Urban Problem folder;

Slayton to Young, 9 May 1968, WMY Jr. Papers, box 84, Urban America Board of Trustees folder.

14. William L. Slayton to Young, 17 December 1968, WMY Jr. Papers, box 97, Urban America folder.

15. Terry Sanford to Young, 24 June 1968; Young to Sanford, 3 July 1968, WMY Jr. Papers, box 83, Urban America folder.

16. Robert C. Weaver, interviewed by author, New York, 16 January 1984.

17. Young to Robert Wood, 24 December 1965, WMY Jr. Papers, box 59, Task Force on . . . Urban Problems, HUD folder; Mahlon T. Puryear to Young, 3 December 1965, WMY Jr. Papers, box 59, Task Force on . . . Urban Problems—Staff Reactions folder.

18. Lyndon B. Johnson to Young, 15 January 1966, WMY Jr. Papers, box 59, Task Force . . . Urban Problems, HUD folder; Robert C. Weaver to Young, 28 November 1966, WMY Jr. Papers, box 60, HUD Advisory Committee folder.

19. H. Ralph Taylor to Young, 6 March 1967, box 66; minutes, HUD Advisory Committee, 1 May 1967; Memorandum for Mr. Puryear, Mrs. Whaley, Dr. Turner et al., n.d., WMY Jr. Papers, box 66, HUD Advisory Committee folder.

20. Andrew Heiskell to A. Philip Randolph, 25 July 1967, A. Philip Randolph Papers, box 2 (misc.), Urban Coalition folder, Manuscript Division, Library of Congress.

21. Andrew Heiskell, interviewed by author, New York, 20 January 1984; "Emergency Convocation: The Urban Coalition," 24 August 1967, Randolph Papers, box 2 (misc.), Urban Coalition folder.

22. Heiskell, interview; Young to Willard Johnson, 16 August 1967, WMY Jr. Papers, box 74, Urban Coalition (Steering Committee) folder.

23. Heiskell, interview.

24. John Gardner, interviewed by author, Washington, D.C., 7 February 1984.

25. Lisle C. Carter Jr. to Young, 18 June 1968, box 86, Urban Coalition folder; Young to Urban Coalition Executive Committee, 9 October 1968, WMY Jr. Papers, box 98, Urban Coalition (Executive Committee) folder.

26. Gardner, interview; Peter Libassi to Young, 21 January 1970, box 117, Urban Coalition Action Council folder; Libassi to Young, 22 May 1970, box 117, Urban Coalition Action Council, Mtg. 5/27 folder; Lowell Beck to Young, 15 August 1970, WMY Jr. Papers, box 117, Urban Coalition Action Council folder.

27. Peter Libassi to Young, 14 October 1969, box 98, Urban Coalition (Steering Committee); Libassi to Young, 10 November 1969, box 99, Urban Coalition Executive Committee 12 May 1969, WMY Jr. Papers, "The Merger of Urban America and the Urban Coalition"; "The Urban Coalition and Urban America, Inc. Merge, 24 February 1970," WMY Jr. Papers, box 116, National Urban Coalition folder.

28. John W. Gardner to Young, 15 October 1968, WMY Jr. Papers, box 85, Urban Coalition folder.

29. Memorandum to the Policy Committee, 28 February 1970, WMY Jr. Papers, box 117, Mtg. Ad Hoc 11 July 1970 Urban Coalition folder; Sol Linowitz to Young, 14 October 1970, WMY Jr. Papers, box 116, National Urban Coalition folder.

30. M. Carl Holman to Young, 27 November 1970, WMY Jr. Papers, box 117, Urban Coalition . . . Mtg. 4-5 December 1970 folder.

31. M. Carl Holman, interviewed by author, Washington, D.C., 24 September 1982; JET, 22 October 1970, WMY Jr. Papers, box 116, National Urban Coalition folder.

32. Young to Adolph Holmes, 10 November 1967, box 312, Urban Coalition folder; John Gardner to Young, 20 November 1968, box 85, Urban Coalition folder; Young and Gardner to Urban League presidents and executive directors, Urban Coalition chairmen and chief executive officers, draft, 11 April 1969; John W. Gardner to Young, 11 April 1969, WMY Jr. Papers, box 98, Urban Coalition Action Council folder.

33. Sterling Tucker to local executive directors, 22 August 1969, box 98, NYC Urban Coalition folder; "Stated Urban Coalition Purpose," box 31, Urban Coalition folder; N.B.

Johnson II to Enid C. Baird, 13 May 1969, and Layhmond Robinson to Young, 12 May 1969, WMY Jr. Papers, box 117, 1970 Urban Coalition (misc.) folder.

34. John W. Gardner to Joseph T. Hughes, 24 September 1968, box 85, Urban Coalition folder; Harold R. Sims to John W. Gardner, 23 June 1970, WMY Jr. Papers, box 116, National Urban Coalition folder.

35. Young to John W. Gardner, 14 July 1970; "The National Urban Coalition: An Urban League View," WMY Jr. Papers, box 117, 1970 Urban Coalition (misc.) folder.

36. Minutes of NUL-NUC meeting, 2-3, 5, 17, 18, 47-49, WMY Jr. Papers, box 30, NUL-National Urban Coalition Meeting folder.

37. "NUC-NUL Liaison Relationships Established at Our Joint Meeting in August," box 118, 1970 Urban Coalition folder; Cernoria D. Johnson, Dorothy K. Newman, and Betti S. Whaley to Young, 24 November 1970, WMY Jr. Papers, box 31, Urban Coalition folder.

38. Nick Katz and Mary Lynn Katz, *A Passion for Equality: George A. Wiley and the Movement* (New York: W.W. Norton, 1977), 57, 92-94, 213-15, 271; George A. Wiley to Young, 13 August 1969; Dean Londa to Betti S. Whaley, 25 August 1969, WMY Jr. Papers, box 180, Welfare Rights folder.

39. Tucker, interview.

40. National Urban League, Inc., grant, 21 November 1968, and Young to Robert W. Scrivner, 18 December 1968, Rockefeller Brothers Fund, project files, NUL, June-December 1968, box 76, Rockefeller Archive Center, North Tarrytown, N.Y.

41. Robert W. Scrivner to Rockefeller Brothers Fund project files, 26 June 1968, NUL June-December 1968, box 76.

42. "A New Thrust for the National Urban League (with Budget Recommendations) August 1968," Ford Foundation Grant, PA 68-897.

43. "Ghetto Power in Action: A Report to the Foundations," by Sterling Tucker, Ford Foundation Grant, PA 68-897.

44. Mel King, *Chain of Change: Struggles for Black Community Development* (Boston: South End Press, 1981), 15, 111-18, 129-30.

45. Young to McGeorge Bundy, 12 September 1968; Ford Foundation Grant, PA 68-897.

46. Mitchell Sviridoff to McGeorge Bundy, 16 September 1968, Ford Foundation Grant, PA 68-897.

47. "National Urban League, Inc.," NUL 1970, Rockefeller Brothers Fund, project files, box 76.

48. "A Prospectus for Foundation Funding, 1970-71," Rockefeller Brothers Fund project files, October 1970, NUL 1970.

49. Young to Hubert H. Humphrey, 29 December 1966; Robert C. Weaver to Young, 28 December 1966; Leonard J. Duhl to Young, 14 February 1967, WMY Jr. Papers, box 56, National Conference on Social Welfare folder.

50. Weaver to Young, 28 December 1966; Young to Leonard Duhl, 9 February 1967; Duhl to Young, 15 February 1967, WMY Jr. Papers, box 56, National Conference on Social Welfare folder.

51. Manuel A. Romero to Young, 9 October 1970, WMY Jr. Papers, box 113, National Conference on Social Welfare folder.

52. Robert J. Brown to Young, 18 July 1969, WMY Jr. Papers, box 93, general correspondence—NASW.

53. Eugene O. Saks to Young, 11 June 1969, WMY Jr. Papers, box 93, affiliates correspondence—NASW.

54. Young to Roger Wilkins, 10 July 1969, box 93, affiliates correspondence; Mitchell Sviridoff to Young, 14 May 1970; Young to Mitchell Sviridoff, 6 May 1970; Young to Roger Wilkins, 23 June 1970; Young to Elliott Richardson, 18 December 1970; Young to John Gardner, 18 December 1970, WMY Jr. Papers, box 111, 1970 NASW.

55. Theodore Levine to Young, 6 March 1970, box 109, 1970 NASW; Virginia Burns to

Young, 15 June 1970; NASW—Metropolitan Washington Chapter—Resolution—D.C. Crime Bill, WMY Jr. Papers, box 111, NASW.

56. Young to William T. Gossett, 23 July 1969, box 93, general correspondence—NASW; Chauncey A. Alexander to Frank T. Wood, n.d., box 110, NASW; Bert J. DeLeeuw to Young, 27 June 1969; box 180, Welfare Rights folder; Alexander to Young, 29 April 1970; Alexander to George A. Wiley, 29 April 1970, WMY Jr. Papers, box 111, 1970 NASW.

57. Audreye E. Johnson, "A Week of History: NABSW," 26-30 May 1968 and "Position Statement of the National of Black Social Workers," tenth annual conference proceedings NABSW, 1979; Audreye E. Johnson, "The National Association of Black Social Workers, Inc.: A View of the Beginning," *Black Caucus Journal, NABSW* 7 (spring 1976): 13-17.

58. Judith R. Millenson to Charles Schooland, 15 April 1969, WMY Jr. Papers, box 93, affiliates correspondence—NASW.

59. Steele, interview; Young to Charles E. Knox, 8 August 1969, WMY Jr. Papers, box 93, general correspondence—NASW.

10. Corporate Philanthropy and Civil Rights

1. "Selected List of Corporation Contributions, 1961-62," "Selected List of Foundation Contributions, 1961-62," Rockefeller Brothers Fund, project files, NUL 1962 folder, box 75.

2. Andrew Heiskell, interviewed by author, New York, 10 January 1984.

3. James A. Linen biography, James A. Linen III '34 file #1, Williamsiana, Williams College, Williamstown, Mass.; James A. Linen, interviewed by author, Greenwich, Conn., 25 September 1982; "Selected Persons"; "Special Notes," WMY Jr. Papers, box 7, Time Tour of Eastern Europe WMY 1966 folder; Lindsley F. Kimball, interviewed by author, Newtown, Pa., 19 June 1984.

4. "Selected Persons"; Young to Robert S. Oelman, 18 November 1966, WMY Jr. Papers, box 7, Time Tour of Eastern Europe WMY 1966 folder.

5. Remarks—James A. Linen—Presidential Dinner—1968 National Urban League Conference, 31 July 1968; speech by James A. Linen, NUL Commerce and Industry Luncheon, Philadelphia, 2 August 1966 (courtesy of James A. Linen, 1982).

6. Address by Young to American Iron and Steel Institute, 22 May 1968, WMY Jr. Papers, box 160, American Iron and Steel Institute folder. On racial discrimination in the iron and steel industry, see Dickerson, *Out of the Crucible.*

7. Speech by Young to American Bankers Association, 26 September 1967; Charles E. Walker to Young, 2 October 1967, WMY Jr. Papers, box 146, American Bankers Association folder.

8. Harry R. Hall to Young, 16 September 1966, WMY Jr. Papers, box 138, Plans for Progress folder; Fred Kremer Jr. to Young, 9 May 1968, WMY Jr. Papers, box 161, Merchandising folder; Grover W. Ensley to Young, 2 June 1969, WMY Jr. Papers, box 179, Mutual Savings Banks.

9. "Visit of Whitney Young . . . to Mississippi," 13-14 November 1968, WMY Jr. files, FBI Records.

10. Howard H. Jones to Young, 18 July 1966; G.D. Bradley to Young, 12 July 1966; Francis S. Quillan to Young, 11 July 1966, WMY Jr. Papers, box 143, Mississippi Statement folder.

11. J.W. Stirling to Mike Goldstone, 7 June 1968; Stirling to R.P. Wagner, 2 October 1968; newspaper clipping, Presentation by Whitney M. Young Jr. . . . before the United Community Funds and Community Councils of America, WMY Jr. Papers, box 181, Shenango Valley Urban League folder.

12. Young to Charles E. Spahr, 21 February 1966, WMY Jr. Papers, box 138, Plans for Progress folder.

13. William R. Simms to Young and Adolph Holmes, 10 June 1968; Clark Donovan to

Holmes, 24 May 1968; Holmes to Young, 27 May 1968, WMY Jr. Papers, box 167, Standard Oil of New Jersey folder.

14. Gilbert W. Fitzhugh to Young, 18 November 1966; Young to Fitzhugh, WMY Jr. Papers, box 7, WMK 1966 Meetings folder; William R. Simms to Young, 13 January 1967, WMY Jr. Papers, box 8, WMY 1967 Luncheons folder.

15. "Special Notes Personalities" on Time-News Tour, 20 October–1 November 1966, WMY Jr. Papers, box 7, Time Tour of Eastern Europe WMY 1966 folder.

16. William R. Simms to Young, 5 December 1966, WMY Jr. Papers, box 7, WMY 1966 Luncheon-Kaiser-Peterson folder.

17. William R. Simms to James A. Linen and W.M. Batten, 1 April 1969; Henry Ford II to Lynn A. Townsend, 20 March 1969; Invitation List, 18 April 1969, WMY Jr. Papers, box 10, WMY 1969 Luncheons.

18. William R. Simms to Young, 1 April 1969, WMY Jr. Papers, box 10, WMY 1969 Luncheons.

19. William R. Simms to J. Paul Austin, 2 December 1968; Simms to Young, 11 December 1968, Atlanta Urban League folder, box 161; Simms to James A. Linen, J.R. Kennedy, and Young, 17 March 1969; Young to Austin, 3 April 1969, WMY Jr. Papers, box 10, WMY 1969 Luncheons folder.

20. "Income by Sources," WMY Jr. Papers, box 148, National Agency Panel folder; Young to Dana S. Creel, 12 December 1969, Rockefeller Brothers Fund, project files, NUL April-December 1969 file, box 76.

21. "1965 Corporate Contributors $500 and Over," WMY Jr. Papers, box 8, WMY 1967 Luncheons folder.

22. William R. Simms to Young, 6 June 1966, WMY 1966 Meetings folder, box 7; Simms to Adolph Holmes, 13 February 1968, WMY Jr. Papers, box 161, Paper Institute folder.

23. William B. Gittens to Young, 26 December 1967; William R. Simms to Adolph Holmes, 13 February 1968, Paper Institute folder, box 161; Charles S. Wolf to Young, 14 October 1969, WMY Jr. Papers, box 177, Fibre Box Association folder.

24. Young to John Lawrence, 28 January 1968; Young to Joseph H. Haggar, 26 January 1968; Young to James J. Ling, 22 January 1968, WMY 1967 Luncheons folder, box 8, William R. Simms to Young, 16 April 1970, WMY Jr. Papers, box 188, Cincinnati folder.

25. Young to Charles E. Spahr, 21 February 1966, WMY Jr. Papers, box 138, Plans for Progress folder.

26. See note 20.

27. "RBF Contributions—National Urban League," Rockefeller Brothers Fund, project files, NUL 1970 folder.

28. Resolution RF 70101, NUL Veterans Affairs 1969-73 folder, box 72, RG 1.2; Resolution RF 64081, Leadership Development 1964-65 folder, box 71, RG 1.2, Rockefeller Brothers Fund, project files.

29. "Lindsley Fiske Kimball," in *Who's Who in America, 1990-91,* vol. 1 (Wilmette, Ill.: Marquis, 1990), 1785.

30. John D. Rockefeller III to Young, 4 April 1968; Young to Rockefeller, 15 April 1968, WMY Jr. Papers, box 81, Rockefeller Foundation folder.

31. Telephone interview, Leland DeVinney to Lindsley F. Kimball, 30 September 1964, Rockefeller Foundation Papers, 200 NUL, Leadership Development, 1964-65 folder, RG 1.2, box 71.

32. Telephone interview, DeVinney to Young, 1 October 1964; Kimball to DeVinney, 5 October 1964; Resolution RF 64081, NUL, Inc. Leadership Development Program, 23 October 1964, Rockefeller Foundation Papers, 200 NUL, Leadership Development, 1964-65 folder, RG 1.2, box 71.

33. Kimball to DeVinney, 5 October 1964, Rockefeller Foundation Papers, 200 NUL, Leadership Development, 1964-65 folder, RG 1.2, box 71.

34. Carson, *In Struggle,* 294-95; Young to John D. Rockefeller III, 12 May 1969, Rockefeller Foundation Papers, 903 WMY Jr. 1969 folder, box 652, correspondence.

35. Young to Dana Creel, 3 December 1970, Rockefeller Brothers Fund, project files, NUL 1970 folder.

36. Leland C. DeVinney to Flora M. Rhind, 11 September 1964, Rockefeller Foundation Papers, 200 NUL, Leadership Development, 1964-65, RG 1.2, box 71.

37. "National Urban League, Inc." (18 November 1965), NUL 1965-66 folder, box 75; Lindsley F. Kimball to David F. Freeman, 12 July 1965, Rockefeller Brothers Fund project files, NUL 1965-66 folder, box 75.

38. Interview, Leland DeVinney to Young, 18 March 1964; J. Kellum Smith to Leland DeVinney, 5 February 1964; Flora M. Rhind to Leland DeVinney, 7 February 1964, Rockefeller Foundation Papers, 200 NUL, U-Z 1964 folder, box 482, general correspondence.

39. "Henry T. Heald," in *Who's Who in America, 1960-1961,* vol. 31 (Chicago: Marquis, 1960), 1279.

40. Lindsley F. Kimball to Henry T. Heald, 11 October 1961; Ford Foundation Grant, PA 61-1417; Henry Steefer Sr. to Heald, 22 November 1961; David R. Hunter to Dyke Brown, 24 April 1962, Ford Foundation Grant, PA 1416.

41. David Hunter memorandum, 30 March 1962, Ford Foundation Grant, PA 61-1417; Hunter to Brown, 24 April 1962; Hunter to Young, 19 September 1962, Ford Foundation Grant, PA 1416; digest of staff discussion with Young, 16 January 1962, NUL Records, series 4, part 2, box 28, Ford Foundation 1962-65.

42. Young to Henry T. Heald, 21 November 1962; Heald to Young, 4 December 1962, Ford Foundation Grant, PA 61-1417.

43. Lindsley F. Kimball to Henry T. Heald, 22 October 1965; Kimball to Joseph M. McDaniel Jr., 22 March 1966; "National Urban League—Improving the Economic Mobility of Negroes," Ford Foundation Grant, PA 66-139.

44. Christopher F. Edley Sr., interviewed by author, New York, 27 June 1984; Clarence Faust to Henry Heald, 9 October 1965, Ford Foundation Grant, PA 66-139.

45. "Paul N. Ylvisaker," in *Who's Who in America, 1988-1989* (Wilmette, Ill.: Marquis, 1988), 3389; Edley, interview.

46. "Christopher F. Edley Sr.," in *Who's Who among Black Americans,* 5th ed. (Lake Forest, Ill.: Who's Who among Black Americans, 1988), 207; Edley, interview.

47. Edley, interview; Christopher F. Edley to Paul Ylvisaker, 2 November 1965, Ford Foundation Grant, PA 66-139.

48. Oscar Harkavy to Marshall Robinson and John R. Coleman, 30 December 1965, Ford Foundation Grant, PA 66-139.

49. "McGeorge Bundy," in *Who's Who in America, 1988-1989,* 425.

50. Young to Bundy, 10 December 1965; Bundy to Young, 13 December 1965, NUL Records, series 1, part 2, box 55, White House 1965.

51. Address by McGeorge Bundy at the annual NUL banquet, 2 August 1966 (courtesy of Bundy, New York University); Mitchell Sviridoff to Bundy, April 1968, Ford Foundation Grant, PA 68-470.

52. Mitchell Sviridoff, interviewed by author, New York, 21 February 1984.

53. McGeorge Bundy, interviewed by author, New York, 10 January 1984.

54. Recommendation in Joseph M. McDaniel Jr. to McGeorge Bundy, 30 November 1966, Ford Foundation Grant, PA 67-76; Sviridoff, interview.

55. Bundy, interview; Charles T. Morrissey interview, Moncure, North Carolina, 8 May 1972, Ford Foundation Oral History Project.

56. Sviridoff, interview.

57. (J.) to Young, 18 January 1967; Thomas E. Cooney Jr. to John Coleman, 22 June 1967; General Support Grant memo (January 1967 to January 1968); Young to Cooney, 1 March 1968, Ford Foundation Grant, PA 67-76. In internal memoranda of various foundations, those who evaluated proposals seem to have deliberately concealed their identities from

outsiders by using only their initials, which were, of course, known to foundation insiders. No only the Rockefeller philanthropies but other foundations cited in these notes pursued this practice.

58. Howard R. Dressner to Young, 15 May 1968; Mitchell Sviridoff to McGeorge Bundy, April 1968, Ford Foundation Grant, PA 68-470.

59. Christopher F. Edley to John Coleman, 15 November 1966, Ford Foundation Grant, PA 67-76.

60. Roger Wilkins, interviewed by author, Washington, D.C., 10 February 1984.

61. Edley to Coleman, 15 November 1966, Ford Foundation Grant, PA 67-76; Roger Wilkins, *A Man's Life: An Autobiography* (New York: Simon and Schuster, 1982), 253; Wilkins, interview.

62. Charles J. Hamilton Jr., interviewed by author, New York, 25 May 1984; Young to Bundy, 13 June 1968, Ford Foundation Grant, PA 67-76.

63. Young to Bundy, 18 November 1970, Ford Foundation Grant, PA 68-470; "A Summary Report: 1968 Summer Program for Participation of Black Student Association Members in Ten Urban League Affiliate Cities," October 1968; Young to Howard R. Dressner, 12 March 1970, Ford Foundation Grant, PA 68-716.

64. Taconic Foundation report, December 1965, p. 31 (courtesy Jane Lee J. Eddy, Taconic Foundation, New York).

65. Young to Stephen R. Currier, 2 January 1962; Enid C. Baird to Jane Lee Eddy, 28 October 1966; report to the Taconic Foundation, 8 July 1966, Taconic Foundation files, NUL folder, 1962-67.

66. Stephen C. Currier to Martin Luther King Jr., 12 June 1963, 8 August 1963, King Papers, box 8, folder 3; Currier to Young, 9 June 1965, NUL Records, series 1, part 2, box 3, CUCRL 1965; Wiley A. Branton to Currier, 15 September 1964, WMY Jr. Papers, box 54, United Civil Rights; William R. Simms to Jane Lee J. Eddy, 10 February 1967, Taconic Foundation files, NUL folder, 1962-67.

67. Gardner, interview.

68. "Grant of $200,000 for a Graduate Fellowship Program," 20 April 1967, NUL memorandum, 13 October 1964, Carnegie Grant Files, NUL Fellowship Program folder.

69. Gardner, interview; "Agenda Sheet—National Urban League—Fellowship for Training in Intergroup Relations"; Interview with Whitney Young, Elizabeth Wiley, and L.M., 27 July 1964; letter to Young, 20 April 1967; letter to Young, 18 November 1964, Carnegie Papers, Grant files.

70. Memorandum, F.M. to L.M. and A.P., 8 April 1969; memorandum F.M. to D.Z.R. and J.D., 17 November 1970; letters to Young, 16 May 1969, 25 November 1970; Young to Alan Pifer, 8 December 1970, Carnegie Grant Files, NUL Executive Development Program folder.

71. "Grant-in-Aid, June 30, 1965, National Urban League"; Young to Everett N. Case, 1 June 1965; Grant-in-Aid, 1 February 1967, National Urban League; Grant-in-Aid, 15 May 1968; Grant-in-Aid, 31 January 1969, Alfred P. Sloan Foundation Grant files, New York.

72. Herbert H. Haines, *Black Radicals and the Civil Rights Mainstream, 1954-1970* (Knoxville: University of Tennessee Press, 1988), 116; Sviridoff, interview.

73. Kimball, interview; Kenneth Thompson, interviewed by author, Charlottesville, Va., 23 November 1987; "John Knowles," in *Who's Who in America*, 38th ed., 1974-75 (Chicago, Marquis Who's Who, 1974), 1732.

11. Washington Insider

1. Henry Steeger Sr. to John F. Kennedy, 23 February 1961, NUL Records, series 1, part 2, box 55, White House 1961-62.

2. Louis E. Martin, interviewed by author, Washington, D.C., 7 February 1984; Harris Wofford, interviewed by author, Philadelphia, 19 June 1984; Memorandum: Young to execu-

tive directors of affiliated organizations, 9 February 1962, NUL Records, Washington bureau, box 15; Carl M. Brauer, *John F. Kennedy and the Second Reconstruction* (New York: Columbia University Press, 1977), 67; Burke Marshall, interviewed by author, New Haven, Conn., 13 February 1984.

3. Martin, interview; Young to Stephen R. Currier, 15 November 1962, Taconic Foundation files, NUL folder, 1962-67; Summary of Points Discussed by the Officers of the National Urban League in Meeting with the President of the United States, Tuesday, 23 January 1962, Washington, D.C., NUL Records, Washington bureau, series 1, part 2, box 59, correspondence, January-August 1962.

4. Tucker, interview; Melvin Miller to Nelson C. Jackson, 10 June 1946, NUL Records, general office file, box A-78, southern regional office, Fort Worth Urban League, January-December 1946; Young to Currier, 15 November 1962, Taconic Foundation files; Young to Cernoria D. Johnson, 26 December 1961; Young to R. Frank Jones, 12 January 1962, NUL Records, Washington bureau, box 15, WMY Jr. correspondence, 26 December 1961-31 December 1962.

5. Cernoria D. Johnson to Young, 31 January 1963; Johnson to Young and Nelson C. Jackson, 7 October 1963, NUL Records, Washington bureau, box 16, WMY Jr. correspondence, January-December 1963.

6. Cernoria D. Johnson to Young, 23 May 1963; Young to Anthony Celebrezze, 16 December 1963, NUL Records, Washington bureau, box 16, WMY Jr. correspondence, January-December 1963.

7. Brauer, *Kennedy*, 68-69; Martin, interview; Wofford, interview.

8. Arthur J. Goldberg to Young, 20 November 1961, President's Committee on Youth Employment folder, box 32; W. Willard Wirtz to Young, 4 July 1963; Young to Wirtz, 2 August 1963, WMY Jr. Papers, box 37, Committee Affiliations Not Accepted folder; Esther Peterson to Young, 18 June 1963; Young to Wirtz, 15 March 1963, NUL Records, series 2, part 2, box 17, Dept. of Labor 1963; Cernoria D. Johnson to Young and Nelson C. Jackson, 9 August 1962, NUL Records, Washington bureau, box 15, WMY Jr. correspondence, 26 December 1961-31 December 1962.

9. Luther L. Terry to Young, 20 April 1961, WMY Jr. Papers, box 34, loose material; Cornelia Knight to Young, 22 November 1961; Young to Knight, 1 December 1961, box 34, Surgeon General's Consultant Group on Nursing folder, WMY Jr. Papers; Robert F. Kennedy to Young, 20 November 1962, NUL Records, Admin. Dept., general files, series 1, part 2, box 41, Peace Corps 1961-62.

10. John F. Kennedy to Young, 22 June 1962, NUL Records, series 1, part 2, box 55, White House 1961-62.

11. Lawrence I. Hewes to Gerhard A. Gesell and Young, 24 March 1963, WMY Jr. Papers, box 37, President's Committee . . . Armed Forces folder.

12. Young to Gerhard A. Gesell, 12 March 1963; Young to Lawrence I. Hewes, 11 July 1963; Reginald A. Johnson to Young, 15 March 1963, WMY Jr. Papers, box 37, President's Committee . . . Armed Forces folder; Claude Organ Jr., interviewed by author, Oklahoma City, 7 February 1987.

13. Young to George W. Culberson, 15 March 1963, WMY Jr. Papers, box 37, President's Committee . . . Armed Forces folder.

14. "Initial Report—Equality of Treatment and Opportunity for Negro Military Personnel Stationed within the United States," Presidential Office Files of John F. Kennedy, 23 June 1963-9 October 1963, JFK Presidential Library, Boston.

15. Robert S. McNamara to Young, 3 September 1963; Young to McNamara, 11 September 1963, WMY Jr. Papers, Speaking Engagements (Not Accepted) 1963 folder.

16. Brauer, *Kennedy*, 43; "Urban League Salutes JFK Housing Edict; Cites Agency's Role In Long Anti-Bias Fight," news bureau, NUL Records, series 4, part 2, box 25, President's Executive Order Barring Discrimination in Housing, 21 November 1962 folder.

17. John F. Kennedy to Young, 27 November 1962, JFK Papers, September-October

1963, JFK Library; Henry Steeger letter; "An Important First Step," NUL Records, Admin. Dept., general files, series 1, part 2, box 43, Program Dept. 1963, Housing, misc. material.

18. Robert C. Weaver to Young, 6 May 1963; Young to Weaver, 17 May 1963; Weaver to Young, 5 July 1963; Young to Weaver, 24 July 1963, NUL Records, Admin. Dept., general files, series 1, part 2, box 43, Program Dept. 1963-65, housing correspondence.

19. "Statement Regarding Implementation of the Executive Order Barring Discrimination in Federally Aid Housing," NUL Records, series 4, part 2, box 26, White House Executive Order 1963 . . . Barring Discrimination in Federally Aided Housing.

20. Brauer, *Kennedy,* 112, 114-15.

21. M.T. Puryear to Clarence D. Coleman, 27 March 1962; Coleman to Louphenia Thomas, 18 October 1962; Puryear to Young, 21 March 1962, NUL Records, Admin. Dept., general files, series 1, part 2, box 6, Program Dept., southern regional office, correspondence 1962; Brauer, *Kennedy,* 230-64.

22. Young, interviewed by Thomas Harrison Baker, 18 June 1969, 1-3, Oral History Collection, Lyndon Baines Johnson Library, Austin, Texas; Theodore W. Kheel, interviewed by author, New York, 19 December 1983.

23. Young interview, 2, LBJ Library.

24. Young interview, 4, LBJ Library; Young to Lyndon B. Johnson, 21 February 1962; Johnson to Young, 27 February 1967; Henry Steeger to Young, 9 April 1962; Summary of Points Discussed by the Officers of the National Urban League in Meeting with the Vice President of the United States, Monday, 9 April 1962, Washington D.C., NUL Records, Washington bureau, box 5, WMY Jr. correspondence, 26 December 1961–31 December 1962.

25. Young to Lyndon B. Johnson, 18 April 1962; telegram, Young to LBJ, 20 June 1962; LBJ to Young, 22 June 1962, Vice President—Civil Rights files, Papers of Lyndon B. Johnson as Vice President, LBJ Library.

26. Arthur A. Chapin to Young, 16 April 1962; Hobart Taylor Jr. to Young, 8 January 1963; Young to Taylor, 10 January 1963; R.M. Mahoney to Taylor, 23 January 1963; Marjorie McKenzie Lawson to Mahlon Puryear, 4 May 1962, NUL Records, series 4, part 2, box 31, Pres. Committee on Equal Employment Opportunity folder.

27. Remarks by Vice President Lyndon B. Johnson, Urban League Dinner, 19 November 1962; Young to LBJ, 21 November 1962, Vice President—Statements 19 October 1961 to 5 December 1962, Papers of Lyndon B. Johnson as Vice President.

28. Young interview, 5-7, LBJ Library; Remarks by V. Pres.—Remarks to Meeting of Negro Leaders, 28 August 1963, Vice President—Statements, Papers of LBJ as Vice President.

29. James Farmer, interviewed by author, Washington, D.C., 8 March 1984; Roy Wilkins, interviewed by Thomas H. Baker, 1 April 1969, 11, Oral History Collection, LBJ Library; appointment file (diary backup), 2 December 1963, box 2, Monday, 2 December 1963, 9:30 a.m. Whitney Young, Papers of LBJ as President.

30. Farmer, interview; Wilkins, interview, 13-14, 22-23; James Farmer, *Lay Bare the Heart,* 293-305; Roy Wilkins with Tom Mathews, *Standing Fast,* 299-301.

31. Wilkins, *Standing Fast,* 295-97, 299-302, 311-12; Wilkins, interview, 13. Clarence Mitchell, the NAACP's Washington lobbyist, stayed on the frontlines pushing passage of the 1964 and 1965 civil rights acts. See Denton L. Watson, *Lion in the Lobby: Clarence Mitchell Jr.'s Struggle for the Passage of Civil Rights Laws* (New York: William Morrow, 1990), 594-625, 645-59.

32. Hobart Taylor Jr. to LBJ, 24 May 1964, White House Central file, Name file, Young folder; Anne to Bill, Ex FG-629-1, box 375, 23 November 1963 to 4 December 1965 folder, Papers of LBJ, President, 1963-69, LBJ Library.

33. John Doar to Young, 15 February 1965, NUL Records, series 1, part 2, box 17, Dept. of Justice 1965.

34. Thurgood Marshall to LBJ, 14 January 1966, LBJ Papers, President, Human Rights, 17 July 1964 to 19 January 1966 folder, box 3, 1963-69, LBJ Library.

35. Young to executive directors of Urban League affiliates, 6 July 1964, NUL Records, series 5, part 2, box 3, Civil Rights Act, Title VI—NUL Statement and Controversy 1964.

36. Lee C. White to Young, 28 April 1964, LBJ Papers, President, 1963-69; White House Central file, Name file, LBJ Library; Young to executive directors, 6 July 1964, NUL Records, series 5, part 2, box 3, Civil Rights Act, Title VI—NUL Statement and Controversy 1964.

37. "Selected Instances of Discrimination and Segregation Which May Involve Title VI of the Civil Rights Act: A Report by the National Urban League," 13 July 1964, NUL Records, series 5, part 2, box 3, Civil Rights Act, Title VI—NUL Statement and Controversy 1964.

38. Young to Lyndon B. Johnson, 22 July 1964, White House Central file, Name file, LBJ Papers, President; Lee C. White to Young, 1 August 1964, NUL Records, series 1, part 2, box 55, White House 1965; LeRoy Collins to Young, 21 December 1964, NUL Records, series 1, part 2, box 16, Federal Government–Community Relations Service, Governor LeRoy Collins folder.

39. Anthony J. Celebrezze to Jack J. Valenti, 16 March 1965, White House Central file, Name file, LBJ Papers, President; Young to John W. Gardner, 20 October 1965, NUL Records, series 1, part 2, box 17, HEW 1965.

40. Orville Freeman to Young, 5 March 1965, NUL Records, series 1, part 2, box 16, Federal Government–Department of Agriculture folder.

41. "Remarks of the President at Howard University, Washington, D.C.," 4 June 1965, LBJ Papers, President, White House Conference to Fulfill These Rights, box 68.

42. Lee C. White to LBJ, 28 September 1965, 5 October 1965, LBJ Papers, President, HU2/MC, 22 January 1963 to 15 November 1965 Human Rights, 22 November 1963 to 6 June 1966, box 22; task forces of the conference, LBJ Papers, President, White House Conference "To Fulfill These Rights," box 68.

43. Joe Califano and Clifford Alexander Jr. to LBJ, 28 October 1965; Alexander to Lee C. White, 30 October 1965; White to LBJ, 2 November 1965, HU2/MC, January 22, 1963 to November 15, 1965, Human Rights Papers, November 22, 1963 to June 6, 1966, White Papers, box 5, Preliminary Plans for Planning folder, LBJ Library.

44. Lee White to LBJ, 2 November 1965; Morris Abrams and William T. Coleman Jr. to Members of the Council for United Civil Rights Leadership, 25 October 1965, HU2/MC, January 22, 1963 to November 15, 1965, Human Rights Papers, box 22, November 22, 1963 to June 6, 1966, LBJ Library.

45. Young to White, memorandum on proposed White House Conference "To Fulfill These Rights," 26 August 1965, NUL Records, series 1, part 2, box 55.

46. Young to M. Carl Holman, 21 October 1965, Civil Rights Leadership folder, White House Conference "To Fulfill These Rights," box 67; White to Young, 16 December 1965, LBJ Papers, President, White House Central file, Name file; Young to Holman, 2 November 1965, NUL Records, series 1, part 2, box 55, White House Conference "To Fulfill These Rights" 1965; Edna A. Hopkins to Young, 24 November 1965, WMY Jr. Papers, box 63, White House Conference . . . correspondence folder.

47. Holman to Young, 26 November 1965; Young to Holman, 14 December 1965; Young to Berl I. Bernhard, 25 April 1966; Bernhard to Young, 19 April 1966, WMY Jr. Papers, box 63, White House Conference . . . correspondence folder.

48. Clifford L. Alexander Jr. to Lee C. White and Harry McPherson, 14 December 1965, WMY Jr. Papers, box 5.

49. Young to M. Carl Holman, 2 December 1965, WMY Jr. Papers, box 63, White House Conference . . . correspondence folder; Young to David Bell, 5 January 1966, box 55, White House Conference "To Fulfill These Rights" 1965; Arthur B. McCaw to Young, 14 June 1966, WMY Jr. Papers, box 63, White House Conference . . . correspondence folder.

50. Bernhard to Young, 19 April 1966; Young to Bernhard, 25 April 1966, WMY Jr. Papers, box 63, White House Conference . . . correspondence folder; Young to NUL Professional Staff, 10 May 1966, WMY Jr. Papers, box 61, White House Conference general folder.

51. Robert Weisbrot, *Freedom Bound: A History of America's Civil Rights Movement* (New York: Plume, 1991), 193; *New York Times,* 1 June 1966.

52. *New York Times,* 3 June 1966; William R. Simms to Young, 6 June 1966, WMY Jr. Papers, box 7, WMY 1966 Meetings folder.

53. Hugh Davis Graham, *The Civil Rights Era* (New York: Oxford University Press, 1990), 261-62, 271; Memorandum: Nicholas Natzenbach to LBJ, 17 March 1966, president's appointment file (diary backup), 13-29 March 1966, box 31; memorandum for the record—civil rights meeting, 15 February 1967, President's appointment file, 2-29-67 to 2-21-67, box 55; memorandum to LBJ, 31 July 1967, White House Central file, Name file, LBJ Library; Charles E. Goodell to Young, 24 April 1968, WMY Jr. Papers, box 83, Urban Affairs Task Forces folder.

54. Young, *To Be Equal* (New York: McGraw-Hill, 1964), 26, 28-31, 33; *Book Week,* 16 August 1964, 6.

55. Young interview, 7-8, LBJ Library.

56. Weisbrot, *Freedom Bound,* 161-64; Young interview, 8, LBJ Library; Andrew T. Hatcher to Young, 7 February 1964, box 55, White House 1964; Hobart Taylor Jr. to Young, 15 April 1964, NUL Records, series 1, part 2, box 19, Poverty Program April-December 1964.

57. Young to Sargent Shriver, 11 February 1965, NUL Records, series 1, part 2, box 19, Poverty Program January-March 1964. The black Johnson officials whom Young noted were Lisle Carter (HEW), Andrew Brimmer (Commerce), Arthur Chapin (Labor), William Seaborn (Agriculture), and George Butler (President's Committee on Employment Opportunity).

58. Young to Sargent Shriver, 31 March 1964; Edwin C. Berry to Young, 24 March 1964, NUL Records, series 1, part 2, box 19, Poverty Program January-March 1964; Shriver to Young, 10 April 1964, NUL Records, series 1, part 2, box 19, Poverty Program April-December 1964.

59. Cernoria D. Johnson to Young, 24 April 1964, NUL Records, series 1, part 2, box 19, Poverty Program April-December 1964; Sargent Shriver to Young, 17 June 1964, NUL Records, series 1, part 2, box 55, White House 1964.

60. Cernoria D. Johnson to Young, 2 February 1965, NUL Records, Washington bureau, series 1, part 2, box 16, WMY Jr. correspondence; Sargent Shriver to Young, 30 March 1965, NUL Records, Washington bureau, box 59, correspondence, January-April 1965; Shriver to Young, 22 December 1965, NUL Records, series 1, part 2, box 40, OEO, August-December 1965.

61. Young to Sargent Shriver, 22 November 1966, NUL Records, Washington bureau, WMY Jr. correspondence 1966; Weisbrot, *Freedom Bound,* 161-66.

62. Joe Califano to LBJ, 4 December 1968, Welfare (WE 8) 1 July 1968, box 22, LBJ Library.

63. Thomas D. Morris to Young, 25 February 1966, WMY Jr. Papers, box 142, Defense Dept. folder; E. Hidalgo to Young, 24 August 1965; Young to E. Hildalgo, 7 October 1965, Navy Department folder, 1965, box 18; Young to Friend, 19 October 1966, NUL Records, Washington bureau, series 1, part 2, box 16, WMY Jr. correspondence 1966.

64. Ansel R. Cleary to Young, 18 June 1965; M.T. Puryear to regional and executive directors, 4 March 1965, WMY Jr. Papers, OJT folder, box 30.

65. Harry C. McPherson to Young, 20 October 1965; Force on . . . Urban Problems folder, box 59; Francis Keppel to Young, 7 August 1964, Advisory Committee on Education folder, box 38, Young to Gene S. Muehleisen, 27 April 1966, WMY Jr. Papers, box 57, Pres. T.'s Commission . . . Justice folder.

66. (Lee C. White) memorandum for the president, 13 January 1965 (notes for discussion with Martin Luther King); Jack Valenti to LBJ, 12 January 1965, Personnel Management folder, box 8, LBJ Library; Ramsey Clark to LBJ, 7 January 1965; Janet Rogan to LBJ, 19 September 1965; John B. Clinton to Rogan, 30 September 1965, White House Central file, Name file, LBJ Library; *Omaha Sunday World Herald,* 23 February 1964.

67. Robert C. Weaver, interviewed by author, New York, 16 January 1984; Young inter-

view, 9, LBJ Library; (Lee C. White) memorandum for the president, 13 January 1965, Personnel Management folder, box 8, LBJ Library.

68. NUL Executive Committee, 18 January 1965, minutes, p. 3, WMY Jr. Papers, box 15, Adm. 1965 Board Committees Exec. Meeting folder; Young interview, 9, LBJ Library.

69. Young interview, 11, LBJ Library; Young, *Beyond Racism: Building an Open Society* (New York: McGraw-Hill, 1969), 1, 8-9.

70. David J. Garrow, *The FBI and Martin Luther King Jr.: From "Solo" to Memphis* (New York: W.W. Norton, 1981), 23-77, 101-72.

71. Memorandum, S.A.C., N.R. to director, FBI (Attention: Assistant Director DeLoach), 7 July 1963; Young to J. Edgar Hoover, 5 August 1964, Hoover to Young, 6 August 1964; memo to W.C. Sullivan re book review of *Beyond Racism,* n.d., WMY Jr. FBI files.

72. J.J. Casper to Mr. Mohr, 5 August 1966, 9 April 1968, WMY Jr. FBI files.

73. Goodell to Young, 24 April 1968; Chuck Sharpe to Enid Baird, 28 April 1968, Urban Affairs Task Force folder, box 83; Young's testimony before the Republican Platform Committee, 29 July 1968, Republican Convention folder, box 166; Young's testimony before the Democratic Platform Committee, 23 August 1968, WMY Jr. Papers, box 162, Democratic National Convention folder.

74. John W. Gardner to Young, 3 December 1968, WMY Jr. Papers, box 85, Urban Coalition folder; Richard M. Nixon, *The Memoirs of Richard Nixon* (New York: Grosset and Dunlap, 1978), 338-39; Nixon, *Four Great Americans: Tributes Delivered by President Richard Nixon* (New York: Doubleday, 1972), 42-43; Farmer, interview; Margaret B. Young, interviewed by author, New Rochelle, N.Y., 7 May 1983.

75. "A Call to Action: Recommendations on the Urban and Racial Crisis," submitted to President Richard M. Nixon by the National Urban League, 20 January 1969; Young FBI files, 1-4, 7-45, 46-47.

76. Young to Richard Nixon, 29 August 1969, WMY Jr. Papers, box 87, Advisory Council on Social Security folder.

77. Graham, *The Civil Rights Era,* 303, 320.

78. Roy Wilkins to Young, 10 February 1969, Organizations: Leadership Conference on Civil Rights folder, box 21; Wilkins to Young, 28 May 1970, WMY Jr. Papers, box 29, Leadership Conference on Civil Rights folder.

79. *New York Times,* 30 June 1970.

80. *New York Times,* 20 July 1970.

81. Leonard Garment, interviewed by author, Washington, D.C., 30 August 1984; Howard J. Samuels to Young, 16 January 1969, Black Economic Development folder, box 88; Maurice H. Stans to Young, 27 May 1970, WMY Jr. Papers, box 107, Federal Reserve Bank of New York.

82. Leonard Garment to Bishop Stephen G. Spottswood, 30 June 1970, Bishop Spottswood, 1968-70 subject file, Container #8, Leonard Garment Papers, Manuscript Division, Library of Congress, James Madison Building, Washington, D.C.

83. Charles E. Walker to Leonard Garment, 10 July 1970, Garment Papers, container 8, Bishop Spottswood, 1968-70 subject file.

84. Garment, interview; James R. Miller to John Ehrlichman, 20 July 1970; Todd R. Hullin to Miller, 31 July 1970, Garment Papers, container 8, Young 1970-71 subject file.

85. Young to Leonard Garment, 14 December 1970, Garment Papers, container 8, Young 1970-71 subject file.

86. Memorandum for the president, 21 December 1970 (meeting with WMY and several cabinet officers), Garment Papers, container 8, Young 1970-71 subject file.

87. Leonard Garment to Richard Nixon, 25 January 1971; Garment to the deputy attorney general et al., 22 December 1970, Garment Papers, container 2, Memorandum to President folder; press conference of Whitney Young, 22 December 1970, Garment Papers, container 8, WMY 1970-71 subject file; Garment, interview; Tucker, interview.

88. Garment to Nixon, 25 January 1971; list of departmental offers to the Urban League,

Garment Papers, container 2, Memorandum to President folder.

89. Press conference of Whitney Young, 22 December 1970, Garment Papers, container 8, WMY 1970-71 subject file.

90. Garment to Nixon, 25 January 1971, Garment Papesr, container 2, Memorandum to President folder.

91. Memorandum for the president, 21 December 1970 (meeting with WMY and several cabinet officers), Garment Papers, container 8, WMY Jr. 1970-71 subject file; Garment, interview; Tucker, interview.

92. Robert Finch to Young, 13 May 1969, box 88, Social Security folder; Young to Cernoria D. Johnson, 17 May 1969, box 88, Social Security folder; Johnson to Young, 8 April 1970, box 103, Advisory Council on Social Security; Johnson to Harold Sims, 29 June 1970; Newman to Young, 29 May 1970, box 106, Advisory Council on Social Security folder 27 May 1970; Robert M. Ball to Young, 18 June 1970, Young to Ball, 18 June 1970, box 104, Advisory Council on Social Security folder; Arthur F. Burns to Young, 18 December 1970, WMY Jr. Papers, Federal Reserve Bank of New York folder.

93. Bob Hope, Billy Graham et al. to Young, 10 June 1970; press release: Honor America Day, 4 June 1970; Young to J. Willard Marriott, 12 June 1970; Young to Richard Nixon, 12 June 1970, WMY Jr. Papers, box 263, correspondence 1970 folder; William Martin, *A Prophet with Honor: The Billy Graham Story* (New York: William Morrow, 1991), 370.

94. Nixon, *Four Great Americans,* 42.

12. On the War Front

1. Carson, *In Struggle,* 183-84, 188; Martin Luther King Jr., "A Time to Break the Silence," in *A Testament of Hope: The Essential Writings of Martin Luther King Jr.,* ed. James M. Washington (San Francisco: Harper and Row, 1986), 232-34; "Interview with Huey Newton," in *Black Protest Thought in the Twentieth Century,* 2d ed., ed. August Meier, Elliot Rudwick, and Francis L. Broderick (Indianapolis: Bobbs-Merrill, 1965), 499, 509.

2. Clifford L. Alexander to LBJ, 7 January 1966, box 41, White House Central file, Name file, WMY Jr. file, LBJ Library; William R. Simms to Young, 6 June 1966, box 7, WMY 1966 Meetings folder; confidential report, n.d., WMY Jr. Papers, box 63, White House Conference-Misc. 1966 folder; M. Carl Holman, interviewed by author, Washington, D.C., 24 September 1982; Weisbrot, *Freedom Bound,* 191, 193, 196.

3. From American Embassy—Saigon—Lodge—State for Bundy. Donnelly from Sieverts, DOD for Vance; White House for Califano, 23 July 1966 (telegrams, Papers of Lyndon Baines Johnson, President, 1963-65, EX FO5 4 September 1965, box 42, FO5 30 June 1966 to 31 August 1966 file, LBJ Library.

4. Text of Cable from Lodge (Saigon 1773), for McGeorge Bundy from Sieverts, 23 July 1966, Lyndon Baines Johnson Presidential Papers, 1963-69, president's appointment file (diary backup), 20-27 July 1966, box 40, LBJ Library.

5. Joe Califano to LBJ, 23 July 1966, 25 July 1966, LBJ Papers, 1963-69, president's appointment file (diary backup), 20-27 July 1966, box 40, LBJ Library; Young to LBJ, 11 August 1966; LBJ to Young, 31 August 1966, EX FO5 4 September 1965, FO5 30 June–31 August 1966, box 42, LBJ Papers, 1963-69; transcript, Clifford L. Alexander Oral History Interview, 17 February 1972, by Joe B. Frantz, 16-17, LBJ Library.

6. Young, "When the Negroes in Vietnam Come Home," *Harper's,* June 1967, 63; *Philadelphia Bulletin,* 1 August 1966, and *Evening Bulletin* (August), newspaper clippings; Gloster B. Current to Young, 5 August 1966, NAACP Records, Urban League folder, 1964-67, box 455, General Office files, series B, Manuscript Division, Library of Congress.

7. Quoted in Garrow, *Bearing the Cross,* 546; *Newsweek,* 15 May 1967; Statement by Young on MLK Jr.'s Stand on the Vietnam War, WMY Jr. Papers, box 211, Vietnam folder.

8. Young, "Vietnam and Civil Rights," 26 April 1967, WMY Jr. Papers, box 211, Vietnam folder.

9. Young, "When the Negroes in Vietnam Come Home."
10. Annual report, Veterans' Affairs (September 1967–September 1968), Rockefeller Foundation Papers, 200 NUL, Veterans' Affairs, 1969-73 folder.
11. Young to J. George Harrar, 16 October 1969; Veterans' Affairs Program (1970 proposal), Rockefeller Foundation Papers, 200 NUL, Veterans' Affairs, 1969-73 folder.
12. Young to J. George Harrar, 18 June 1970; Young to J. Kellum Smith, 18 December 1970, Resolution RF 70101–National Urban League, Inc.–Veterans' Affairs Program, National Urban League–Veterans' Affairs Program Expansion Proposal, June 1970; Rockefeller Foundation Papers, 200 NUL, Veterans' Affairs, 1969-73 folder.
13. American Observers at the Vietnamese Elections, National Security file–Country file, Vietnam Elections 1G (3) September-October 1967 folder, box 65, LBJ Library; Samuel Freeman, "Election of 1967 (South Vietnam)," in *Dictionary of the Vietnam War,* ed. James S. Olson (Westport, Conn.: Greenwood Press, 1988), 131.
14. Robert W. Gilmore to Young, 27 June 1967; Terry A. Knopf to Young, 24 August 1967, South Vietnam Elections folder; Rodney Shaw to Young, 25 August 1967; Leonard Beerman et al. to Young, 25 August 1967, WMY Jr. Papers, box 8, 1967 Vietnam folder.
15. Telegram (1): Secretary of State of American Embassy—Saigon, September 1967; telegram (2): American Embassy—Saigon to Secretary of State, September 1967; telegram: American Embassy—Saigon to Secretary of State, August 1967; Walt W. Rostow to LBJ, 1 September 1967, National Security file-Country file, box 65, Vietnam Elections 1 G(2), 13 August-5 September 1967 folder, LBJ Library.
16. Freeman, "Election of 1967," 131; *New York Times,* 5 September 1967; James B. Antell to Young, 11 September 1967, WMY Jr. Papers, box 8, South Vietnam Elections folder.
17. Charles H. Alspach to Young, 7 September 1967, box 8, South Vietnam Elections folder; Theodore E. Brown to Young, WMY Jr. Papers, box 65, American Negro Leadership . . . Africa folder.
18. *Chicago Sun-Times,* 6 September 1967; Young to General William C. Westmoreland, 26 September 1967; William H. Marsh to Young, 22 September 1967; Robert D. Levine to Young, 7 September 1967, WMY Jr. Papers, box 8, South Vietnam Elections folder.
19. Notes on Negro GIs in Vietnam prepared for Whitney M. Young Jr., 6 September 1967; Young to Leonard J. Holshey, 26 September 1967, WMY Jr. Papers, box 8, South Vietnam Elections folder.
20. Hubert H. Humphrey to Young, 26 November 1968; Hubert H. Humphrey Papers, Vice Presidential files, 1965-68; XY folder, Control files 1968 We-Z-General files-Corres. John G. Stewart.
21. Walter Issacson, *Kissinger: A Biography* (New York: Simon and Schuster, 1992), 159; Linda Kelly Alkana, "Moratorium Day Demonstrations" in Olson, *Dictionary of the Vietnam War,* ed. 290-91, 317.
22. Young to NUL trustees, 7 October 1969; Young to Susan Werbe, 8 October 1969, WMY Jr. Papers, box 22, Vietnam Moratorium folder.
23. Draft statement by WMY Jr., n.d., WMY Jr. Papers, box 22, Vietnam Moratorium folder; *New York Times,* 14 October 1969; Garrow, *Bearing the Cross,* 546.
24. John T. Smith to Young, 3 December 1969; Henry Loeb to Young, 9 October 1969; Wayne Babovitch to Young, 6 October 1969, WMY Jr. Papers, box 22, Vietnam Moratorium folder; *New York Times,* 14 October 1969.
25. "Vietnam—The Peace Dividend," by WMY Jr., 3 September 1969, WMY Jr. Papers, box 217, Vietnam—The Peach Dividend folder.

13. The Ties That Bind

1. Young to Frank Buckner, 6 April 1965, WMY Jr. Papers, box 131, Men's Club . . . Baptist Church . . . Aurora, Illinois, folder.
2. Address by WMY Jr. before the Antioch Baptist Church, 75th anniversary banquet,

Cleveland, Ohio, 4 October 1968; T.G. Shirreffs to Young, 18 September 1968, WMY Jr. Papers, box 161, Antioch Baptist Church folder.

3. Wyatt Tee Walker to Young, 20 September 1967, box 146, Canaan Baptist Church folder; Ulysses B. Blakeley to Young, 15 June 1968, box 161, Caucus folder; Francis A. Kornegay to Enid C. Baird, 29 April 1968; background information for Mr. Young's presentation at African Methodist Episcopal Zion Church, 10 May 1968, WMY Jr. Papers, box 160, AME Zion Church folder.

4. Joseph L. Griffin to Young, 29 June 1963, box 125, Speaking Engagements (Not Accepted) 1963; John H. Adams to Young, 7 January 1964, WMY Jr. Papers, box 128, Speaking Engagements (General).

5. Frank L. Patterson to Young, 3 October 1965, box 131, Men's Club . . . Baptist Church . . . Aurora, Ill. folder; Andrew E. Whitted to Young, 25 March 1966; To Mr. Young . . . re Business and Professional Night, St. Catherine AME Zion Church, 9 May 1966, box 142, St. Catherine AME Zion Church folder; M. Moran Weston to Young, 19 February 1968, WMY Jr. Papers, box 167, St. Philip's Church folder; *Reaching Out: An Epic of the People of St. Philip's Church* (Tappan and New York: Custombook, 1986), 62-66.

6. Stephen Gill Spottswood to Young, 12 April 1968, box 160, AME Zion Church folder; Edward A. Freeman to Young, 25 April 1969, box 185, Baptist Congress folder; Norris S. Curry to Young, 17 April 1970, background information for Mr. Young's presentation before the Christian Methodist Episcopal Church, Memphis, 13 May 1970, WMY Jr. Papers, box 188, CME Church folder; King, *Daddy King*, 77-79, 203; Coretta Scott King, *My Life with Martin Luther King Jr.* (New York: Holt, Rinehart and Winston, 1969), 172.

7. Margaret B. Young, interviewed by author, New Rochelle, N.Y., 11 May 1984; Young to Lawrence M. Channing, 27 December 1961, box 32, Unitarian Service Committee folder; Young to G. Robert Hohler, 23 September 1964, box 38, Committee Affiliations (misc.) 1964; Young to Peter H. Samson, 30 December 1970, WMY Jr. Papers, box 120, White Plains Community Church folder.

8. Wesley, *Alpha Phi Alpha*, 599-600; William A. Muraskin, *Middle-Class Blacks in a White Society: Prince Hall Masonry in America* (Berkeley: University of California Press, 1975), 43-85, 193-236; Charles H. Wesley, *The History of the Improved Benevolent and Protective Order of Elks of the World* (Washington, D.C.: Association for the Study of Negro Life and History, 1955), 419-20.

9. Leon E. DeKalb to Young, 1 February 1963; address by Young at the public meeting, Gamma Iota Lambda chapter, Alpha Phi Alpha Fraternity, Cornerstone Baptist Church, Brooklyn, 31 March 1963, 2-3, 6, WMY Jr. Papers, box 125, APA Fraternity, Inc., folder.

10. Frank W. Morris Jr. to Young, 25 March 1963, WMY Jr. Papers, box 125, APA Fraternity, Inc., folder.

11. Young to T. Winston Cole, 17 April 1963, box 125, APA Fraternity, Inc., folder; Lionel H. Newsom to Young, 25 June 1967, 17 July 1967, WMY Jr. Papers, box 146, APA folder.

12. Joseph Mason Andrew Cox, *Great Black Men of Masonry* (New York: Alpha Book, 1982, 1987), 359; Clarence D. Coleman to Nelson C. Jackson, 8 October 1962, NUL Records, Admin. Dept., general files, series 1, part 2, box 6, Program Dept., southern regional office, correspondence 1962.

13. John G. Lewis to Young, 23 May 1963, box 127, Prince Hall folder; Arthur Swaby to Young, 8 September 1965, WMY Jr., box 131, Prince Hall Masons folder.

14. Charles A. Dargan to Young, 17 June 1963; Young to Dargan, 1 July 1963; Dargan to Young, 5 July 1963, WMY Jr. Papers, box 125, Speaking Engagements folder.

15. "Hobson R. Reynolds," in *Who's Who among Black Americans*, 4th ed. (Lake Forest, Ill.: Who's Who among Black Americans, 1985), 704; Wesley, *Elks*, 411-12; Andrew Buni,

Robert L. Vann of the Pittsburgh Courier: Politics and Black Journalism (Pittsburgh, University of Pittsburgh Press, 1974), 218-19.

16. Hobson R. Reynolds to Young, 27 July 1962; Young to Reynolds, 1 August 1962; Reynolds to Young, 6 August 1962, WMY Jr. Papers, box 122, Elks Convention folder.

17. J.F. Simmons to Young, 17 October 1962; Reynolds to Young, 18 December 1962; Young to Reynolds, 4 January 1963, WMY Jr. Papers, box 122, Elks Convention folder.

18. Reynolds to Young, 23 February 1965; letter to Young, 2 April 1965, WMY Jr. Papers, box 130, Elks folder.

19. Hobson R. Reynolds and Young, "A Special Message to Officers and Members of the Improved Benevolent and Protective Order of the Elks of the World," 1968 annual convention, New York Hilton Hotel, 24-30 August 1968, WMY Jr. Papers, box 163, Elks folder.

20. Frank Huntley to Young, 13 December 1965; Young to Huntley, 29 January 1966, WMY Jr. Papers, box 7, WMY 1966 Ohio State Elks folder.

21. Young to James F. King, 5 July 1963, WMY Jr. Papers, Frontiers International folder, Speaking Engagements (Not Accepted) 1963.

22. June Granger Branche to Young, 18 February 1962; Eunice J. Jones to Young, 4 May 1962; Helen G. Edmonds to Young, 11 June 1962; Young to Edmonds, 20 June 1962, WMY Jr. Papers, box 123, The Links, Inc., folder.

23. Young to Mrs. Leo M. Mervis, 8 March 1966; Young to Vivian J. Beamon, 30 March 1966, WMY Jr. Papers, box 137, Links folder.

24. Ronald H. Brown to Young, 18 March 1970; Vivian J. Beamon to Young, 2 April 1970, WMY Jr. Papers, box 189, Links folder.

25. "Mollie Moon," in Jessie Carney Smith, *Notable Black American Women* (Detroit: Gale Research, 1992), 760; "Mollie Moon," in Darlene Clark Hine, Elsa Barkley Brown, and Roslyn Terborg-Penn, eds., *Black Women in America: An Historical Encyclopedia* (Brooklyn: Carlson, 1993), 2:810-11; Aleathia H. Mayo to Margaret Young, 13 July 1971, WMY Jr. Papers, box 264, correspondence 1971 folder.

26. Pauli Murray, *Pauli Murray: The Autobiography of a Black Activist, Feminist, Lawyer, Priest, and Poet* (Knoxville: University of Tennessee, 1987), 353; Young to Pauli Murray, 29 November 1963, NUL Records, Washington bureau, box 16, WMY Jr. correspondence, January-December 1963.

27. Sterling Tucker to Young, 3 December 1963; Cernoria D. Johnson, 6 December 1963, NUL Records, Washington bureau, box 16, WMY Jr. correspondence, January-December 1963; Betti Whaley, interviewed by author, Washington, D.C., 30 August 1984.

28. Cernoria D. Johnson to Young, 1 November 1962, NUL Records, Washington bureau, box 15, WMY Jr. correspondence, 26 December 1961–31 December 1962; Deighton O. Edwards Jr. to Young, 10 April 1969, WMY Jr. Papers, box 176, Bankers folder.

29. Clarence D. Coleman to Young, 26 October 1962, NUL Records, Admin. Dept., general files, series 1, part 2, box 6, Program Dept., southern regional office, correspondence 1962; Norman B. Houston to Young, 24 April 1962; Young to Houston, 2 May 1962, WMY Jr. Papers, box 123, National Insurance Association folder.

30. Address of Young before the 42d annual convention of the National Insurance Association, Los Angeles, 27 July 1962, WMY Jr. Papers, box 123, National Insurance Association folder.

31. Carlton B. Goodlett to Young, 14 August 1962; Young to Goodlett, 27 August 1962, WMY Jr. Papers, box 123, National Insurance Association folder.

32. Notes for Whitney M. Young, Opening Session 6th Imhotep National Conference on Hospital Integration, 25 May 1962, box 123, Imhotep Conference folder; Edward S. Cooper and W. Montague Cobb to Young, 7 June 1965, box 132, NMA folder; Haynes Rice to Young, 23 August 1968, WMY Jr. Papers, box 160, American Hospital Association folder.

33. Quoted in Smith, *A Black Educator*, 180; Rufus B. Atwood to Young, 30 November 1961; Young to Atwood, 12 December 1961, 20 June 1962, WMY Jr. Papers, box 123, Kentucky State Commencement folder.

34. William J. Trent Jr., interviewed by author, Greensboro, N.C., 19 October 1983; Young to Trent, 5 September 1963, UNCF Archives 24:1, fiche #1708, RG 3, series Bio. Young to Zuniga, United Negro College Fund, New York; Vernon Jordan, interviewed by author, Washington, D.C., 10 February 1984.

35. Young, "Today's Graduate Returning to the Ghetto," WMY Jr. at Hampton Institute, 3, 7-8, box 154, Hampton Institute folder; Marion Brown to Carl Alan Thomas, 23 September 1966; Rembert Stokes to Young, 23 January 1967, WMY Jr. Papers, box 151, Wilberforce folder.

36. L.H. Pitts to members of the board of trustees of Miles College, 14 April 1964, box 39, Miles College folder; E.P. Murchison to Young, 1 July 1963, WMY Jr. Papers, box 7, Adm. WMY 1963 folder.

37. Lucius Pitts to Young, 13 July 1964; Young to Roger Blough, 3 August 1964, WMY Jr. Papers, box 39, Miles College folder; telegram, Young to Pitts, 16 January 196?, WMY Jr. Papers, box 67, Miles College folder.

38. Rosemary Jackson to Young, 27 October 1965, NUL Records, series 1, part 2, box 49, SCLC folder.

39. Wyatt Tee Walker to Young, 27 August 1962; address of WMY Jr. before the sixth annual convention of the Southern Christian Leadership Conference, 27 September 1962, WMY Jr. Papers, box 124, SCLC folder.

40. Young to Martin Luther King Jr., 28 October 1964; King to Young, 3 November 1964, King Papers, box 18, NUL file #5, May 1964-July 1965.

41. Charles H. Butler Sr. to Young, 2 August 1963, box 125, Speaking Engagements (Not Accepted) 1963 folder; Mildred Williams and Lana Cook to Young, 27 November 1969; Harry D. Owens to Young, 25 January 1970, box 187, Speaking Engagements (Not Accepted), January-April 1969 folder; James A. Gay III to Young, 23 December 1968; Charles L. Kellar to Young, 24 March 1969, WMY Jr. Papers, box 174, Speaking Engagements (Not Accepted) January-April 1969.

42. Young to John R. Coleman, 9 September 1966; Coleman to T. Cooney, N. Dennis, C. Edley, M. Feldman, A. Ferguson, G. Perkin, R. Schmid, and E. Staples, 27 September 1966; T.E. Cooney to Coleman, 5 October 1966; Alan D. Ferguson to Coleman, 6 October 1966, Ford Foundation Grant, PA 67-76.

43. Young to Roy Wilkins, 18 September 1967, NAACP Records, Urban League folder, 1964-67, General Office files, series B, box 455, Manuscript Division, Library of Congress; meeting of NAACP-Urban League Staff, 20 December 1967, WMY Jr. Papers, box 23, Delta Airlines folder.

44. Bayard Rustin to Community Leaders, N.P., WMY Jr. Papers, box 65, Freedom Budget folder.

45. Minutes, A. Philip Randolph Institute, National Executive Board, 19 September 1966, New York; Young to Eugene H. Buder, 1 February 1967; Subcommittee Statement, n.d.; Young to Andrew F. Brimmer, 13 December 1966; Young to William F. Butler, 13 December 1966, WMY Jr. Papers, box 65, Freedom Budget folder.

46. Andrew F. Brimmer to Young, 31 January 1967; "Comments on a 'Freedom Budget' for All Americans"; William F. Butler to Young, 6 January 1967, WMY Jr. Papers, box 65, Freedom Budget folder.

47. Robert G. Long to Young, 31 March 1965; H. Claude Hudson to Martin Luther King Jr., 31 March 1965; Kivie Kaplan to Young, 19 April 1965, WMY Jr. Papers, box 131, March on Montgomery folder.

48. Transcript, Sterling Tucker Oral History Interview, 21 April 1969, by Thomas Baker, Lyndon Baines Johnson Library, Washington, D.C., 7 March 1984, p. 15.

49. Tucker, interview (Dickerson).

50. Press release: WMY Jr. on the Poor People's March, 28 April 1968; M.T. Puryear to Urban League Staff, 9 May 1968; Young to Ralph D. Abernathy, 14 May 1968; Young to local

executive directors, regional directors, Washington bureau, NUL Staff, 31 May 1968, WMY Jr. Papers, box 31, SCLC folder.

51. Layhmond Robinson to Young, 11 June 1968, WMY Jr. Papers, box 166, Poor People's March folder.

52. Robinson to Young, 11 June 1968; address by Young at Washington March, 19 June 1968, WMY Jr. Papers, box 166, Poor People's March folder.

53. Malcolm X to Young, 31 July 1963; Young to Malcolm X, 7 August 1963, WMY Jr. Papers, box 125, Speaking Engagements (Not Accepted) 1963 folder; telegram: Young to Robert Kennedy, 12 May 1964, NUL Records, series 1, part 2, box 55, White House 1964.

54. "Black Power," editorial by WMY Jr., 9 July 1968, WMY Jr. Papers, box 194, Black Power folder.

55. Dittmer, *Local People,* 389, 393, 395-96.

56. *New York Times,* 22 June 1967.

57. Ann Tanneyhill to Guichard Parris and Alexander J. Allen, 24 July 1967, WMY Jr. Papers, box 30, National Conference on Black Power folder.

58. Hubert H. Humphrey to Young, 31 October 1966, Hubert H. Humphrey Papers, correspondence by Name: X-Y 1966, Vice Presidential files, 1965-68, General correspondence by Name: 1966 U-Z, 23 F 180F.

59. Tanneyhill to Parris and Allen, 24 July 1967, WMY Jr. Papers, box 30, National Conference on Black Power folder.

60. August Meier and Elliott Rudwick, *CORE: A Study in the Civil Rights Movement, 1942-1968* (New York: Oxford University Press, 1973), 3-9, 26-27, 135-58.

61. James Farmer to Young, 20 June 1962; Young to Farmer, 26 June 1962, core 1962 folder; Farmer to Young, 25 June 1964; Young to Farmer, 7 July 1964; Clarence D.M. Funnye to Young, 14 October 1964, NUL Records, series 1, part 2, box 13, core 1964 folder; Farmer to Young, 14 July 1965, WMY Jr. Papers, box 134, White House Conference on Education folder; Meier and Rudwick, *CORE,* 380-408, 412.

62. Floyd B. McKissick to McGeorge Bundy, 11 January 1967; S.M. Miller to John R. Coleman, 26 June 1967; Coleman to Bundy, 13 July 1967; Young to Bundy, 18 August 1967, Ford Foundation Grant, PA 67-446.

63. McKissick to Bundy, 25 June 1968; Mitchell Sviridoff to Bundy, 15 July 1968; letter to McKissick, 25 July 1968, Ford Foundation Grant, PA 67-446.

64. Roy Innis to Young, 1 July 1968; *Long Island Newsday,* 8 July 1968, WMY Jr. Papers, box 162, 1968 CORE Convention folder; *New York Times,* 7 July 1968, 9 July 1968.

65. Thomas Adams to executive director, 9 July 1968; Young to Adams, 15 July 1968; W.H. Wheeler Jr. to Young, 13 August 1968; Walter G. Hooke to Young, 8 July 1968; Joseph Freitas Jr. to Young, 17 July 1968; Price M. Cobbs to Young, 26 July 1968; William R. Hudgins to Young Jr., 25 July 1968; Millicent H. Fenwick to Young, 7 July 1968; Young to Fenwick, 15 July 1968, WMY Jr. Papers, box 162, 1968 CORE Convention folder.

66. Young to Floyd B. McKissick, 13 January 1969, WMY Jr. Papers, box 21, Organizations: McKissick Enterprises folder.

67. Dunbar S. McLaurin to Young (through Adolph Holmes), 5 September 1969; Specific working paper for the NUL banking proposal: letter draft for WMY's signature, WMY Jr. Papers, box 19, Adm. 1969 Black Economic Development folder.

68. Alexander J. Allen to members of the Cabinet, 13 February 1969; Young to Russell Bingham, 18 March 1969, WMY Jr. Papers, box 21, Organizations-Committee for Unified Newark folder.

69. Leroi Jones to Young, 8 January 1970; WMY Jr. Statement, 30 January 1970, WMY Jr. Papers, box 188, Newark folder; Amiri Baraka, *The Autobiography of Leroi Jones/Amiri Baraka* (New York: Freundlich Books, 1984), 290.

70. Percy Steele, interviewed by author, Oakland, Calif., 1 March 1988; letter to Young, 29 December 1969, WMY Jr. Papers, box 4, WMY 1969 folder.

71. George Reedy to LBJ, 7 September 1965, Lee White Collection, box 4 (1266/1267),

Civil Rights folder; Harry C. McPherson Jr. to LBJ, 12 September 1966, Harry C. McPherson Jr. Collection, box 22 (1439), McPherson Civil Rights folder, LBJ Presidential Library.

72. Harry McPherson to LBJ, 29 July 1967; Willard Wirtz to LBJ, 28 July 1967; letter to Martin Luther King, n.d.; George Christian to LBJ, 31 July 1967, McPherson Collection, box 32 (1753), McPherson [Riots] (1), McPherson [Riots] (3) folders, LBJ Presidential Library; Hubert H. Humphrey to Young, 8 November 1965, NUL Records, series 1, part 2, box 18, Office of the Vice President folder.

73. Hubert H. Humphrey to I. Myrtle Carden, 14 February 1947, correspondence-FEPC folder; Humphrey to James T. Wardlaw, 7 April 1948, Urban League-Minneapolis folder, Mayorality files, 1945-48, Minneapolis Committees, Commissions, Offices; Frank L. Stanley to John Stewart, 28 September 1966, CR Orgs. Correspondence and misc. by Sub. Summer Task Force: July-August 1966, Vice Presidential files, 1965-68, Civil and Human Rights; Bruce Terris to Bill Walsh, 5 December 1967, "Contacts with Negro Activists," Vice Presidential files, Civil and Human Rights, corr. and misc. by date 1967-68, Humphrey Papers; Humphrey to Young, 8 November 1965; Young, "Rights Program Downgraded," 3 November 1965, newspaper article, NUL Records, series 1, part 2, box 18, Office of the Vice President folder.

74. Terris to Walsh (Contacts with Negro Activists), 5 December 1967, Vice Presidential files, Civil and Human Rights, corr. and misc. by date, 1967-68, Humphrey Papers.

75. Jim Gaither to LBJ, 5 April 1968, 8:35 A.M., 4:50 P.M.; Joe Califano to LBJ, 5 April 1968, 11:22 A.M., president's appointment file (diary backup), box 95, 5 April 1968, LBJ Library.

76. Harry McPherson and Joe Califano to LBJ, 5 April 1968, president's appointment file (diary backup), box 95, 5 April 1968, LBJ Library.

14. Home to Africa

1. G. Mennen Williams to Young, 1 December 1962; Young to Williams, 4 and 1. January 1963; Jean Drew Lightfoot to Young, 9 August 1963, NUL Records, series 1, part 2, box 18, Dept. of State folder 1963; Possible Project with National Urban League, 18 June 1962; Chester Carter to Cernoria D. Johnson, 19 June 1962; Johnson to Young, 21 June 1962; Johnson to Franklin H. Williams, 5 July 1962, NUL Records, Washington bureau, box 15, WMY Jr. correspondence, 26 December 1961–31 December 1962; Franklin H. Williams, interviewed by author (telephone), 6 August 1984; Vivian C. Mason to Young, 1 November 1961; Sargent Shriver to Young, 29 November 1961, NUL Records, Admin. Dept., general files, series 1, part 2, box 41, Peace Corps 1961-62.

2. Telegram: Young to LBJ, 12 July 1967; LBJ to Young, 15 July 1967, LBJ Papers, President, 1963-69, National Security-Defense, box 200, ND 19/CO 52 file, LBJ Library.

3. Memorandum on American Negro Leadership Conference on Africa, March 1967; Theodore E. Brown to Young, 7 June 1967, 6 September 1967, WMY Jr. Papers, box 65, American Negro Leadership Conference on Africa (ANLCA) folder; Brown to Robert Scheer, 29 May 1969, WMY Jr. Papers, box 88, ANLCA folder.

4. Memorandum on ANLCA, March 1967, WMY Jr. Papers, box 65, ANLCA folder; Roy Wilkins to Young, 8 April 1966; Brown to Young, 8 April 1966, 12 October 1966; Young to Brown, 21 October 1966, WMY Jr. Papers, box 29, ANLCA folder.

5. Brown to Young, 22 April 1967; telegram: ANLCA to LBJ, 25 April 1967; Brown to Roy Wilkins, A. Philip Randolph, Martin Luther King Jr., Whitney Young Jr., Floyd McKissick, Dorothy Height, 10 May 1967, WMY Jr. Papers, box 65, ANLCA folder.

6. Theodore E. Brown to Dorothy Height, Martin Luther King, A. Philip Randolph, Roy Wilkins, and Young, 21 March 1967; ANLCA statement to the Nigerian government, n.d.; Brown to Young, 21 April 1967; Brown to Roy Wilkins, Whitney Young, A. Philip Randolph, and Martin Luther King, 7 June 1967; Young to Brown, 25 August 1967, WMY Jr. Papers, box 65, ANLCA folder.

7. George M. Houser to Young, 2 March 1967; memorandum on ANLCA, March 1967; Young to Houser, 24 April 1967, WMY Jr. Papers, box 65, ANLCA folder.

8. Frank T. Wilson, ed., "Living Witnesses: Black Presbyterians in Ministry—James Herman Robinson," *Journal of Presbyterian History* 51 (winter 1973): 367-70; James H. Robinson to Young, 1 June 1965; Young to Robinson, 3 June 1965, WMY Jr. Papers, box 128, Speaking Engagements (Not Accepted) May to August 1965.

9. A. Philip Randolph to Young, 22 June 1966; Arthur Q. Funn to Young, 30 June 1966; Guichard Parris to Young, 8 July 1966; Young to Randolph, 15 July 1966, WMY Jr. Papers, box 53, A. Philip Randolph Institute (advisory) folder; Randolph to Young, 12 June 1970; "An Appeal by Black Americans for United States Support to Israel"; Young to Charles Hightower, 7 October 1970, WMY Jr. Papers, box 103, A. Philip Randolph Institute folder; Lewis V. Baldwin, *Toward the Beloved Community: Martin Luther King Jr. and South Africa* (Cleveland: Pilgrim Press, 1995), 41; Bayard Rustin to Friend, 28 August 1970.

10. Edward E. Anderson to Young, 22 May 1968; Frank E. Ferrari to Young, 16 July 1968, box 160, African American Institute folder; Young to Margaret B. Young, 1969, WMY Jr. Papers, box 269, correspondence 1969 folder.

11. Young to Margaret B. Young, 3 March 1971, Private Papers of Margaret B. Young, Denver; Thomas Wyman, interviewed by author, New York, 24 January 1984.

12. Wyman, interview; Ramsey Clark, interviewed by author, New York, 16 January 1984; death certificate, Young, Lagos State Government, 13 March 1971, WMY Jr. Papers, box 264, correspondence 1971; *New York Times*, 12 March 1971, 13 April 1971.

13. *New York Times*, 13 and 17 March 1971; Richard M. Nixon, *Four Great Americans*, 44, 47.

14. Margaret B. Young to Young Sr., 27 April 1971, WMY Jr. Papers, box 264, correspondence 1971.

Bibliography

Archival Collections

Frankie V. Adams Papers, Robert W. Woodruff Library, Atlanta University Center

Horace Mann Bond Papers, Archives, University of Massachusetts, Amherst

Rufus E. Clement Papers, Robert W. Woodruff Library, Atlanta University Center

Carnegie Corporation of New York Grant Files, New York

Ford Foundation Grant Files, Ford Foundation Archives, New York

Leonard Garment Papers, Manuscript Division, Library of Congress, Washington, D.C.

General Education Board Papers, Rockefeller Archive Center, North Tarrytown, New York

Human Rights Papers, Lyndon Baines Johnson Presidential Library, Austin, Texas

Hubert H. Humphrey Papers, Minnesota Historical Society, St. Paul

Papers of Lyndon Baines Johnson, President, 1963-69, Lyndon Baines Johnson Presidential Library, Austin, Texas

Papers of Lyndon Baines Johnson as Vice President, Lyndon Baines Johnson Presidential Library, Austin, Texas

John F. Kennedy Presidential Office Files, John F. Kennedy Presidential Library, Boston

Martin Luther King Jr. Papers, Martin Luther King Jr. Center for Nonviolent Social Change, Atlanta

Arthur C. McCaw Personal Papers, Kissimmee, Florida

Ralph E. McGill Papers, Robert W. Woodruff Library, Special Collections, Emory University, Atlanta

National Association for the Advancement of Colored People (NAACP) Records, Manuscript Division, Library of Congress, Washington, D.C.

National Security File—Country File, Lyndon Baines Johnson Presidential Library, Austin, Texas

National Urban League Records, Manuscript Division, Library of Congress, Washington, D.C.

Charles Henry Parrish Jr. Papers, University Archives and Records Center, William Ekstrom Library, University of Louisville

President's Appointment File (Diary Backup), Lyndon Baines Johnson Presidential Library, Austin, Texas

Rockefeller Brothers Fund Papers, Rockefeller Archive Center, North Tarrytown, New York

Rockefeller Foundation Papers, Rockefeller Archive Center, North Tarrytown, New York

Alfred P. Sloan Foundation Files, Alfred P. Sloan Foundation, New York
Social Welfare History Archives, University Libraries, University of Minnesota, Minne-
    apolis
Taconic Foundation Files, Taconic Foundation, New York
Lee C. White Papers, Lyndon Baines Johnson Presidential Library, Austin, Texas
White House Central File, Name File, Lyndon Baines Johnson Presidential Library, Aus-
    tin, Texas
Margaret Buckner Young Personal Papers, Denver, Colorado
Whitney M. Young Jr. Papers, Columbia University Libraries, New York
Whitney M. Young Jr. FBI files, J. Edgar Hoover Building, Washington, D.C.
Whitney M. Young Sr. Papers, Blazer Library, Kentucky State University, Frankfort
Governor Luther Youngdahl Papers, Minnesota State Archives, Manuscripts Division,
    Minnesota Historical Society, St. Paul

Secondary Sources

Anderson, Jervis. *A. Philip Randolph: A Biographical Portrait.* New York: Harcourt Brace
    Jovanovich, 1972.
———.*Bayard Rustin: Troubles I've Seen.* New York: Harper-Collins, 1997.
Bacote, Clarence A. *The Story of Atlanta University: A Century of Service, 1865-1965.*
    Atlanta: Atlanta University, 1969.
Baldwin, Lewis V. *Toward the Beloved Community: Martin Luther King Jr. and South
    Africa.* Cleveland: Pilgrim Press, 1995.
Baraka, Amiri. *The Autobiography of Leroi Jones/Amiri Baraka.* New York: Freundlich Books,
    1984.
Berman, William C. *The Politics of Civil Rights in the Truman Administration.* Columbus:
    Ohio State University Press, 1970.
Bernstein, Barton J., ed. *Politics and Policies of the Truman Administration.* Chicago:
    Quadrangle Books, 1972.
Brauer, Carl M. *John F. Kennedy and the Second Reconstruction.* New York: Columbia
    University Press, 1977.
Bruner, Richard. *Whitney M. Young Jr.: The Story of a Pragmatic Humanist.* New York:
    David McKay, 1972.
Buchanan, A. Russell. *Black Americans in World War II.* Santa Barbara, Calif.: Clio Books,
    1977.
Buckley, Tom. "'Whitney Young: Black Leader or 'Oreo Cookie?'" *New York Times Maga-
    zine,* 20 September 1970, 32-33, 74-77, 80-85
Buni, Andrew. *Robert L. Vann of the Pittsburgh Courier: Politics and Black Journalism.*
    Pittsburgh: University of Pittsburgh Press, 1974.
Burk, Robert F. *The Eisenhower Administration and Black Civil Rights.* Knoxville: Univer-
    sity of Tennessee Press, 1984.
Butler, Jon H. "Communities and Congregations: The Black Church in St. Paul, 1860-
    1900." *Journal of Negro History* 56 (April 1971): 118-34.
Carson, Clayborne. *In Struggle: SNCC and the Black Awakening of the 1960s.* Cambridge:
    Harvard University Press, 1981.
Chafe, William H. *Civilities and Civil Rights: Greensboro, North Carolina, and the Black
    Struggle for Freedom.* New York: Oxford University Press, 1980.
Channing, Steven A. *Kentucky: A Bicentennial History.* New York: W.W. Norton, 1977.

Cleghorn, Reese. "The Angels Are White: Who Pays the Bills for Civil Rights?" *New Republic,* 17 August 1963, 12-14.

Cone, James H. "Martin Luther King Jr., Black Theology—Black Church." *Theology Today* 40 (January 1984): 409-20.

Cox, Joseph Mason Andrew. *Great Black Men of Masonry.* New York: Alpha Book, 1982, 1987.

Dalfiume, Richard. "The 'Forgotten Years' of the Negro Revolution." *Journal of American History* 55 (June 1968): 90-106.

Davis, Allison. *Leadership, Love, and Aggression: The Psychological Factors in the Making of Four Black Leaders.* New York: Harcourt Brace Jovanovich, 1983.

Dickerson, Dennis C. "Eugene Percy Roberts: Black Physician and Leader." *New York State Journal of Medicine* 85 (April 1985): 143-44.

———. *Out of the Crucible: Black Steelworkers in Western Pennsylvania, 1875-1980.* Albany: State University of New York Press, 1986.

———. *Religion, Race, and Region: Research Notes on A.M.E. Church History.* Nashville: A.M.E. Sunday School Union, 1995.

Dittmer, John. *Local People: The Struggle for Civil Rights in Mississippi.* Urbana: University of Illinois Press, 1994.

"Does State FEPC Hamper You?" *Business Week,* 25 February 1950, 114-17.

English, James W. *Handyman of the Lord: The Life and Ministry of the Reverend William Holmes Borders.* New York, Meredith Press, 1967.

Esbjornson, Robert. *A Christian in Politics: Luther W. Youngdahl.* Minneapolis: T.S. Denison, 1955.

Farmer, James. *Lay Bare the Heart: An Autobiography of the Civil Rights Movement.* New York, Arbor House, 1985.

Forman, James. *The Making of Black Revolutionaries.* Washington, D.C.: Open Hand, 1972, 1985.

Garrow, David J. *The FBI and Martin Luther King Jr.: From "Solo" to Memphis.* New York: W.W. Norton, 1981.

———. *Bearing the Cross: Martin Luther King Jr. and the Southern Christian Leadership Conference.* New York: William Morrow, 1986.

Gavins, Raymond. *The Perils and Prospects of Southern Black Leadership: Gordon Blaine Hancock, 1884-1970.* Durham, N.C.: Duke University Press, 1977.

Graham, Hugh Davis. *The Civil Rights Era.* New York: Oxford University Press, 1990.

Haines, Herbert H. *Black Radicals and the Civil Rights Mainstream, 1954-1970.* Knoxville: University of Tennessee Press, 1988.

Hine, Darlene Clark, Elsa Barkley Brown, and Roslyn Terborg-Penn, eds. *Black Women in America: An Historical Encyclopedia.* Vol. 2. Brooklyn: Carlson, 1993.

Horton, John Benjamin. *Not without Struggle.* New York: Vantage Press, 1979.

Howard, Victor B. *Black Liberation in Kentucky: Emancipation and Freedom, 1862-1884.* Lexington: University Press of Kentucky, 1983.

Issacson, Walter. *Kissinger: A Biography.* New York: Simon and Schuster, 1992.

Jacoway, Elizabeth, and David Colburn, eds. *Southern Businessmen and Desegregation.* Baton Rouge: Louisiana State University Press, 1982.

Johnson, Audreye E. "The National Association of Black Social Workers, Inc.: A View of the Beginning." *Black Caucus Journal, NABSW* 7 (spring 1976): 13-17.

Karger, Howard Jacob. "Phyllis Wheatley House: A History of the Minneapolis Black Settlement House, 1924-1940." *Phylon* 47 (March 1986): 79-90.

Katz, Nick, and Mary Lynn Katz. *A Passion for Equality: George A. Wiley and the Move-ment.* New York: W.W. Norton, 1977.

King, Coretta Scott. *My Life with Martin Luther King Jr.* New York: Holt, Rinehart and Winston, 1969.

King, Martin Luther Sr., with Clayton Riley. *Daddy King: An Autobiography.* New York, William Morrow, 1980.

King, Martin Luther Jr. *A Testament of Hope: The Essential Writings of Martin Luther King Jr.* Edited by James M. Washington. San Francisco: Harper and Row, 1986.

King, Mel. *Chain of Change: Struggles for Black Community Development.* Boston: South End Press, 1981.

Lomax, Louis E. *The Negro Revolt.* New York: Harper and Row, 1962.

Loveland, Anne C. *Lillian Smith: A Southerner Confronting the South.* Baton Rouge: Loui-siana State University Press, 1986.

Low, W. Augustus, and Virgil A. Clift. *Encyclopedia of Black America.* New York: McGraw-Hill, 1981.

Manis, Andrew M. *Southern Civil Religions in Conflict: Black and White Baptists and Civil Rights, 1947-1957.* Athens: University of Georgia Press, 1987.

Markoe, John P., S.J. "Omaha De Porres Center." *Interracial Review* 21 (February 1950): 24.

Martin, William. *A Prophet with Honor: The Billy Graham Story.* New York: William Morrow, 1991.

Mayer, Michael. "With Much Deliberation and Some Speed: Eisenhower and the Brown Decision." *Journal of Southern History* 52 (February 1986): 43-76.

Mead, Frank S., and Samuel S. Hill. *Handbook of Denominations in the United States.* 8th ed. Nashville: Abingdon Press, 1985.

Meier, August, and Elliott Rudwick. *CORE: A Study in the Civil Rights Movement, 1942-1968.* New York: Oxford University Press, 1973.

Meier, August, Elliot Rudwick, and Francis L. Broderick, eds. *Black Protest Thought in the Twentieth Century.* 2d ed. Indianapolis: Bobbs-Merrill, 1965.

Mihelich, Dennis N. "World War II and the Transformation of the Omaha Urban League," *Nebraska History* 60 (fall 1979): 401-23.

Moore, Jesse T. Jr. *A Search for Equality: The National Urban League, 1910-1961.* Univer-sity Park: Pennsylvania State University Press, 1981.

Morris, Aldon D. *The Origins of the Civil Rights Movement: Black Communities Organiz-ing for Change.* New York: Free Press, 1984.

Morrison-Reed, Mark D. *Black Pioneers in a White Denomination.* Boston: Beacon Press, 1980.

Muraskin, William A. *Middle-Class Blacks in a White Society: Prince Hall Masonry in America.* Berkeley: University of California Press, 1975.

Murray, Pauli. *Pauli Murray: The Autobiography of a Black Activist, Feminist, Lawyer, Priest, and Poet.* Knoxville: University of Tennessee, 1987.

The National Cyclopaedia of American Biography. Vol. 1, *1953-1959.* New York: James T. White, 1960.

Nixon, Richard M. *Four Great Americans: Tributes Delivered by President Richard Nixon.* New York: Doubleday, 1972.

———. The Memoirs of Richard M. Nixon. New York: Grosset and Dunlap, 1978.

Olson, James S., ed. *Dictionary of the Vietnam War.* Westport, Conn.: Greenwood Press, 1988.

Parris, Guichard, and Lester Brooks. *Blacks in the City: A History of the National Urban League.* Boston: Little, Brown, 1971.

Payne, Charles M. *I've Got the Light of Freedom: The Organizing Tradition and the Mississippi Freedom Struggle.* Berkeley: University of California Press, 1995.

Polk, Donna Mays. *Black Men and Women of Nebraska.* Lincoln: Nebraska Black History Preservation Society, 1981.

Pride, Richard A., and J. David Woodard. *The Burden of Busing: The Politics of Desegregation in Nashville, Tennessee.* Knoxville: University of Tennessee Press, 1985.

Reed, Adolph Jr. *The Jesse Jackson Phenomena: The Crisis of Purpose in Afro-American Politics.* New Haven: Yale University Press, 1986.

Rucker, Clifford E. "The Governor's Interracial Commission of Minnesota: An Administrative History." M.A. thesis, University of Minnesota, 1955.

Sitkoff, Harvard. "The Detroit Race Riot of 1943." *Michigan History* (fall 1969): 183-206.

———. "Harry Truman and the Election of 1948: The Coming of Age of Civil Rights in American Politics." *Journal of Southern History* 37 (November 1971): 597-616.

———. "Racial Militancy and Interracial Violence in the Second World War." *Journal of American History* (December 1971): 661-81.

———. *A New Deal for Blacks.* New York: Oxford University Press, 1978.

———. *The Struggle for Black Equality, 1954-1980.* New York: Hill and Wang, 1981.

Smith, Gerald. *A Black Educator in the Segregated South: Kentucky's Rufus B. Atwood.* Lexington: University Press of Kentucky, 1994.

Smith, Jeffrey H. "The Omaha De Porres Club." *Negro History Bulletin* 33 (December 1970): 194-99.

Smith, Jessie Carney. *Notable Black American Women.* Detroit: Gale Research, 1992.

Solberg, Carl. *Hubert Humphrey: A Biography.* New York: W.W. Norton, 1984.

Spangler, Earl. *The Negro in Minnesota.* Minneapolis: T.S. Denison, 1961.

Tucker, David M. *Lieutenant Lee of Beale Street.* Nashville: Vanderbilt University Press, 1971.

Watson, Denton L. *Lion in the Lobby: Clarence Mitchell Jr.'s Struggle for the Passage of Civil Rights Laws.* New York: William Morrow, 1990.

Weisbrot, Robert. *Freedom Bound: A History of America's Civil Rights Movement.* New York: Plume, 1991.

Weiss, Nancy J. *The National Urban League, 1910-1940.* New York: Oxford University Press, 1974.

———. *Whitney M. Young Jr. and the Struggle for Civil Rights.* Princeton: Princeton University Press, 1989.

Wesley, Charles H. *The History of Sigma Pi Phi.* Washington, D.C.: Association for the Study of Negro Life and History, 1954, 1969.

———. *The History of the Improved Benevolent and Protective Orders of Elks of the World.* Washington, D.C.: Association for the Study of Negro Life and History, 1955.

———. *The History of Alpha Phi Alpha: A Development in College Life.* Chicago: Foundation, 1961.

Who's Who in America, 1964-65, vol. 33 (Chicago: A.N. Marquis, 1964),

Who's Who in America, 1984-85, 43d ed., vol. 1 (Chicago: A.N. Marquis, 1984)

Who's Who in Colored America, 1928-1929. New York: Who's Who in Colored America Corp., 1929.

Wilkins, Roger. *A Man's Life: An Autobiography.* New York: Simon and Schuster, 1982.

Wilkins, Roy, with Tom Matthews. *Standing Fast: Autobiography of Roy Wilkins.* New York: Viking Press, 1982.

Wilson, Frank T., ed. "Living Witnesses: Black Presbyterians in Ministry-James Herman Robinson." *Journal of Presbyterian History* 51 (winter 1973): 367-70.

Woodson, Carter G. *The Negro Professional Men and the Community.* Washington, D.C.: Association for the Study of Negro Life and History, 1934.

Wright, George C. "The Founding of Lincoln Institute." *Filson Club History Quarterly* 49 (January 1975): 57-70.

———. "The Faith Plan: A Black Institution Grows during the Depression." *Filson Club History Quarterly* 51 (October 1977): 334-36.

———. *Life behind a Veil: Blacks in Louisville, Kentucky, 1865-1920.* Baton Rouge: Louisiana State University Press, 1985.

———. *Racial Violence in Kentucky, 1865-1940: Lynching, Mob Rule, and "Legal Lynchings."* Baton Rouge: Louisiana State University Press, 1990.

———. *A History of Blacks in Kentucky, 1890-1980.* Frankfort: Kentucky Historical Society, 1992.

Wright, Richard R. Jr., ed. *Encyclopedia of African Methodism.* Philadelphia: A.M.E. Church, 1947.

Wynn, Neil A. *The Afro-American and the Second World War.* New York: Holmes and Meier, 1975.

Yarbrough, Tinsley E. *A Passion for Justice: J. Waites Waring and Civil Rights.* New York: Oxford University Press, 1987.

Young, Andrew. *An Easy Burden: The Civil Rights Movement and the Transformation of America.* New York: HarperCollins, 1996.

Young, Whitney M. Jr. "History of the St. Paul Urban League." M.A. thesis, University of Minnesota, 1947.

———. "Review of Social Work Today." *Phylon* 15, no. 2 (1954): 219;

———. "Participation of Citizens." *Phylon* 19, no. 1 (1958): 96.

———. "Attitude Survey on Desegregation." *Phylon* 19, no. 4 (1958): 425-26.

———. "The Role of the Community Organizer in Desegregation." *Journal of Orthopsychiatry* (June 1956): 452-55.

———. *To Be Equal.* New York: McGraw-Hill, 1964.

———. "When the Negroes in Vietnam Come Home." *Harper's,* June 1967, 63-68.

———. *Beyond Racism: Building an Open Society.* New York: McGraw-Hill, 1969.

Young, Whitney M. Jr., and Frankie V. Adams, comps. *Some Pioneers in Social Work: Brief Sketches.* Atlanta: Atlanta University Press, 1958.

Young, Whitney M. Jr., and Carl Holman. "A Second Look: The Negro Citizen in Atlanta." Atlanta: Committee for Cooperative Action, 1960.

Interviews by Dennis C. Dickerson

Ralph D. Abernathy, Atlanta, 26 October 1983

Mrs. Ralph Adams, Omaha, 7 July 1982

Enid Baird, Brooklyn, 11 January 1984

Wiley Branton, Washington, D.C., 8 February 1984

McGeorge Bundy, New York, 10 January 1984

George O. Butler, Washington, D.C., 1 February 1985

Bertha Calloway, Omaha, 5 July 1982

Mr. and Mrs. Joseph Carroll, Indianapolis, 23 April 1982
Lauren Young Casteel, Denver, 19 June 1982
Kenneth B. Clark, New York, 13 September 1984
Ramsey Clark, New York, 16 January 1984
Clarence Coleman, Atlanta, 28 July 1982
Betty Corbin, Omaha, 6 July 1982
Lavonne Curtis, Omaha, 9 July 1982
N. Phillips Dodge, Omaha, 7 July 1982
Lillian Dorsey, Omaha, 9 July 1982
Richard S. Dowdy, New Haven, Conn., 13 February 1984
Christopher F. Edley Sr., New York, 27 June 1984
Herman C. Ewing, Memphis, 23 August 1985
James Farmer, Washington, D.C., 8 March 1984
Margaret Fischer, Omaha, 8 July 1982
Harold Fleming, Washington, D.C., 6 March 1984
Dr. Arthur Flemming, Washington, D.C., 7 March 1984
John Gardner, Washington, D.C., 7 February 1984
Leonard Garment, Washington, D.C., 30 August 1984
Lloyd Garrison, New York, 12 January 1984
Mr. and Mrs. Ashley Gaskins, Minneapolis, 4 August 1982
Mitchell Ginsberg, New York, 24 January 1984
Jack Greenberg, New York, 27 January 1984
James S. Griffin, St. Paul, 11 October 1983
Charles J. Hamilton Jr., New York, 25 May 1984
Andrew Heiskell, New York, 10 January 1984
Genevieve Hill, Atlanta, 27 July 1982
M. Carl Holman, Washington, D.C., 24 September 1982
John Jacob, New York, 19 December 1983
Sophie Y. Jacobs, New York, 27 December 1983
Dr. Thomas Jarrett, Atlanta, 29 July 1982
Vernon Jordan, Washington, D.C., 10 February 1984
Thomas W. Kheel, New York, 19 December 1983
Representative Mae Street Kidd, Louisville, Ky., 20 July 1982
John C. Kidneigh, St. Paul, 3 August 1982
Lindsley F. Kimball, Newtown, Pa., 19 June 1984
Gisela Konopka, Minneapolis, 5 August 1982
Edward S. Lewis, New York, 11 January 1984
Hylan Lewis, New York, 13 September 1984
James Linen, Greenwich, Conn., 25 September 1982
Florence Logan, St. Paul, 13 October 1983
Eleanor Young Love, Louisville, Ky., 19 July 1982
Howard L. Love, Little Rock, Ark., 21 July 1984
John W. Mack, Los Angeles, 29 February 1988
Burke Marshall, New Haven, Conn., 13 February 1984
Louis E. Martin, Washington, D.C., 7 February 1984
Dr. Benjamin E. Mays, Atlanta, 27 July 1982
Arthur McCaw, Kissimmee, Fla., 29 July 1982
Arthur McWatt, St. Paul, 12 October 1983

Martin Meyerson, Philadelphia, 29 June 1985
Dr. Claude Organ, Oklahoma City, 17 February 1987
Guichard Parris, New York, 14 December 1983
Estyr Peake, St. Paul, 12 October 1983
Dr. A.B. Pittman, Omaha, 7 July 1982
Judge Elizabeth Pittman, Omaha, 9 July 1982
Ersa Hines Poston, Washington, D.C., 24 September 1982
William Ramsey, Omaha, 6 July 1982
Samuel Robinson, Lincoln Ridge, Ky., 20 July 1982
Walter Rock, North St. Paul, 4 August 1982
Charles F. Rogers, St. Paul, 3 August 1982
Burns Roper, New York, 4 December 1983
Harvey C. Russell Jr., New York, 16 January 1984
Bayard Rustin, New York, 11 January 1984
Judge Benjamin Shobe, Louisville, Ky., 20 July 1982
Sargent Shriver, Washington, D.C., 7 February 1984
Eugene Skinner, Omaha, 6 July 1982
Theodore Sorensen, New York, 12 January 1984
Henry Steeger, New York, 17 January 1984
Percy Steele, Oakland, 1 March 1988
Mitchell Sviridoff, New York, 21 February 1984
Kenneth Thompson, Charlottesville, Va., 23 November 1987
William J. Trent Jr., Greensboro, N.C., 18 October 1983
Sterling Tucker, Washington, D.C., 7 March 1984
James T. Wardlaw Sr., Minneapolis, 4 August 1982
Robert C. Weaver, New York, 16 January 1984
Betti Whaley, Washington, D.C., 30 August 1984
Mrs. Aminda Wilkins, Jamaica, N.Y., 22 February 1984
Roger Wilkins, Washington, D.C., 10 February 1984
Mrs. Alfred Williams, St. Paul, 3 August 1982
Alyce Wilson, Omaha, 8 July 1982
Harris Wofford, Philadelphia, 19 June 1984
Thomas Wyman, New York, 24 January 1984
Margaret B. Young, New Rochelle, N.Y., 5 November 1982 and 7 May 1983, 11 May
    1984

Other Interviews

Sterling Tucker, interviewed by Thomas Harrison Baker, 21 April 1969, Oral History
    Collection, Lyndon Baines Johnson Presidential Library, Austin, Texas
Roy Wilkins, Roy, interviewed by Thomas Harrison Baker, 1 April 1969, Oral History
    Collection, Lyndon Baines Johnson Presidential Library, Austin, Texas.
Margaret Buckner Young, interviewed by Betty Barnes, New Rochelle, N.Y., 13 Novem-
    ber 1975, Oral History Research Office, Columbia University, New York.
Whitney M. Young Jr., interviewed by Thomas Harrison Baker, 18 June 1969, Oral
    History Collection, Lyndon Baines Johnson Presidential Library, Austin, Texas.

Index

Abernathy, Ralph D., 101, 299–300
Abrams, Morris B., 250
ACCA. *See* Atlanta Committee for Cooperative Action
activism, 49–51, 62–64, 76, 85, 106, 111–12. *See also* Black Power
Adams, Frankie, 129
Adams, John, Sr., 60
Adams, Ralph, 81, 82, 85
Adams, Rev. John Hurst, 285
Africa: American blacks and, 311–17; Young's interest in, 130
African American Institute, 315–16
Agriculture Department, discrimination in, 250
Ahmann, Matthew, 167
Albany (GA), 163, 164
Alexander, Clifford, 250–51, 252, 271, 273
Alexander, Sydney, 85
Alfred P. Sloan Foundation, 156, 202, 219, 234, 235
Allen, Alexander J., 85, 142, 169
Allen, Ivan, 191
Allen, Nimrod, 50
Allen, Rev. Charles L., 113
Allport, Gordon W., 122
Alpha Phi Alpha, 48, 49, 286–87
American Association of Medical Social Workers, 92–93
American Bankers Association, 212
American Bar Association, 205
American Can, 218
American Negro Leadership Conference on Africa, 312–13
American Nurses' Associations, 240
American Paper Institute, 218
ANCLA. *See* American Negro Leadership Conference on Africa
Anderson, Charles W., Jr., 14
Anderson, Marian, 56
Andrews, Regina, 130, 131

Antioch Baptist Church, 284
antiwar movement, 281
apartheid, 312–13, 314–15
Astor, Mrs. Vincent, 186
Atlanta, 112–15; civil rights movement in, 106–9; liberalism in, 110–11
Atlanta Committee for Cooperative Action, 109–11
Atlanta Negro Voters League, 107–8
Atlanta University. *See* School of Social Work, Atlanta University
Atwood, J.L., 216
Atwood, Rufus B., 27, 295
Austin, J. Paul, 217

Bacon, Emery, 104
Baird, Enid C., 233
Baker, Ella, 165
Balenger, Lillian Parks, 50
banking industry: black employment and, 212; funding of urban initiatives, 307
Banner, Warren, 103
Baraka, Imamu Amiri, 6, 303, 307–8
Batten, William M., 216–17
Beamon, Vivian, 291
Beesley, Eugene S., 211
Berea College, 9
Bernhard, Berl I., 252–53
Berry, Edwin "Bill," 85, 130, 131, 172, 233, 256, 291
Beyond Racism, 260
Binger, James H., 211
Bingham, Russell, 307
Birmingham Urban League, 156–57
Bishopric, Karl, 174
black(s): in Atlanta, 107–11, 111; in Boston, 124, 125–126; churches, 50, 52–53, 83–84, 284–86; colleges, 295–97. *See also specific institutions;* Council for United Civil Rights Leadership and, 179; economic unrest during World War

II, 42–43; in freedom rides and sit-ins, 163; ghettos, 185–86; middle class, 14, 50–51, 200; migration during World War I, 12; in National Urban Coalition, 194; responses to slum clearance, 72–73; self-help and, 134; in St. Paul, 51; support for Young, 3, 81–84, 284–95; teachers, segregation and, 73–75; in urban agencies, 185; urban grassroots activity, 199–200; veterans, aid to, 140, 270, 272, 273, 275–77; in Vietnam, 272, 275, 280; voter registration and, 173, 244
Black Economic Development Conference, 221
black employment: in Atlanta, 111; in banking industry, 212; in federal government, 241; in iron industry, 212; in Minnesota, 43, 45–48; in Nebraska, 59–65; in skilled jobs, 146–48
Blackie, William, 211
black Muslims, 287
Black Panther Party, 205, 269, 308
Black Power, 5–6, 213–214, 215, 220, 300–310, 311
black women: gender roles and, 292–93; organizations, 291–93
Blake, Eugene Carson, 167
Blakeley, Rev. Ulysses B., 284
Blough, Roger, 297–97
Bohanon, M. Leo, 57, 59, 64, 85, 130, 131
Bond, Horace Mann, 130
Bookbinder, Hyman, 256
Borders, William Holmes, 107, 109, 112
Boston: urban renewal in, 123–27; Young's postgraduate study in, 122–28
Boston Community Development Program, 123–24
Boston University, 122
Boston Urban League, 202
boycotts. See bus boycotts
Branch, Rev. Emanuel, Jr., 284
Brandeis, 122
Branton, Wiley, 178, 181, 244
Brawley, James P., 111
brewery industry, job discrimination in, 64
Bridgeport, Connecticut, 151
Brimmer, Andrew F., 299
Brisco, M.M., 215
Bronfman, Edgar M., 216
Broom, W.W., 315, 316
Brown, H. Rap, 192, 303, 308
Brown, Theodore E., 257, 279, 312–13

Brown v. Board of Education, 4, 88–89, 98, 135
Bruce, Audrey, 177
Buchanan v. Warley, 8
Buckingham, George M., 215
Buckley, Tom, 2, 183
Buckner, Eva Carter, 28
Buckner, Frank, 28, 315
Buckner, Margaret. See Young, Margaret
Buffalo Urban League, 142
Bundy, McGeorge, 192–93, 227–29, 230, 232, 305
Burke, Harry A., 74, 75
Burns, Arthur F., 282
bus boycotts, 89, 101, 107, 135
business: in National Urban Coalition, 191; support of National Urban League, 151, 154, 155, 158; support of Young, 293–94. See also corporate funding
bus terminals, freedom rides and, 163
Butler, George O., 132
Butler, William F., 299

Cahill, Edward, 113
Califano, Joseph, 251, 257, 273, 310
Callender, Eugene, 186
Calloway, N.O., 172
Cambridge. See Boston
Cannon, Joseph F., 276
capital punishment, 180
Carmichael, Stokely, 168, 214, 300, 302, 303, 308
Carnegie Corporation, 219, 234–35; National Urban League fellowship program and, 144–46; support of National Urban League, 136
Carroll, Joseph A., 25
Carson, Clayborne, 162
Carswell, G. Harold, 263
Carter, Lisle C., Jr., 193, 231, 239, 252
Case, Everett N., 234, 235
Catholicism, desegregation and, 80
Cavanagh, Jerome, 191
Celebrezze, Anthony, 249
Chambers, Maurice, 217
Chapman, Earl, 170
Cheaney, Henry C., 27
Chicago Housing Authority, 123
Chicago Urban League: civil rights activism and, 172; funding of, 233
churches: black, 50, 52–53, 83–84, 284–86; desegregation in, 80; white, civil rights and, 113

CPSIA information can be obtained
at www.ICGtesting.com
Printed in the USA
LVHW090317180619
621521LV00001B/1/P

9 780813 190815